# South Wales and the Rising of 1839

KU-114-300

John Frost

Dr. William Price
(*Welsh Folk Museum, St. Fagans*)

Zephaniah Williams

William Lloyd Jones

Rebel Leaders, 1839

# South Wales
# and the Rising of 1839

Ivor Wilks

GOMER PRESS, 1989

*First impression: softback edition — 1989*

© Ivor Wilks

First published in hardback by Croom Helm in 1984

ISBN 0 86383 605 4

This volume is published with the support of the Welsh Arts Council

Printed in Wales by J. D. Lewis and Sons Ltd., Gomer Press, Llandysul, Dyfed.

# CONTENTS

# MAPS, FIGURES AND TABLES

To Daniel Hughes and Mary Hinton,
who chose the 4th of November 1839 for their wedding;
and to their last surviving grandchild, my Mother.

# PREFACE

In 1839 the turmoil that was endemic to the condition of south Wales assumed a new form: ironworkers and colliers took to arms in a bid to win, for labour, autonomy within the evolving industrial capitalist system. The roots of the workers' movement lay deep in the Welsh past, its immediate causes in the grim circumstances of the workplace. Chartism was a catalyst, the rising in November the result. Almost a century and a half later the events of 1839 retain their place in the sensibilities of the people. In the centre of Newport, Gwent, is the contemporary John Frost Square, named after the Welsh chartist. There is a high-rise building, Chartist Tower, and a café, Frostbite. The pedestrian passes from one part of the development to another by way of a tunnel, one wall adorned with a splendid mosaic depicting the march of the ironworkers and colliers on Newport. In 1980 the Islwyn Folk Club presented *The Chartists,* a musical dramatisation of the rising by Wynford Jones, and the album that was released proved highly popular.[1]

In south Wales the rising of 1839 has remained part not only of the decorative but also of the usable past. The hunger marchers in the 1930s compared themselves to the men of 1839, and the analogy was present in the minds of miners' leaders like Aneurin Bevan, then active in the creation of secret anti-fascist workers' freedom groups.[2] Recently a Chartist Rally has become one of the major shows put on by the Labour Party in south Wales each year. It is held at Blackwood, where the rebels set up their headquarters in 1839. The rally in 1980 followed immediately after the Welsh rugby team had lost 3-23 to New Zealand at Cardiff Arms Park. 'If it had been the English who had beaten us', remarked one of the organisers, 'we would have cancelled the rally, because everyone would have been in the pubs!' The respectable parliamentarians who annually exhort the faithful to emulate the struggles of the old Welsh chartists would doubtless be highly dismayed to have their advice taken.[3]

This study of the rising is quite patently a partisan one, and I do not know how it could be otherwise. What passes for objectivity is all too commonly a subscription to conventionally received opinion. The standard view of early industrial Wales was developed — 'underdeveloped' might seem a more appropriate term — by bourgeois historians attached to a mystical belief in the imperial destiny of the English nation. Here

1

I have sought to place the movement of 1839 in a more appropriate setting, as an episode in Welsh history in general and Welsh working-class history in particular. It will harm none of us to keep in mind the 'categorical demand in examining any social question' made by Lenin 70 years ago, in *The Rights of Nations to Self-Determination*, that 'the question be formulated within definite historical limits, and if it refers to a particular country . . . the specific features that distinguish that country from others within the same historical epoch be taken into account'.

The origins of this book are to be found in seven articles I contributed to the *Welsh Republican* in 1954-5. They were written from the Gold Coast and the database on which they were constructed was inadequate. They were the writings of an angry man too young to have participated in the anti-Nazi struggle except passively, by being bombed, but old enough to have served in the Middle East and seen the state of Israel born, then so full of socialist promise. In the mid-1950s I watched the people of the Gold Coast preparing themselves for the independence that was soon to come, and I reflected on the sorry state of the Wales I had left in 1953. The articles were indeed written in anger, but I do not disown them; many of their themes have survived a more careful scrutiny.

By far the most important source for the events of 1839 is the evidence taken by the magistrates in Newport in the weeks after the rising. This is extant in the form of official transcripts, to be found in the Newport Public Library and among the Home Office and Treasury Solicitors' papers in the Public Record Office, and in reports of the proceedings made independently by newspaper correspondents. Not infrequently these latter produced fuller texts than the court clerks. Space has not allowed all versions of the evidence to be cited. I have therefore referred the reader to the specific source I have used after ensuring that it was at least as full as any other text available to me. It must always be borne in mind that those who gave evidence seldom did so willingly. They were concerned to incriminate themselves and their comrades as little as possible. The chronicler of the rising has therefore to rely heavily upon witnesses who for the most part concealed more than they revealed. The full extent of the rebel organisation can probably never be known. It was perhaps the difficulties inherent in investigating a movement so shrouded in secrecy that led me to make an extensive use of direct quotations from the sources. I adopted this course, however, for more specific reasons, in part to convey something of the 'flavour' of the period and in part because, over the years, the meanings of many words and expressions have changed subtly and sometimes not so subtly. I have declined to become locked into precise definitions of such terms as 'rising', 'insurrection', 'working class', 'middle class' or whatever. I cherish that degree of vagueness that makes for civilised discourse, and can only say that I use such terms in much the sense that they were used in the sources I cite.

My debts are many. I have received much help from librarians, archivists and others of like persuasion, particularly in the National Library of Wales, the British Library, the Public Record Office, Newport Public Library, Cardiff Central Library, Gwent Record Office and Northwestern University Library (and above all, its interlibrary loans section). I am most grateful to the American Philosophical Society for two grants from the Penrose Fund, and to the Northwestern University Research Grants Committee for two grants; these much facilitated the research process. The many individuals who have helped and encouraged me in a variety of ways will, I hope, understand that I cannot name them all. But Harri Webb was as supportive of my work in the 1950s as he was in the 1980s. Jeff Holden and Jean Allman both read and commented on the manuscript and the former shared in the travails of research. Jane Taylor spotted numerous typing errors and more serious infelicities, and Michael Culhane provided encouragement more valuable than she perhaps realises. Brian Davies generously made available to me drafts from his forthcoming study on Welsh chartism. I must also record the debt I owe to Gwyn A. Williams's scintillating writings, which I read and re-read whenever doubts assailed me. It is conventional but still necessary to add that none of these good people, named or unnamed, is in any way responsible for my errors of commission or omission.

Ivor G. Hughes Wilks,
Evanston

## Notes

1. Steam Pie Records, Pontllanfraith, Blackwood.
2. Hywel Francis and David Smith, *The Fed. A History of the South Wales Miners in the Twentieth Century* (London, 1980), pp. 192-8, 250, 299.
3. *The Times*, 3 Nov. 1980. *South Wales Argus*, 30 Oct. 1981.

# PREFACE TO THE 1989 EDITION

The hundred and fiftieth anniversary of the south Wales rising of 1839 is being commemorated this year. The bold bid for power, by miners, ironworkers and artisans, continues to retain its hold upon the Welsh imagination.

The first edition of this book appeared in early 1984. The following year David J. V. Jones published a remarkably similar study, *The Last Rising. The Newport Insurrection of 1839*. Citing many of the same sources, Jones subscribed to many of the same conclusions, and most especially to the view that a revolutionary situation did indeed exist in south Wales in 1839. The thousands of armed rebels who entered Newport on the night of 3-4 November were no mere rioters. They operated within the framework of a carefully formulated plan to seize power over the whole of the coalfield and its ports.

Reviews of *South Wales and the Rising of 1839* were, by and large, complimentary. Some writers of a Marxist persuasion thought the book unduly nationalistic, others of a nationalist persuasion thought it unduly Marxist. With all due deference to their opinions, I do not think that they got it quite right. I attempted to take account of both class and (Welsh) national factors in the mix which produced the rising, but argued that the national factors must be treated as a major, but by no means only, determinant of the particular form that class struggle took in south Wales. It is in this sense that I speak of the 'peculiarities' of Wales. This was seen by one reviewer as an assault upon the premises of E. P. Thompson's *The Making of the English Working Classes*. His wife, Dorothy Thompson, abused the pages of *Albion* to launch a petty and ill-informed personal attack upon me. The suggestion that, in the early nineteenth century, the trajectories of Welsh and English working class history differed significantly was apparently an anathema to her. I remain convinced of my argument. David Jones concurs, remarking that 'the special nature of Welsh industrial society and Welsh Chartism helped to bring about a revolutionary situation on this side of the border . . .'

I must express my gratitude to a cherished friend, Delwyn Phillips, who encouraged me to approach Gomer Press; to Dyfed Elis-Gruffydd of that Press, for the enthusiasm of his response to my approach; to David Croom of Routledge, for generously making the softback rights available to Gomer; and to the Welsh Arts Council for a grant in aid of publication.

*August,* 1989

# Part I: PROLOGUE

You men of Gwent and Gwalia
From Neath to Ebbw Vale,
Sing us a song of triumph
Out of a Celtic tale.

(Idris Davies, *The Angry Summer*, Faber and Faber, 1943)

O! ye who love glory, *we* heed not the story
Of Waterloo won with the blood of the brave,
But we dare the rough storm, in the cause of reform,
Then let the red banner triumphantly wave.

(Welsh chartist song, 1839)

Come, hail, brothers, hail the shrill sound of the horn;
For ages deep wrongs have been hopelessly borne;
Despair shall no longer our spirits dismay,
Nor wither the arm, when upraised for the fray;
The conflict for freedom is gathering nigh.
We live to secure it, or gloriously die.

(Hugh Williams of Carmarthen, 'The Horn of Liberty', 1839)

# 1 WALES: THE INDUSTRIAL NATION

The Edwardian conquests of 1282-3 marked the final stages in the reduction of Wales to the status of an English colony. In *pura Wallia*, as earlier in the March of Wales, government and commerce came to be dominated by settlers, for the most part from England, planted on lands appropriated for the purpose.[1] The great anti-colonial struggle of the early fifteenth century engulfed the country in civil war, but Owain Glyn Dŵr's vision of a Welsh nation founded on the medieval institutions of Parliament, Church and University took shape, faltered and died within the space of a decade. The new penal laws of Henry IV made aliens of the Welsh in their own country (other than those who took to the hills and a life of banditry), but failed to arrest the decay of lordship in both the Principality and March of Wales.[2] The colonial status of Wales was finally legislated out of existence by acts of the English Parliament of 1536 and 1542.[3] With the so-called 'union' of England and Wales — the earlier act referred to Wales being 'incorporated united and annexed' — the rights of the Crown's English subjects were formally extended to all Welsh persons and, by enactments intended to eradicate all manner of traditional Welsh tenure including the practice of partible inheritance, the stage was set for the rising class of entrepreneurial gentry to establish its ascendancy over the affairs of the Welsh shires.[4] Wales had undergone the passage from the late medieval to the early modern world.

Under the Tudor monarchy and in the revolutionary seventeenth century the gentry of Wales (whether by origin native or 'incomer') celebrated their release from the restraints of the old order by the avid and relentless pursuit of land and with it office and political preferment.[5] Younger sons sought advancement in the trades and professions in London and the provincial towns of England, and even further afield in the colonies.[6] Among the Welsh bards were those, Siôn Tudor, Simwnt Fychan, Edmwnd Prys, Tomos Prys and others, who were not insensitive to the evils of the times. They criticised the gentry for landgrabbing, for the unscrupulous exploitation of their tenantry, and for their venality in office, and they saw that their acculturation into English ways and adoption of the English language threatened the very fabric of traditional Welsh society.[7] By the turn of the seventeenth century the poets could lament the decline of patronage; thus, for example, Owain Gruffydd (in Anthony Conran's unforgettable translation),

> And as I go, not a house I've seen
> Ready for praise, as it once had been —
> Serious song has gone from the scene,
>    There wants to hear me not one of the throng!
> Pure Welsh they do not willingly use:
> Twice better than the cywydd's muse
>    Is the pampered note of the English tongue.[8]

By the eighteenth century the affairs of Wales had come to be dominated by a small number of landlords of great power and wealth. There were, perhaps, several score of them. Many were members of the peerage and had access to lucrative offices, often sinecures, under the Crown. They were part of what has been called 'the broad, acquisitive, astute, ruthless and flexible oligarchy of England'.[9] Below them in the social order were the county gentry, whose sedulous cultivation of their pedigrees from the chiefly houses of medieval times (the 'royal tribes of Wales') contrasted oddly with their equally sedulous cultivation of the manners of well-born Englishmen. They had no harsher critics than the Welsh essayists of the early nineteenth century. 'The good days of the Principality seem to have departed with the misguided family of the Stuarts', wrote one:

> Had the higher ranks then shewn a dignified indifference to the ridicule that it became fashionable to attach to their nation, all would have been well . . . But instead of combating English prejudices, they fostered them; instead of aiding to elucidate national antiquities, they were themselves the foremost to bring the pursuit into contempt: they began to affect an ignorance of the Welsh language, and to echo the commonplace declamations against it that they heard elsewhere, allowing themselves to be deceived by the puerile self-sophism, that when they had forgotten the Welsh language, their own origin would be forgotten.[10]

Aspiring to a style of life that their small estates could not support, many of the county gentry were in financial difficulty, their lands mortgaged and their capital insufficient for agricultural improvement. Their survival as a class was possible only at the expense of the tenantry.[11]

Throughout most of the eighteenth century the level of industrial development in Wales was low and the units of production small. Coal, lead and copper were mined, and slate quarried, extensively but not intensively. Iron was smelted often from inferior grade ores at little charcoal furnaces dependent upon adequate local supplies of timber. The Tawe and Neath Valleys were the centres of copper and brass manufacture. Flannel was produced in many districts, but it was only late in the century that the first factories were established in mid-Wales.[12] Early industry used relatively little labour, and then often on a part-time |basis. The mass of the Welsh people, whether tenant farmers or cottagers and labourers, was locked into a system of peasant production on upland pastures. They were beset |by an indifferent climate, poor soils, bad communications and shortages of land made all the worse by an oppressive landlordism. They lived at a level of semi-subsistence, producing all that was necessary to sustain the family but obliged to send store animals and farm produce to the market in order to pay rents, tithes and taxes. The rhythm of life was punctuated by the great droves of livestock into England.[13] It is doubtful whether the peasantry of the lowland districts, where cereal cultivation replaced stock-rearing, was significantly more favoured. 'The distresses of many of these people', it was remarked in 1794, ' . . . simply arise from the difficulties they must encounter in maintaining themselves, their wives (and often large families) in comfort, with what they earn, notwithstanding their labours are from dawn to night, and many of them sober, discreet, and industrious.'[14] Unremitting poverty and overpopulation had to be relieved by emigration; by the middle of the century the movement of Welsh families to the rising industrial centres of Shropshire and south Staffordshire was one that was substantial if difficult to quantify.

The religious revivals in Wales in the middle decades of the eighteenth centry were appropriate to a people who could see little hope of earthly rewards. The genius of Griffith Jones created the 'circulating' schools and with them mass literacy in Welsh. But the literature to which the masses gained access was almost exclusively devotional in character. For the most part it was written by Anglican clergymen under the patronage of Anglican landowners and, designed to strengthen the moral fibre of the Welsh peasantry, it did so by inculcating the virtue of obedience to authority.[15] Popular culture withered under the impact. In the second half of the century high culture, by contrast, was revitalised. The intellectual revival was nurtured in the cosmopolitan environment of London. The Cymmrodorion Society was founded there in 1751 to promote Welsh literature, history, agriculture and trade. It ceased to function (temporarily) in 1787. Its place had been taken by the less élitist and politically more bold Gwyneddigion, founded in 1771, and its two radical 'tendencies' (as we might now say): the Cymreigyddion for Welsh speakers and the Caradogion for English. Under the skilful guidance of Owen Jones (Owain Myfyr) and William Owen (later Owen Pughe) a new interest in the Welsh past developed side by side with a new concern for the Welsh future. The movement nurtured a new breed of Welsh patriots and radicals, the *gwladwriaethwyr*. Their roots lay in old Dissent but their thinking was profoundly affected by the experience first of the American and then of the French revolutions. 'These new intellectuals of Wales', Gwyn A. Williams has written,

> were operating in precisely the same manner and to precisely the same rhythm as their counterparts in Europe during the age of revolution, those minority peoples emerging, in the eyes of their spokesmen, from a 'non-historic' existence, the Czechs, the Catalans, Serbs, Croats, indeed some Venezuelans, some Argentines and some Americans.[16]

Edwards Williams (Iolo Morganwg) reached far back into the Welsh past, and in the *gorsedd* found a concept of a self-regulating and egalitarian community that in fact owed more to the revolutionary republicanism of contemporary France than to the druidism of antiquity. John Jones (Jac Glan y Gors) wrote *Seren Tan Gwmmwl* ('Star under a Cloud') in 1795 and *Toriad y Dydd* ('Break of Day') in 1797, and thereby introduced his countrymen to the writings of Thomas Paine. In 1798 Thomas Roberts of Llwynrhudol violently attacked tithes and the Church in his *Cwyn yn erbyn Gorthrymder* ('Complaint against Oppression'). Radical journals, short-lived in the tradition of most such enterprises, were launched in rapid succession, the *Cylchgrawn Cymraeg* of Morgan John Rhys in 1793, the *Trysorfa Gymmysgedig* of Thomas Evans (Glyn Cothi) in 1795, and the *Geirgrawn* of David Davies of Holywell in 1796. William Jones of Llangadfan in the uplands of central Wales — 'a rank republican and leveller' according to a contemporary — chronicled the oppressive dominion of the Saxon in his country. 'We, the poor remnants of Ancient Britons', he wrote in an address intended for American readers,

> are confined in the mountains of Wales, cultivating an ungrateful soil, whose production is insufficient to support its occupiers. The

tendency of our boasted constitution to accumulate property into few hands, and the present wretched mode of taxing the produce of labour and the necessities of life, has of late increased the number of our poor into an alarming degree, and must sooner or later reduce the labouring classes into a servile dependency or absolute slavery, and which the insatiable avarice of the landed gentry has partly effected in our country.[17]

The Welsh 'Jacobin' movement has been recently treated with great sensitivity by Gwyn A. Williams.[18]

From 1 February 1793 Britain had been formally at war with republican France, and Pitt took advantage of the wave of populist anti-French sentiment to legislate an extension of the definition of treason and a limitation on the rights of association. Jacobinism was virtually outlawed. The Welsh *gwladwriaethwyr* were subjected to official harassment and Thomas Evans was jailed and pilloried. Their potential constituency ravaged by the ascendant reactionary fervour, they became almost to a man propagandists of emigration to North America: it was, they decided, only there that a new Welsh nation, free of oppression, could be founded. Their vision of the *gwladfa* (where, in the event, neither their revolutionary nor their national aspirations were to be realised) concealed from them the rapid transformation of the homeland that was taking place under the impact of industrialisation.

In the mid-eighteenth century Wales was an impoverished and under-developed peasant country ruled by an oligarchy of influential land-owners. By the mid-nineteenth century it had become an industrial nation. Power had passed into the hands of a plutocracy of ironmasters, coalowners, rentier-landlords and financiers, and the overall structure of the economy was approximating ever closer to that of England. In 1841, of the employed population of Wales, 27.3 per cent still worked in agriculture compared with 18.8 per cent in England, but 43.3 per cent were engaged in the manufacturing and extractive industries and related services compared with 51 per cent in England. The change was located principally in south Wales where, in the two counties of Glamorgan and Monmouth, only 14.8 per cent of the employed population worked in agriculture but 61.3 per cent in industry.[19] It was a result of a surge in the growth of the iron industry on the south Wales coalfield in the late eighteenth century.

In 1788 there were only 15 iron furnaces on the coalfield, and 7 of them still smelted with charcoal. The total annual make of iron was estimated at about 12,500 tons.[20] By early 1839 there were 122 furnaces in blast in south Wales, with a make of about 454,000 tons.[21] In 50 years production of iron had thus increased thirty-six-fold, and the advance in technology may be measured by the average annual output of a furnace: 833 tons in 1788 and 3,720 tons in 1839. The growth of the workforce is charted in the early censuses. In the iron-working district in Monmouthshire the population of the parish of Bedwellty, for example, grew from 619 in 1801 to 22,413 in 1841, and that of Trevethin from 1,472 to 14,042. In Glamorganshire Merthyr Tydfil was a parish of 7,705 people in 1801, and of 34,977 in 1841. Equally spectacular was the rate of capital formation. That of the Cyfarthfa ironworks increased from £14,369 in 1790 to £103,908 in 1798,[22] and, to judge from the movement of its shares, the capital value of the Dowlais ironworks rose from about £7,000 in 1782 to about £38,400 in 1792 and £61,000 in 1798.[23] Such were the key aspects of industrialisation in south Wales: labour and capital mediated by technology. In 1788 south Wales had accounted for about 20 per cent of the total production of iron in England and Wales. By 1839 the proportion had risen to 43 per cent. 'The iron trade continued rapidly to increase', wrote Harry Scrivenor in 1841; 'the great addition was principally in Wales, where the manufacture . . . may be considered as of modern growth.'[24] It was indeed not so much the *direction* as the *rate* of change that gave the Welsh industrial experience its singularly violent character.

The ironworks that proliferated in the late eighteenth and early nineteenth centuries were located on the eastern section of the south Wales coalfield, in the mountainous country of western Monmouthshire, eastern Glamorganshire and southernmost Breconshire (see Map 1.1).[25] Most of them were situated on the relatively gently dipping north crop of the coal, where ironstone, limestone, building stone and water were also all available in close proximity. They were integrated concerns, that is, the ironmasters ran their own collieries and iron mines. The independent sale-coal collieries tended to be located towards the interior of the mineral basin, where the deep cut of the rivers facilitated access to the seams by levels and cross headings following the rise of the coal. Even in the 1830s pits were the exception rather than the rule other than at collieries that were situated like Risca near the steeply dipping coal measures of the south crop. The iron-working and mining districts, the 'disturbed districts' as they became known in the late 1830s, had the character of an industrial enclave in the early nineteenth century such that they were sometimes also called the 'Black Domain' (a name that failed to achieve currency).[26] To their

**Map 1.1: South Wales. Early Nineteenth-century Population Centres and Approximate Limits of the Coalfield**

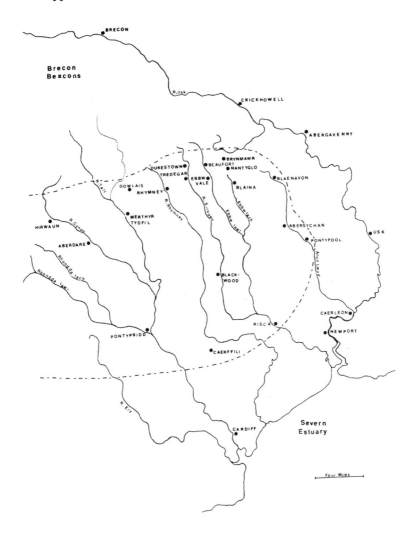

east lay the hilly farming country that rolled away from the valley of the Usk to the Welsh border along the Wye and Monnow, and to their north, beyond the heads of the valleys and the rim of the coalfield, the empty moorlands reached up to the greater heights of the Bannau

Brycheiniog, the Brecon Beacons. To the west, where the coal seams were thought to dip so deep that they could not be won, the land was also still rural in character. In 1836 the Rhondda appeared 'a wild and mountainous region where Nature seemed to reign in stern and unbroken silence amidst her own eternal rocks',[27] and the parish of Ystrad Dyfodwg, which included much of the Rhondda, only grew in population from 542 in 1801 to 748 in 1841.

The greater part of the manufacture of the ironworks was moved southwards to the Severn shore. There, on the estuaries of Taff and Usk, lay the ports of Cardiff (Caerdydd) and Newport (Casnewydd). Each was linked with the industrial hinterland by canals and connecting tramroads. The Glamorganshire Canal from Merthyr Tydfil to Cardiff was formally opened in 1794, and in 1812 a branch was constructed to Aberdare in the Cynon valley. The Monmouthshire Canal was in full operation by 1796. It ran the few miles from Newport to Bassaleg, whence a western branch was made to Crumlin on the Afon Ebwy or Ebbw River and an eastern one to Pontnewynydd on the Afon Lwyd. The Pontnewynydd branch was linked with the Brecon and Abergavenny Canal in 1812.[28] Hadfield estimated that by 1840 about £1½ million had been spent on the construction of the inland waterways and tramroads, perhaps some £800,000 on the former and £700,000 on the latter.[29] The tonnage of iron carried by the canal companies to Newport and Cardiff over the years 1821 to 1839 documents the growth both of the industry and of the ports (Figure 1.1).[30] The development of the export trade in coal, of the bituminous coal intended principally for household use, was rather later than that in iron. It was predicated upon the coalowners gaining access to the inland transportation system constructed to facilitate the movement of iron rather than coal. In 1799 Newport shipped only 18,359 tons of coal and Cardiff an estimated 7,000 to 10,000 tons.[31] (In that same year Swansea shipped 251,430 tons, though of semi-anthracitic coals more suitable for industrial than household use.) Twenty-five years later, in 1824, 375,759 tons of coal were exported through Newport and 19,713 through Cardiff.[32] Coal, however, was often stockpiled at the ports when the market was weak, and the shipping figures are a poor guide to production. Unfortunately the statistics for the quantities of coal consigned to the two ports via the canal companies are defective before 1830. The movement of coal in the 1830s, when production appears to have levelled off, is shown in Figure 1.2.[33] The population of Newport grew from 1,423 in 1801 to 13,766 in 1841, and of Cardiff from 1,870 to 10,077.

**Figure 1.1: Iron Carried to Newport by the Monmouthshire Canal Company and to Cardiff by the Glamorganshire Canal Company, 1821-39**

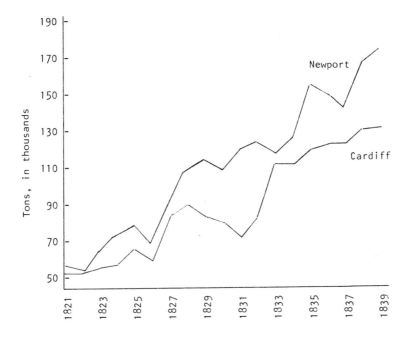

An estimated 436,800 tons of iron were smelted at the works in the hinterland of Newport and Cardiff in 1839.[34] The quantity of coal mined in the region in the same period can only be guessed. In 1839 Joseph Johnson, with 'very great difficulty' but the 'utmost exactness', calculated the amount of coal consumed in the manufacture of iron. He maintained that three tons of coal were needed to make one ton of iron at the furnaces, and a further 1.9 tons of coal were used in refining, puddling and rolling the make into the standard No. 2 bar.[35] Upwards of two million tons of coal, then, would have been required to sustain the iron industry at its 1839 level. This was mined at the collieries owned by the ironworks. In addition about 730,000 tons of coal mainly from the independent collieries were consigned to Newport and Cardiff through the canal companies.[36] Some coal was also sold locally for domestic consumption. The total quantity of coal mined in or

**Figure 1.2: Coal Carried to Newport by the Monmouthshire Canal Company, and to Cardiff by the Glamorganshire Canal Company, 1830-9**

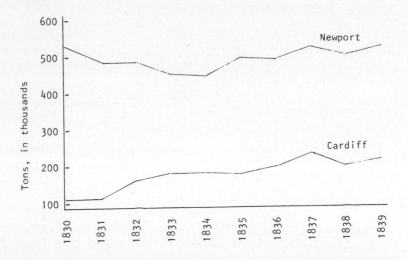

about 1839 is therefore unlikely to have been less than three million tons.[37]

The early iron industry in south Wales had access to adequate supplies of labour but the search for capital was an unremitting one. Increasingly companies began to supply part of that capital from their own resources by the reinvestment of profits, but new sources had still to be found to sustain growth and undertake the modernisation of old plant. In the 1830s a surge of money into south Wales occurred as a result of the formation of joint stock companies, an innovation in the iron industry. The Blaenavon Iron and Coal Company was floated in 1836 with an authorised capital of £300,000, and it purchased the old Blaenavon Ironworks from Thomas Hill for £220,000.[38] In the same year the Monmouthshire Iron and Coal Company was formed with an authorised capital of £300,000 to build the new Victoria and Abercarn works. By October 1839 £168,000 had been expended: £4,000 on wharves at Newport, £25,000 on Abercarn and the remainder on Victoria where a new township of 220 houses had already been built. The costs of completing the projects were estimated at a further £102,000.[39] In the short term the switch from private to public ownership, from family partnerships to joint stock companies, gave rise to grave problems during the deep recession in the iron trade in the early 1840s, and neither the Blaenavon nor the Monmouthshire Iron and Coal Companies succeeded. Ultimately, however, the public companies were to make possible the continued expansion of industry. The Welsh economy began to acquire its own distinctive characteristics and to develop its own particular markets.[40] In the second half of the nineteenth century it experienced sustained and rapid growth when the economies of England and Scotland were relatively stagnant. 'The inverse relation between phases of growth in Welsh and English coalfields between 1850 and 1913', Brinley Thomas remarked, 'is the key to the understanding of the evolution of the Welsh economy in that period.'[41]

Well over a century ago Charles Wilkins of Merthyr Tydfil pointed out that it was industrialisation that had saved Wales from replicating the Irish experience in the nineteenth century. The ironmasters and coalowners of Wales, he wrote,

> have not only fairly kept pace with the increase of population, and employed thousands at substantial wages, in comparison with the payment of agricultural labour, but they have prevented Wales from presenting the same condition as now exists in Ireland . . . The mere tillage of the soil could not have employed the population. Down in the agricultural counties of Cardigan, and Carmarthen, stalwart sons gain the rudiments of farming, but as they grow up they are compelled to look abroad for means of sustenance. If there were no iron or coal works, sufficient labour could not be had; even England could not, except in harvest time, employ the thousands of willing honest hands eager to be employed, and the result would be either semi-starvation in their own country, or excessive emigration to Australia and America.[42]

The thesis has recently been restated by Brinley Thomas. Industrialism, he argued, saved the language and culture of Wales from virtual extinction in the nineteenth century:

> Industrial development was on such a scale that Wales was able to retain a large proportion of the indigenous stock which was displaced from the country-side . . . Given a miracle, Wales, like Denmark, might have found her Grundvig; but it is much more likely, when we think of the physical disabilities of Welsh agriculture, that she would have been caught, like Ireland, in the vicious circle of mass emigration.[43]

In 1802 a local newspaper circulating in north Wales could inform the 'great numbers' about to emigrate to America that there was plenty of work in south Wales.[44]

If industry saved the Welsh nation from extinction, it did so at a price. It was J.L. and Barbara Hammond who saw that south Wales provided a paradigm of the social consequences of rapid and intensive industrialisation. It gives, they wrote, 'perhaps the most complete picture of the worst features of the Industrial Revolution', and they found an analogue to the Welsh experience in the mining towns and plantations of colonial Africa half a century later. There, they argued, it was also the case that 'the restraints of tradition, of a common history, of experience in government, were all wanting',[45] that is, that there was little or nothing, past or present, to mediate the gap between those who owned the means of production on the one hand and those who had only their labour to sell on the other. Not even a community of language bound the mass of the Welsh (or African) workers to those who came to preside over their lives, determining the hours that they worked and the wages they were paid, and often owning the houses in which they lived and the stores at which they shopped.

The new proletariat of south Wales lacked any constitutional access to political power. It showed itself, none the less, remarkably capable of autonomous action. In the early decades of the nineteenth century the level of turmoil on the coalfield rose steeply. The great strikes of 1816, 1822 and 1830 were testimony to the seemingly inexorable growth of working-class power. The clandestine organisation of the Scotch Cattle acted vigorously to promote a sense of working-class solidarity, and imposed its stern Scotch Law on those who flouted the imperatives of the emerging proletarian commonwealth. In 1831 the workers of Merthyr rose in revolt and for a few brief days challenged the ascendancy of the civil and military authorities. At that point, Gwyn A. Williams has remarked, 'the prehistory of the Welsh working class comes to an end. Its history begins.'[46] The south Wales insurrection of November 1839 belongs to the early phases of that history.

In May 1839 a writer in the *Western Vindicator* commented,

The Welshmen are completely alive to the evils resulting from the present state of society and government, and they are uniting in thousands to bring about the *requisite change* . . . Let but the local agitators do their duty in the mother tongue, and scatter widely the principles we espouse, and there will soon be created in Wales the finest democratic army in the world.[47]

Six months later, almost to the day, the forecast seemed to have come true. On Sunday, 3 November, the communities of ironworkers and colliers were systematically 'scoured', that is, ablebodied men were impressed into the ranks of an insurgent force that grew to one of many thousands. The next day several columns of workers marched into Newport. 'Is this the beginning of the *servile war* which was predicted as the inevitable consequence of the Whig oppression of the labouring classes?' asked the *Morning Herald.*[48] But Newport had been put into a state of defence by a company of the 45th Regiment of Foot. The attackers were forced to retire, leaving upwards of a score of their number dead. Word had it that a second attack on Newport was imminent and that other columns were poised to move against Brecon, Abergavenny, Monmouth, perhaps Cardiff. The government in London responded swiftly to the threat, despatching the remainder of the 45th Regiment and a brigade of the Royal Horse Artillery to the support of the companies of the 12th and 45th Regiments and the troops of Lancers already in south Wales. In late 1839 the coalfield was under *de facto* if not *de jure* military occupation. At the very least events there had shown that the participation of the workers in the instruments of their own domination was minimal. They aspired to establish the highest possible degree of working-class autonomy within the new industrial system and to curb the hegemonic impulse of the plutocracy of ironmasters, coalowners, landlords and financiers. At issue was the extent of the commonwealth of the workers: of the degree of dependence of capital on labour or of labour on capital.

## Notes

1. R.R. Davies, 'Colonial Wales', in *Past and Present*, 65 (Nov. 1974), pp. 3-23.
2. R.R. Davies, *Lordship and Society in the March of Wales, 1282-1400* (Oxford, 1978), pp. 426-7, 465-6. J. Goronwy Edwards, *The Principality of Wales 1267-1967* (Caernarvonshire Historical Society, 1969), pp. 20-6.
3. William Rees, 'The Union of England and Wales', in *Transactions of the Honourable Society of Cymmrodorion* (1937), pp. 27-100. P.R. Roberts, 'The Union with England and the Identity of "Anglican Wales" ', in *Transactions of the Royal Historical Society*, 22 (1972), pp. 49-70.
4. T. Jones Pierce, 'Landlords in Wales. A. The Nobility and Gentry', in Joan Thirsk (ed.), *The Agrarian History of England and Wales*. Volume IV. 1500-1640 (Cambridge, 1967), pp. 368-9. T. Jones Pierce, *Medieval Welsh Society* (Cardiff, 1972), especially pp. 369-89.
5. Jones Pierce, 'Landlords in Wales', pp. 370-81. Glanmor Williams, *Religion, Language and Nationality in Wales* (Cardiff, 1979), pp. 148-70.
6. Williams, *Religion, Language and Nationality*, pp. 171-99. A.H. Dodd, *The Character of Early Welsh Emigration to the United States* (Cardiff, 1953),

pp. 6-18.

7. J. Gwynfor Jones, 'The Welsh Poets and their Patrons, c. 1550-1640', in *Welsh History Review*, 9, 3 (June 1979), pp. 268-77.

8. Gwyn Jones (ed.), *The Oxford Book of Welsh Verse in English* (Oxford, 1977), pp. 110-11.

9. Gwyn A. Williams, *The Search for Beulah Land* (New York, 1980), p. 8.

10. Anon, 'The Anti-national Spirit of the Welsh Borders', in *The Cambrian Quarterly Magazine and Celtic Repertory*, II, 8 (Oct. 1830), pp. 471-2. For a recent attempt to refurbish the image of the gentry, see Williams, *Religion, Language and Nationality*, pp. 166-7.

11. P.F. Roberts, 'The Decline of the Welsh Gentry in the Eighteenth Century', in *National Library of Wales Journal*, XIII (1963-4).

12. For a useful summary of these developments, see E.D. Evans, *A History of Wales 1660-1815* (Cardiff, 1976), pp. 136-68.

13. The history of rural Wales in the eighteenth century remains relatively unstudied. David W. Howell, *Land and People in Nineteenth-Century Wales* (London, 1977), has no counterpart for the previous century and makes little reference back to it. But see D. Moore (ed.), *Wales in the Eighteenth Century* (Swansea, 1976). For the drovers, see R.J. Colyer, *The Welsh Cattle Drovers* (Cardiff, 1976).

14. John Fox, *General View of Agriculture in the County of Monmouth* (Brentford, 1794), p. 18.

15. Geraint H. Jenkins, *Literature, Religion and Society in Wales, 1660-1730* (Cardiff, 1978), p. 263.

16. Williams, *Beulah Land*, p. 11.

17. Gwyn A. Williams, *Madoc. The Making of a Myth* (London, 1979), p. 91.

18. Gwyn A. Williams, *The Welsh in their History* (London, 1982), especially pp. 48-61; *Beulah Land*, pp. 7-80; *Madoc*, pp. 89-117 A pioneering work in the field is Thomas Evans, *The Background of Modern Welsh Politics 1789-1846* (Cardiff, 1936), especially Ch. 2. For John Jones, Owen Jones, William Owen Pughe, Thomas Roberts, Edward Williams and others, see *The Dictionary of Welsh Biography down to 1940* (London, 1959).

19. Domestic servants are not included in these figures, since they cannot be distributed between the agricultural and industrial sectors. The source of the statistics is British Parliamentary Papers, *Abstracts of the Answers and Returns. Occupation Abstracts, 1841, Part I, England and Wales* (1844), Preface, pp. 22-3 and table facing p. 52. Figures are adjusted to include Monmouthshire in Wales.

20. Harry Scrivenor, *A Comprehensive History of the Iron Trade* (London, 1841), pp. 85-7. For the earlier industrial history of the region, see D. Morgan Rees, *The Industrial Archaeology of Wales* (London and Vancouver, 1975), pp. 29-62.

21. Joseph Johnson, 'On the State and Prospects of the Iron Trade in Scotland and South Wales, in May 1839', *Cambrian* (29 June 1839). David Mushet, *Papers on Iron and Steel, Practical and Experimental* (London, 1840), p. 415. Scrivenor, *Iron Trade*, p. 292. By 1811 there were said to be 22 furnaces fired by coal in Monmouthshire alone, with a make of about 44,000 tons (or an average of 200 tons per furnace), and several still fired by charcoal, see Charles Hassall, *General View of the Agriculture of the County of Monmouth* (London, 1812), pp. 10-14.

22. A.H. John, *The Industrial Development of South Wales 1750-1850* (Cardiff, 1950), p. 41.

23. Alan Birch, *The Economic History of the British Iron and Steel Industry 1784-1879* (London, 1967), p. 70. John Lloyd, *The Early History of the Old South Wales Iron Works (1760 to 1840)* (London, 1906), pp. 23-33.

24. Scrivenor, *Iron Trade*, p. 121.

25. Location of the early ironworks and collieries has been much facilitated by John Prujean's 'Map of the Iron-works and Collieries', 1843, Gwent County Record Office, D.38.28, and by 'Plan of the Canals and Railroads communicating with the Town of Newport Monmouthshire', 1839, Public Record Office, London, TS.11/496.

26. David J.V. Jones, *Before Rebecca. Popular Protests in Wales 1793-1835* (London, 1973), p. 86. The name 'Black Domain' was presumably coined by analogy with that of the 'Black Country' of south Staffordshire.

27. Thomas Roscoe, *Wanderings and Excursions in South Wales* (London and Birmingham, [1836] ), p. 245.

28. Charles Hadfield, *The Canals of South Wales and the Border* (Cardiff and London, 1960), Chs 6-8.

29. Ibid., p. 19.

30. Scrivenor, *Iron Trade*, pp. 123, 126, 293-4.

31. John, *Industrial Development*, p. 191. John's estimated figure for shipments from Cardiff may be wrong. An amount of a mere 313 tons is given in British Parliamentry Papers, *Report of the Commissioners appointed to Inquire into the Several Matters relating to Coal in the United Kingdom*, Vol. 3, C.435-2 (1871), Appendix to Report of Committee E, p. 6.

32. Ibid., Appendix to Report of Committee E, p. 67.

33. Ibid., Report of Committee E. p. 51 (Glamorganshire Canal), and *Glamorgan, Monmouth and Brecon Gazette and Merthyr Guardian* (henceforth referred to as *Merthyr Guardian*), 4 May 1844 (Monmouthshire Canal). I am grateful to Brian Davies for drawing my attention to the latter figures.

34. Mushet, *Iron and Steel*, pp. 414-5. The computation of 75 tons per week per furnace has been applied to all the 112 furnaces in blast in the hinterland of Cardiff and Newport. A return for 1836 shows that about 350,000 tons of iron were smelted in the same district in that year, *Cambrian* (16 Feb. 1839).

35. *Cambrian* (29 June 1839). See also Mushet, *Iron and Steel*, p. 307, who makes the lower estimate of 2 to 2½ tons of coal per ton of pig iron when smelting without hot blast.

36. Surpluses of coal from the ironworks were sometimes sent for sale at the ports, see J.H. Morris and L.J. Williams, *The South Wales Coal Industry 1841-1875* (Cardiff, 1958), pp. 82-90, and E.W. Evans, *The Miners of South Wales* (Cardiff, 1961), pp. 12-13.

37. This topic is also discussed in Morris and Williams, *South Wales Coal Industry*, pp. 6-8.

38. J. Knight, 'The Blaenavon Iron and Coal Company, 1836-1864', in *Bulletin of the Board of Celtic Studies*, XXVIII, 4 (May 1980), passim.

39. *Monmouthshire Merlin*, 27 May and 10 June 1837; *Merthyr Guardian*, 23 Nov. 1839.

40. In 1843, during the deep recession in the home market for iron, the agent of the Dowlais works was able to obtain an order for 12,000 tons of railway iron in Poland, see Birch, *British Iron and Steel Industry*, p. 168. For the development of the French market for Welsh steam coal, see J.E. Vincent, *John Nixon. Pioneer of the Steam Coal Trade in South Wales* (London, 1900), pp. 101-53.

41. Brinley Thomas (ed.), *The Welsh Economy* (Cardiff, 1962), p. 189.

42. Charles Wilkins, *Wales, Past and Present* (Merthyr, 1870), p. 234.

43. Thomas, *Welsh Economy*, pp. 27-8. Brinley Thomas, *Migration and Urban Development* (London, 1972), pp. 179-81. The thesis is supported by Alan Conway, 'Welsh Emigration to the United States', in *Perspectives in American History*, VII (1973), p. 271, and, with some qualifications, by Glanmor Williams, 'Language, Literacy and Nationality in Wales', in *History*, LVI (1971), pp. 10-13.

44. A.H. Dodd, *The Industrial Revolution in North Wales* (Cardiff, 1933),

citing *Chester Chronicle*, 20 Aug. 1802.
45. John L. and Barbara Hammond, *The Rise of Modern Industry* (New York, 1926), pp. 158-9.
46. Gwyn A. Williams, *The Merthyr Rising* (London, 1978), p. 230.
47. *Western Vindicator*, 4 May 1839. Italics original.
48. *Morning Herald*, 6 Nov. 1839. Italics original.

# 2 THE SOUTH WALES RISING THROUGH THE EYES OF THE PRESS

Brief accounts of the attack on Newport on 4 November 1839 reached several London newspapers in time for inclusion in the second editions the next day. *The Times, Morning Herald, Morning Chronicle* and *Sun*, for example, carried reports from their local correspondents that a body of armed men from the hills had entered Newport, had engaged the regular soldiers in fire, and had been put to flight. The *Sun* referred to 'an immense body' of assailants, *The Times* and *Herald* put their number at seven thousand or eight thousand, and the *Chronicle* at a thousand. Several correspondents reported that other bodies of men were marching on Brecon and some added that an attack on Monmouth was rumoured to be imminent. The immediate reaction of the London editors was apparent from the headlines they chose: 'Riots at Newport' (*Herald*), 'Alarming Chartist Riots at Newport' (*The Times*), 'Dradful [sic] Chartist Riots at Newport' (*Chronicle*), and 'Alarming and Fatal Riot' (*Sun*).

By 6 November a fuller picture of the events in south Wales was beginning to emerge. *The Times*'s correspondent reported that the workers ('the ignorant mountaineers of South Wales') had been convinced that they should create a 'kingdom of Chartism' by the popular demagogue Henry Vincent, but that it was only after he had been jailed in early May that they began to make serious plans 'for seizing the whole of South Wales to erect a Chartist kingdom'. Secrecy was preserved, he wrote, 'from the fact of the mountaineers universally making use of the Welch [sic] language', until,

> the men began their march from the 'hills' in the neighbourhood of Merthyr, etc., armed with muskets, guns, pikes, swords, crowbars, pickaxes, etc . . . and proceeded towards Newport, with the intention of dividing into various columns; one to attack and keep in check the soldiers at Newport, another to keep in check those stationed at Brecon, while a third marched to Monmouth to liberate Vincent. After which they were unitedly to seize the whole of South Wales.

The correspondent thought that at least 20,000 men had been mustered, a figure that seems to have excluded those from the eastern valleys. From reports reaching Bristol the *Herald*'s man guessed that between 40,000 and 50,000 men had joined the rebel ranks. Otherwise he told much the same story. The magistrates learned that 'the 4th of November had been fixed upon as the period for simultaneous attacks in Newport, Brecon, and Monmouth' and this information, he wrote,

> proved to be too correct, for on the 3d [sic] the general rising commenced – the mines and levels in the mountains were deserted – the furnaces were blown out, and the deluded advocates of chartism commenced their threatened march upon Newport.

The *Chronicle* for the same day, 6 November, revised its estimate of the numbers of men involved in the attack on Newport, citing one source for putting it at 20,000 and another at 10,000: 'blowing out all the furnaces as they proceeded, and pressing every man into their service, chiefly from the neighbourhood of Blackwood, Pont-y-pool, and Caerfilly'. The major London papers all relied upon correspondents in Bristol for their early coverage of the attack, and they in turn obtained their information from the despatches sent from Newport to the Bristol magistrates, requesting troops, and from the verbal reports of those who had made the passage of the Severn after the fighting.[1] As more and more accounts came in, so it became clear that the 'riots' of the earliest newspaper headlines were in fact very much more than that. Just what more became a matter of sustained comment.

A leader writer for the *Morning Herald* displayed something like a touch of admiration for the 'iron men [who] descended from the mines and levels of the mountains upon the town of Newport'. He had no doubts, however, about the gravity of the situation. 'Wales', he wrote,

> where rebellion never reared its head – where insurrection was unknown since the reign of HENRY IV until the disastrous sway of the whigs was inflicted upon England, has become the scene of revolutionary doctrines, violence, and bloodshed. The horrors of a chartist 'little war' have fallen upon the QUEEN'S dominions, which have been untainted with the blood of civil slaughter since the days of OWEN GLENDOWER.

The writer dismissed any idea that the 'little war' was only a particularly violent industrial dispute between masters and men. It was, he maintained, 'unequivocally of political origin' and he invited comparison with Ireland:

> . . . chartist violence has stained the soil of Wales with the blood of civil slaughter. Thus the hitherto most peaceful part of the kingdom has been rendered by whig misrule as *volcanic* as Ireland, only the flames burst out sooner: the Irish haters of the 'Saxons', whether white-boys, white-feet, or ribandmen, preferring the work of midnight assassination to open fighting in the light of day . . . The Welch hills have suddenly poured down a tumultuous torrent of desperate men, who, unlike the Irish barbarians, rushed upon the musket balls and bayonets of the military.[2]

The London *Courier* saw the matter in much the same light. 'The Chartist movement in South Wales', its leader writer observed,

> has commenced with a fury which seems to have taken the Government by surprise, and yet exhibits a degree of long previous preparation and organisation, which will leave their ignorance, if ignorant they were, without excuse . . . It will be seen that this insurrection, for it cannot be softened down to a mere riot, has been marshalled upon a most formidable footing, that an almost entire population has been embarked on it, a population proverbially excitable, and easily rendered, by wrongs real or imaginary, as hot as their furnaces.[3]

Within a few days of the rising a near consensus had emerged in the major newspapers on its magnitude if not its causes. 'An organised and armed insurrection has broken out in the counties of Monmouth and Glamorgan', *The Times* announced in its first leader of 7 November, and a few days later explained its stance:

> We feel that we have called that by the name of riot which should have been styled 'an insurrection'; for a riot is, strictly speaking, some sudden outbreak of popular fury, arising from some excitement of the moment; while here there has been sufficient evidence to show that this was no momentary outbreak, but a long-planned insurrection, deeply organized, managed with a secrecy truly astonishing, and which has been defeated only by concurrent acts of Providence.[4]

The events in south Wales, urged the *Manchester Guardian*, 'cannot, with any propriety, be denominated riots or outrages – but which, amounting as they do, to a direct levying of war against the queen's troops and the queen's authority, can be considered in no other light than as treasonable and rebellious insurrection ... '⁵

From 7 November onwards reports of the examinations conducted by the magistrates in south Wales were becoming available to the London and provincial editors, supplementing the flow of extemporary information. On 9 November, too, the local weekly newspapers appeared, and added much new detail to what was already available. That a large part of the population of industrial south Wales had taken up arms in rebellion was a source of acute embarrassment to the whig government and of some immediate satisfaction to the tory opposition. Wales became for a time a central issue in English politics. The editors had to confront the situation there and offer their readers some understanding of the unanticipated turn of events. For this task they were ill prepared. To most of them the affairs of Canada, India and other distant parts of England's far-flung empire were more familiar than those of its oldest possession of all.

The *Sun* was remarkable for the rapidity if not the lucidity of its attempt to establish a whig position. Its evening edition of 5 November carried a short leader on the matter. After the English chartists had rejected violence in pursuit of their aims, agitators turned their attention to Wales and in particular to 'the rude population of the mining districts about Newport'. By their actions the rebels – 'these madmen in Wales' – had set back the cause of reform and had united 'the higher and middle classes in dire hostility against their Charter'. The next day the whig *Morning Chronicle* confessed to finding the affair at Newport 'most inexplicable'. The Welshmen differed from the English chartists, its writer argued, for 'there is something in the disposition of the Welsh to embrace Chartism in its worst features, and to rush on to destruction, which deserves to be inquired into'. The writer's rather marginal contribution to that inquiry was to point to the distress caused by the expulsion of cottagers from the Crown wastes.⁶ A day later, however, the *Chronicle* did succeed in formulating a coherent whig position. First, it was suggested, the rising in Wales resulted from a combination of circumstances not reproduced elsewhere in the British Isles:

In no part of the country could an organization be formed, with so little interruption, as in a district where the lower orders speak almost universally a language unknown to the educated classes. In no part of the country is there such facility for obtaining arms as in a district of iron-works. The population are numerous, too, and naturally brave to temerity.

Second, the writer urged that the rising could not possibly have succeeded for 'there was never in the history of the world, a successful insurrection of mere working men'. And with that comforting thought in mind he went on to suggest that ignorance of the English language was at the root of the turmoil. 'It reflects no great credit on successive governments', he observed, 'that a large population should have been suffered to accumulate in this mining district with no provision for dispelling their ignorance.'[7] The belief that rebellion sprang from ignorance was in fact to become the key factor in the whig government's approach to the Welsh problem.

For the tory editors the approach to the rising virtually dictated itself. In their pursuit of power, proclaimed the *Morning Herald*, the whigs had encouraged jacobinism, 'doctrines subversive of monarchy, of order, of constitutional freedom'. The government had already succeeded 'in adding to the embarrassments of the empire *two successive rebellions* in Canada'. Now it was faced with 'insurrectionary movements' in Wales. The whigs, the writer maintained, 'are ever found in the one extreme or the other — either *stimulating the licentious violence of mobs, or making tyrannical thrusts at the constitutional liberties of the people*'.[8]     *The Times* was even shriller. The Welsh insurrection, it announced, 'is the offspring of Lord Melbourne's own loins. It is the spawn of Whiggery in office, truckling to sedition for its daily bread.'[9] None of the tory papers missed the fact that one of the Welsh leaders was the John Frost of Newport who an earlier whig Home Secretary, Lord John Russell, had seen fit to approve as magistrate. 'In what light could the ignorant and excitable population of Monmouthshire and Glamorganshire view this appointment?' asked the *Courier*; truly, it remarked, the government 'have sown the wind, and are now reaping the whirlwind'.[10] Russell had indeed later dismissed Frost from the magistracy, but, argued *The Times*, for the wrong reason: 'not by reason of his being a seditious revolutionist, but for the higher crime of rudeness and impertinence to the Whig Secretary of State'.[11]

Even the tory editors recognised, however, that the Welsh uprising required some rather more convincing analysis. The leader writer for the *Courier* found it in the backwardness of the Welsh and in the growth of religious dissent:

In addition to the prevalence of the grossest ignorance, for few can even read, and a very large proportion neither speak nor understand English, all the intercourse of life being carried on in the Welsh language, the majority of the people are generally sectarians of the lowest class and most degraded habits. It is no uncommon thing to find their most popular preacher a blacksmith or other low mechanic . . . [12]

For *The Times* this came uncomfortably close to conceding the whig position. Accordingly it devoted a lengthy editorial to a restatement of the correct tory line. 'They tell us', it argued,

that the Welch people are untaught. Well, then, if rebellion be the fruit of ignorance, why is Wales now, for the first time during centuries, in rebellion! They tell us that if the Welch clergy were to have taught the people in their native tongue, they would have fallen a less easy prey to the inculcation of criminal councils. Why, it is a known fact that *all* the parochial clergy throughout Wales are bound to understand the Welch tongue, and to officiate in it every Sabbath. Again, we are informed that if the magistrates could address the people in their 'native tongue', their exhortations would have been more attended to, and the progress of conspiracy would have been better watched and detected. This is purely ignorant and childish twaddle.

In its eagerness to establish its own position *The Times* did not allow awkward facts to stand in the way. 'The people of the mining districts', it roundly proclaimed, 'are not Welch exclusively, nor are the majority Welchmen. They are composed of English, Irish, Scotch, of whom none, or hardly five in a hundred, are acquainted with the Welch dialect.' The matter of language thus set aside with scant respect for reality, the writer felt able to identify the true problem:

No, the fountain of the mischief is more tangible and specific. A restless and unruly spirit has been spread among the working classes by those who, for profligate and selfish ends, desired to shake all pre-existing power, and to draw to themselves whatever portions of the monarchy should remain unblighted. Conservatism, or the principle of stability, upheld by all that was most independent, virtuous, enlightened, and noble in the land, stood as a barrier against the principle of unwholesome change, pushed onwards by poverty, profligacy, and desperation. The Whigs became vassals to this demon power, to it they have sold themselves, and with it – nay, through it – they are at this moment about to perish.[13]

The indignation of *The Times* became uncontainable when it learned that the Home Secretary, Lord Normanby, had written to the mayor and magistrates of Newport to convey the queen's approval of their conduct 'on the occasion of the outrage recently committed in the town of Newport'. It must be a hoax, commented the paper:

To find the Home Minister describing the late proceedings at Newport by the comparatively mild word 'outrage' will startle, we think, equally those who have read the accounts of those proceedings, and those who have contented themselves with merely ascertaining that there have been numerous commitments for HIGH TREASON of persons engaged in them. 'Outrage', my Lord Normanby! We pray you to recollect that *you are not in Ireland now!*[14]

Consistent whig and tory attitudes to the Welsh rising did emerge in the press. The chartist editors by contrast failed to develop any common position, and nothing illustrated more clearly the extent to which the issue of 'physical force' divided the radical politicians. The *Charter*, a London weekly which claimed on its masthead to be 'established by the Working Classes', took the impeccable line that the aristocratic and middle classes had driven the Welsh workers into rebellion:

These classes – by a long series of legislative acts – have reduced the 'masses' to a state of poverty, and then goaded them to despair and a reckless contempt for danger, by an insolent mockery of their wretchedness. The monopolists, as they would be, of all that is essential to social comfort and enjoyment, cannot, for the souls of them, forget the good old creed in which they were suckled, – that capital is everything, labour nothing.

Nevertheless the writer found the events in south Wales both 'extraordinary and deplorable', and proceeded to explain his choice of adjectives:

We say extraordinary, as well as deplorable, for it has never fallen to our lot to read of an insurrectionary movement which appeared to be at once so destitute of high purpose, and so characterised by

sheer folly . . . We know not with whom the insane project originated, but are disposed to give the credit of it to some base myrmidon
of the Whigs, whose object was at once to humiliate and punish a
body of enthusiastic and generous, but undisciplined men.[15]

No hint of the identity of the supposed agent of whig perfidy was
offered.

The *Northern Star*, a chartist weekly published from Leeds, was
known to be more sympathetic to the 'physical force' concept. Its
leader writer − probably the editor, William Hill − disclaimed any
direct knowledge of the situation in south Wales, but expressed his
belief that 'it is not a light sense of wrong which has converted the
peaceful hills of Cambria into mountain fastnesses of war'. Grievances,
he thought, 'which could thus excite the sympathies of a whole population in one movement for redress can have been of no ordinary
character'. He inclined to attribute the rising to the repressive quality
of government. 'The simplest movements of an ordinary social character were construed into crimes, and made to furnish nurture to the
terror of the law', he wrote; 'thus deprived of all protection of the law,
what wonder if the people should lose some portion of their habitual
respect for the law.'[16] In its next issue a week later the paper returned
to the matter with an apology for its earlier lack of enthusiasm. 'We
inclined last week', it confessed, 'to view the recent outbreak, as the
madness of a few, heightened by the colouring of the Government
artists.' Now, however, it felt able to place 'the stamp of reality' on its
observations on the rising:

That it was a mountain torrent long pent up until continued oppression, and multiplied insult, prematurely burst the dams, we now
believe. That other and nobler motives than plunder, devastation, or
merely the supply of immediate want, urged the assailants to the
attack is manifest from the fact that many are sworn to be in good
and constant employment.[17]

Of all the chartist weeklies the *Western Vindicator*, published from
the west of England, had been the most active in the dissemination of
ultra-radical ideas in south Wales, and it had carried a number of
features in Welsh. Curiously enough the issue of 26 October contained
an editorial apologia for the decline of chartism. 'That the spirit of
Chartism does not at present render itself so apparent as it did some
time since, may, perhaps, be admitted', it allowed, 'but does it follow

necessarily, that it has ceased to be . . . ? The Chartists do exist. They bide their time.' It is difficult not to detect a subterfuge here. Certainly the first issue of the paper after the attack on Newport came out with the bold headline, 'Revolution in Wales'. The stand was firm:

> We, being somewhat conversant with the history of the revolutions which have taken place in other nations, and having made it our business to ascertain the causes of these revolutions, foretold that nothing could avert a physical revolution in this country . . . When we reflect upon the state of the country, and consider how our friends have been cast into dungeons, there to die of starvation, we are not at all surprised at what has taken place near our borders.

Indeed, in the rising of the Welshmen the *Vindicator* found an example to be followed:

> Oh, Englishmen! let not the sturdy sons of Walia eclipse your glory;
> be up and stirring, and hold yourselves in readiness, for
> > Now's the day and now's the hour
> > To resist oppression's power.[18]

In the tense situation which prevailed in late 1839 the paper's rhetoric was unlikely to escape the attention of the government. *The Times* ensured that it did not. It reproduced the offending passages and accused the *Western Vindicator* of 'inflaming the minds of the deluded people and exciting them to rebellion'.[19] By 18 November the Home Secretary had taken the decision to prosecute the publisher.[20] The editor made a belated attempt to dissociate his paper from any suspicion of complicity in the rising by printing Letter XXXIX of the pseudonymous Publicola. 'No person', urged the columnist, 'could have been more surprised at the late riots in Newport than ourselves; we are now in the dark as to the intentions of the Welshmen who created these riots.'[21] But time had run out for the *Western Vindicator*. Copies of the paper for 30 November were seized by the magistrates in south Wales, and early in December the Home Secretary approved its suppression.[22]

In their attitudes towards the Welsh insurrection tory and whig writers alike showed themselves affected by a whiggish sense of destiny, though the tories did not of course regard the current whig administration as an acceptable arbiter of that destiny. The inexorable course of English history, towards the supremacy of Parliament and the rule of law, was seen as guaranteeing the liberty and well-being of the sub-

jects. Many of the chartist spokesmen, increasingly inclined to constitutional agitation and class collaboration, concurred in this view of
affairs. Events such as those which convulsed south Wales in late 1839
were therefore assumed to be aberrations. They were an affront to
history. But in fact they revealed the weakness of the hegemonic control
of the British state over one more part of its dominions: Wales, that is,
began to look like another Ireland. It is in the nature of a paradox that
in the circumstances many of the English publicists assumed the role of
apologists for the Welsh insurrection. They sought to explain it away as
the result of repressive government or unbridled reform, or Welsh backwardness, or irresponsible agitation. None sensed that the armed struggle
which the Welsh workers waged against the regimen of ironmasters and
coalowners signalled the appearance of a distinctly new conjunction of
national and class interests.

## Notes

1. Only the correspondent of the *Morning Chronicle* identified his sources,
namely, the guard of the Cardiff mail; Mr Giradon, brother of the Bristol coroner;
Captain Jeffries of the Usk-Newport steam packet; Captain Allen of the Bristol-
Cardiff steam packet; and three passengers. The twice weekly *Manchester
Guardian* was exceptional in receiving its earliest reports of the rising from Pontypool rather than Newport.
2. *Morning Herald*, 6 Nov. 1839. Italics original.
3. *Courier*, 6 Nov. 1839.
4. *The Times*, 11 Nov. 1839.
5. *Manchester Guardian*, 9 Nov. 1839.
6. *Morning Chronicle*, 6 Nov. 1839.
7. Ibid., 7 Nov. 1839.
8. *Morning Herald*, 6 Nov. 1839. Italics original.
9. *The Times*, 7 Nov. 1839.
10. *Courier*, 6 Nov. 1839.
11. *The Times*, 7 Nov. 1839.
12. *Courier*, 6 Nov. 1839.
13. *The Times*, 9 Nov. 1839.
14. Ibid., 13 Nov. 1839. Italics original.
15. *Charter*, 10 Nov. 1839.
16. *Northern Star*, 9 Nov. 1839.
17. Ibid., 16 Nov. 1839.
18. *Western Vindicator*, 9 Nov. 1839.
19. *The Times*, 12 Nov. 1839.
20. Public Record Office, London, HO.41/15: Home Sec. to P.B. Purnell,
18 Nov. 1839.
21. *Western Vindicator*, 30 Nov. 1839. For 'Publicola', see Thomas Evans, *The
Background of Modern Welsh Politics 1789-1846* (Cardiff, 1936), pp. 132-3. He is
assumed to be David Rees, editor of *Y Diwygiwr*.
22. *Monmouthshire Merlin*, 14 Dec. 1839.

# Part II: CLASSES IN CONFLICT

Bogey, bogey, one pound ten,
All for the masters, none for the men.

(Early nineteenth-century south Wales children's song)

Among brown hills and black hills
    And hills bleak and bare
They have given us hovels
    And a bed and a chair
And told us to labour
    And not to desire
The cake of the countess,
    The wine of the squire.

(Idris Davies, *The Angry Summer*, Faber and Faber, 1943)

In green and gracious valleys among the hills of Gwent
We never saw the sunshine, to earth our backs were bent,
Like a toiling slave an early grave was all we had to gain,
So we struck like men and struck again, but our struggle was in vain.

(Harri Webb, *Rampage and Revel*, Gomer Press, 1977)

# 3 LANDOWNERS, CAPITALISTS AND THE GROWTH OF INDUSTRY

In the aftermath of the November Rising one essayist identified among its causes the lack of a local squirearchy able to exercise a 'moral influence' over the ironworkers and colliers.[1] He wrote from Dublin and clearly had little insight into the nature of the new proletariat created by industry. He was quite correct, however, about the disappearance of the old local landed gentry. Its extraordinary decline (a 'rush toward extinction') in the eighteenth century has been the subject of a recent study.[2] By the turn of the century Monmouthshire and Glamorganshire were dominated by an oligarchy of great magnates, most notably the Nevills, Earls of Abergavenny; the Somersets, Dukes of Beaufort; the Stuarts, Marquesses of Bute; the Morgans of Tredegar Park; and the Hanburys of Pontypool.

The Barony of Abergavenny had been created for Edward Nevill (died 1476), youngest son of the Earl of Westmorland. His successors in the barony and later earldom showed little interest in Wales, for their principal estates lay in the south of England and in the border counties. Nevertheless, of the 18 ecclesiastical livings which Henry Nevill controlled in the early nineteenth century, half were in Monmouthshire.[3] The Somerset connection with Wales was almost as old. It was established by Charles Somerset (died 1526), an illegitimate son of the Duke of Somerset. He was a strong supporter of Henry Tudor, and married into the ancient Welsh house of the Herberts of Pembroke. Most of the Beaufort lands were in Wales, and the dukes were continuously and intensively involved in Welsh affairs. In the early nineteenth century it was remarked that the Somerset 'ramifications in church and state are almost untraceable'.[4] By virtue of his estates in south Wales alone, Henry Charles Somerset (died 1835), the sixth Duke, held the lord lieutenancies of Monmouthshire and Breconshire, in which capacities he directed operations against the workers at the time of the great strike of 1816. He also received the rents for Monmouthshire in the Duchy Court of Lancaster; controlled the parliamentary seat for Monmouth Boroughs and one of the seats for the shire; was patron of seven ecclesiastical livings in Breconshire and Monmouthshire; and was, *inter alia*, lord of the manor of Newport.[5]

By contrast, the Stuarts were newcomers to Wales. 'No one', it has been remarked, 'would have mistaken the Stuarts of Cardiff Castle for the old gentry of Glamorgan with whom they were often at odds.'[6] In the eighteenth century the Glamorgan estates of the Herberts of Pembroke passed through the female line to Herbert, second Viscount Windsor, and thereafter, again through the female line, to John Mount-stuart, Baron Cardiff, fourth Earl and later first Marquess of Bute (died 1814).[7] His successor John, second Marquess (died 1848), came to exercise an influence in the affairs of Glamorganshire comparable to that of the Somersets in Monmouthshire. He held the lord lieutenancy of the shire (and so followed closely the activities of the rebels in 1839), controlled the parliamentary seat for Cardiff; was patron of six livings in Glamorganshire and one in Monmouthshire; and was, *inter alia*, lord of the castle and manor of Cardiff.[8]

The Morgans of Tredegar Park near Newport were not to obtain a peerage until 1859, when Sir Charles Morgan (died 1875), became first Baron Tredegar, but the family claimed descent from the eleventh-century Cadifor Fawr, lord of Cil-sant in west Wales. In 1792 the main line failed. In that year Judge-Advocate General Sir Charles Gould (died 1806) acquired through his wife the name of Morgan, some 40,000 acres of land yielding revenues of £30,000 a year, and control of the parliamentary seats for Breconshire and Brecon Boroughs and of one of those for Monmouthshire.[9] Entry to estates through the female line, instanced by Herbert Windsor, John Mountstuart and Charles Gould, was not uncommon. The Glamorgan lands of Thomas Lewis of Van passed through his daughter to Other Windsor, third Earl of Plymouth (died 1732),[10] and a moiety of those of Charles Mathew of Castell-y-Mynach through his daughter to Charles, first Baron Talbot and Lord Chancellor of England (died 1737).[11]

The growth and consolidation of the great estates in southeast Wales has still to be fully studied.[12] Clearly the penchant of the old Welsh families for marrying their daughters into the English aristocracy much affected the composition of the landowning class. Agricultural rents, political preferment and auspicious marriages were the buttresses of oligarchy, and few of the magnates in south Wales showed any early appreciation of the mineral wealth of their properties. An exception to this generalisation were the Hanburys of Pontypool. Their connection with south Wales extended back to the second half of the sixteenth century, when Richard Hanbury acquired interests in forges and furnaces in Monmouthshire at Tintern, Monkswood, Machen, Abercarn and Pontypool.[13] A series of well-chosen marriages in the seventeenth and eighteenth centuries brought the family appointments under the Crown, seats in Parliament and more land. On the accession of George III to the throne, Capel Hanbury was offered a peerage. A friend of John Wilkes and sympathiser with the cause of liberty, he declined it. In the early nineteenth century his grandson, Capel Hanbury Leigh (the last an assumed name), expanded and modernised the Pontypool works, presided over his extensive estates, and was serving as Lord Lieutenant of Monmouthshire at the time of the rising in 1839.[14]

The Hanburys apart, it is a measure of the general lack of interest in industry that the south Wales magnates continued, to the end of the eighteenth century, to lease mineral rights over their lands at what were virtually nominal rents, asking no royalties on the minerals won. In 1748, for example, Herbert, Viscount Windsor, leased for £26 a year for 99 years the rights over part of the Herbert estates he had inherited: a tract of land extending from Dowlais Top southwards to Gelligaer. The cost to the lessee appears to have been under a halfpenny per acre per year.[15] On it the Dowlais ironworks were later constructed. In 1765 William, Baron Talbot, and Michael Roberts of Cardiff, joint heirs to the old Mathew estates, leased mineral rights over 4,000 acres in the parish of Merthyr for 99 years at £100 a year, or 6d an acre.[16] The Cyfarthfa works were built on it. Even a quarter of a century later, when the signs of industrial growth were quite apparent, mineral rents remained remarkably low. In 1789 Henry, Earl of Abergavenny, leased the rights under 12,000 acres of land in northern Monmouthshire for 21 years at £1,300 a year, or 2s 2d an acre, still with no royalties.[17] The Blaenavon works were constructed there.

In 1812 Charles Hassall argued that it was pride that deterred the 'Cambrian' landowners from involving themselves in the early iron trade.[18] It was clearly more. Wales was relatively remote from the London market, its communications were notoriously bad, and its impoverished peasantry were nevertheless conservatively attached to the land. It was not at all obvious in the later eighteenth century that the iron industry in south Wales could achieve competitiveness with the older and more advanced works in the west midlands and north of England. There was little incentive for the landowners to invest their money in such speculative ventures. Yet no other sources of capital on the appropriate scale were available in Wales for, despite its annexation to England in 1536, it had participated only peripherally in those developments which transformed England over the next two centuries into the world's first industrial capitalist nation. Specifically, the Welsh economy had been totally dominated by the requirements of the

English markets and the conditions did not exist for the emergence of an indigenous (or national) Welsh bourgeoisie. It is true that there were a few Welshmen, surviving members of the old local gentry, who were quick to see in industry a possible alternative to complete penury. Thomas Lewis of Llanishen (who already owned several small charcoal-fired furnaces) and Thomas Price of Caerffili, for example, began to erect the first blast furnace at Dowlais in 1758. They were, however, unable to supply the capital — a modest £4,000 — necessary to complete the project, In 1759 they were forced to launch a company with 16 shares of £250 each and they acquired seven partners: four were merchants of Bristol and one the well-known Bersham ironmaster Isaac Wilkinson.[19]

The foundation of the Dowlais works was exceptional in that the initiative was taken by local entrepreneurs. In requiring immediate inputs of outside capital, however, the development of the works set a pattern. John Lloyd, that excellent chronicler of the south Wales iron industry, remarked that the Welshmen had enterprise and skill but lacked 'the staying power of sufficient capital behind them . . . and left the field for English promoters and English capitalists to exploit and to capture'.[20] He depicted, in vivid terms, the events which drastically changed the coalfield in the late eighteenth century. 'A whole troupe of English ironmasters', he wrote,

> invaded the Welsh Hills, the indigenous Welsh inhabitants being either lookers-on, or hewers and drawers for those who, with capital and skill, soon changed the solitudes of the high plateau land and the valleys and slopes of the mountains, from a solitude into a teeming hive of human industry.
>
> The Welsh looked on and wondered at the changes effected before their eyes: great furnaces being erected in every direction, and money lavishly expended by strangers, of whom they scarcely knew the names and nothing as to where they came from, except from Staffordshire, London, or Bristol.[21]

The first of the great south Wales ironmasters was Anthony Bacon. In the 1730s and early 1740s he had run a successful business at White-haven in Cumbria, dealing in the coal trade to Ireland and the tobacco trade to the colony of Maryland (where he resided for a time). In the mid-1740s he moved his offices to London, and in the next decade extended his interests to West Africa. In 1764 he succeeded John Wilkes as member of Parliament for Aylesbury, at which time he held several government contracts for the supply of slaves to the West Indian colonies.[22] The next year, in partnership with his relative, William Brownrigg of Whitehaven, Bacon founded the Cyfarthfa ironworks at Merthyr.[23]

With considerable prescience, Anthony Bacon entered the gun-founding business in 1773. Initially he acted as broker for the newly invented solid-bored cannon between John Wilkinson of Bersham, Broseley and Bilston, who claimed the patent, and the Board of Ordnance in London. In this venture Bacon was already associated, by mid-1774, with the Yorkshire-born London ironmonger, Richard Crawshay, though the arrangement was apparently not such as to preclude intense rivalry between the two. With the outbreak of the American War in 1775, Wilkinson's patent was cancelled in the national interest and Bacon announced his readiness to produce the new cannon at his Cyfarthfa works. In 1777 Brownrigg relinquished his partnership with Bacon for some £1,500, but by that time the latter had already entered into a formal association with Crawshay in London. Business boomed with the supply not only of cannon and shot, but also of coal and victuals, to the armies in America.[24] In or about 1777 Bacon acquired the leases of the defunct Plymouth ironworks in Merthyr (which had been started by John Wilkinson's father, Isaac, and manager, John Guest), and in 1780 he rented the moribund Hirwaun works (started by the Worcestershire ironmaster John Maybery), and revived them with an injection of new capital.[25]

The west Midlands ironmaster Francis Homfray, who owned a furnace near Broseley in Shropshire and a forge near Kinver in Staffordshire, was brought to Merthyr by Anthony Bacon in 1782. It may be that rumours that Bacon had traded with *both* sides during the American War affected his standing with the Board of Ordnance,[26] or it may be that Bacon anticipated that, with the end of the war, the market would shift from munitions to bar iron. Whichever the case, for a token rent Bacon leased a mill and foundry at Cyfarthfa to Homfray, and informed the Board of Ordnance that Homfray would henceforth take over his orders for cannon.[27] Homfray relinquished the works to David Tanner of Monmouth only two years later.[28] Before returning to England, however, Homfray obtained several mineral leases on small properties around Merthyr for his sons, Jeremiah, Thomas and Samuel, and there they erected the Penydarren ironworks.[29] Two of the sons were to play a major part in the expansion of the industry in south Wales. Samuel Homfray managed Penydarren very successfully and in 1800 built the Tredegar works on land leased from the Morgans of

Tredegar Park.[30] Jeremiah Homfray started the Ebbw Vale works in 1789, the Abernant works in 1801, and in 1803 he took a lease on Hirwaun. The Pen-y-cae lands on which the Ebbw Vale works were built belonged to Henry Lewis, a local freeholder. He was reluctant to sell to Jeremiah Homfray until his wife reminded him that he probably had little choice. *'Gwerth ê. Cofiwch y brad y cyllyll hirion. Saeson ydyw ef'*, she is reported to have said, speaking to more than thirteen centuries of history: 'Sell it. Remember the treachery of the long knives. He is an Englishman.'[31]

Anthony Bacon died in 1786. The trustees of his estate rented the Cyfarthfa works to Richard Crawshay; the Plymouth works to Bacon's manager and friend, Richard Hill; and the Hirwaun works to Samuel Glover, Birmingham merchant and proprietor of the Abercarn Forge which drew its supplies of pig iron from Hirwaun.[32] It was Richard Crawshay, however, who assumed the commanding position in the Welsh iron industry previously held by Bacon, and the ramifications of his interests were highly extended ones. His sister, Elizabeth, married twice. Her first husband joined Crawshay's London firm but, as a result of his early death, the post was taken by her second husband, Robert Thompson from Grayrigg in Westmorland. In the mid-1790s Thompson held a one-sixteenth share in Dowlais, but sold it to buy the Tintern Abbey works on the Wye.[33] He also had banking interests in Chepstow. Robert Thompson's brother, William, was a merchant in the City of London. He too acquired various partnerships in south Wales: in the Aberdare ironworks in 1799, in the Tredegar works (with Samuel Homfray) in 1800, and in the Penydarren works (*vice* Samuel Homfray) in 1819.[34] William Thompson died a bachelor. His heir was his nephew William, son of a third brother James Thompson. The junior William Thompson, known as Alderman Thompson, added the proprietorship of Penydarren to his many other interests which included the seat in Parliament for the City of London. The interlocking nature of the Crawshay, Homfray and Thompson concerns is reflected in the marriages between the families. The wife of Richard Crawshay, grandson of the founder of Cyfarthfa, was Mary Homfray, granddaughter of Francis Homfray who founded Penydarren. The brother of the younger Richard Crawshay, William Crawshay jr., was married to Elizabeth Homfray, sister of Mary. When Elizabeth Crawshay née Homfray died in 1813, William Crawshay jr. remarried. His second wife was Isabel Thompson, sister of Alderman Thompson and niece of the elder Richard Crawshay's brother-in-law![35]

Richard Crawshay, founder of the Cyfarthfa dynasty, had another sister, Susannah, who married a Yorkshire farmer, John Bailey. Two of their sons, Joseph and Crawshay Bailey, were given positions in the Cyfarthfa works. Richard Crawshay's daughter, Charlotte, made a marriage which brought a touch of aristocratic sensibility to her eminently bourgeois family. Her husband was Benjamin Hall (of Christ Church, Oxford, and Lincoln's Inn), elder son of the Chancellor of Llandaff.[36] In 1803 Crawshay and Hall purchased the Union ironworks in the Rhymney Valley,[37] and in 1808 the former acquired the Abercarn works from the Glover estate and immediately made them over to his son-in-law as a gift.[38] By his will of 1809 and codicils of 1810 Richard Crawshay bequeathed the Union works to Hall, but divided Cyfarthfa between Hall with a three-eighths share, his son William Crawshay with a like share, and his nephew Joseph Bailey with a quarter.[39] Bailey immediately sold out his share to William Crawshay, and in partnership with the Cyfarthfa manager Matthew Wayne leased the moribund Nantyglo ironworks from Thomas Hill and Co. In 1820 Wayne withdrew, and Crawshay Bailey took up his partnership.[40] Wayne went on to found the small Gadlys ironworks on land leased from the Marquess of Bute.[41] Joseph and Crawshay Bailey, having revived the Nantyglo works, acquired the Beaufort works from the Kendalls in 1833.[42]

Gwyn A. Williams has aptly referred to the 'Bacon-Crawshay empire'.[43] It was an empire built on the profits of the Atlantic trade in tobacco and slaves and, when war intervened, on the booming demand for munitions. In the aftermath of the American struggle Richard Crawshay explored the possibility of settling Welsh ironworkers in Pennsylvania;[44] the project nicely reflects both the Atlantic connections and the hegemonic impulse of his empire. In the late eighteenth century that empire dominated the iron industry in south Wales. It was not, however, co-extensive with it. Indeed, for a time its dominion was threatened by a rival 'Wilkinson-Guest empire'. The Wilkinsons, Cumbrians perhaps of Salopian origins, were among the pioneers — not least in technology — of the iron industry in north Wales and the west midlands of England. Isaac Wilkinson took over the old ironworks at Bersham, near Wrexham, in 1753, and his son John joined him there within a year or two.[45] In the late 1750s and early 1760s John Wilkinson built up the Bradley ironworks at Bilston, on the south Staffordshire coalfield, and the New Willey works at Broseley, on the Severn in Shropshire. In the same period Isaac Wilkinson became the first of the English ironmasters to show an interest in the development of the industry in south Wales. In 1759 he took a one-sixteenth share (for £250) in the Dowlais company launched by the two early Welsh entrepreneurs,

Thomas Lewis and Thomas Price. He brought to the company his patent of 12 March 1757 for a new type of blowing-engine, on which he was to be allowed a royalty on the make.[46] In 1762 he sold his share in Dowlais.[47] It seems that he needed the capital, little though it was, for a new venture.

Among John Wilkinson's experienced managers at the Broseley works was John Guest. At the end of 1763 Isaac Wilkinson of Wrexham and John Guest of Broseley obtained mineral leases in the Merthyr area from the Earl of Plymouth at £60 a year.[48] On the land the first Plymouth works were started probably in mid-1765, when Guest had already arrived in Merthyr.[49] The history of the venture is highly obscure. It is clear, however, that by 1767 Guest had gone on to become manager of Dowlais. Left to his own resources and gravely under-capitalised, Isaac Wilkinson for a time persisted. He leased a small property in Cwm Canaid in 1768, for £18 a year,[50] and spent £200 opening a coal pit on it. A protracted dispute with the colliers, however, reduced him to penury. He relinquished his Merthyr interests (which Anthony Bacon took over in or about 1777) and moved to Bristol, where he died in 1784.[51] John Guest managed the Dowlais works with great success and in 1782 bought himself into the partnership by acquiring six of its sixteen shares for £2,600.[52] Dowlais was to flourish under the Guests, but the 'Wilkinson-Guest empire' had faltered and collapsed. Only the participation of John Wilkinson in it might have changed the situation, but he had built up a different empire based on Wrexham, Broseley and Bilston.

In the late eighteenth century the cost of erecting a single blast furnace with ancillary plant appears to have been around £13,000 to £14,000.[53] Since not even the wealthiest of entrepreneurs had the flow of cash necessary to build a large works of several furnaces, the industrialisation of south Wales involved a relentless pursuit of capital. That capital came for the most part from Bristol and London merchants and bankers, who appeared as partners in every company. Such were the Harfords and the Formans, to take two examples. The Harfords, of Worcestershire background, were merchants and bankers in Bristol.[54] James Harford and his sons, with John Partridge, formed a company (a 'Committee of Tradesmen') specifically, it seems, to enter the south Wales iron industry. They acquired interests in the Monmouth forges and Melingriffith works in the 1780s,[55] and in 1791-2, as Messrs Harford, Partridge and Co., entered into a partnership with Thomas Hill and others to erect the Nantyglo works. They also provided two-thirds of the capital for the purchase and expansion of Ebbw Vale. In 1796 the company obtained full control of the Ebbw Vale works and, between 1799 and 1818, of the Sirhowy works.[56] The Formans, merchants of London, provided the Homfrays with most of the capital for the erection of the Penydarren works in 1784, and backed the construction of the Tredegar works by Samuel Homfray in 1800. They were also partners in the Aberdare Iron Company around 1799, and launched the Bute works in 1825.[57]

By the end of the eighteenth century the industrialisation of south Wales was proceeding vigorously. Many of the great ironworks were in full blast and Lloyd's 'whole troupe of English ironmasters' had arrived on the coalfield, some to fail and others to succeed beyond their expectations. It was curious, Charles Hassall thought in 1812,

> that the Saxon race of men should have been almost the sole adventurers who have in latter times brought this wealth into action, and by their ingenuity, perseverance, and adventurous spirit, have raised many a noble fortune, and laid the foundations of many more.[58]

The reasons are to be found in the singular history of Wales. Yet Hassall's observation has to be qualified with respect to the participation of those he called 'the Britons' not in iron but in coal, for local entrepreneurs played a major part in the development of the export trade in that latter commodity.

Even as late as the 1830s few of the coalowners employed as many as 100 men. Most of the collieries were worked by levels which could be started with only a small outlay of capital.[59] Those entrepreneurs who were successful in entering the export trade through Newport and Cardiff were for the most part local men drawing upon their own relatively meagre savings supplemented, perhaps, with small loans. Thomas Powell of Newport (Buttery Hatch, Bryn, Gelligroes and Gelligaer collieries) and Walter Coffin of Bridgend (Dinas collieries), two of the most successful, switched to coal from timber and tanning respectively.[60] Thomas Prothero (Woodfield and Place) and Thomas Phillips (Cwrt-y-bella and Manmoel) were Newport solicitors (and the latter mayor of that town at the time of the 1839 Rising) who invested their earnings and other gains in coal. Neither belonged by background even to the lesser gentry: Prothero's grandfather was a currier in Usk,[61] and Phillips's father a labourer at the Ebbw Vale ironworks.[62] Other coalowners had started as subcontractors or gaffers in the coal workings attached to the ironworks. Of their number were, it seems, Lewis and Rosser Thomas (Carngethin, Glanddu, Tir Adam,

Union, Pencoed and Rose collieries), and Moses Moses (Waterloo) who was able to construct his surface equipment only with a loan of £800 from Benjamin Hall.[63]

Of crucial importance in the industrial transformation of south Wales was the development of an infrastructure of canals, tramroads and port facilities. Parliament approved the construction of the Glamorganshire Canal in 1790 and of the Monmouthshire Canal two years later. The authorised capital of the former was £60,000 with a reserve of £30,000, and of the latter £120,000 with a reserve of £60,000. The largest shareholders in the Glamorganshire Canal Company were the ironmasters and their business associates. Richard Crawshay, members of his family, and his London partner William Stevens severally subscribed £18,100, and the next largest block of shares were those purchased by the Harfords of Bristol for £6,000.[64] Among the investors in the Monmouthshire Canal Company those representing the iron interests were again prominent. The Harfords subscribed £7,500, the largest block of shares, and Thomas Hill of the Blaenavon works put up £4,500. But capital was also attracted from new sources. The Staffordshire manufacturer Josiah Wedgwood subscribed £7,000. More to the point, however, the great landowners of south Wales who had been so long reluctant to risk their money in iron or coal began to invest heavily in the infrastructure. Sir Charles Morgan of Tredegar Park subscribed £5,200 to the Monmouthshire Canal Company, and Henry Somerset, fifth Duke of Beaufort, £4,700.[65] Morgan already owned wharves in Newport and stood to make immediate financial gains from the canal. The Duke of Beaufort took steps to construct his own wharf there in or about 1793, but the burgesses of the town were able successfully to contest his title to the land.[66]

Nothing, perhaps, signalled the *rapprochement* of aristocratic and bourgeois interests more clearly than the marriage of Sir Charles Morgan's daughter, Jane, to Samuel Homfray. Indeed, Morgan entered into a virtual business partnership with his son-in-law. In 1800 he leased him the mineral rights over some 3,000 acres of land for 99 years at a mere £500 a year. Morgan stipulated, however, that Homfray invest at least £40,000 in the new Tredegar ironworks and that all his business should be done through the Morgan wharves in Newport and by Morgan ships.[67] Morgan himself made a further investment in the Sirhowy tramroad which much facilitated the movement of goods between the Tredegar works and Newport; specifically, he subscribed £4,000 for the construction of the one-mile section that ran through Tredegar Park.[68] The tramroad was opened in 1805, and Morgan died the following year. His successor, another Sir Charles, shared his father's interests. In 1807 he and Samuel Homfray formed the Tredegar Wharf Company to build new warehouses and quays at Newport and nearby Pillgwenlly.[69] In 1835 the Newport Dock Act was passed by Parliament. Construction started immediately, and the Town Dock was opened in 1842. Sir Charles Morgan, his brother-in-law Samuel Homfray, and the Harfords were among the leading promoters.[70] Meanwhile, in Cardiff, events had proceeded even more rapidly. The Bute Ship Canal Act was passed in Parliament in 1830, and the Bute West Dock was opened in 1839. Its promoter was John Stuart, second Marquess of Bute, who invested about £300,000 in it.[71] His interest in port facilities extended back at least into the 1820s,[72] but for a time he had contemplated entering the iron industry as such. In the early 1830s he had plans made for the erection of an ironworks with ten blast furnaces at Rhymney.[73]

Revenues from the canals, tramroads and docks represented the immediate returns on investment. By the early 1830s the so-called 'golden mile' where the Sirhowy tramroad crossed Tredegar Park alone yielded Morgan about £3,000 annually.[74] The landowners, however, also benefited from the rising value of their mineral properties. The lease which Thomas Hill of the Blaenavon works had obtained from the Earl of Abergavenny in 1789, for 21 years at £1,300 a year, was renegotiated in 1806 at £5,200 a year and £500 for each furnace over nine.[75] The Dowlais works had been established on a tract of land leased, as we have seen, from the Windsor estate in the mid-eighteenth century for 99 years at £26 a year. The freehold passed by inheritance to the Stuarts, and the second Marquess of Bute litigated for redress, claiming that the iron company had worked both the coal and the iron ore inefficiently. In 1828 the annual rent was raised to £30,000 for the remainder of the term.[76]

The social boundary between the landowning aristocracy and the industrial *haute bourgeoisie* was eroded by the increasing involvement of landowners in industry. It was eroded still further as some industrialists purchased country estates, invaded Parliament, and acquired baronetcies and, exceptionally, peerages.[77] Little but a matter of pedigree distinguished Joseph Bailey, for example, from the true born aristocrat. Bailey retired from active involvement in the ironworks in 1830. He established his seat at Glanusk Park near Crickhowell, and purchased extensive estates in Wales and the English border counties. He served as high sheriff for Monmouthshire in 1823; was elected member of Parliament for Worcester in 1835 and for Breconshire in 1847; and was made a baronet in 1852. His son Joseph also entered Parliament, as member for Sudbury in Suffolk in 1837 and for Herefordshire in 1841.[78] Josiah John Guest, grandson of John Guest of Broseley and Dowlais, became

MP for Honiton in Devon in 1825 and for the newly created constituency of Merthyr in 1832. In 1833 he married Charlotte, daughter of the ninth Earl of Lindsay, and in 1838 he acquired his baronetcy.[79] Unlike Joseph Bailey, however, he remained active in industry and built Dowlais into the largest ironworks in the world (which did not prevent Charlotte Guest worrying that her husband was 'in trade'[80]). Joseph Bailey's brother, Crawshay Bailey, took the seat in Parliament for the Monmouth boroughs, but he too remained wedded to industry.[81] A public statement he made in 1839 expresses the quintessence of the new capitalist mentality. 'What was the state of this valley fifty years ago?' he asked of the Ebbw Fach;

> nothing could be heard from Brynmawr to Aberbyg but the solitary sound of a blacksmith's hammer, with some 200 inhabitants: but now may be heard the sound of machinery employed in converting the mineral that then lay buried under these mountains into finished iron, and we see a population of 10,000 souls. And what was I thirty years ago, and what did I possess? I owe all that I have to my own industry, and I would sacrifice my life rather than lose the property I have so acquired.[82]

But he too finally retired late in life to a country estate near Abergavenny.

The typical ironmaster was envisaged by a writer in 1840, an ironmaster himself, as living 'at a distance from any town, surrounded exclusively by the habitations of his workmen, in the gloomy recesses of the mountains'. He likened the proprietors of the works to 'those little continental princes who on a summer's day can walk from the boundary of their kingdom on the one side unto the neighbouring kingdom on the other, without experiencing any very serious degree of fatigue'.[83] But there is more than a touch of romanticism in this. The typical ironmaster and his family spent much of their time in London or the county towns and spas of England. William Crawshay jr., grandson of the founder of Cyfarthfa, approximated as closely as anyone to the idea of the ironmaster as 'prince', but if he built the gothic pile that is Cyfarthfa Castle in Merthyr in 1825 (for £30,000), he also rented and then purchased Caversham Park and its classical mansion in Berkshire.[84] Henry Scale of Aberaman got it right. 'The Masters', he wrote, 'are *very few* and very distant towards their men excepting *in the works*.'[85] They left those works for much of the time in the hands of a plenitude of officials: chief managers; managers and undermanagers of furnaces, forges, collieries and mines; mineral agents; book-keepers and cashiers; surgeons, and the rest. Necessarily resident on the coalfield, the works officials were a key element in the new industrial middle class. Their number included some Welshmen who often had risen from the ranks of the skilled workers (though usually in different works).[86] The majority, however, came from Scotland and England. 'The cause of such an arrangement', it was remarked in 1839, 'is obvious at a glance. The numbers of persons who, according to their station in life, might be reckoned upon as eligible for such situations, are few in Wales; and of those few, the bulk are not sufficiently educated.'[87] Needless to say, the class interests of the officials were closely bound up with those of their employers.

Contemporary writers drew attention to the absence of a sizeable lower middle class or petty bourgeoisie on the coalfield. 'The fact is that in Wales the population are divided into two great extremes', it was observed; 'there are the very rich, and the ordinary labourer; while but few middle men.'[88] The smallness of the shopocracy particularly stimulated comment. 'All the men who have saved money', wrote Henry Scale, 'immediately leave this part of the country and settle elsewhere — Cardiff, Swansea, Neath, etc.'[89] The matter was widely perceived to result from the prevalence, despite its technical illegality, of the truck, or company shop, system. It came to the attention of the government's commissioner, Seymour Tremenheere, in the course of his inquiry into the causes of the insurrection. 'Where, in a population of from 3,000 to 5,000 persons, the only shop of any consideration, perhaps the only shop at all, is that of the Company', he observed,

the influence of an intermediate class between the half-a-dozen persons in superior station and the large mass of day-labourers and their families, is entirely excluded . . . Where the truck system does not exist, or where it is not compulsory on those employed to conform to it, a middle class is gradually springing up, notwithstanding the disadvantages with which it has to contend. The individuals composing it still remain only a fraction of the community; but in them the uninstructed workman is able to observe the effect of decent, orderly and frugal habits, in a sphere not too far removed for imitation; receiving insensibly the lessons of habitual example proceeding from an intelligence superior to his own.[90]

Nevertheless the lower middle class or petty bourgeoisie was a force to be reckoned with in such towns as Merthyr and Pontypool, and in the ports of the coalfield, where shopkeepers, publicans, master artisans, clerks, teachers and the like resided in considerable numbers. Aspiring to unambiguous middle-class status, they were for the most part of working-class origins: 'the *Shopkeepers* and *Publicans*', as Scale remarked, 'have Brothers and Cousins and Nephews *all Workmen*'.[91]

Contemporaries found difficulty in characterising a middle class so amorphous in composition as to include the few great ironmasters at the one extreme and the numerous small shopkeepers at the other. They spoke, indeed, not of a middle class but of the middle classes. In an address 'To the Middle Classes of the Iron and Coal Districts of South Wales' the pseudonymous Junius faced the issue squarely. 'I know it to be a matter of some difficulty', he wrote,

> to describe you correctly, either individually or collectively, from the circumstances that some of you, in habits and manners of life, approximate to that class which is above you, called the Aristocracy; whilst, on the other hand, there are many of you but one degree removed from the working people.

He settled on a definition that went to the heart of the matter. The middle classes, he decided, were 'persons living upon the labour of the working classes . . . engaged from year to year in the calculations and speculations of trade and commerce'.[92] Their great folly, he warned them, was 'to look down with contempt upon that man, be he miner, collier, fireman, mechanic, weaver, tailor, or shoemaker, who labours daily with his hands, and maintains himself honestly and creditably by the sweat of his brow'.[93] The peculiar circumstances of industrialisation in south Wales, where class distinctions were powerfully reinforced by national ones, brought the middle and working classes into a state of armed confrontation in 1839. In August of that year Junius saw clearly the momentous events portended by the growing workers' movement. 'Middle classes of the Iron and Coal Districts of South Wales', he wrote,

> I beg of you to examine carefully into this present movement, which, whatever may be its termination, will necessarily affect you greatly. I pray of you not to measure it by any thing of the kind ever seen or heard of in England before, not to mistake it as the precursor of riots similar to those which have taken place in Merthyr, and some other places, some time past. Far different are the men, and widely different the objects . . . [94]

## Notes

1. *Dublin Review*, VIII, 15 (Feb. 1840), p. 275.

2. J.P. Jenkins, 'The Demographic Decline of the Landed Gentry in the Eighteenth Century: a South Wales Study', in *Welsh History Review*, 11, 1 (June, 1982), pp. 31-49.

3. [John Wade], *The Extraordinary Black Book* (London, 1832), p. 650.

4. Ibid., p. 572.

5. For the Somerset interests see [John Wade], *The Black Book; or, Corruption Unmasked!* (London, 1820), pp. 78, 395, 442, 444, and [Wade], *Extraordinary Black Book*, pp. 122, 572, 647, 651, 669. For the Welsh connections of the family see *The Dictionary of Welsh Biography down to 1940* (London, 1959), pp. 916-19, and David Williams, *John Frost. A Study in Chartism* (Cardiff, 1939), pp. 3, 27-9.

6. E.D. Davies, *A History of Wales 1660-1815* (Cardiff, 1976), p. 183.

7. *Dictionary of Welsh Biography*, pp. 59-60.

8. For the Butes see John Davies, *Cardiff and the Marquesses of Bute* (Cardiff, 1981), [Wade], *Extraordinary Black Book*, pp. 647, 653, 669.

9. *Dictionary of Welsh Biography*, pp. 635-7. John Lloyd, *The Early History of the Old South Wales Iron Works (1760 to 1840)* (London, 1906), pp. 135-6. Leslie W. James, *The Morgans of Tredegar* (Museum and Art Gallery Publications, Newport, 1977), passim. Williams, *John Frost*, pp. 5-9.

10. Lloyd, *Old South Wales Iron Works*, pp. 99-100. *Dictionary of Welsh Biography*, p. 546.

11. J. Barry Davies, 'The Mathew Family of Llandaff, Radyr and Castell-y-Mynach', in *Glamorgan Historian*, XI (n.d.), pp. 171-87. Lloyd, *Old South Wales Iron Works*, pp. 50, 97.

12. But see, for example, P.D.G. Thomas, 'Society, Government and Politics', in Donald Moore (ed.), *Wales in the Eighteenth Century* (Swansea, 1976).

13. M.B. Donald, *Elizabethan Monopolies. The History of the Company of Mineral and Battery Works 1568-1604* (Edinburgh and London, 1961), pp. 3-4, 61, 97-100, 109-41.

14. Richard Hanbury Tenison, 'The Hanburys of Pontypool', in *Monmouthshire Medley*, I (1976), pp. 19-28.

15. Lloyd, *Old South Wales Iron Works*, pp. 20-2. It is assumed that this is the tract 'at least eight miles long and four wide' referred to by B.H. Malkin, *The Scenery, Antiquities and Biography of South Wales* (1804), p. 174, though the account is inaccurate in several respects.

16. Lloyd, *Old South Wales Iron Works*, pp. 48, 50.

17. Ibid., pp. 160-1.

18. Charles Hassall, *General View of the Agriculture of the County of Monmouth* (London, 1812), p. 19.

19. Lloyd, *Old South Wales Iron Works*, pp. 20-30, 37. The date of 1758 is supplied by Harry Scrivenor, *A Comprehensive History of the Iron Trade* (London, 1841), p. 360.

20. Lloyd, *Old South Wales Iron Works*, p. 131.

21. Ibid., pp. 132-3.

22. L.B. Namier, 'Anthony Bacon, M.P., an Eighteenth Century Merchant', in W.E. Minchinton (ed.), *Industrial South Wales 1750-1914* (London, 1969) (reprinted from *Journal of Economic and Business History*, II (1929), pp. 20-70).

23. Lloyd, *Old South Wales Iron Works*, pp. 48-50. Scrivenor, *Iron Trade*, p. 360, states that the works were built in 1767.

24. Namier, 'Anthony Bacon', pp. 78-84, 104 note 114. A useful account of Crawshay's rise from office boy to ironmonger is that by his grandson, see Lloyd,

*Old South Wales Iron Works*, pp. 209-10.
  25. Lloyd, *Old South Wales Iron Works*, pp. 11-15, 50.
  26. Namier, 'Anthony Bacon', pp. 78, 103 notes 93 and 94, discounts the suggestion that Bacon supplied arms to the American rebels, and notes that similar accusations were levelled against John Wilkinson. Capitalism and patriotism, however, have always been uneasy partners, and there is a fairly early source for the statement about Bacon, see W.H. Smyth, *Nautical Observations on the Port and Maritime Vicinity of Cardiff* (Cardiff, 1840), p. 8.
  27. Lloyd, *Old South Wales Iron Works*, p. 51. Namier, 'Anthony Bacon', p. 85.
  28. Lloyd, *Old South Wales Iron Works*, pp. 52, 54. Bacon's will shows that Francis Homfray still held the lease of the Cyfarthfa mill and foundry in 1785.
  29. Ibid., p. 87. A.H. John, *The Industrial Development of South Wales 1750-1850* (Cardiff, 1950), p. 33. Scrivenor, *Iron Trade*, p. 360, reports that the Penydarren works were built in 1785.
  30. Lloyd, *Old South Wales Iron Works*, pp. 139-42.
  31. Ibid., pp. 15-16, 87, 116-20, [151. *Dictionary of Welsh Biography*, p. 364. Charles Wilkins, *The South Wales Coal Trade and its Allied Industries* (Cardiff, 1888), p. 172.
  32. Lloyd, *Old South Wales Iron Works*, pp. 15, 56, 74-7, 157-60.
  33. Ibid., pp. 33, 36, 205.
  34. Ibid., pp. 41, 90, 122, 140.
  35. For the Crawshay family see J.P. Addis, *The Crawshay Dynasty: a Study in Industrial Organisation and Development, 1765-1867* (Cardiff, 1957), and the more popular but less reliable M.S. Taylor, *The Crawshays of Cyfarthfa Castle. A Family History* (London, 1967).
  36. *Dictionary of Welsh Biography*, p. 334.
  37. Lloyd, *Old South Wales Iron Works*, pp. 131-3.
  38. Ibid., pp. 64, 160.
  39. Ibid., pp. 65-7.
  40. Ibid., pp. 166-74.
  41. Ibid., pp. 127-8.
  42. Ibid., pp. 178-82.
  43. Gwyn A. Williams, *The Merthyr Rising* (London, 1978), p. 24.
  44. David Williams, 'John Evans's Strange Journey', in *Transactions of the Honourable Society of Cymmrodorion* (1948), p. 117.
  45. For the Bersham works, see A.N. Palmer, 'John Wilkinson and the Old Bersham Iron Works', in *Transactions of the Honourable Society of Cymmrodorion* (1897-98). Palmer does less than justice to the career of Isaac Wilkinson, for which see W.H. Chaloner, 'Isaac Wilkinson, Potfounder', in L.S. Pressnell (ed.), *Studies in the Industrial Revolution* (London, 1960), pp. 23-51.
  46. Lloyd, *Old South Wales Iron Works*, pp. 23-30.
  47. Chaloner, 'Isaac Wilkinson', p. 44.
  48. Lloyd, *Old South Wales Iron Works*, pp. 72-3.
  49. Charles Wilkins, *History of the Iron, Steel, Tinplate, and Other Trades of Wales* (Merthyr Tydfil, 1903), p. 42; *Wales, Past and Present* (Merthyr, 1870), pp. 330-1. Scrivenor, *Iron Trade*, gives 1766 as the date of the Plymouth works.
  50. Lloyd, *Old South Wales Iron Works*, p. 50.
  51. Chaloner, 'Isaac Wilkinson', pp. 45, 48-51. John, *Industrial Development*, p. 77. Chaloner states that Isaac Wilkinson acquired the Cyfarthfa works in 1767. His sources possibly confused Cyfarthfa and Plymouth (and, indeed, we do not know what name the latter had at the time of Wilkinson and Guest).
  52. Lloyd, *Old South Wales Iron Works*, p. 33.
  53. The Homfray brothers built Penydarren in 1786, originally with one blast

furnace, with a capital of £14,000, see John, *Industrial Development*, p. 33. The Blaenavon works, with three furnaces, were erected in 1788-9 for £40,000, see J. Knight, 'The Blaenavon Iron and Coal Company, 1836-1864', in *Bulletin of the Board of Celtic Studies*, XXVIII, 4 (May 1980), p. 632. In 1791-2 the Nantyglo works, with two furnaces, were built for £27,316, see Lloyd, *Old South Wales Iron Works*, p. 166. In 1802 Jeremiah Homfray's Abernant works, with three furnaces, cost £40,000, see John, *Industrial Development*, p. 34, and Lloyd, *Old South Wales Iron Works*, pp. 116-22.

54. Arthur Gray-Jones, 'Quaker Ironmasters in Monmouthshire (1796-1842)', in *Monmouthshire Medley*, III (1978), pp. 97-8.

55. Ibid., p. 91. Lloyd, *Old South Wales Iron Works*, pp. 107-8, 206.

56. Lloyd, *Old South Wales Iron Works*, pp. 148-9, 151-3, 166-9. Among its other interests the company also held a lease for pit timber on part of the Morgan estates, ibid., p. 139.

57. Ibid., pp. 41, 122, 129, 140. John, *Industrial Development*, pp. 33-4.

58. Hassall, *Agriculture of the County of Monmouth*, p. 19.

59. The Risca colliery on the southern rim of the coal was exceptional. In 1810 it was worked by four pits and three levels, and £60,000 had been invested in it, see John, *Industrial Development*, p. 27. Not only the capital of Risca, but much of the workforce, appears to have been transferred from the Bristol and Somerset coalfield. John, ibid., p. 28, suggests that the size of a 'normal capital unit' in south Wales was £7,500 to £10,000. It could not have been so high for a colliery worked only by levels.

60. J.H. Morris and L.J. Williams, *The South Wales Coal Industry 1841-1875* (Cardiff, 1958), p. 13. E.D. Lewis, *The Rhondda Valleys* (London, 1959), p. 41. E.D. Lewis, 'Pioneers of the Cardiff Coal Trade', in *Glamorgan Historian*, XI (n.d.), passim.

61. Williams, *John Frost*, p. 19.

62. Gray-Jones, 'Quaker Ironmasters', p. 93, but see also Williams, *John Frost*, p. 57.

63. John, *Industrial Development*, p. 37.

64. Charles Hadfield, *The Canals of South Wales and the Border* (Cardiff and London, 1960), p. 91. William Stevens had joined Bacon and Crawshay's London business in 1781, see Namier, 'Anthony Bacon', pp. 85, 98. He was named an executor in Bacon's will.

65. Hadfield, *Canals of South Wales*, pp. 127-8.

66. Williams, *John Frost*, p. 26.

67. Lloyd, *Old South Wales Iron Works*, pp. 139-42.

68. Hadfield, *Canals of South Wales*, p. 136.

69. Ibid., p. 138.

70. Ibid., p. 147.

71. Ibid., p. 106.

72. Ibid., pp. 101, 103-4.

73. Cardiff Central Library, Bute MSS, XIV (plans, surveys, etc.).

74. Williams, *John Frost*, p. 22.

75. Lloyd, *Old South Wales Iron Works*, pp. 160-1. Knight, 'Blaenavon Iron and Coal Company', p. 634.

76. Lloyd, *Old South Wales Iron Works*, pp. 43-4. The dispute between Bute and the Dowlais Iron Company continued for many years. It was active in 1839 for example, see J.E. Vincent, *John Nixon* (London, 1900), pp. 55-64.

77. For recent studies of the theme in comparative contexts, see Martin J. Wiener, *English Culture and the Decline of the Industrial Spirit 1850-1980* (Cambridge, 1981), and Arno J. Mayer, *The Persistence of the Old Regime* (New York, 1981).

78. *Dictionary of Welsh Biography*, pp. 21-2.

79. Ibid., pp. 321-2.

80. Earl of Bessborough (ed.), *Lady Charlotte Guest, Extracts from her Journal 1833-1852* (London, 1950), pp. 131-3.

81. *Dictionary of Welsh Biography*, pp. 20-1.

82. *Report of the Proceedings at the Great Anti-Chartist Meeting*, held at *Coalbrook Vale, Monmouthshire, On Monday, April 29th, 1839* (Monmouth, [1839]) p. 2.

83. G.S. Kenrick, *The Population of Pontypool and the Parish of Trevethin; situated in the so-called 'Disturbed Districts'* (London, 1840), pp. 28-9.

84. The analogy with the 'prince' could be pursued. Tales are still told of the time when 'Cronshay' – which Crawshay is unclear – exercised *droit de seigneur*; to secure a job a worker might have to send a daughter to the 'big house' for the night.

85. Cardiff Central Library, Bute MSS, XX/75: Scale to Bute dd. 19 Nov. 1839. Italics original.

86. This observation is based upon the testimony collected by R.H.Franks in 1841, see British Parliamentary Papers, *Children's Employment Commission. Appendix to First Report of Commissioners. Mines*, Part II (1842).

87. *Merthyr Guardian*, 16 Oct. 1839.

88. Idem.

89. Cardiff Central Library, Bute MSS, XX/75: Scale to Bute dd. 19 Nov. 1839.

90. British Parliamentary Papers, *Minutes of the Committee of Council on Education with Appendices and Plans of School Houses*, Part II (1839-40), Report by Seymour Tremenheere, p. 216.

91. Cardiff Central Library, Bute MSS, XX/75: Scale to Bute dd. 19 Nov. 1839. Italics original.

92. *Western Vindicator*, 24 Aug. 1839.

93. Ibid., 31 Aug. 1839.

94. Ibid., 24 Aug. 1839.

# 4 THE WORKING-CLASS COMMUNITY: WAGES, PRICES AND HOUSEHOLDS

Six months before the workers of south Wales rose in rebellion, Henry Vincent described the situation in those parts of the coalfield he had recently visited. 'These beautiful tracts of country', he wrote,

> studded over with extensive establishments of iron, the raising of coal, etc. – peopled by a hard-working, honest, and kind-hearted population – afford materials for serious reflection, as to the causes of degradation and slavery among the masses. The men of Monmouthshire and Breconshire obtain a higher rate of wages than do the working classes of other parts of the kingdom – but they toil more like horses than men. The work of the pits and the iron manufactures, with the blazing furnaces, is of a very laborious nature – though the men perform it with a cheerfulness truly astonishing.[1]

Vincent's observations were very much to the point. The spokesmen for the workers in 1839 were as much concerned with the severity of the conditions of labour as with the level of wages as such. The most recent surge in the demand for iron had started in the late summer of 1837, when the price of bar iron rose rapidly from £6 to £9 the ton in south Wales and made corresponding advances on the London market.[2] Prices were maintained throughout 1838 and 1839. Wages rose accordingly, and in late 1839 they were regarded as having reached an all-time high.[3] Real wages at the independent sale-coal collieries were significantly lower than at the ironworks, but in that sector too they had shown considerable advances over the last few years.

Throughout the iron industry wages were commonly based on 'jobwork by the piece'.[4] Production rested on an intricate series of arrangements, adjustable from month to month, by which the ironmasters agreed to pay so much per ton for specified quantities of coal cut, iron ore mined, pig iron smelted, or the pig refined, puddled and rolled.[5] The gangs of labourers in the collieries, mines and other works were supervised by 'butties' or 'gaffers', that is, skilled workers who were often employed on fixed contracts that afforded them a security denied to those working under them. William Thomas, master puddler at Tredegar, was recruited by the Dowlais Company 'for seven years, at and for £10 a month, and to be provided with house rent and firing. – Dated 25th Sept. 1837.' David Hopkin agreed to work for the same company 'as a roll-turner, (or to make himself generally useful in any other situation under them), for two years, commencing on or before the 25th day of December, 1837, for five pounds per month'.[6] Such men constituted, if the term is to be permitted, an aristocracy of labour.

The ironmasters fixed the piece-rates by reference to the prevailing market price of finished iron.[7] The rates for puddling tended to set the level of earnings throughout the works,[8] for the skills of the puddler were in great demand and the job was regarded as physically the most arduous in the whole industry not excepting that of the collier.[9] The rise in the price of Welsh bar iron on the London market from 1837 to 1839, and the increase in the earnings of the puddler in the same period, are shown in Table 4.1.[10] It may be that, as a rule of thumb, the puddler was awarded an extra penny a ton for each rise of a shilling a ton in the market price, but the figures cannot be matched with sufficient precision to be sure of this.

**Table 4.1: Prices of Iron and Payment to Puddlers, 1837-9**

| Year | Average price of S. Welsh bar iron in London, per ton | Payment to puddler per ton, Plymouth works | Wage increase per shilling rise in price |
|------|-------------------------------------------------------|--------------------------------------------|------------------------------------------|
| 1837 | £ 9 11s 3d | 6s 3d | – |
| 1838 | £ 9 14s 7d | 6s 7d | 1.2d |
| 1839 | £10  5s 0d | 7s 3d | 0.76d |

Between 1837 and 1839 the average weekly earnings of the puddler at the Plymouth works rose from 30s to 35s. Table 4.2 shows the increases over a wider range of occupations.[11] The differences in the percentage increments over the two years presumably reflect the need for colliers, puddlers and carpenters at the ironworks. Figures for wages at three works in 1839, in the Merthyr, Tredegar and Pontypool districts, are presented in Table 4.3.[12] The comparability of the data is imperfect, but a broad compatibility is evident.

In 1839, then, the workers in the iron industry had seen their wages rise year after year in all occupations, though more steeply in some than others. Employment, moreover, was constant. The ironmasters were able to maintain full production throughout the year. They were sufficiently heavily capitalised not to have to realise profits immediately and, if

Table 4.2: Increase in Wages, Plymouth Works, 1837-9

| Occupation | 1837 | 1838 | 1839 | Increase, 1837-9 | Per cent increase |
|---|---|---|---|---|---|
| COLLIERIES AND MINES | | | | | |
| Colliers* | 22s 6d | 24s 0d | 27s 0d | 4s 6d | 20 |
| Miners | 19s 7d | 21s 3d | 21s 3d | 1s 8d | 7 |
| FURNACES, FORGES AND MILLS | | | | | |
| Refiners | 33s 0d | 33s 0d | 35s 0d | 2s 0d | 6 |
| Puddlers | 30s 0d | 32s 0d | 35s 0d | 5s 0d | 16.7 |
| Heaters | 36s 0d | 38s 6d | 38s 6d | 2s 6d | 7 |
| ARTISANS | | | | | |
| Carpenters | 17s 6d | 18s 9d | 21s 0d | 3s 6d | 20 |
| Smiths | 18s 6d | 20s 0d | 20s 0d | 1s 6d | 8 |

*subject to an average deduction of 3s a week for candles, gunpowder and tools

short-term falls in the demand for finished iron occurred, they were able to stockpile the bar at their wharves rather than cut back production and lay off labour. The independent coalowners were not in so advantageous a position. Few if any of them were able to ride out even the regular seasonal fluctuations in the market. It was in the spring and summer that the coal merchants built up their stocks to meet the following winter's household demand and (somewhat paradoxically) it was in the winter months that the coalowners found the greatest difficulty in moving their produce. They either laid off colliers or put them on short time.

At the ironworks and the independent collieries alike the earning capacity of the collier was fixed by the price paid for the ton of coal cut and by the quantity he could cut. The price was generally set at 2s the ton in the ironworks.[13] Some of the sale colliery proprietors offered the same, for example, Thomas Powell at Gelligaer.[14] Others offered a few pence more in order to attract labour. The Cartwights paid 2s 2d at Waterloo colliery in 1839, and in 1841, when prices were falling, Aaron Crossfield was still paying his cutters from 2s 1d to 2s 4d at the Gwrhay and Pan-y-fan levels while Lewis and Rosser Thomas were apparently offering as much as 2s 7d at Argoed.[15] The amount of coal cut in the day varied with the nature of the seam. At Gwaun-yr-eirw in the Lower Rhondda, which supplied the Treforest works, it was reckoned that a man could cut 1½ tons a day;[16] the levels were presumably being driven into the No. 3 Rhondda seam. At Gelligaer, on the more accessible Mynddislwyn seam, a cutter might raise somewhat over 2

## Table 4.3: Wages at Selected Ironworks, 1839

| Occupations | Plymouth works | | Tredegar works | Varteg works |
|---|---|---|---|---|
| **COLLIERIES AND MINES** | | | | |
| Colliers | 27s 0d* | ) | 22s to 24s | 22s 6d |
| Miners | 21s 3d | ) | | |
| | | ) | | |
| **FURNACES, FORGES AND MILLS** | | | | |
| Furnacemen | 35s 0d | | 35s 0d | 20s to 30s |
| Puddlers | 35s 0d | ) | | 40s |
| Heaters | 38s 6d | ) | 35s 0d | |
| | | ) | | |
| Rollers | | | 50s to 60s | 50s to 60s |
| **ARTISANS** | | | | |
| Fitters up | | ) | | |
| Smiths | 20s 0d | ) | 25s 0d | |
| Pattern-makers | | ) | | |
| Carpenters | 21s 0d | | 21s 0d | |
| Moulders | | | 24s 0d | |
| Masons | | | 20s 0d | |
| **UNSKILLED WORKERS** | | | | |
| Labourers | | | 14s to 16s 4d** | 12s to 15s |
| Boys | | | | 4s to 12s |
| Women | | | | 7s to 7s 6d |

*subject to an average deduction of 3s a week for candles, gunpowder and tools
**based on a daily rate of 2s to 2s 4d

tons a day.[17] From record books to which he had access, probably those of Dowlais, Tremenheere found that some cutters raised 70 or 80 tons a month, or about 2½ tons a day, while others raised only 40 or 50 tons, or around 1½ a day;[18] it must be assumed that the former were using more assistant cutters. The data may be taken as indicating that a basic wage for a collier in 1839 was about 21s a week, that is, the proceeds of 1½ tons of coal cut daily, seven days a week, at 2s the ton. Colliers at the ironworks clearly did earn such wages throughout the year; few at the independent collieries could have done so.

'The work about this neighbourhood', observed the cashier at Waterloo colliery, 'is very uncertain, which uncertainty often proves injurious to the men; in winter they suffer much, as few vessels arrive for coal at Newport.'[19] At Gilfach Fargoed colliery work came to a standstill for almost four months in the year.[20] In general from March to May cutters' wages were perhaps a little higher at the independent collieries than at the ironworks; by report, they averaged about 22s 6d a week in 1838, and 25s 8d in 1839.[21] Over the entire year, however, the situation was quite different. At Penllwyn and Gellideg cutters were said to have earned an average weekly wage of no more than 10s for 1840; at Gwrhay colliery, 12s; and at Dinas, 16s.[22] The agent at Rock colliery remarked that a cutter assisted by one or two boys might earn from £9 to £10 a month for some months in the year, but less than £4 for others. 'What they lose in bad months', he added, 'is never made up by good work.'[23] A haulier at Gwrhay complained that sometimes he received 9s 6d a week, sometimes 4s and sometimes nothing.[24]

In the matter of wages the sale-coal colliers clearly had more cause for grievance than their counterparts in the iron industry. Their distress was compounded by the prevalence of the truck system — 'the mode of remunerating labour by part payment in goods'.[25] More than the ironmasters, the independent coalowners promoted the system vigorously despite its illegality. Operating on narrower margins of profit than the ironmasters, they used truck to recover part of the money they had laid out in wages. Prices were commonly marked up by 15 to 20 per cent or more in the company shops, so that the worker lost at least 3s or 4s in the pound on his purchases,[26] and it was widely believed that fraudulent weights were also often used.[27]

R.H. Franks of the Children's Employment Commission perceived the effects of the truck system with clarity. 'In many parts of Glamorganshire and Monmouthshire', he reported,

the wages of the working collier population are very rarely paid in money, but a shop in the neighbourhood, not professedly in the hands of the proprietors of the works, advances goods to the workmen employed in the mine on account of the proprietors; the books of the shop and the books of the colliery are checked on the pay-day at the same offices, and the balance, if any, is handed over to the men. It very often happens, however, that the men unfortunately have nothing to receive for months together.[28]

The problem was put more graphically by Howell Lyshon, a collier at Carngethin: 'no man can pay his way because of these shops, everything is overcharged; besides the weight is bad, and there is no one to look to this, and the men are afraid to speak for fear of being turned off'.[29] Joseph Thomas of Pontllanfraith, a smith, pointed out another aspect of the situation: 'the truck system of dealing is so common in the collieries of this district that our markets are closed; in the village of

Blackwood the whole supply is monopolised by the company's shop. The market-house is closed. There is a terrorism existing over the men, and they dare not speak out.'[30]

The real value of wages has to be measured against the prices of those commodities necessary to the sustenance of the working-class community. A number of household budgets are on record for the 1839-41 period. Seymour Tremenheere reported two, 'as not unfair specimens of the mode in which high wages are appropriated'.[31] One was for a collier, the other for a furnaceman. Both were employed by an iron company, perhaps Dowlais. Both were married and both had four children. Both owned their own cottages and therefore paid no rent. Both were assisted at work by their eldest sons, in each case 13

**Table 4.4: Household Budgets, 1839**

| Commodity | Price | Expenditure per month | |
| | | Collier | Furnaceman |
| --- | --- | --- | --- |
| Rent | | Nil | Nil |
| Flour | 13s 6d/bushel | £2  0s 6d | £2  0s 6d |
| Butter | 1s 0d/pound | 8s 0d | 12s 0d |
| Sugar | 8d/pound | 5s 4d | 6s 8d |
| Tea | 6d/ounce | 3s 9d | 4s 6d |
| Cheese | 7½d/pound | 6s 3d | 3s 9d |
| Bacon or ham | 8d/pound | 5s 4d | 8s 0d |
| Fresh meat | 7d/pound | 11s 8d | 14s 0d |
| Potatoes* | | 6s 0d | Nil |
| Currants | 10d/pound | 5d | 5d |
| Raisins | 7d/pound | 3d | 3½d |
| Blue, starch, pepper, mustard, etc. | | 10d | 10d |
| Soap | 7d/pound | 3s 6d | 2s 4d |
| Clothes, shoes, etc. | | 16s 0d | 18s 0d |
| Tobacco | 5s 4d/pound | 2s 8d | 2s 8d |
| Malt** | 3s 1½d/peck | Nil | 9s 4½d |
| Beer** | | 6s 0d | Nil |
| Candles (for house) | 7d/pound | 7d | 7d |
| Candles (for work) | 7d/pound | 4s 8d | Nil |
| Gunpowder | 6½d/pound | 6s 6d | Nil |
| Total Expenditure | | £6  8s 3d | £6  3s 11d |
| Wages | | £6 10s 0d | £6 10s  0d |
| Balance | | 1s 9d | 6s  1d |

*furnaceman presumably grew his own potatoes
**furnaceman presumably brewed beer

years of age. Both earned about £6 10s a month; 'those of the collier', noted Tremenheere, 'were above, those of the furnace-man rather below, the average at present generally attainable'. The expenditures of the two households, which Tremenheere had selected for comparability, are shown in Table 4.4.

These budgets may be compared with three reported for 1841, for workers in somewhat different circumstances.[32] Edward Beddow was a miner at the Rhymney ironworks; he was aged 30 and had a wife and a one-year-old child. Thomas Rees was a miner at the Cyfarthfa works; he was aged 28, and had a wife with a two-year-old child. And William Hodge, a labourer at Cyfarthfa, was aged 37 and had a wife but no children. Each of the three households was dependent on one income. The 1841 data have been converted from a weekly to a monthly base, assuming the former to be one-quarter of the latter. It will be remarked that no expenditures on clothing and beer are shown in the 1841 budgets; for this reason the balances shown in Tables 4.4 and 4.5 are not comparable. From the quantity of soap and candles purchased by Beddow it may be inferred that he was an underground worker, though it is unclear why he made no purchases of gunpowder. From the quantity of cheese obtained it seems likely that his wife did a little petty trading in that commodity. Rees, who bought neither powder nor candles, may have been an ore miner working on the patch.

The five budgets span the range from skilled to unskilled workers, but all five men were employees of large ironworks. Regrettably, no similar data have been found for workers at the sale-coal collieries, where it was a recurrent complaint that earnings were totally absorbed in the settlement of accounts at the company shops. In 1841 John Evans, who had attempted to open a school near Blackwood with little success, remarked how men would obtain provisions from the shop in order immediately to barter them for drink in the beerhouses. 'Nothing can exceed the mischief of the shops', he claimed; 'I frequently myself take goods from the colliers instead of money; the colliers have no money; I can't do anything else; I can't express myself strongly enough on this subject. There is very seldom any balance for the working man to receive; they are screwed down to the lowest possible pitch.'[33] The elderly Phillip Lloyd was one of those to voice the workers' grievances vividly. Born in or about 1783 in Swansea, where his father was employed at the copper works, Lloyd had first gone to work underground when he was 16. He moved to the Blackwood district in 1809 or 1810, where he was employed at the Rock colliery and later at the Waterloo. In 1838 he was seriously injured in a roof fall. Three

## Table 4.5: Household Budgets, 1841

| Commodity | Price | Expenditure per month | | |
| --- | --- | --- | --- | --- |
| | | Beddow | Rees | Hodge |
| Rent and coal | | 14s 0d | 12s 0d | 9s 0d |
| Flour | 2½d/pound | 16s 8d | 11s 8d | 12s 6d |
| Butter | 1s 0d/pound* | 6s 0d | 5s 2d | 5s 2d |
| Sugar | 9d/pound | 6s 0d | 4s 0d | 2s 8d |
| Tea | 6d/ounce** | 6s 0d | 4s 6d | 3s 0d |
| Cheese | 7d/pound | 14s 0d | 4s 8d | 2s 4d |
| Bacon | 8d/pound | 5s 4d ) | 6s 0d | ( 3s 0d |
| Fresh meat | | 8s 0d ) | | ( 6s 0d |
| Potatoes | ½d/pound | 2s 0d | Nil | Nil |
| Salt | ½d/pound | 2d | Nil ) | 6d |
| Pepper | 1d/pound | 4d | Nil ) | |
| Soap | 8d/pound | 4s 0d | 1s 0d | 1s 0d |
| Tobacco | 5s 0d/pound | 2s 6d | 2s 6d | 3s 8d |
| Candles | 8d/pound | 5s 4d | Nil | Nil |
| | Total Expenditure | £4 10s 4d | £2 11s 6d | £2  8s 10d |
| | Wages | £5  4s 0d | £3  0s 0d | £2 10s  0d |
| | Balance | 13s 8d | 8s 6d | 1s  2d |

*10½d a pound at Cyfarthfa
**4½d an ounce at Cyfarthfa

years later he reflected on his subsequent situation:

> Was off work some months, which much distressed me, as things are very queer about this place; work is very uncertain, and wages paid upon the truck system; and as the storekeepers are either contractors or have some interest in the works, we pay through the noose [sic] for everything, and when we run a little in debt in the winter season [when] we have no work, we are screwed out of every penny when work sets in again, and the storekeeper keeps every shilling of our wages till he is satisfied; and I have not seen, nor have many of the men, money for months . . . I have seven children. Three boys are working below, and one girl (my daughter) works in the mine for William Morgan, who has lost his leg and cannot do much. Have not been able to give my children schooling, nor can many do so from paying so high for the necessaries of life, and especially the mode of payment we are compelled to submit to.[34]

Phillip Lloyd was typical enough in having to deny his children schooling. Though it was perceived by most of the workers and many of the employers as an evil, the employment of young children was prevalent throughout industry. For the first few years of life children were the responsibility of their mothers, 'the objects', so Franks remarked, 'of tender maternal solicitude'.[35] This stage in the life cycle was abruptly terminated when they started work. Boys were given jobs occasionally as early as the age of four and quite commonly at five or six. Girls were seldom sent to the works before the age of eight or nine, though many were kept at home to assist their mother, as it was said, 'in cleaning, scouring, nursing, and fetching water, which latter is a heavy and fatiguing part of a girl's duty'.[36] Once a child started at the works the mother apparently considered herself free from all specifically *maternal* responsibilities. 'The child follows a new teacher, a new instructor', wrote Franks; 'the father or the employer becomes the object of his imitation; he drinks, smokes, and swears, the child follows his example, and children of seven years of age, and even less, will be found to enter in their expenses at the shop their supply of tobacco ...'[37]

The employment of very young children resulted from a custom known as 'privilege of work'. Again it is Franks who describes it most perceptively:

> no matter the infant's age, strength, or capacity, into the mine he must be taken to enable his father to claim an extra tram of coals: that is to say, supposing a given number of men working a colliery, and the quantity of coal desired to be raised being limited, the full day labour of a collier not being required, it is obvious that each workman must be reduced below his usual work: to remedy this, in the case of men with a family, the system of privileges seems to have been devised, and by this means the married man works for himself and perhaps a full day's work; by this circuitous mode of giving the man with a family a chance of extra work, the unfortunate child, who of course is of little use to his father, is taken into the unwholesome atmosphere from his mother's side, and deprived of the slender means of education afforded.[38]

At Argoed colliery a cutter was given an extra tram on every four for a young child.[39] At the Rhymney ironworks four trams a week were allowed for younger children and seven for older.[40] It is less clear how the system worked at the furnaces and mills, though it certainly extended to them.

Very small children might stay at work only a few hours a day, and if they received any remuneration it was whatever their fathers (or others adults responsible for them) chose to give them.[41] As they acquired experience of the workplace, however, they might come on to the company payrolls in jobs for which adults, because of bulk, were unsuitable. Children under eleven, both male and female, were commonly employed as air-door keepers underground, and were paid 6d to 8d a day. 'I been down about three years; I don't know my own age', said William Richards, air-door keeper at Buttery Hatch (who was in fact not yet eight); 'when I first went down I couldn't keep my eyes open; I don't fall asleep now, I smoke my pipe; earns 8d a-day; it is not every day'.[42] Older children, in the ten to seventeen age bracket, might become hauliers at about 14s a week, junior cutters at 10s to 15s a week paid by the piece, and in some collieries carters – a particularly onerous job – at 9s to 10s.[43] There was much competition for such jobs, and the works received numerous applications from fathers hoping to place a child in regular company employment.[44] The additional income usefully supplemented that of the family for, as Franks reported, 'the collier boy is, to all intents and purposes, the property of his father (as to wages) until he attains the age of 17 years, or marries; his father receives his wages, whether he be an air-door boy of five years of age or a haulier of 15'.[45] Joseph Head, to give one example, had been taken underground at the age of six, and two years later he had been taught how to handle horses and trams by his brother. As a 14-year-old haulier at Gwrhay colliery, Joseph Head was earning 12s a week. The wage was paid to his father, who allowed him 6d to 1s a week for beer and tobacco.[46] Thomas Jenkins, to take a somewhat different experience, had also started work underground at the age of six. Four years later he was working at Cwrt-y-bella colliery as an assistant to a cutter who was not his father but who paid his father 2s 6d a week for his services.[47]

A variety of jobs in the works were open to girls, for example, as fillers and limestone-breakers at the furnace tops, as patch workers at the iron ore mines, and as pilers in the mills. Those of eight years and thereabouts might earn no more than 2s 6d to 3s a week, and those of 17 and 18 up to 7s.[48] Many girls, however, were put into domestic service by their parents, especially on farms in rural areas. They usually worked for their maintenance for the first two years, after which they were paid 40s to 60s a year in addition.[49] Understandably, the girls themselves generally preferred employment at the ironworks, where they could make more money with a working day of only twelve hours![50]

Tremenheere commented on the high incidence of early marriage among working-class men. 'They take their wives', he reported, 'from the coke-hearths, the mine and coal-yards, or other employments about the works . . .'[51] The contractor at Gilfach Fargoed colliery was more specific. 'Colliers about this quarter marry very early', he maintained; '17 and 18 is the average and it is not uncommon for lads to get married at 14 and 15 years of age.'[52] Inspection of the census returns suggests that men were in fact most commonly in their early to mid-twenties when they married. G.S. Kenrick remarked that it was frequent for girls to marry at 15 or 16.[53] The census returns suggest that the late teens were more usual. Marriage often occurred after pregnancy and sometimes following the birth of the first child, and it was rare for men to evade the responsibilities of parenthood; at least one ironworks dismissed those who 'do not marry the females who proved with-child'.[54] Franks referred to the 'first important act' of a wife in celebration of her new status; it was to 'open an account at the shop for goods, clothing, food, etc.'[55] It will be apparent from the samples of working class households given in Table 4.6 below that some married couples were able to rent a house of their own (David and Susan Rees, Household 1) and that some had to take up lodgings (Evan and Ann Evans, Household 2). It was rare for a married man to remain in his parental household, but it seems to have been not uncommon for him to move for a time into his wife's family home. This last situation, however, cannot readily be identified in the census books because of the daughter's change in name at marriage. More extensive family reconstruction is necessary to determine the incidence of such 'matrilocal' arrangements, that is, of daughters remaining with mothers and being joined by husbands.

Table 4.6 does not show different *kinds* of working-class families but different *stages* in the development cycle of the working-class household.[56] David Rees of the Victoria ironworks had a wife and one small child; he provided lodgings for a blacksmith, his wife and family; for a miner and his wife; and for two puddlers who were presumably unmarried (Household 1). The household of Benjamin Davies, who was employed by the same ironworks, is essentially similar in structure. However, whereas Rees had only one child to support, Davies had four; the units of lodgers had accordingly increased from four to five to yield a little extra income (Household 2). James James of Nantyglo headed a household that was in its most advanced form. He and four of his sons were in employment, and there was neither need of nor space for

**Table 4.6: Specimen Working-class Households, 1841**

| Household 1 | Household 2 | Household 3 |
|---|---|---|
| David Rees, 30, puddler | Benjamin Davies, 27, collier | James James, 40, miner |
| Susan Rees, 23 | Joanna Davies, 23 | Sarah James, 40 |
| Samuel, 18 mths | Richard, 7 | William, 20, miner |
| John Griffith, 23, puddler | Catherine, 4 | Benjamin, 15, miner |
| Rees Lewis, 40, puddler | Elizabeth, 3 | Susan, 15 |
| James Probert, 35, smith | Sarah, 1 | Margaret, 14 |
| Eleanor Probert, 35 | Abraham John, 17, collier | James, 12, miner |
| Emma, 16 | Thomas George, 23, collier | John, 10, miner |
| Price, 13 | John Thomas, 27, fireman | David, 6 |
| Caroline, 11 | John Thomas, 4 | Ann, 6 |
| William, 7 | Evan Evans, 35, carpenter | |
| John Evans, 33, miner | Ann Evans, 19 | |
| Susan Evans, 33 | Maria, 6 mths | |
| | Evan Owens, 25 | |

| Household 4 | Household 5 | Household 6 |
|---|---|---|
| William Morgan, 45, miner | William Thomas, 60, collier | Mary Feredy, 30 |
| Mary, 15 | Ann Thomas, 50 | Ann, 12 |
| Elizabeth, 15 | Isaac, 20, collier | Thomas, 9, labourer |
| David, 10 | Thomas, 16, collier | Elvira, 6 |
| David Williams, 25, collier | David Owen, 35, hawker | Amelia, 3 |
| Margaret Williams, 20 | Joseph Williams, 20, collier | John Wilson, 30, baker |
| John, 3 | John Thomas, 30, collier | Rachel Wilson, 20 |
| | David Richards, 15, puddler | Mary Ann, 10 mths |
| | | Charles Scarle, 20, linen weaver |
| | | Ema [?] Burriss, 8, female servant |

lodgers (Household 3). We shall meet James James and two of his sons in a different context, as members of No. 11 Section of Blaina which lost one of its number in the attack on Newport in 1839. Household 4, that of William Morgan of Nantyglo, represents the next stage in the cycle. His older children had presumably all left home and his wife was, perhaps, dead. Lodgers had been taken in once again in order to maintain the financial viability of the household. It is quite likely that in this case Margaret Williams was a daughter of William Morgan, and David Williams his son-in-law, but it is impossible to be sure. Last in the sequence, the household of William Thomas of Victoria was in an advanced stage of decay (Household 5). Its existence was threatened by the possibility of the deaths of the parents as well as by the departure from it of the two remaining sons. Four units of lodgers – in fact four lodgers – had taken their place within it.

It was very rare for a married woman to remain in employment, for her services were crucial in running the household. With the assistance of her younger daughters she was responsible for feeding and arranging bathing facilities not only for her husband and sons but also for her lodgers.[57] Clearly lodgers must be seen as an integral part of the working-class household at most stages in its cycle. They also sustained those households the cycle of which was threatened by untoward circumstances, most frequently the death by accident of the head of family. Household 6 in Table 4.6 is a rather special case of this. William Farraday (or Feredy) of Blackwood had died in the fighting at Newport in 1839. His widow, 'a poor woman, with an infant in her arms, and in an agony of distress', threw herself on the mercy of the Newport bench, and, so it was reported, 'in the most touching strain, preferred some prayer to the magistrates, the purport of which, the Welsh dialect of the poor creature, rendered more indistinct by intermitting sobs and exclamations, prevented us from understanding'.[58] But, finding the magistrates unhelpful, Mary Farraday overcame her distress and succeeded in holding together her family; in 1841 one of her young sons had found a labouring job and she had taken in a complement of lodgers.

At the request of Seymour Tremenheere, G.S. Kenrick of the Varteg works prepared a detailed survey of the parish of Trevethin, of which Pontypool was part. The average number of persons to a house, he found, was six, and to a sleeping room, over three. 'But it must be remembered', he remarked, 'that the iron works are never idle, and some of the men work at night and others during the day; so that when six o'clock strikes, one set of men leaves their beds, and is succeeded by those who have been working all day.' The lodgers, he found, were about a fifth of the total population; he counted 3,537 of them, of whom about 3,000 were single men. They were, he thought, the most disorderly element in the community:

These men can earn plenty of money; have not much occasion for it; scorn to lay it by for a rainy day; have not many resources from education, or amusements at home; and therefore fly to the beer-shop for excitement, where they spend their evenings in dissolute company, and where they learn bad habits . . . [59]

Kenrick regarded the beershops as 'the proper nursery for all kinds of sedition and disturbance'.[60] His view was fully shared by employers in other parts of the coalfield. Thomas Prothero pointed out, quite rightly, that all the chartist lodges were based on beershops and public-houses (the latter able to sell spirits as well as beer).[61] Henry Scale bemoaned 'the cursed Beer Act', which had converted 'hundreds of Cottages into Sedition Shops'.[62] And W.T. Harford Phelps, a solicitor with interests in ironworks and collieries, saw the beershops as 'seminaries of sedition, and nurseries of treason, tending to demoralise and brutalize the population'. They should, he thought, be abolished, and he believed that without them the November Rising — 'the conspiracy which has lately broken out, and spread such terror throughout the country' — would not have been possible.[63] Such comments undoubtedly had substance. The beershops were the exclusive preserve of the workers. They were virtually impenetrable to the police spy or informer, and it was indeed in them that the preparations for the rising were made.

The beershop was an ubiquitous feature of the working-class community. Circumstances in the ironworks and collieries were certainly such as to stimulate an undeniable thirst, and grossly overcrowded living conditions mandated the existence of public places of relaxation.[64] The working man after labour has no resort but the beer-shop', wrote Franks; 'his boy accompanies him, his daughter often passes the evening there.'[65] Tremenheere saw a beershop's clientele as a tightly interlocked group. 'The public-house or the beer-shop is at hand', he wrote, 'kept perhaps by a relation, a connexion, or a friend, or in which he [the worker] is sure to find many of his friends assembled.'[66] Observers seldom failed to be impressed by the sheer number of the drinking establishments. A temperance missionary travelling between the ironworks in 1836 reported 120 beershops along a three-miles stretch of road.[67] A place of refreshment every 44 yards might seem something of a record or something of an exaggeration, but perhaps not. Of the 151 houses in Dukestown, 33 sold drink.[68] The village of Tongwynlais in Taff Vale had a total population of no more than 200 people; they were served by seven beershops or public-houses.[69] There was one beershop to every 13 or 14 houses in Blackwood (and about the same ratio of latrines!),[70] and in Trevethin parish there were 170 licensed drinking places, or one to every 17 houses, not counting the unlicensed 'bid-alls'.[71] The complaint of the foreman of Maesmawr colliery that 'there are more people at the public-house than at the chapel'[72] was one repeated by many of his contemporaries, and seems to echo the familiar distinction between *pobl y dafarn* and *pobl y capel*, tavern folk and chapel folk.[73] The furnace manager at Abersychan could argue the inadvisability of stopping the works on Sundays, since the men would be more likely to spend the day in the beershops than the chapels.[74]

In the five central parishes of the coalfield, Merthyr, Bedwellty, Aberystruth, Trevethin and Mynyddislwyn, there were twelve churches (six with Sunday schools) and 93 chapels (80 with Sunday schools) in 1839: a ratio of one place of worship to every 800 or so of the population.[75] No adequate statistics of attendance are available, though in the parish of Trevethin, for example, Kenrick reckoned that the number of people who regularly attended church or chapel was of much the same order as the number of those who never attended.[76] In 1841 the commissioners on the employment of children met with an ignorance on religious matters that clearly surprised them. 'I do not know what you mean by catechism, or religion; never was told about God', testified the nine-year-old Morgan Lewis, a puller-up at the Plymouth ironworks; 'the sky is up above, and no one ever told me about Jesus Christ; cannot say what he is'.[77] Ann Davis, who was aged 14 or 15 and wheeled trams at Waun Wyllt colliery, was equally assured in her innocence. 'Have heard something about Jesus Christ', she allowed; 'can't say who he is; indeed, I do not know who God is – no, nothing do I know about him. Never heard what prayer means . . .'[78]

In the 1830s few of the workers were more than a generation or two removed from the land, but the ancient ritual enactments to ensure the well-being of livestock and crops had become irrelevant to life on the coalfield (where 'the twin kings of the earth are Coal and Iron'[79]). The new proletariat had yet to renegotiate its contract with a god who offered it not the harvest of the land but the wages of industry. It had yet to learn how to propitiate a god whose wrath was manifest in the explosion of firedamp, the fall of rock, the blow-out of a furnace, the runaway tram or the epidemic of cholera.[80] The great religious revivals that swept the coalfield (and that had so much to do with the cholera) had yet to gather momentum.[81] It was not, perhaps, that the religious impulse had withered; rather that it had become transformed into a fierce commitment to establishing the political kingdom on earth. The emphasis which the Calvinists placed upon obedience to authority was not such as to commend their creed to the mass of the workers prepared to overturn the established order in pursuit of a better life.

In the aftermath of the November Rising spokesmen for the

employers expressed their puzzlement that it should have occurred at a
time when the workers enjoyed a relative prosperity. 'They have no
master grievance to complain of', it was argued in the *Merlin*:

> Work there was and is in abundance for the honest and industrious.
> Unlike the ill-fed and worse-paid Manchester and Birmingham opera-
> tive, their wages were high, and amply sufficient for the maintenance
> of themselves and families. They could stand in the attitude of inde-
> pendence, and look on increasing families without decreasing hopes.
> Still, at the bidding of a few madmen, thousands of them 'rush like a
> torrent from the hills', and precipitate themselves on a peaceful and
> enterprising town . . . [82]

Seymour Tremenheere made a very astute comment on the attitudes
behind such a stance. 'Nearly the whole body of employers', he remarked, 'acted on Bentham's theory that the masters had no responsibility beyond paying the men their wages; everything else that they
wanted the men had to do for themselves.'[83] A liberal in politics,
Tremenheere was in fact appalled by what he saw of the working-class
townships clustered around the ironworks. 'Next to nothing was done for
the comfort and convenience of life among the work-people', he wrote
in his memoirs.[84] He commented on the poor roads ('in wet weather,
ankle deep in black mud'); on the absence of any sewage system; on the
few gardens to be seen; and on the omnipresence of debris and smoke
from the mines and furnaces. 'The people', he reported to London,

> are for the most part collected together in masses of from 4,000 to
> 10,000. Their houses are ranged round the works in rows, sometimes
> two to five deep, sometimes three stories [sic] high. They rarely
> contain less than from one to six lodgers in addition to the members
> of the family, and afford most scant accommodation for so many
> inmates. It is not unusual to find that 10 individuals of various age and
> sex occupy three beds in two small rooms. Far worse instances might
> be given.[85]

What Tremenheere failed to sense was that the workers saw their circumstances as a result not so much of neglect as of oppression. Henry
Vincent described the conditions under which men, women and children
toiled; thus, he remarked, 'the whole population are reduced to a state
of perpetual servitude'.[86] In his address to the middle classes of south
Wales the pseudonymous Junius expanded on the topic. 'Believe me',

he wrote,

> there is something more in hand with the people at the present time than a mere question of a rise or fall in wages. They feel the degradation of being bound by laws, oppressive and tyrannical in their nature, made by persons who know nothing of their condition and their wants. They have felt there is no security for their rights — no respect for their feelings — no hope of any amelioration from a Parliament elected by you — the middle classes. They have been robbed of the fruits of their labour, and their poverty and misery laughed at by worthless and wicked men. They have been slaves, and from all appearances they are determined to be so not much longer.[87]

Nothing illustrates more starkly the sense of degradation and oppression to which Junius referred than the interpretation which working-class women put on the new Poor Law. Kenrick reported their great alarm:

> 'Is it true that Government means to destroy all the children under three years of age?' Others said, 'Do you want to send them to Van Dieman's Land?' At Blaenavon a woman observed, 'It is said the Poor Law only allows us to have three children!' Nearer Pontypool some women turned their backs upon the querists. Others said, 'Oh I heard by the papers that you wanted to destroy all the children under four years of age, and I find now that the report is true!'[88]

Kenrick commented that such beliefs on the part of the workers showed 'an unnatural distrust of their rulers'. In the circumstances of south Wales in the late 1830s it is not at all obvious why the workers should have reposed their trust in a government which represented so faithfully the interests of property and disregarded so totally those of labour. The collier Thomas Thomas of Waterloo was much taken by the way the chartist leader William Lloyd Jones made the point. 'What sort of Law was ours to protect Money and not Persons', Jones had asked;

> we as workmen who worked underground ought to earn more money than any one else and what risk we ran underground of our lives . . . after we went in the morning we did not know whether we should return home at night alive or not.[89]

## Notes

1. *Western Vindicator*, 4 May 1839.

2. *Merthyr Guardian*, 2 Sept. 1837. *Monmouthshire Merlin*, 26 Aug. and 9 Sept. 1837. Harry Scrivenor, *A Comprehensive History of the Iron Trade* (London, 1841), p. 409.

3. *Cambrian*, 4 Jan. 1840.

4. British Parliamentary Papers, *Children's Employment Commission. Appendix to First Report of Commissioners. Mines.* Part II (1842), pp. 469-580, Report by Robert Hugh Franks (henceforth Franks Report, 1842), and pp. 581-720, Report by Rhys William Jones (henceforth Jones Report, 1842). Franks Report (1842), p. 503: testimony of William Williams and John Jones.

5. For a contract of 1801 for driving a new level at 18s the yard, see John Lloyd, *The Early History of the Old South Wales Iron Works* (London, 1906), p. 18.

6. *Merthyr Guardian*, 13 Jan. 1838. The master-workmen were often made responsible for paying the men under them, see British Parliamentary Papers, *Minutes of the Committee of Council on Education with Appendices and Plans of School Houses*, Part II (1839-40), pp. 207-18, Report by Seymour Tremenheere (henceforth Tremenheere Report, 1840). Tremenheere Report (1840), p. 214.

7. E.W.Evans, *The Miners of South Wales* (Cardiff, 1961), p. 19, citing the observations on this point made by William Crawshay in 1825.

8. Alan Birch, *The Economic History of the British Iron and Steel Industry 1784-1879* (London, 1967), p. 263.

9. Samuel Griffiths, *Guide to the Iron Trade of Great Britain* (London, 1873), p. 166 [misnumbered].

10. Franks Report (1842), p. 483. Scrivenor, *Iron Trade*, p. 409.

11. Franks Report (1842), p. 483.

12. Idem, for the Plymouth works. *The Times*, 15 Nov. 1839, for the Tredegar works, and compare W.N. Johns, *The Chartist Riots at Newport*, 2nd edn (Newport, 1889), p. 13. For the Pontypool district, see PRO, HO.73/55: report by Sir Edmund Head, Asst. Poor Law Commissioner, July 1839, and compare G.S. Kenrick, *The Population of Pontypool and the Parish of Trevethin; situated in the so-called 'Disturbed Districts'* (London, 1840), p. 16.

13. Tremenheere Report (1840), p. 213.

14. Franks Report (1842), p. 526: testimony of William Jenkins.

15. Ibid., pp. 536, 537, 547: testimony of Samuel Jones, James Harper, John Morgan.

16. Ibid., p. 525: testimony of Arnold Butler.

17. Ibid., p. 526: testimony of William Jenkins.

18. Tremenheere Report (1840), p. 213.

19. Franks Report (1842), p. 536: testimony of Samuel Jones.

20. Ibid., p. 532: testimony of David Davies.

21. Ibid., p. 484.

22. Ibid., pp. 543, 537, 522: testimony of Edward Rees, James Harper, Thomas Haynes.

23. Ibid., p. 541: testimony of John Jones.

24. Ibid., p. 548: testimony of Griffith George.

25. Tremenheere Report (1840), p. 216.

26. Franks Report (1842), pp. 531, 544: testimony of John Pickford, Sarah Tobay.

27. Ibid., pp. 531, 536: testimony of John Williams, Howell Lyshon.

28. Ibid., pp. 482-3.
29. Ibid., p. 536: testimony of Howell Lyshon.
30. Ibid., p. 544: testimony of Joseph Thomas.
31. Tremenheere Report (1840), pp. 213-14.
32. Jones Report (1842), pp. 703-4.
33. Franks Report (1842), p. 545: testimony of John Evans.
34. Ibid., p. 536: testimony of Phillip Lloyd.
35. Ibid., p. 481.
36. Ibid., p. 482.
37. Ibid., p. 481.
38. Ibid., p. 482.
39. Ibid., p. 546: testimony of Thomas Pierce.
40. Jones Report (1842), p. 631: testimony of John Evans *et al.* For calculating privilege the tram (or dram) was reckoned at one ton of coal, see Franks Report (1842), p. 532: testimony of David Davies. Some collieries allowed no privilege for those under seven years, ibid., p. 545: testimony of William Evans, and compare p. 544: testimony of William James.
41. Jones Report (1842), p. 584.
42. Franks Report (1842), p. 534: testimony of William Richards.
43. Ibid., pp. 474-5, 548.9: testimony of Elias Jones, George Johnson.
44. Jones Report (1842), pp. 603, 627: testimony of George Gaskill, William Thomas.
45. Franks Report (1842), p. 482.
46. Ibid., p. 538: testimony of Joseph Head.
47. Ibid., p. 539: testimony of Thomas Jenkins.
48. Ibid., p. 512: testimony of Hannah Pritchard, Mary Haddock. Jones Report (1842), p. 622: testimony of Margaret Williams.
49. Franks Report (1842), pp. 528-9: testimony of Richard Andrews.
50. Ibid., p. 482.
51. Tremenheere Report (1840), p. 212.
52. Franks Report (1842), p. 532: testimony of David Davies.
53. Kenrick, *Population of Pontypool*, pp. 10-11.
54. Franks Report (1842), pp. 522, 528-9: testimony of Thomas Thomas, Richard Andrews.
55. Ibid., p. 482.
56. Public Record Office, HO.107/742, Nantyglo examples, and HO.107/750, Victoria and Blackwood examples.
57. Franks Report (1842), p. 481.
58. *Monmouthshire Merlin*, 16 Nov. 1839.
59. Kenrick, *Population of Pontypool*, pp. 6-7, 11-12.
60. Ibid., p. 16.
61. *Monmouthshire Merlin*, 23 Nov. 1839.
62. Cardiff Central Library, Bute MS, XX/75: Scale to Bute, 19 Nov. 1839.
63. *Monmouthshire Merlin*, 23 Nov. 1839.
64. W.R. Lambert, 'Drink and Work-Discipline in Industrial South Wales, c. 1800-1870', in *Welsh History Review*, 7, 3 (June 1975), pp. 289-306.
65. Franks Report (1842), p. 482.
66. Tremenheere Report (1840), p. 214.
67. *Preston Temperance Advocate*, 8 Aug. 1836.
68. Sir John Pakington, House of Commons, 19 Feb. 1840, cited in J.L. and B. Hammond, *The Age of the Chartists* (London, 1930), p. 161.
69. Franks Report (1842), p. 517: testimony of Jabez Thomas.
70. Ibid., pp. 541-2: testimony of Thomas Felton, Evan Jones.
71. Kenrick, *Population of Pontypool*, p. 18.

72. Franks Report (1842), p. 517: testimony of Jabez Thomas.

73. For the distinction in a modern context, see David Jenkins, 'Aber-porth', in Elwyn Davies and Alwyn D. Rees (eds.), *Welsh Rural Communities* (Cardiff, 1960), pp. 12-23, 42-3, 61 note 8. For a caution on this matter, see Gwyn A. Williams, *The Merthyr Rising* (London, 1978), p. 82.

74. Franks Report (1842), p. 542: testimony of Evan Jones.

75. Tremenheere Report (1840), pp. 216-17.

76. Kenrick, *Population of Pontypool*, p. 19.

77. Franks Report (1842), p. 511: testimony of Morgan Lewis.

78. Ibid., p. 514: testimony of Ann Davis.

79. Charles Wilkins, *The South Wales Coal Trade* (Cardiff, 1888), title page, citing Kilsby Jones.

80. At the Penydarren ironworks alone, 30 or 40 men with missing limbs were to be seen in 1841, see Jones Report (1842), pp. 654-5: testimony of John Pritchard. The magistrates who conducted the investigations into the November Rising were thoroughly confused by the number of one-legged men involved.

81. E.T. Davies, *Religion in the Industrial Revolution in South Wales* (Cardiff, 1965), pp. 55-61.

82. *Monmouthshire Merlin*, 9 Nov. 1839. The paper had been founded by R.J. Blewitt in 1829, and in 1839 was edited by his nephew, Edward Dowling, when Blewitt was MP for Monmouth boroughs and Deputy Lieutenant for Monmouthshire.

83. E.L. and O.P. Edmonds, *I was There. The Memoirs of H.S. Tremenheere* (Eton Windsor, 1965), pp. 37-8.

84. Idem.

85. Tremenheere Report (1840), p. 208.

86. *Western Vindicator*, 4 May 1839.

87. Ibid., 24 Aug. 1839.

88. Kenrick, *Population of Pontypool*, p. 9.

89. Newport Public Library, Chartist Trials 1839-1840, 24 vols., XV, doc. 443: evidence of Thomas Thomas.

# 5 STRIKES, COMBINATIONS AND THE CLASS STRUGGLE

In the early nineteenth century the south Wales coalfield was in a state of constant civil unrest and violence. Over the half century preceding the rising of 1839 the iron industry had shown spectacular growth. In 1788 the total make of iron was estimated, so we have seen, at 12,500 tons and by 1839 it had risen to about 454,000 tons. Advances in technology lowered costs of production and the price of iron fell over the period, enabling the industry to maintain its competitiveness in both the insular and overseas markets. Merchant bar iron sold at the south Wales ports for around £15 the ton in 1803, and for around £9 5s in 1839.[1] This long-term development did not, however, proceed evenly. Phases of expansion alternated with ones of contraction, and it has been remarked that iron was a 'boom and slump industry *par excellence*'.[2] It was these movements in the economy that dictated the particular forms which the working-class struggle took in south Wales. Roundly, short-term contractions in the iron trade generated strikes and riots; long-term growth was the precondition of combination and ultimately unionisation.[3] Further, turmoil (strikes and riots) and conspiracy (combination and union) underpinned the revolutionary political consciousness which emerged in the period, though they were not the only determinants of it.[4]

Typically, early strikes were immediate, almost spontaneous, responses to downturns in the economy, when reductions in wages were threatened or made. Other grievances (notably about truck) usually resurfaced. Rioting was a characteristic feature of the strike, though the level of violence was usually low. Marching gangs travelled the hills, bringing out the men in other and sometimes distant works. Strikes tended to collapse as abruptly as they had broken out, for as recession deepened so the ironmasters began to reduce the make and lay workers off; jobs and not wages thus became the issue. Early strikers, therefore, never achieved all and seldom many of their aims, but they did accumulate tactical experience. The great strikes of 1816, 1822 and 1830 were followed by the Merthyr Rising of 1831, which metamorphosed from strike into riot and, briefly, into open rebellion.

The early combinations were societies (or clubs or lodges) of fixed and limited membership, committed to the promotion of working-class causes. They were, in the nature of the case, local in operation, though frequently they became linked together in loose associations extending across the coalfield. Many such early combinations were concerned with the provision of sickness, injury and death benefits for their members. These were the Friendly Societies which operated legally and indeed often enjoyed the approval and even patronage of the ironmasters and coalowners. In time many of them merged into larger organisations such as the Oddfellows or the Druids, or the Order of True Ivorites which added to its other functions the promotion of the Welsh language. Other combinations were quite different in their aims, seeking the autonomous working-class regulation of wages, hours of work and recruitment of labour. They were essentially terroristic in operation and illegal. The Scotch Cattle, as these combinations were each and all known, existed in most districts of the coalfield. They acted without central direction (a source of strength rather than weakness granted their clandestine character), but there was collaboration between different groups. They were active from at least the 1820s, and continued to be so in 1839. They tended to be the most visible when, with an upturn in the iron trade, labour was being taken on at the works and wages were rising; they monitored the situation closely in order to preserve the bargaining power of the workers. The Scotch Cattle did not lead strikes, but they did act against strike-breakers.

In the 1820s and 1830s conditions on the coalfield were still inimical to the development of a third sort of combination, the trade union, committed to the provision of strike benefits and therefore able to initiate and direct strikes. An attempt to establish such unions was made in mid-1831, when branches of the Friendly Society of Coal-Mining, affiliated to the National Association for the Protection of Labour, sprang up over the coalfield. The movement collapsed within six months.[5] A second attempt was made at the beginning of 1834, when branches of the Grand National Consolidated Trades Unions were opened. Again the movement collapsed within a few months.[6] The NAPL and the GNCTU were both Owenite in inspiration, but the particular industrial system which had fostered their growth in England was very different from that of south Wales, which was even less likely to promote their success. The Scotch Cattle were to continue their activities through the 1840s and at least into 1850. They had their rural counterpart in the Rebecca groups of the early 1840s, which also acted without central direction yet co-operated in seeking redress of their grievances. The Scotch Cattle and Rebecca shared a distinctive *modus operandi* that is still perhaps to be seen in certain forms of present-day

Welsh protest.[7]

The nineteenth century opened in south Wales with riots which spread from Merthyr to many other parts of the coalfield. Food prices rather than wages were the central issue.[8] One of the earliest strikes for wages was that which brought out the puddlers of Dowlais for a month in 1810.[9] The price of iron was relatively steady at the time, and there does not appear to have been any general threat to wages; at issue was the remuneration of *skilled* labour. The first general strike was to be that of 1816. The average price of bar iron at the south Wales ports was £12 a ton in 1815; in 1816 it was £8.[10] Wages were reduced. Colliers and miners around Merthyr saw their money drop from 21s a week at the beginning of 1816 to 18s in the spring and to 15s by the autumn.[11] In June an Abergavenny magistrate warned the Home Office in London that the coalfield was seething with discontent and that emissaries from Merthyr were visiting all the other works.[12] The recession deepened when the price of south Wales bar iron on the London market, which had so far been sustained, fell from £13 10s a ton in September to £10 in October.[13] On 15 October further reductions in wages were announced at the Tredegar works. The strike started there the next day. The Tredegar men marched to Merthyr, and the Plymouth and Cyfarthfa works were stopped. To William Crawshay jr. 'the enemy' had entered the gates, and 'in too great strength to oppose with any probability of success'.[14] The strike spread to other parts of the coalfield. Rumours circulated that the strikers had obtained firearms and pikes, that they were casting large quantities of bullets, and that an attack upon the arms depot at Brecon was projected. Whatever the truth in these reports, the arrival on the coalfield of several companies of the 55th Regiment of Foot (supported by the Monmouthshire Yeomanry, the Royal Glamorgan Militia and the Swansea Cavalry) was sufficient to deter all but the most militant of the workers from risking an armed confrontation. By the end of October the strike was over, but the coalfield remained in a highly inflamed state and it was necessary to station more regular soldiers there to maintain order.[15]

The iron trade picked up in 1817, when bar iron averaged £12 a ton at Newport and Cardiff. Prices held fairly steady in 1818 and 1819, but began to fall again in 1820. The average price for 1821 was only £8. On the London market south Wales iron fell below £9 for the first time ever in November of that year.[16] In December the ironmasters moved to restore their competitiveness in the market. Since transport costs from south Wales added about £1 to the price of the ton in London, some proprietors agreed to sell for £7 while others were prepared to go still lower.[17] Again, wages were threatened. The strike of 1822 started in Nantyglo, after Joseph Bailey reduced from 2s 4d to 1s 3d the price offered the collier for the ton of coal cut.[18] It spread rapidly across the Monmouthshire valleys, and the level of violence rose when the strikers attempted to prevent supplies of coal reaching the ironworks. Tramways and rolling stock were destroyed, and on 2 May soldiers of the Scots Greys and the Chepstow Yeomanry escorting coal wagons from Crumlin to Ebbw Vale were obliged to fight their way through. On the night of 5-6 May a half-mile section of the Sirhowy tramroad was torn up.[19] By that time, however, the strike had begun to collapse. Men had returned to work at Clydach, Sirhowy and Beaufort at the end of April. The Ebbw Vale and Blaenavon men were back by late May. The last to give in were the Tredegar men, on 17 June.[20] Some concessions were won by the workers about the payment of wages in cash, and strike leaders in custody were released, among them Josiah Evans ('the Commander') of Blaenavon and Harri Lewis ('Cotton Balls') of Ebbw Vale. The reductions in wages, however, stood.

In the course of 1824 the iron trade began to recover, and the industry enjoyed a short boom in the first half of 1825 when south Wales bar iron reached £15 10s a ton in London. A downturn in trade was apparent by August, and the price of iron fell slowly throughout 1826 and 1827. In May 1828 it dipped below £9 again, in March 1829 below £8, and in November of that year below £7. In January 1831 it hit a record low of £6. The iron trade remained in deep recession throughout 1831 and 1832.[21] The first reductions in wages were made in the spring of 1826. They were immediately followed by brief strikes in the Merthyr district, which the ironmasters countered with the threat of a lock-out, and by more extended strikes at the Monmouthshire works. By mid-June opposition to the reductions had collapsed almost everywhere; only the Ebbw Vale and Nantyglo men held out for a while longer.[22] As the recession deepened, so the ironmasters began to reduce their make. They sent surplus coal for sale at Newport. This in turn affected the price of that commodity, and the proprietors of the sale-coal collieries announced wage cuts on 24 March 1827. The colliers struck immediately, and did not resume work until early May when the coalowners finally agreed to moderate the wage reductions.[23] By the beginning of 1829 the situation had worsened across the whole coalfield. Wages continued to fall throughout that year, payment in cash became less and less common, and unemployment rose. Strikes were called at a number of ironworks and collieries, but little was achieved.[24] Then, in the third week of March 1830, work was stopped at most of the sale-coal collieries. The strikers demanded the maintenance of existing wage levels, the payment weekly of at least 10s in cash, the abolition of truck, and cuts in production to raise the price of coal. Patrols of workers brought to a halt the movement of all coal by tramroad or canal to Newport.[25] The coalowners were sufficiently intimidated to accept (or appear to accept) most of the strikers' demands, and work was resumed on 3 April.[26]

The effects of the long recession were particularly keenly felt in Merthyr if only because of the heavy concentration of population there dependent on the ironworks. By the end of 1830 a quarter of the furnaces had been closed down, and wages had fallen. Yet Merthyr remained remarkably calm during that year, perhaps because the level of class conflict there was moderated by the existence of a large town middle class within which political radicals and reformers – most of them 'fairly orthodox petty-bourgeois democrats' – could thrive.[27] All this changed late in the spring of 1831. Crawshay introduced new reductions in the wages of the ironstone miners at Cyfarthfa and Hirwaun which first affected their pay packets on 23 May. The following day he laid off 84 puddlers. The shock effect of these measures was critical, for Crawshay was the ironmaster generally considered the most sympathetic to the workers.[28] On 30 May a demonstration in support of parliamentary reform was taken over by those committed to more immediate aims, notably the abolition of the Merthyr Court of Requests (which had powers to distrain property in settlement of small debts), and the regulation of wages ('no miner or collier should take a stall vacated by another except at an increased price').[29] On 1 June Thomas Llewellyn led a party of Merthyr men to Aberdare, forced the ironmaster Richard Fothergill to retract a statement about wages being too high in Merthyr, and attacked the company shop. On the following day Lewis Lewis yr Heliwr led bands of men through Merthyr town. They spent much of the day restoring distrained property to its owners, and then proceeded to sack the Court of Requests. In the course of the night of 2-3 June the ironworks were one after the other stopped: Cyfarthfa, Penydarren, Dowlais and Plymouth. The magistrates sent out urgent requests for troops.

On 3 June the workers attempted to storm the Castle Inn in Merthyr, where the magistrates had established their headquarters. It was defended by about 80 men of the Argyll and Sutherland Highlanders, who had force marched in from Brecon. The assault left 16 soldiers wounded, and about a score of workers dead. Under cover provided by the newly arrived Royal Glamorgan Militia, the magis-

trates extricated themselves from the town and set up a new headquarters in Penydarren House. The workers scoured the district around
Merthyr for powder, weapons and recruits, and set up posts on the
hills. On 4 June they blocked the Brecon road with boulders to prevent
the baggage and ammunition of the Highlanders from being brought
up, and on the Aberdare road they ambushed and disarmed a detachment of 34 men of the Swansea Cavalry. Later in the day representatives
of the workers met with the magistrates and ironmasters in Penydarren
House. Wages were discussed, but the outcome of the talks is unclear.
Certainly there was a lull in hostilities on 5 June, a Sunday. The workers
made use of it to send emissaries and marching gangs to the Monmouthshire ironworks to summon people to a mass meeting above Dowlais
the next day. Estimates of the number who responded ranged from
12,000 to 20,000. Lt. Colonel Richard Morgan, senior officer at Penydarren House, took a gamble. Leaving the defence to pensioners and
special constables, he mustered all the available troops — Highlanders,
Militia and Yeomanry — and on 6 June intercepted the Monmouthshire workers at Dowlais Top. Before the muskets and bayonets of the
soldiers, the marchers faltered and then dispersed. The episode was
critical in its effect. By the evening of the same day the Merthyr
workers had abandoned the struggle. On 7 June they began to go back
to work.[30]

Eight years later, in the aftermath of the November Rising of 1839,
several analysts of the political scene raised the matter of its relationship to the Merthyr Rising. 'The deplorable carnage, by military executions, at Merthyr Tydfil, some years ago', argued a leader writer for the
*Morning Herald*,

> arose out of a local quarrel between some ironmasters and their men,
> and had no connection with revolutionary designs . . . It was the
> mode of suppressing it which gave that disturbance the appearance
> of a political insurrectionary movement, *which it certainly was
> not*.

1831 was essentially a strike, he claimed, and 1839 a revolutionary
'little war'.[31] The editor of the *Merthyr Guardian* took issue with this.
Wages, he maintained, were not the real issue in 1831, for the Merthyr
rebels wanted parliamentary reform in order to legislate radical changes:
'a division of property; that every man should possess his three or four
acres of land; that he should have to labour at most for four hours a
day; together with several other equally chimerical projects'. The

risings of 1831 and 1839 were then, he claimed, both revolutionary in their aims.[32] Henry Scale of Aberaman went further and detected the origins of 1839 in 1831. 'Chartism, – my Lord', he wrote to Bute,

> began in 1830-31. – altho' it was then called by *another* name the populace understood it in the same sense that they do now – a Reforming of society . . . The words 'Remember Paris' and 'think of the Poles' were in the mouths of many of the so called ignorant men of the Mountains in June 1831, and the distress – (hunger that will break thro' stone walls) – then existing, soon induced the mass of the population to lend a ready ear to the Demagogues whose ultimate view went far beyond a mere riot for increased wages.[33]

All these analyses contained elements of truth. The 1831 Rising did occur in a period of deep recession and wages were an issue. In the abruptness with which it both broke out and collapsed it did display a characteristic feature of early strikes. But what made 1831 more than a particularly riotous strike was indeed its ideological content. In this respect, as Gwyn A. Williams remarked, it 'brought a pre-history to an end',[34] and many of its revolutionary themes were to be heard again in 1839. But the 1839 Rising differed from that of 1831, and indeed from the great strikes of 1816, 1822 and 1830, in a very significant respect: it occurred during a time not of slump but of modest advance in the iron trade. On 3-4 November work was stopped throughout most districts of the coalfield, and certainly in that regard the 1839 Rising can be seen as a collective action against the employers in the tradition of the earlier strikes.[35] But the stoppage of work, the mobilisation of the men which followed, and the march on Newport, had all been planned over a period of several months, and cells of activists – 'Sections of Ten' – had been secretly organised in the works and collieries. In such aspects the influence of the early combinations is to be seen, and we may be sure that the men of the Scotch Cattle were not unrepresented in the rebel conclaves of 1839.

In the early nineteenth century the Friendly Societies that sprang up on the coalfield were commonly restricted to a maximum of 201 members, who met regularly once a month when dues were collected (usually about 1s for the fund and 2d towards the convivialities). Each society had a strongly local character, and seldom varied its meeting place. The movement was not an exclusively male one. A 'Society of Women' – clearly of working women – was for example founded at

Merthyr in 1806, and met at Twyn-y-Waun.[36] The members of a society were enjoined to secrecy about its proceedings on pain of fine or expulsion. It is therefore impossible to know whether they sometimes used the society as a cover for other activities, in particular, ones directed to the improvement of wages (for such has been suggested of some of their counterparts in England[37]). This would seem unlikely in the case, for example, of the 'Society of Craftsmen and Others' which was founded in 1807 and met at the Beaufort Arms, for the ironmasters Richard Crawshay and Benjamin Hall were chosen as its treasurers.[38] Generally speaking, however, wages and such matters were the purview of other associations often though not consistently described as 'union societies', which may have borrowed features of their internal organisation from the friendly societies but were otherwise quite different in their ends and in the means they used to pursue those ends.

Old Evan Powell of Tredegar knew much of the Scotch Cattle, and set down his memories in 1884:

> The objects of this organization were to prevent strangers being taught the art of mining, to fix the limits of the number of miners, to restrict the output of minerals, and to protect the interests of the workmen by obtaining for them the highest possible rate of wages . . . No miner was allowed to take a stranger underground without the sanction of these societies, with the exception of miners' children. This sanction was conditional, the stranger had to pay a certain sum to the nearest society.[39]

Powell made no distinction between the union societies and the Scotch Cattle; they were one and the same. Earlier, in 1839, Henry Scale had seen the Cattle more as the executive arm of the unions. 'The Scotch Cattle', he wrote, 'ruffians so-called, executed the secret orders of these societies.'[40] And in that same year Thomas Prothero of Newport gave yet another account of the matter. The first union societies (he actually called them 'Trades' Unions') were established by the 'mountaineers' immediately following the repeal of the Combination Acts in 1824. They were, he claimed,

> at first conducted openly and without offence – men were suffered to join or not, and they remained unmolested. They were very soon, however, converted into secret associations, and a system of coercion and terrorism of the worst character was carried on throughout the country – the leaders and chief conspirators bearing

the name of Scotch Cattle.[41]

Prothero may have been right that the earliest union societies were overt in their activities; as a coalowner himself, he should have known. But he was certainly wrong in his chronology, for the earliest clandestine operations of the Scotch Cattle predate the repeal of the Combination Acts. Evan Powell referred to action taken against a miner in Shop Row, Tredegar, in 1821.[42] He may have been mistaken about the date. Oliver Jones associates the rise of the Cattle specifically with the aftermath of the great strike of 1822, when actions were taken in Tredegar, Nantyglo and elsewhere against workers who had broken ranks.[43] This is veridical. And the Cattle were certainly operating at the time of the local strike of Clydach colliers in mid-1823, when notices in English and Welsh were posted threatening those who were returning to work: ' . . . the Bull and his friends are all alive, and the vale of Llamarch is wide, and woe shall be to you, since death you shall doubtless have all at once, you may depend on this'.[44] It is Evan Powell again who provides the clue to the circumstances in which the Scotch Cattle most probably originated. 'A characteristic feature in the disposition of workmen in general is', he wrote,

that whenever trade prospers and wages are advanced their minds are easily agitated, and, singularly, a method is adopted with a view to redress their hypothetical wrongs. During these prosperous times a masquerading mob, termed 'Scotch Cattle', made its appearance, and secret societies were established from Hirwaun to Pontypool.[45]

The prosperous times he referred to were the boom years of late-1817 to early-1820, when the price of south Wales bar iron on the London market seldom fell below £12 and peaked at £14 10s.[46] The emergence of a movement committed to the improvement of wages, by regulation of the size of the labour force and of output, appears highly appropriate in the strong market of those years.

Each phalanx of the Scotch Cattle was headed by its Bull, or *Tarw*.[47] His followers were therefore the Cattle, or Herd. The mode of operation of the Bull and Cattle was to 'scotch' those who undermined the solidarity of the working-class community. 'Scotching', it was later recollected, 'was a means employed by the ignorant and dissatisfied workman to coerce his fellow-labourer, and prevent him working otherwise than according to the united decree, determined at meetings held for that purpose.'[48] The 'scotch' was also the wedge which, inserted into a wheel, brought a tram to an abrupt halt.[49] A majority of scotchings were directed against working-class violators of working-class mores, a minority against petty officials at the works and collieries, company shopkeepers and the like, who were also perceived as having broken Scotch Law. 'Destruction of furniture, bodily violence, and in some instances murder', wrote Evan Powell, 'were weapons which these combinations did not scorn to employ in order to carry out their objects.'[50] To avoid the risk of identification, it was unusual for a herd to carry out scotchings in its own locality. Whatever and wherever their business, however, the herds conducted it with a fine sense of guerrilla theatre. The Bulls often wore horns, the Cattle frequently assumed female attire, and the entire herd lowed, mooed and blew horns as it moved from place to place.[51] Charles Wilkins maintained that the history of the Scotch Cattle extended back to the years before Waterloo.[52] He was correct only in the sense that the movement undoubtedly had its own prehistory. It was one that reached back into the Welsh peasant past, to the masquerades of the *ceffyl pren*, 'the wooden horse', through which the community disciplined its miscreants, and of the Mari Lwyd, with which it enlivened its Christmas and New Year.[53]

In sentencing three ironworkers to death for their part in the food riots of 1800, Justice Hardinge remarked on their belief 'that by *terror alone*, without *actual mischief*, a reform of the market price would be accomplished by their spirit'.[54] His observation is of relevance to later times. The Scotch Cattle were at their most effective when the very possibility of punitive action was sufficient to deter the would-be transgressor. When violations of Scotch Law did occur, the culprit might expect to receive several warnings before being visited by a herd. A typical enough example is the well-known notice dated Hoarfrost Castle, 19 April 1832, and 'signed' with a bull's head in red:

To all Colliers, Traitors, Turncoats and others.
We hereby warn you the second and last time. We are determined to draw the hearts out of all the men above-named, and fix two hearts upon the horns of the Bull; so that everyone may see what is the fate of every traitor — and we know them all. So we testify with our blood.[55]

When violence became necessary, it was used 'according to the extent of the violation of the rules'.[56]

Most scotchings went unnoticed by the press other than at those times of heightened tension when magistrates had to leave their mansions and soldiers their barracks for a spell of duty among the natives. The cycles of activity and inactivity which recent writers have seen in the history of the Scotch Cattle may therefore be exaggerated by the vagaries of the data.[57] Be this as it may, there can be little doubt that the number of scotchings increased appreciably after 1831. The change reflected the heightened consciousness of working-class power after the great strike of 1830 and the Merthyr Rising of 1831 and, more particularly, a growing concern with immigration. Charles Wilkins reported that the workers had been, until 1830,

> in the habit of introducing large numbers of men from every shire in Wales to the full acquaintance of iron making and coal cutting, and thus, by making labour cheap, had rendered wages less. It was observable, after the Strike had ended, that men guarded more secretly the knowledge gained by a long apprenticeship in the caverns of the earth, or by the blinding heat of the forge, and old workmen say that the knowledge gained by that Strike led to the exercise of more care in guarding the secrets of their work, and caused eventually better times.[58]

A set of union rules was made public in 1831. We know neither how this secret document leaked out nor where it originated (though Merthyr and Blackwood are both possibilities).[59] It reveals clearly the strong concern of skilled or semi-skilled workers to protect their jobs from the competition of outsiders. The rules are those of a 'friendly Society of Coal Mining', that is, of one of the early trade unions in south Wales affiliated to the Lancashire union of the same name. The initiates subscribed to ten articles. The first, second, ninth and tenth were on the preservation of secrecy, and the sixth on the drawing of strike benefits. The other five regulated labour:

> 3rd. I will never instruct any person in the art of Coal Mining, Sinking, Tunnelling or Boring, or Engineering, or any other department of my work, except an obligated Brother or Brothers, or an apprentice. So help me God.
> 4th. I will never work any work where an obligated Brother has been unjustly injured off, or for standing up for his price, or in defence of his trade. So help me God.
> 5th. I will never take any more work than I can do myself in one day, except necessity requires me to do so, and if I do I will employ

none but an obligated Brother, and will pay him according to the Master's price, or according to his work. So help me God . . .

7th. I will never injure an obligated Brother, nor any thing belonging to him, before I acquaint him of his foreseen dangers. So help me God.

8th. I never will in a boasting manner make known how much money I can get, or in how short a time. So help me God.

The archaic language gives a touch of unreality to the rules, but there was nothing unreal about the herds which drove the Irish out of the Varteg works: not because they were Irish but because they were taking wages below what was considered the acceptable level.[60]

It is unnecessary here to calendar the many operations of the Scotch Cattle of which record does survive.[61] So extensive were their visitations in mid-1834 that it was remarked, 'no person can travel from Risca to Tredegar without shuddering at the works of violent and wanton devastation that presents itself to the eye'.[62] In that year the Scotch Cattle claimed to have 9,000 'faithful children'. If the figure has any real relationship to the total number of initiates across the coalfield, then it may indicate the existence of some 40 to 50 herds in all.[63] Whatever the case, neither the local authorities nor London could ignore the challenge to bourgeois order presented by the Scotch Cattle. Their first concerted effort to deal with the matter was made in 1832.

At the beginning of that year the proprietors of the Blaina works reduced the wages of colliers. The workers struck, and blackleg scab labour was brought in. Bulls' heads appeared painted in red on the doors of the newcomers' lodgings. On 17 February two scotchings took place at the Cornish Pit. The ironmasters offered a reward of £15 for information and the Home Office authorised the payment of a further £100. The Scotch Cattle extended operations to the ironworks in Beaufort, Tredegar and Ebbw Vale, and to sale-coal collieries at Blackwood, Argoed and Trelyn (Fleur-de-lis). Troops were moved in.[64] On 4 May the beleaguered proprietors held a veritable council of war at Abergavenny. It was attended by twelve magistrates and thirteen ironmasters from all districts of the coalfield and by representatives of the military. The meeting resolved,

that the abuses of the Truck System and particularly the nonpayment of the Workmen in money have been the principal Original Causes of the illegal combinations of the Workmen called the 'Scotch Cattle System' whereby the rioters have lately endeavoured to prevent the peaceable Workmen from labouring for their Masters who have felt it necessary to reduce their wages in order to meet the unexampled depression of the Trade . . .

The ironmasters agreed (not for the first or the last time) to abolish truck, and proceeded to declare war on the Cattle: that is, 'to unite with the magistrates to the utmost of their power to put an end to the Scotch Cattle system of intimidation'.[65] They envisaged this objective attainable through the creation of a special task force, the Mountain Police. It was a project that Abergavenny's rector and magistrate, William Powell, had put to the Home Office some weeks before.[66] But the meeting failed to develop any immediate initiative, and the Scotch Cattle continued their operations virtually unimpeded.

By the early summer of 1834 the situation had reached crisis proportions. With the approval of the Home Office, magistrates, ironmasters and coalowners met at Rhymney on 13 June. This time they decided to require all their workers to sign, on pain of dismissal, a pledge to belong to neither union society nor Scotch herd.[67] The timing was crucial; after a very modest recovery in late-1833 and early-1834, the market for iron was contracting once more and there was very little incentive for the ironmasters to maintain high outputs. The workers refused to sign the pledge at only four places, the Cyfarthfa, Blaenavon, Hirwaun and Varteg works. At the first three they were immediately locked out, but the Varteg was kept going with the assistance of special constables.[68] In London the Home Secretary encouraged the creation of the Mountain Police. He refused to sanction the issue of firearms to the new force, but sent 100 cutlasses and accoutrements.[69] The workers gave way. By mid-August the Hirwaun men, who had held out the longest, signed the pledge. The Scotch Cattle, however, remained as active as ever. But something had changed. Perhaps the generous rewards offered for information about the Cattle did indeed produce informers, or perhaps the herds simply became careless. Once in 1834 and once in 1835 the anonymity of the herd was breached, and members were apprehended and brought to trial.

On 28 October 1834 two scotchings were carried out in Argoed. In the course of the operation the gun of one of the assailants burst. It wounded Joan Thomas, the wife of a blackleg collier, and Edward Morgan, a member of the herd. Joan Thomas died several days later, her husband having been too scared to seek immediate medical attention for her. Badly wounded, Edward Morgan made his way home, and was arrested shortly after. Joan Thomas's killer apparently escaped to

America. The unfortunate Morgan — he was 32 years old and a lapsed Baptist well versed in the scriptures — was tried, found guilty of complicity in murder and executed before a large crowd at Monmouth Gaol on 6 April 1835. He died expressing the wish 'that content would be restored among the working classes'.[70] The Bull on the occasion of the action in Argoed was apparently a man of Staffordshire origins, Ned Lolly; 'of quiet harmless disposition, of good education, and superior manner', his involvement in the affair was only revealed much later.[71]

The actions of the Scotch Cattle against Thomas Rees, a young ex-collier turned preacher at Rock, also ended in disaster for the herd. Rees was highly unpopular. Unable to live on the monthly stipend of 10s allowed him by the chapel, he had opened a shop. It seems that he ran it as a truck shop in collusion with the local coalowners, whose interests he faithfully represented in his sermonising on the evils of the union societies. On the night of 18-19 July 1834 a herd some 40 to 50 strong, using tram plates as battering rams, destroyed his shop and appropriated all his goods.[72] Rees refused to bow to Scotch Law, and it was necessary to visit him again six months later. His house was wrecked in the usual style and he was beaten. On this occasion, however, the identity of many members of the herd became known. John James (Shoni Coal Tar), William Jenkins, John Griffith and Thomas Jarman were all brought to trial, while others, David Hughes (Dai'r Diawl) and Edward Howells among them, eluded capture.[73] James and Jenkins were condemned to death, but the sentence was commuted to transportation for life. Awaiting removal from Monmouth Gaol, they made a determined and almost successful attempt at escape.[74] Thomas Rees, the object of their attention, went on to become one of the most influential members of the nonconformist establishment in south Wales. He was the Thomas Rees D.D. of Beaufort who liked to address himself to the problems of the Welsh workers, commending them 'for their loyalty and submission to their superiors'. The queen had no more loyal supporters than her 'warm-hearted subjects', he assured his public in 1864:

Ever since the incorporation of Wales with England, the loyalty of the Welsh nation to their Saxon rulers has been perfectly unswerving, notwithstanding the occasional effusions of frenzied poets and hot-headed orators against the Saxon invaders. Who has ever heard, from the days of Henry VIII, to the present hour, of secret clubs and traitorous plots in Wales to upset the Government, such as have from time to time disgraced Ireland?[75]

Rees had conveniently ignored the Scotch Cattle of the tumultuous 1830s and the risings that marked the beginning and end of that decade.

The year 1839 opened with a scotching at Brynmawr, where Evan Thomas had failed to get permission to introduce a stranger to 'the art and mystery of mining'. He ignored several warning notices, and on 17 January his house was sacked and he himself was severely beaten.[76] Four months later 150 men from Brynmawr took part in a massive Whit Monday demonstration at Blackwood.[77] There they heard John Frost and William Lloyd Jones — no men of the Scotch Cattle these, but a Newport draper and Pontypool watchmaker — expound the principles of the People's Charter. Through the 1820s and 1830s the class struggle in south Wales had intensified as workers learned, from the strike, the power of collective action in the redress of common grievances and, from the combination, the effectiveness of disciplined organisation in the pursuit of specific goals. The spread of chartism from England into Wales in the late 1830s was to give a new direction to the struggle. Conversely, however, chartism in Wales was to be mutated from a popular front for the reform of Parliament into an armed movement for the creation of a workers' republic. In April 1839 Thomas Jenkins of Carmarthen had written 'Liberty's Address to the Welsh'. Three stanzas will convince the reader, if not of his poetical excellence, at least of his awareness that class and national oppression were inseparable in the Welsh context.

> Sons of Cambria! — come, arise
>   And no longer be
> Serfs enslaved, whom all despise
>   Who have known of me;
> Will ye longer wear your chains? —
> Still disgrace your native plains?
>
> Will ye always bow so meek,
>   To the imperious nod
> Of a haughty race who seek
>   To rule you by the rod? —
> Say — shall ignorance and pride
> Still the sons of Wallia guide?

Shall the stupid, haughty crew
   Still enjoy your gains?
Fresh demands shall they pursue?
   Faster bind your chains?
Burst your shackles — and be free! —
   Sons of Cambria! — follow me![78]

## Notes

1. Harry Scrivenor, *A Comprehensive History of the Iron Trade* (London, 1841), pp. 409-10.
2. See Alan Birch, *The Economic History of the British Iron and Steel Industry, 1784-1879* (London, 1967), pp. 122-33.
3. This formulation differs somewhat from that offered by M.J. Daunton, 'The Dowlais Iron Company in the Iron Industry, 1800-1850', in *Welsh History Review*, 6, 1 (June 1972), pp. 33-4. Daunton correlates combination activity with upturns and downturns in trade.
4. For a sociological treatment of turmoil, conspiracy and revolution, see Ted Gurr, 'Psychological Factors in Civil Violence', in *World Politics*, XX, 2 (1968). I use the word 'turmoil' but not 'conspiracy' in Gurr's sense.
5. E.W. Evans, *The Miners of South Wales* (Cardiff, 1961), pp. 39-47.
6. Ibid., pp. 52-7.
7. See the rather uneasy remarks on the Scotch Cattle of Ystradgynlais in Hywel Francis and David Smith, *The Fed. A History of the South Wales Miners in the Twentieth Century* (London, 1980), pp. 63, 107, 299 note 13. See, more importantly, their Ch. 2, passim. There is a multiplicity of movements in contemporary Wales that seem, in one respect or another, to lie in the tradition of the old Scotch Cattle: Meibion Glyndwr and Rhys Gethin, Eagles of Eryri, Guardians of Wales, Mudiad Amddiffyn Cymru, and so forth.
8. David J.V. Jones, *Before Rebecca. Popular Protests in Wales 1793-1835* (London, 1973), pp. 206-20.
9. Charles Wilkins, *History of the Iron, Steel, Tinplate, and Other Trades of Wales* (Merthyr Tydfil, 1903), p. 126.
10. Scrivenor, *Iron Trade*, p. 410.
11. Jones, *Before Rebecca*, p. 71.
12. PRO, H.O. 42/151: Rev. William Powell to Home Secretary, dd. 15 June 1816.
13. Scrivenor, *Iron Trade*, p. 409.
14. Glamorgan Record Office, Dowlais Iron Company records, Crawshay to J.J. Guest, dd.16 Oct. 1816. See Jones, *Before Rebecca*, p. 76.
15. The fullest treatment of the 1816 strike is that by David J.V. Jones, 'The South Wales Strike of 1816', in *Morgannwg*, XI (1967), and *Before Rebecca*, pp. 69-85. Interesting local detail is to be found in Oliver Jones, *The Early Days of Sirhowy and Tredegar* (Tredegar Historical Society, 1969), pp. 76-8.
16. Scrivenor, *Iron Trade*, pp. 409-10.
17. Evans, *Miners of South Wales*, pp. 15, 28-9.
18. Jones, *Before Rebecca*, p. 98.
19. Ibid., pp. 100-2.
20. Evans, *Miners of South Wales*, p. 16.
21. Scrivenor, *Iron Trade*, p. 409.

22. Evans, *Miners of South Wales*, p. 21.
23. Ibid., pp. 22-3.
24. Ibid., pp. 31-2, 35.
25. Jones, *Before Rebecca*, pp. 100-1.
26. Evans, *Miners of South Wales*, pp. 36-7.
27. Gwyn A. Williams, *The Merthyr Rising* (London, 1978), pp. 34-71, 75.
28. Ibid., pp. 99-101.
29. Ibid., pp. 110-11. Jones, *Before Rebecca*, pp. 139-41.
30. These events are described in detail in Williams, *Merthyr Rising*, pp. 109-64, and Jones, *Before Rebecca*, pp. 141-50.
31. *Morning Herald*, 6 Nov. 1839. Italics original.
32. *Glamorgan, Monmouth and Brecon Gazette and Merthyr Guardian* (henceforth referred to as *Merthyr Guardian*), 16 Nov. 1839.
33. Cardiff Central Library, Bute MSS XX/69: Henry Scale to Bute dd. 14 Nov. 1839. Italics original.
34. Williams, *Merthyr Rising*, p. 72.
35. See Charles Wilkins, *The South Wales Coal Trade and Its Allied Industries, from the Earliest Days to the Present Time* (Cardiff, 1888), p. 278: 'One of the earliest and most general strikes was in the Chartist outbreak, 1839-40, when honest labour was neglected for training, and in some cases for possible physical contingencies, and meetings where the illusory shadow was grasped at, and the practical wages, small as they were, lost.'
36. *Rules and Orders to be observed by a Society of Women* (William Williams, Merthyr Tydfil, 1806).
37. E.P. Thompson, *The Making of the English Working Class* (Harmondsworth, Middlesex, 1968), p. 199.
38. *Rheolau a Threfniadau, i sylwi arnynt gan Gwmdeithas o Grefftwyr ac Eraill*, Job James (Merthyr Tydfil, 1820).
39. Evan Powell, *History of Tredegar. Subject of Competition at Tredegar 'Chair Eisteddfod' held February the 25th, 1884* (Newport, 1902), p. 41.
40. Cardiff Central Library, Bute MSS XX/69: Scale to Bute dd. 14 Nov. 1839.
41. *Morning Chronicle*, 23 Nov. 1839. For a slightly different text, see *Monmouthshire Merlin*, 23 Nov. 1839.
42. Powell, *History of Tredegar*, p. 44.
43. Oliver Jones, 'The Scotch Cattle', in Goronwy, Alun Hughes, *Men of no Property* (Gwasg Gwenffrwd, Caerwys, 1971), p. 21; *Sirhowy and Tredegar*, p. 79. PRO, H.O. 52/23: T. Wood to Home Sec. dd. 6 Oct. 1833.
44. John Lloyd, *The Early History of the Old South Wales Iron Works (1760 to 1840)* (London, 1906), p. 195. For the Clydach strike, see Evans, *South Wales Miners*, pp. 25-6.
45. Powell, *History of Tredegar*, p. 41.
46. Scrivenor, *Iron Trade*, p. 409.
47. Welsh *tarw*, 'bull', echoes *taro*, 'to smite, strike out at'. The bull was the 'smiter' *par excellence* of the familiar animal world.
48. Ignotus, *The Last Thirty Years in a Mining District* (London, 1867), p. 3. The value judgements are those of the pseudonymous Ignotus rather than his informants.
49. Jones, 'Scotch Cattle', p. 24.
50. Powell, *History of Tredegar*, pp. 41-2.
51. The theatre of the Scotch Cattle involved much verbal punning. Jones, *Before Rebecca*, pp. 96-7, 'clutching at straws', suggested that the Scotch Cattle took their name from the Scotch (Scots) Greys, who were indeed used against the workers in 1822. Jones was on the track. Note Welsh *gre, gyr*, 'herd'.

The *Gre Scotch* of the workers opposed the Scotch Greys of the government!
52. Wilkins, *Trades of Wales*, pp. 178-9.
53. O. Jones, 'The Scotch Cattle', p. 24. D.J.V. Jones, *Before Rebecca*,
p. 105. Williams, *Merthyr Rising*, pp. 29, 77. Ignotus, *Last Thirty Years*, p. 64,
first noted the similarity to 'our Christmas "merryluid" '.
54. Cardiff Great Session, 8 April 1801, see Jones, *Before Rebecca*, p. 215.
55. PRO, H.O. 52/21. The notice was first published in Ness Edwards, *The
History of the South Wales Miners* (London, 1926), p. 30. The influence of the
events in Merthyr in 1831 is perhaps discernible in the word 'Reform' written
across the bull's head.
56. Powell, *History of Tredegar*, p. 42.
57. Evans, *Miners of South Wales*, p. 48. Jones, *Before Rebecca*, p. 259,
note 79.
58. Wilkins, *Trades of Wales*, p. 160.
59. The rules were published as an appendix to A Looker On, *On the Oaths
Taken in the Union Club. A Dialogue between Thomas Cadogan and David
Nathaniel, Colliers* (Morgan Evans, High Street, Newport, 1831), pp. 11-12. The
body of the work is a fictitious conversation in which the theme is developed that
union oaths 'are not obligations to be kept, but sins to be repented of'. A case
can be made for attributing the tract to Thomas Revel Guest, the devout
Methodist brother of the proprietor of the Dowlais works. Certainly T.R. Guest
wrote a *Plain Address to Unionists* in the same year, in which much the same
arguments are made, see M. Elsas (ed.), *Iron in the Making: Dowlais Iron
Company Letters, 1782-1860* (Cardiff, 1960), p. 612, and Williams, *Merthyr
Rising*, pp. 213-14. If this attribution is correct, then the union rules may have
been among those documents seized by the Merthyr magistrates in the course
of the rising. There are, however, difficulties in this view, not least that the tract
was published in Newport rather than Merthyr. The printer, Morgan Evans, is
known to have undertaken work for Thomas Prothero, see James Ifano Jones, *A
History of Printing and Printers in Wales to 1810, and of Successive and Related
Printers to 1923. Also, a History of Printing and Printers in Monmouthshire to
1923* (Cardiff, 1925), p. 245. There is, then, at least the possibility that the tract
was written or inspired by Prothero, who had colliery interests in the Blackwood
district. It is worthy of note that Morgan Evans's printing shop was fired into
during the attack on Newport in 1839, see John Warner and W.A. Gunn, *John
Frost and the Chartist Movement in Monmouthshire* (Newport, 1939), p. 38 (who
wrongly named the printer Morgan Davies).
60. *Monmouthshire Merlin*, 10 May 1834. O. Jones, *Sirhowy and Tredegar*,
p. 83, remarks that the Scotch Cattle must surely have been represented in the
early trade unions and 'must have stiffened their discipline'.
61. The major primary sources for the Scotch Cattle are the local newspapers,
and PRO, H.O. 40/23, H.O. 52/19, 21, 23 and 25.
62. *Monmouthshire Merlin*, 26 July 1834. Some herds became nothing more
than 'criminal bands', wrote Oliver Jones, 'Scotch Cattle', p. 23, 'whose sole aim
was to rob and plunder'. There were, argues Evans, *South Wales Miners*, pp. 50-1,
'at least as many criminals as idealists among the Scotch Cattle'. Banditry did
flourish in the disturbed times. One group had its base near Blackrock, and
preyed on those travelling the Abergavenny road. Another, of house-breakers,
operated in the Blackwood district, and its members disguised themselves somewhat in the manner of the Scotch Cattle, see *Monmouthshire Merlin*, 16 Sept.
1837 and *Merthyr Guardian*, 20 Jan. 1838. Nothing, however, suggests that these
were renegade Scotch herds; indeed, the Blackwood gang turned out to be one of
immigrant Somerset men.
63. *Merthyr Guardian*, 17 May 1834. Herds often numbered between 150 and

200 persons. It is therefore possible that the Scotch Cattle followed the precedent of the friendly societies in limiting the membership of a herd to 201. If so, then 9,000 'faithful children' would be 45 full herds.

64. PRO H.O. 40/30: Col. Love to Melbourne, dd. Cardiff, 10 April 1832, and Love to Somerset, dd. Cardiff, 20 April 1832. *The Times*, 21 April and 1 May 1832. *Monmouthshire Merlin*, 12 May 1832.

65. PRO, H.O.40/30: Love to Melbourne, dd. Brecon, 5 May 1832.

66. PRO. H.O. 41/12: S.M. Phillipps to J.B. Bruce at Merthyr, dd. Whitehall, 9 June 1834.

67. PRO, H.O. 52/53: Bute to Home Office, dd. Cardiff, 16 June 1834.

68. *Monmouthshire Merlin*, 26 July and 2 August 1834. *Cambrian*, 26 July and 2 August 1834.

69. PRO H.O. 41/12: Phillipps to Bruce dd. 18 June, and Phillipps to Bute dd. 26 June 1834.

70. *Monmouthshire Merlin*, 4 and 11 April 1835.

71. The pseudonymous south Welsh writer, Ignotus, learned the identity of the Bull from an informant who had known him well, *Last Thirty Years*, p. 5. Ignotus, pp. 6-7, reports that Ned Lolly finally fled the coalfield, afraid of being implicated in the murder of a constable at Blackwood. Jones, *Before Rebecca*, p. 97, reads far too much into Ignotus's references to Ned Lolly.

72. *Monmouthshire Merlin*, 26 July 1834.

73. Ibid., 4 April 1835.

74. Ibid., 3 May 1835.

75. Thomas Rees, *Miscellaneous Papers on Subjects Relating to Wales* (London, 1867), p. 14. For the life of Rees, see John Thomas, *Cofiant T. Rees, D.D., Abertawy* (Dolgellau, 1888).

76. *Merthyr Guardian*, 26 Jan. 1839.

77. Ibid., 25 May 1839.

78. Hugh Williams (ed.), *National Songs and Poetical Pieces, dedicated to the Queen and her Countrywomen* (London, 1839 [in fact, 1840]).

# 6  WORKS, WORKERS AND THE WORKING MEN'S ASSOCIATIONS

The London Working Men's Association was founded in June 1836, with William Lovett as secretary and Henry Hetherington as treasurer. It was conceived as an exclusive club committed to agitation for social and political improvement through lawful means. Members of the middle classes were ineligible for full membership, and in practice few day labourers were regarded as sufficiently educated to be admitted. Artisans and skilled workers dominated its ranks. In February 1837 the London WMA announced its political programme, namely, to petition Parliament to reform (indeed, transform) itself by the introduction of universal adult suffrage, equal representation, secret voting by ballot, annual general elections, the abolition of property qualifications for candidates and a six-hour working day for members at a salary of £400 a year. In subsequent months the association worked in collaboration with a number of radical members of Parliament to embody the proposed reforms, with some amendments, in a draft bill. It was published on 8 May 1838, and became known as the People's Charter.[1]

The middle months of 1838 were momentous ones in the development of the chartist movement, and the London WMA was obliged to share power with other bodies. The London Democratic Association became active in May. It was a revival of the East London Democratic Association which had been launched by George Julian Harney and others at the beginning of 1837, and like its predecessor it was committed to revolutionary working-class politics in the republican tradition of Thomas Paine.[2] In Leeds the Great Northern Union was founded. It represented the views of Feargus O'Connor who had launched the highly successful *Northern Star and Leeds General Advertiser* the previous November, and who inclined to the belief that Parliament would have to be coerced rather than persuaded into any major reform. In July the Birmingham Political Union, which had long advocated the presentation to Parliament of a people's petition for reform, now adopted the idea of creating a sort of shadow Commons — the General Convention of the Industrious Classes. The London WMA incorporated the concept of the Convention into its programme, and the Birmingham Political Union declared its support for the People's Charter. With these events the chartist movement assumed something

like its mature form. The London WMA and the Birmingham Political
Union dominated the moderate centre, flanked on the left by a number
of more or less extreme organisations, factions and tendencies committed to some combination of revolutionary politics and direct action.
The latter part of 1838 saw a fierce struggle between moderates and
extremists for control of the delegates to the General Convention, which
had been scheduled to open in London early in February the next year.
At a skilfully managed meeting at the Palace Yard, Westminster, on 17
September the London WMA succeeded in excluding all members of
the London Democratic Association from the slate of London delegates. Over the next two months, however, the Democratic Association
forged a series of working alliances with such provincial groups as the
Northern Political Union, and revolutionaries like Dr John Taylor
and Robert Lowery began to appear on the list of delegates. Harney himself, who had emerged as national leader of the London Democratic
Association, was chosen as delegate by Norwich, Newcastle upon Tyne
and Derby. In London old members of the WMA like Henry Vincent and
Robert Hartwell attempted to move the organisation leftwards to make
co-operation with the London Democratic Association possible. By the
end of 1838 it was clear that the struggle between radicals and revolutionaries and between 'moral force' and 'physical force' men would
be taken to the floor of the General Convention.[3]

In these events Wales played a part even if a peripheral one.
Throughout 1837 the London WMA had systematically extended its
influence beyond the metropolis. Selected members were designated
'missionaries' and empowered to open branch associations. Their
earliest efforts were directed principally to the north of England where,
among others, Henry Hetherington and Henry Vincent toiled in the
middle months of 1837. Both were to become involved in Welsh affairs,
but only later. The first branch to be established in Wales was that at
Carmarthen. It was founded by Hugh Williams, a close friend of Hetherington, early in 1837. A solicitor by occupation and middle class in
status, Williams was ineligible for membership of the London WMA. He
became, none the less, secretary of the Carmarthen WMA and went on
to open other branches in west Wales at Swansea and Llanelli. He was
granted honorary membership of the London WMA in January 1838.[4]
The first missionary proper to be sent to Wales by the London WMA
was Hetherington. It reveals something of the counsel that prevailed at
the time, that he was sent not to the ironworking districts of south
Wales but to the flannel-manufacturing towns of mid-Wales, Welshpool,
Newtown and Llanidloes. Branches of the WMA were founded there in

November 1837.[5]

The Bristol WMA was opened in October 1837 with a Welshman, Morgan Williams, as its chairman.[6] The earliest branches to be established in Monmouthshire, those at Pontypool and Newport, were probably its offshoots. The former was founded in January 1838 by Samuel Shell, who appears to have been a Bristol man (and whose son, George Shell, was to die in the attack on Newport).[7] The latter, Newport, was started in July 1838 by William Edwards, a baker who also had Bristol connections.[8] Aware of the challenge which the London WMA faced from less moderate organisations, Hugh Williams ot Carmarthen moved to secure the loyalty of the branches in south and west Wales. At the end of August 1838 he sent an emissary, William Jenkins, to visit them.[9] The Pontypool and Newport associations, like those of Swansea, Llanelli and Carmarthen itself, dutifully signalled their support for the position of the London WMA.[10] As a result of the same initiative a new branch was opened in Merthyr in October. Its secretary was the flannel manufacturer, Morgan Williams.[11]

The first of the Welsh delegates to the General Convention was chosen on 10 October 1838. This was Charles Jones of Welshpool. Intended for the church, Jones had been disowned by his family when he abruptly turned his back on that career and took up radical causes.[12] The next delegate, John Frost, was not chosen until 30 November. A former mayor and presently a magistrate of Newport, Frost had come out in support of the People's Charter exactly a month earlier.[13] He was chosen to represent Newport, Pontypool and a newly opened branch at Caerleon.[14] The selection of Welsh delegates was completed on 25 December when Hugh Williams was chosen at Merthyr.[15] Subsequently Carmarthen and Swansea also gave him their endorsement.[16] It will be noted that all three delegates were of middle-class status, Williams and presumably Jones by birth and Frost, perhaps, by ascent from the petty bourgeoisie. There can be little doubt, moreover, that in the few working men's associations that existed in Wales at that time artisan and petty bourgeois interests were preponderant. The *Address and Rules* of the Newport branch were closely based on those of the London WMA. They identified 'the *intelligent* and *influential* portion of the working classes' (emphasis original) as the target group; extended honorary membership to 'persons not of the working classes but whom the Members believe are sufficiently identified with them;' and allowed the members to decide each application on its merits since 'there are great differences of opinion as to where the line should be drawn which separates the working classes from the other portions of society'.[17]

In the early months of 1839 many new associations, or 'chartist lodges' as they were often called, sprang up in the ironworking and mining districts of the coalfield. Local initiative was frequently taken by artisans and craftsmen if only because they had hours of work sufficiently flexible to enable them to undertake the necessary organisation; shoemakers were particularly well represented among the lodge secretaries and treasurers. Publicans commonly allowed their premises to be used as lodge headquarters; it was, among other things, good for business. The coalfield was divided into five more or less well defined districts, the 'disturbed districts' as they came to be known. Leaders emerged who put their own distinct imprint on the development of the movement in each district. They were, in a sense, chartist 'bosses' whose power based on the control of labour threatened that of the ironmasters and coalowners based on the command of capital.

Morgan Williams, secretary of the Merthyr lodge, dominated the affairs of the wider district. The son of a Unitarian minister, he had become an Owenite socialist in the early 1830s. In 1834 he collaborated with John Thomas in launching the bilingual *Gweithiwr* or *Worker* and at the end of that year he was one of those most active in securing the election to Parliament of the first member for Merthyr, the newly radicalised Josiah John Guest.[18] As owner of a small manufactory, Williams was distinctly middle class in standing. So too was the leader of the Pontypridd district chartists, Dr William Price. Son of an Anglican clergyman and erstwhile Fellow of Jesus College, Oxford, Price himself became a Member of the Royal College of Surgeons in 1821. In the 1830s he was employed at the Chain Cable works at Pontypridd, and he too had supported Guest's election in 1834.[19] Price's radicalism was complemented by a cultural nationalism that was to take a highly idiosyncratic form in his later years.[20]

A third district extended across the heads of the valleys. There Zephaniah Williams dominated the movement. He had long been active in radical causes and in 1830 was one of the founders of the Tredegar branch of the National Union of the Working Classes.[21] Early in 1839 he gave up his position as master collier and mineral agent at the Sirhowy ironworks to become landlord of the Royal Oak Inn near Blaina.[22] Born in Argoed, Williams came from yeoman farmer background. Of very different origins was William Lloyd Jones of the Pontypool district. He was the son of a tradesman in Bristol. Abandoning a career as a strolling actor, Jones settled down in Pontypool in 1833 to combine watchmaking with keeping the Bristol House beershop.[23]

Lastly, the Newport baker William Edwards controlled the Blackwood district. He claimed to have been active in radical politics since 1816, and had been a dissenting preacher before opening his bakery in or about 1836.[24]

In 1839 Morgan Williams and William Lloyd Jones were around 30 years of age, and William Price, Zephaniah Williams and William Edwards were in their early to mid-forties. All were Welsh, and Welsh was the first language certainly of Price and the two Williamses. None was working class in origin, though Edwards and Jones belonged to the petty bourgeoisie rather than the bourgeoisie. With the exception of Jones, all had been previously active in radical politics. It was these men who were to build up the chartist movement in south Wales in 1839. Of the five it was William Edwards who played perhaps the most critical role. His importance in the period has tended to be neglected, however, for at the time of the November Rising he had already been in gaol for six months.

William Edwards effectively launched a campaign to mobilise the workers in the chartist cause at a meeting at Pontnewynydd on 1 January 1839. The two local delegates to the General Convention were billed to speak. John Frost did, making one of his infrequent appearances in the hills, but Hugh Williams did not. Two guest speakers were also announced, Feargus O'Connor and Henry Vincent. Only Vincent arrived. The authorities had their spy present, one David Jones, and he made notes of what was said.[25] Edwards took the chair and set the tone of the meeting by declaring his readiness to die for the People's Charter. Frost attacked government sinecures and made some humourous references to the queen's grooms of the bedchamber, and Vincent argued that the whole edifice of government must be toppled and with it the monarchy. The tory *Merthyr Guardian* saw the meeting, and those that followed on 2 and 3 January at Newport and Caerleon, as attacks upon the whig administration, and pronounced them harmless enough – 'none of them calculated, certainly, to set the Severn on fire'.[26] The paper was soon to change its tune for over the next four months Edwards succeeded in organising the most restless and turbulent section of the population: the workers in the sale-coal collieries around Blackwood. He was, he wrote in his brief memoirs, constantly in the hills 'giving publicity to the heart-cheering principles of the People's Charter' and everywhere, he claimed, 'the brave colliers and miners . . . nobly rally round the standard of liberty'.[27] At the beginning of April Edwards could boast of having 'five thousand able fellows like myself at Blackwood whom I can call by a blow of my

Horn to support the cause if required'.[28] He also maintained contact with the chartist leaders at the ironworks. He visited Blaina, Nantyglo and Beaufort on 1 April and afterwards described Zephaniah Williams and David Lewis of the Brynmawr lodge as 'two of the best Chartists I ever met'.[29] A few weeks later Dr William Price came over from Pontypridd to join William Edwards in Blackwood, there to expound the ideas of Thomas Paine to the colliers in Welsh.[30] It was probably Price, impressed by the resolution of the Blackwood chartists, who urged Morgan Williams in Merthyr to discuss common strategies with the Monmouthshire leaders. Morgan convened a meeting at Dukestown on 30 April. Certainly William Edwards and William Lloyd Jones attended it, for the next day – May Day – they addressed public meetings in the neighbourhood.[31]

In the drive to organise the ironworkers and colliers the two delegates to the General Convention from south Wales played little part. The Convention opened in London on 4 February 1839. John Frost took his seat on that day, but Hugh Williams did not do so until 10 May, giving as his reason professional engagements of a 'peremptory and important kind'.[32] Frost was engaged at the time in a spirited exchange with the Home Secretary, Lord John Russell, about the compatibility or otherwise of his being both a magistrate and a chartist. From this Frost gained kudos at the Convention. At the end of February he was among those given three weeks' leave of absence by the Convention in order to visit their constituencies and rally support for the charter.[33] He declined the mission and Vincent was sent instead. It seems clear that Frost relished the limelight of the Convention and was most reluctant to leave it. When he did so in late March it was part of a carefully staged, theatrical move. On 21 March the Home Secretary had finally revoked Frost's commission as a magistrate. Eight days later Frost was in the Gloucestershire town of Stroud, where Vincent joined him. It was Lord John Russell's parliamentary constituency. At a large public meeting which both he and Vincent addressed, Frost secured election as Stroud delegate to the General Convention. He then announced his intention of standing against Russell at the next parliamentary elections.[34] The challenge laid down, Frost travelled to Newport. William Edwards scheduled him to speak at Pontypool on 5 April. Frost, however, broke the engagement and returned to London.[35] Thereafter he was to regard himself as representing not only south Wales in the chartist assembly, but also the west of England.[36]

Understandably, the Welsh ironworkers and colliers came to view Frost with considerable distrust, a matter which will be pursued in

Chapter 9. For Vincent, in contrast, they developed a strong affection. Vincent was also in attendance at the General Convention, and on 23 February he had launched the *Western Vindicator* from Bristol. Nevertheless, he found time to pay several visits to south Wales and on two occasions, in late March and late April, he accompanied William Edwards on his tours of the hills.[37] The huge, rough Edwards and the slight, graceful Vincent made a strange but effective pair, for both were powerful orators in their respective styles. At the Pontypool meeting of 5 April, which Frost had missed, Edwards likened himself to Moses, ready to lead his people against their oppressors.[38] When Vincent arrived in Wales two weeks later to join Edwards, he took up the same theme. 'When the time for resistance arrives', he told an audience in Newport on 19 April,

> let your cry be to your Tents of Israel, and then with one voice, one heart and one blow – Perish the privileged orders. Death to the aristocracy. Up with the people and the Government they have established.[39]

Four days later Edwards and Vincent were in Nantyglo and Blaina, in Zephaniah Williams's bailiwick. There, according to a hostile witness who subtly distorted what was said, Edwards spoke of the need

> to do away, by force of Chartist pikemen, all law, religion, order, customs, rights, and properties that may happen to stand in the way of the necessary or desirable proceedings of *us* – the working classes, who only want to have *great wages*, – and unlimited *rights* in exchange for whatever quantity of labor we may see fit and proper to perform; – and no more.[40]

The rhetoric was all too much for the authorities. Early in May the Newport magistrates issued warrants for the arrest of Edwards, Vincent and two other members of the Newport WMA, John Dickenson and William Townsend. All were lodged in Monmouth Gaol to await trial at the Summer Assizes on charges of unlawful assembly, conspiracy and riot. Dickenson and Townsend received six months sentences, Edwards nine months and Vincent twelve months.[41] Edwards and Vincent were, however, tried a second time on sedition charges at the Lent Assizes in 1840, when the former was given a further 14, and the latter 12, months.[42] Neither Edwards nor Vincent could, in a sense, have had cause for complaint; in the judges and juries they had indeed encountered the class enemy to which they had so often made reference in their speeches. Clearly both had come to see parliamentary reform as at most only a gesture in the direction of revolution. It seems likely that Edwards was influenced, perhaps through Vincent, by the advanced jacobin views current in the left-wing factions of the chartist movement. It seems impossible that he was not much affected, and Vincent through him, by his sustained contact with the workers of south Wales whose commitment to direct action had been manifest over several decades, most dramatically in the Scotch Cattle.

As a result of the activities of William Edwards and the other district leaders, with the support of the many local lodge officials, the chartist movement in south Wales became decisively proletarianised. The working men's associations on the coalfield in 1839 bore little resemblance in social composition to their ultimate progenitor, the London WMA of 1836. The change that had occurred was interestingly treated in an article in the Carmarthen paper, *The Welshman*, which may possibly have been penned by Hugh Williams himself. Certainly the writer was someone sympathetic to chartism in the form that the early members of the London WMA had conceived it, and certainly he deplored the insurrection and saw it as a result of the transfer of power within the movement from the skilled workers, artisans and craftsmen to the proletarian masses. 'There are', he argued,

large bodies of really intelligent men, overlookers and operatives in the Iron and Coal Works, etc., who thoroughly acquaint themselves with the principles of political economy, are well versed in the history of their country, including its government, and general statistics, and having made up their minds, that the constitution of the laws, and the present state of society, are not adapted to each other; consequently they seek a change which they are persuaded would be for the better; but they seek it only by employing the moral powers of evidence, argument, union, and perseverance. These men are firm opponents to the physical force system, and have formally withdrawn themselves from all lodges and associations, which have practically advocated that system by partaking in the recent outrages. These we may venture to denominate the original and legitimate Chartists.

It is easy to recognise in this a reference to men like Samuel Etheridge, the radical Newport printer and publican. One of the early members of the WMA in that town, he became its secretary in January 1839. He resigned from the association six months later in protest against the extremism of many of the members.[43] At the time the lodge numbered about 600 persons and Etheridge classed about 50 of them as 'tradesmen'.[44]

With the withdrawal of the 'really intelligent men' from the chartist lodges, so the contributor to *The Welshman* argued, power passed to another class 'possessing considerable information, with far less judgment, and greater impetuosity, than the former'. He thought their range of knowledge remarkable considering their lack of English, but deplored their methods of seeking redress for their grievances:

> It is astonishing to what an extent men, who do not understand a sentence of English, are informed, and accurately too, of practices in Church and State, which all but *Conservatives* concur in condemning as abuses, more or less gross. They know all about the Civil List, and the spiritual rent-roll — they can give an undeniable detail of sinecures, pensions, jobs, and official salaries — of fat Bishoprics and lean Curacies — they compute the amount of national taxation, and by a practical arithmetic of their own, divide its charge among the community, giving themselves, at least, their full quota — and then, seeing they are not at all consulted in laying on the burden, they are seized with a strong desire to fling it off; less solicitous about the means, than the accomplishment of their object. These are the physical force, or spurious Chartists; who think a Revolution would be a good thing, because it would get rid of all the aforesaid grievances, by a grand explosion — not taking thought for the manifold new evils which might come upon them instead.

There was, however, yet another class of workers for whom the writer had no good word. It was, perhaps, a sort of lumpenproletariat that included new immigrants with neither roots nor families on the coalfield. 'The third class — and alas! an exceedingly numerous one', he wrote,

> is made up of the ignorant, the depraved, and the idle, who become the ready tools of their more knowing, but violent compatriots, and constitute the great mass of silly enthusiasts, who rush upon their own destruction, in the pursuit of no definite object, like the imbeciles and unfortunates, who recently signalized their errant folly at Newport.[45]

Partisan though the writer was in his hostility to the 'physical force' option, his analysis of the changing structure of the Welsh movement was undoubtedly well informed.

Henry Scale expressed surprise that the authorities were so slow to recognise the nature of the threat presented to them as the chartist organisers extended their activities into the ironworking and mining communities. 'They are ready enough to stop a Union for wages', he remarked, 'but a Union for *Social and Political Reforms* so-called — miscalled I should say — excites no notice whatsoever.'[46] At the very beginning of 1839 Henry Vincent had returned to England from his first campaign in south Wales already much enthused by what he had seen. 'Associations', he claimed,

> are forming all over the hills of Monmouthshire, Glamorganshire, and Breconshire; and in a short time there will not be a village in the western part of Monmouthshire, and the eastern part of Glamorganshire, which will not have its association for obtaining the people's charter.[47]

When John Frost arrived in London for the opening of the General Convention on 4 February, he announced that 'in Monmouthshire alone there had been formed, within three months, twenty branches of the Working Men's Association, and there were 15,000 or 20,000 men determined upon having their rights'.[48] By the time of the rising in November there were, according to Zephaniah Williams, about 50 lodges on the coalfield, and 'in each from 100 to 1,300 members'.[49] It is no longer possible to reconstruct fully the proliferation of the lodges over the period. Many of them kept good records, but in the aftermath of the attack on Newport most lodge officers prudently destroyed them. The papers of the Brynmawr Association were seized by a detachment of the 12th Regiment that made an unanticipated foray into the rebel strongholds on 4 November, but they are not known to have survived.[50] One cache of material did come briefly to light, seemingly in the late nineteenth century. An iron chest containing what must have been the records of the Blaina lodge were found there, bricked up in a wall at the Rolling Mill Inn. 'I burned them', said the proprietor at the time, 'because they were some old papers about the Chartists and could hardly be deciphered.'[51] In the absence of such records the spread of the lodges is best examined with reference to the distribution of the labour force over the coalfield.

In the early nineteenth century the old parishes, where coal from

**Figure 6.1: The 'Disturbed Districts'**

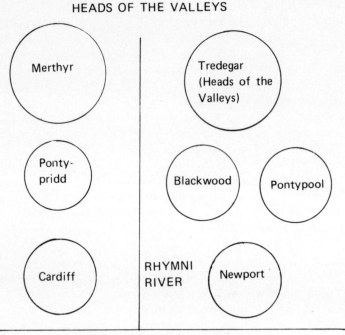

one might be brought to bank in another, had become largely irrelevant to the life of the industrial region.[52] The old boundary between Monmouthshire and Glamorganshire along the Rhymney River did, however, retain its importance. It divided those works and collieries linked by canal and tramroad with Cardiff on the one hand from those linked by canal and tramroad with Newport on the other. The industrial hinterland of Cardiff comprised two districts based upon Merthyr and Pontypridd, and that of Newport three districts based on Tredegar, Pontypool and Blackwood. Those who planned the strategy of the rising did so on the basis of these 'disturbed districts', assigning to each a distinct operational role. This matter will be treated in Chapter 8. Data on the labour force in each district are compiled in Tables 6.1 to 6.6 from the chronologically most relevant source available, principally the report which the commissioners on the employment of children produced in 1841 and presented to Parliament in 1842.[53] The data are not complete, although they cover all but the smallest of the works and

## Map 6.1: South Wales ca. 1839. Ironworks, Tinworks and Principal Sale-coal Collieries

Ironworks and tinworks ★
Principal sale-coal collieries □

Four Miles

## KEY

*Ironworks and tinworks*
1 Hirwaun. 2 Cyfarthfa. 3 Dowlais. 4 Penydarren. 5 Plymouth. 6 Aberdare.
7 Gadlys. 8 Abernant. 9 Rhymney. 10 Bute. 11 Tredegar. 12 Sirhowy. 13 Beaufort.
14 Ebbw Vale. 15 Victoria. 16 Nantyglo. 17 Coalbrookvale. 18 Blaina and C
Cwmcelyn. 19 Clydach. 20 Garnddyris. 21 Blaenavon. 22 Varteg. 23 British.
24 Pentwyn and Golynos. 25 Pontypool and Blaendare. 26 Pontrhydrun. 27 Pont-
newydd. 28 Abercarn. 29 Machen. 30 Pontymister. 31 Chain Cable. 32 Taff Vale.
33 Treforest. 34 Pentyrch. 35 Melingriffith.
For key to Sale-coal collieries, see p. 104.

collieries (see Map 6.1).

The northwesternmost of the districts embraced the valleys of Taff and Cynon above their junction at Abercynon. It was dominated by the town and (since 1832) parliamentary borough of Merthyr Tydfil. It included the cluster of great ironworks around Merthyr itself (Dowlais, Cyfarthfa, Penydarren and Plymouth) and the lesser works in the Cynon Valley (Hirwaun, Aberdare, Abernant and Gadlys). In 1839 over 121,000 tons of iron were consigned by canal company to Cardiff from these eight works, perhaps about three-quarters of the tonnage being in manufactured iron and the remainder in pig.[54] Dowlais, largest of all the ironworks in south Wales and probably anywhere, had 15 furnaces in blast and produced 40,495 tons of iron in 1839.[55] Its labour force was fairly evenly divided between ironworkers in the stricter sense, and colliers and miners: 1,004 people were employed at the blast furnaces, 1,365 at the forges and mills, 1,482 at the iron mines and patches, and 1,230 in the coal pits and levels.[56] It was claimed that 1,500 tons of coal were cut daily to meet the requirements of the works.[57]

Little coal was yet produced for sale in the Merthyr district in the 1830s. The only independent colliery of any size was that run by the Thomas family at Waun Wyllt and Craig a few miles south of Merthyr Tydfil, where Robert Thomas had been the first to win the famous Four Foot seam of steam coal in the mid-1820s. In 1839 the colliery produced about 26,000 tons of coal.[58] Thomas Wayne was next to prove the same seam at Cwmbach in the Cynon Valley in 1837, but in 1839 the enterprise was still very small and no information on labour has been found.[59]

Data on the workers' organisations in the district are scant. Morgan Williams presided over the affairs of the Merthyr Tydfil WMA, and at his factory at Pen-yr-Heolgerrig he produced uniform waistcoats for the lodge men and aprons for the women.[60] The branch often met in a schoolroom near the smithy of another of its leading members, David John.[61] It was the largest of all the Welsh lodges. In April or May 1839 the card or 'ticket' numbered 2,601 was issued to one of those later to be killed in the fighting in Newport,[62] and in June membership was

*Sale-coal collieries*
1 Craig and Waun Wyllt. 2 Dinas. 3 Gelliwion. 4 Maesmawr. 5 Craig-yr-Allt. 6 Llancaiach. 7 Top Hill. 8 Gelligaer. 9 Gilfach Fargoed. 10 Union, Glanddu, Tir Adam, Pencoed, Rose. 11 Plas. 12 Buttery Hatch. 13 Carngethin. 14 Gellideg. 15 Bryn. 16 Gelligroes. 17 Hafod-yr-isclawdd. 18 Manmoel (Mamhole). 19 Argoed and Cwmcrach. 20 Cwrt-y-bella and Gwrhay. 21 Waterloo. 22 Rock. 23 Woodfield. 24 Penllwyn. 25 Penycoedcae and Kendon. 26 Trinant. 27 Cwm Dws. 28 Risca.

**Table 6.1: Merthyr District Works, Sale-coal Collieries and Labour Force**

| Works | Labour Force by Age and Sex, 1841 | | | | | | Totals |
|-------|---------|---|-------|---|----------|---|--------|
| | Over 18 | | 13-18 | | Under 13 | | |
| | M | F | M | F | M | F | |
| *Iron* | | | | | | | |
| Dowlais | 4,082 | 200 | 372 | 158 | 327 | 53 | 5,192 |
| Penydarren | 1,605 | 94 | 166 | 49 | 140 | 17 | 2,071 |
| Plymouth | 1,350 | 140 | 330 | 140 | 190 | 75 | 2,225 |
| Cyfarthfa  )<br>Hirwaun  ) | ? | ? | ? | ? | ? | ? | 4,500* |
| Aberdare  )<br>Abernant  ) | 780 | 80 | 174 | 31 | 89 | 6 | 1,160 |
| Gadlys | ? | ? | ? | ? | ? | ? | 150* |
| *Sale-coal* | | | | | | | |
| Craig and Waun Wyllt | 28 | 4 | 13 | 3 | 0 | 2 | 50 |
| | | | | | | | 15,348 |

*estimated from output of iron

said to be increasing at the rate of 100 and more a week.[63] In July over £87 was sent from Merthyr to the fund for the defence of the chartist prisoners: £20 was earmarked for the Llanidloes defendants and the remainder for Vincent, Edwards and comrades.[64] The sum was presumably raised by a special levy on the members, though there is no clear evidence on the point. The amount might be the proceeds of a sixpenny levy on some 3,500 members, for when the lodge ordered a uniformed church parade in early August, 3,000 turned out (though the *Merthyr Guardian* argued, improbably, that only a few hundred of them were chartists).[65] In both the levy and the church parade, however, members of the nearby Dowlais lodge most likely participated. It was believed to have had about 1,000 members in October 1839,[66] but its affairs were shrouded in such secrecy that even J.J. Guest knew little about them.[67] The Merthyr Tydfil and Dowlais lodges aside, only one other is known to have existed in the district, at Aberdare. Its secretary was the weaver John Williams and the shoemaker Thomas Evans also held office.[68] In November 1839 its membership was thought to be upwards of 400; earlier in the year it had contributed £14 to the chartist prisoners' defence.[69]

To the south of the Merthyr district and also in the hinterland of Cardiff lay the growing town of Pontypridd (or Newbridge as it was then known), at the junction of Rhondda and Taff. It was the centre of a district that extended into the lower Rhondda Valley to the west, and along Taff Vale to the south. The independent sale-collieries in the vicinity of Gelligaer and Llanfabon are treated as part of this district since the coal they produced was transported through Pontypridd to Cardiff. The district differed markedly in character from that of Merthyr. The ironworks did not command the rich mineral resources of those situated on the northern rim of the coalfield, and were engaged in founding rather than smelting. The Treforest works near Pontypridd, for example, had to depend on the Hirwaun furnaces for supplies of pig iron and upon the Gwaun-yr-Eirw colliery in the lower Rhondda for most of the supplies of coal. Production of the ironworks was in the range of 3,000 to 4,000 tons of manufactured iron a year, and none of them employed as many as a thousand workers (Table 6.2). The

**Table 6.2: Pontypridd District. Works, Sale-coal Collieries and Labour Force**

| Works | Labour Force by Age and Sex, 1841 | | | | | | Total |
| | Over 18 | | 13-18 | | Under 13 | | |
| | M | F | M | F | M | F | |
|---|---|---|---|---|---|---|---|
| *Iron (and Tin)* | | | | | | | |
| Taff Vale | 70 | 0 | 10 | 0 | 18 | 0 | 98 |
| Chain Cable | 140 | 0 | 40 | 0 | 20 | 0 | 200 |
| Treforest* | 175 | ? | ? | ? | ? | ? | 245 |
| Pentyrch** | 450 | 0 | 185 | 0 | 165 | 0 | 800 |
| Melingriffith | 65 | 20 | 10 | 5 | 30 | 10 | 140 |
| *Sale-coal* | | | | | | | |
| Dinas | 301 | 0 | 32 | 0 | 81 | 0 | 414 |
| Gelliwion | 22 | 0 | 4 | 0 | 0 | 0 | 26 |
| Maesmawr | 130 | 0 | 15 | 0 | 12 | 0 | 157 |
| Craig-yr-Allt | 35 | 0 | 10 | 0 | 1 | 0 | 46 |
| Gelligaer† | ? | ? | ? | ? | ? | ? | 80 |
| Top Hill† | ? | ? | ? | ? | ? | ? | 40 |
| Llancaiach† | ? | ? | ? | ? | ? | ? | 27 |
| | | | | | | | 2,273 |

*including Gwaun-yr-Eirw colliery
**including Coed-y-Bedw and Lan collieries and Garth Fach iron mine
†corrected for 1839 from Bute MSS, XX/133

total amount of coal sent from the district by canal company to Cardiff in 1839 was almost 179,000 tons.[70] It originated from a scatter of collieries of which Walter Coffin's at Dinas on the Rhondda, George Insole's at Maesmawr in Taff Vale, and Thomas Powell's at Gelligaer midway between the Taff and Rhymney Valleys, were the largest. The other sizeable labour force in the district was that employed by the

Taff Vale Railway Company. In 1839 about 1,000 men were working on construction of the line, which was to be opened in 1841.[71]

The existence of three lodges in the district is clearly attested: Pontypridd, Dinas and Nelson. The distribution of works and collieries, however, did not permit the high level of organisation found in the vicinity of Merthyr. The Pontypridd lodge frequently held its meetings at the rocking-stone on the common above the town. Its secretary was a weaver named Francis,[72] but Dr William Price dominated the proceedings. The leader of the Cwm Rhondda colliers at Dinas was William David whose father, also William David, kept a shop at Pen-y-Graig.[73] At the beginning of September 1839, the local magistrates reported that 'among the mining and manufacturing population of Dinas and New-bridge [Pontypridd] three fourths of the people are Chartists'.[74] A meeting called at Pontypridd on 3 July drew 600 people, presumably from the Pontypridd and Dinas lodges, and William Lloyd Jones came over from Pontypool to share the platform with William Price and William David.[75] A few weeks later Pontypridd contributed £5 15s 6d and Dinas £4 5s 0d to the fund for the chartist prisoners.[76]

On 22 April 1839 a meeting took place at Blackwood between Dr William Price and William Edwards of Newport.[77] It was probably the occasion on which Price agreed to undertake the organisation of the men in the Nelson area, at the Gelligaer, Top Hill and Llancaiach collieries. Both Price and William David were active there in early May, when the lodge was perhaps founded.[78] It met at the Colliers' Arms near Nelson, kept by Morgan Morgan, and it was run by two local colliers, Thomas Giles and the ex-soldier William Owen.[79] Owen collected £1 19s 0d for the chartist prisoners. If we assume it to have represented a sixpenny levy, then about 80 men had joined the lodge by the middle of the year.[80]

The northernmost district of the coalfield was one that extended across the heads of the valleys of Rhymney, Sirhowy, Ebbw Fawr, Ebbw Fach and Clydach. The new town of Tredegar, with a population of over 7,000 in 1841, had emerged as the effective centre of the district though the unruliness of its people deterred the local authorities from developing it as a market town.[81] The ten ironworks (Table 6.3) together consigned 113,197 tons of iron by canal company to Newport in 1839.[82] No independent collieries of any size are known to have been operating in the district in that year.

About a dozen working men's associations (including one women's group) are known to have existed in the district. The Rhymney lodge drew its members from the Bute and Union ironworks, both of which

**Table 6.3: Heads of the Valleys District. Works and Labour Force**

| Works | Labour Force by Age and Sex, 1841 | | | | | | Total |
|---|---|---|---|---|---|---|---|
| | Over 18 | | 13-18 | | Under 13 | | |
| | M | F | M | F | M | F | |
| *Iron* | | | | | | | |
| Rhymney (Union-Bute) | 1,900 | 110 | 213 | 72 | 177 | 22 | 2,494 |
| Tredegar | 2,100 | 150 | 230 | 86 | 179 | 12 | 2,757 |
| Sirhowy | 728 | 40 | 72 | 92 | 31 | 12 | 975 |
| Ebbw Vale | 1,202 | 76 | 129 | 49 | 129 | 19 | 1,604 |
| Nantyglo ) Beaufort ) | 3,170 | 250 | 203 | 135 | 131 | 11 | 3,900 |
| Victoria | 155 | 11 | 48 | 10 | 30 | 5 | 259 |
| Coalbrookvale | ? | ? | ? | ? | ? | ? | 800* |
| Blaina and Cwm Celyn | ? | ? | ? | ? | ? | ? | 850* |
| Clydach | 945 | 46 | 181 | 46 | 110 | 23 | 1,351 |
| | | | | | | | 14,990 |

*estimated from output

were operated by the Rhymney Iron Company. It contributed £7 15s 0d to the prisoners' fund, which is the only indication of its size that has been found.[83] In the next valley, that of the Sirhowy, there were three large lodges in the vicinity of Tredegar itself. The oldest was that at Dukestown, where Zephaniah Williams had been resident until his move to Blaina early in 1839. Its headquarters was the Star (Twyn-y-Star) Inn, though there is some conflict in the record as to whether the proprietor was John Morgan (Morgan the Star) or Evan Evans (Ianto Darlwm).[84] A second lodge met at the Miners' Arms in Sirhowy, where a local branch of the National Union of the Working Classes had been started in 1830, and a third, the Tredegar lodge proper, at the Red Lion in what is now Commercial Street.[85] These three lodges served the Tredegar ironworks, a Homfray concern, and the Sirhowy ironworks, a Harford concern, which together employed upwards of 3,500 workers. There were, apparently, two other lodges in the immediate vicinity of Tredegar.[86] They were probably branches opened as the older lodges became too large for easy management. One of them had its headquarters at the Horse and Jockey in Dukestown, a beershop kept by William Rees.[87] The lodges in and around Tredegar were reported to have contributed £11 17s 0d to the prisoners' fund.[88] The amount seems very low; either the lodges had set the levy at only a penny or two or the records of the sums raised are defective.

The next valley moving eastwards is that of Ebbw Fawr. Three lodges are known to have existed in it, the Ebbw Vale and Beaufort, the

Rassa and the Victoria. The Ebbw Vale and Beaufort WMA was by far the largest of the three. The collier George George enrolled in it probably in June 1839; certainly he paid his first dues in that month. His lodge number was 1,174.[89] It may be inferred that of the 3,000 or so workers at the Ebbw Vale and Beaufort plants (Harford and Bailey concerns respectively), somewhat over a third had joined by the early summer. The Rassa lodge was probably opened as the movement grew, specifically to serve those Beaufort workers whose homes were distant from the meeting place of the Ebbw Vale and Beaufort WMA. Its headquarters was at the house of Llewellyn Davies. John Thomas, a tailor, was the secretary, and on 3 November the Beaufort miner John Powell enrolled as No. 324.[90] No report of the contribution of the Ebbw Vale and Beaufort lodge to the prisoners' fund has been found. The 13s 3d sent from 'Upper Ebbw Vale' came, presumably, from the Rassa lodge.[91] Lower in the valley the Victoria lodge served the ironworks of that name. The labour force was small and so, too, must have been the WMA membership.[92]

Largest of the associations in the valley of Ebbw Fach was that at Blaina. Its headquarters was at the Royal Oak Inn in Coalbrookvale, which was kept by Zephaniah Williams. In mid-1839 membership appears to have been around 450[93] and it had reached over 750 by late October.[94] The members were drawn principally from the Coalbrookvale works owned by the Brewers and the Blaina and Cwm Celyn works owned by the Browns. A women's lodge was also held at the Royal Oak.[95] In August the chartist prisoners' defence fund received 10s 9d from Blaina and £5 from Coalbrookvale. It may be assumed that the women's lodge subscribed the former sum and the men's the latter.[96] A little higher in the valley lay the Nantyglo works run by Crawshay Bailey. Its workers were organised in the Brynmawr lodge, which used the King Crispin beershop at Waunhelygen on the hills above the town as headquarters; its proprietor, David Lewis, was high in the chartist councils on the coalfield. The branch contributed £3 to the defence fund in mid-1839.[97] Further east still, in the valley of Clydach, was the Llanelli lodge. Its membership was drawn from the Clydach Iron Company's works, but little is otherwise known about it.

The fourth of the 'disturbed districts' was that occupying the basin of the coalfield (Table 6.4). Centre of the district was the growing town of Blackwood or Coed-duon, where the rebels established their command for the attack on Newport in November. The economy of the district was based upon the sale of bituminous coal. Most of it was cut from the relatively accessible Mynyddislwyn seam. In the late 1830s it was estimated that about 150 acres were being worked, yielding between 3,000 and 4,000 tons of coal per acre annually.[98] Most of the 518,916 tons of coal sent to Newport in 1839 originated from the Blackwood district.[99] The independent collieries were still small concerns. Lewis and Rosser Thomas were among the leading proprietors but employed fewer than 500 men at their Carngethin, Glanddu, Tir Adam, Union and Pencoed levels and Rose pit. Thomas Powell of Newport employed only about 400 or so men at Buttery Hatch, Bryn and Gelligroes, and at Gelligaer in the Cardiff hinterland, and Martin Morrison had under 300 men in his pits and levels at Trinant, Penycoedcae, Kendon and Cwm Dws. Few of the coalowners operated on even these modest scales.

**Table 6.4: Blackwood District. Sale-coal Collieries, Works and Labour Force**

| Works | Labour Force by Age and Sex, 1841 | | | | | | Total |
| | Over 18 | | 13-18 | | Under 13 | | |
| | M | F | M | F | M | F | |
|---|---|---|---|---|---|---|---|
| *Sale-coal* | | | | | | | |
| Gilfach Fargoed | 50 | 0 | 7 | 0 | 12 | 0 | 69 |
| Union, Glanddu, Tir Adam, Pencoed, Rose | 198 | 0 | 50 | 0 | 39 | 0 | 287 |
| Carngethin | 114 | 0 | 30 | 0 | 12 | 0 | 156 |
| Hengoed | 30 | 0 | 15 | 0 | 7 | 0 | 52 |
| Plas | 30 | 0 | 15 | 0 | 8 | 0 | 53 |
| Buttery Hatch | 80 | 0 | 56 | 0 | 22 | 0 | 158 |
| Bryn | 30 | 0 | 8 | 0 | 7 | 0 | 45 |
| Gelligroes | 50 | 0 | 16 | 0 | 12 | 0 | 78 |
| Gellideg and Penllwyn | 79 | 0 | 19 | 0 | 16 | 0 | 114 |
| Woodfield | 59 | 0 | 4 | 0 | 1 | 0 | 64 |
| Rock | 88 | 0 | 35 | 0 | 9 | 0 | 132 |
| Argoed and Cwmcrach | 80 | 0 | 41 | 0 | 20 | 0 | 141 |
| Manmoel and Cwrt-y-bella | 90 | 0 | 30 | 0 | 10 | 0 | 130 |
| Pen-y-fan and Gwrhay | 59 | 0 | 14 | 0 | 13 | 0 | 86 |
| Waterloo | 57 | 0 | 26 | 0 | 7 | 0 | 90 |
| Penycoedcae, Kendon and Trinant | 150 | 0 | 40 | 0 | 22 | 0 | 212 |
| Cwm Dws | 60 | 0 | 12 | 0 | 15 | 0 | 87 |
| Risca | 250 | 0 | 50 | 0 | 15 | 0 | 315 |
| *Iron (and Tin)* | | | | | | | |
| Abercarn | ? | ? | ? | ? | ? | ? | 150* |
| Pontymister | ? | ? | ? | ? | ? | ? | 350* |
| Machen | ? | ? | ? | ? | ? | ? | 140* |
| | | | | | | | 2,909 |

*estimated from output

For convenience a number of enterprises which lay near the south crop of the coal have been included in the Blackwood district. The Risca colliery, worked by John Russell and Co., was atypical. It was geared to production for the steam packet boats, and deep pits were dropped because of the steep dip of the seams on the crop. Welsh workers considered the colliery a particularly dangerous one, and much of the labour was recruited from the Kingswood pits near Bristol. It was said that none of the men took part in the November Rising.[100] A number of small iron and tin works also lay near the south crop. The only three of size, Abercarn, Pontymister and Machen, together sent only 4,434 tons of iron to Newport in 1839.[101]

The oldest of the working men's associations in the district was that at Blackwood itself. Owen Davies and several other shoemakers had founded it early in 1839, but control was soon taken over by the colliers.[102] It met at the Coach and Horses, the proprietor of which, Richard Pugh, served as treasurer. There was also a women's lodge in Blackwood, the Female Patriotic Association.[103] The Blackwood women subscribed £2 to the chartist defence fund in July 1839, and the men £10.[104] A further £2 13s 3d was collected by the lodge secretary, William Barwell, a few weeks later.[105] At least eight other lodges existed in the district. Each was associated with one or several collieries, and each had its headquarters at a local beershop or public house. Those which are known to have contributed to the defence fund are Pontllanfraith (£5 0s 6d), Fleur-de-lis (£2 11s 0d), Gelligroes (£1 10s 0d), Argoed (£1 5s 6½d) and Crumlin (£1 1s 11d).[106] No return has been noted for the Maes-y-cwmer, Llanhilleth and Croespenmaen lodges. The size of the labour force in the district casts doubt on William Edwards's claim in April, that he could call together 5,000 'able fellows' with a blast of his horn. Whatever the Blackwood workers lacked in numbers, however, they made up for in their zeal for the cause, and they were among the most ardent of those who took to arms in November.

The easternmost, and last, district of the coalfield was one that extended along the valley of Afon Lwyd. Its natural centre was the old market town of Pontypool, with a population of just over 12,000 in 1841. The larger of the ironworks in the district (Table 6.5) sent between 12,000 and 13,000 tons of iron to Newport in 1839. None, therefore, had the manufacturing capacity of the great works along the northern rim of the coalfield in the Merthyr and Tredegar districts. The many collieries appear to have been producing almost exclusively for the local iron and tin works.

**Table 6.5: Pontypool District. Works and Labour Force**

| Works | Labour Force by Age and Sex, 1841 | | | | | | Total |
|---|---|---|---|---|---|---|---|
| | Over 18 | | 13-18 | | Under 13 | | |
| | M | F | M | F | M | F | |
| *Iron (and Tin)* | | | | | | | |
| Garnddyris and Blaenavon | 1,490 | 26 | 216 | 54 | 148 | 37 | 1,971 |
| Varteg | ? | ? | ? | ? | ? | ? | 1,474* |
| British | 1,007 | 50 | 125 | 22 | 92 | 4 | 1,300 |
| Pentwyn and Golynos | 1,079 | 46 | 133 | 15 | 80 | 3 | 1,356 |
| Pontypool and Blaendare | 920 | 30 | 160 | 18 | 70 | 2 | 1,200 |
| Pontrhydrun Tin | 36 | 13 | 3 | 6 | 9 | 4 | 71 |
| Pontnewydd Tin | 32 | 8 | 9 | 0 | 1 | 1 | 51 |
| | | | | | | | 7,423 |

*labour force for 1840; works closed in 1841

Four working men's associations are known to have existed in the district, at Pontypool, Pontnewynydd, Abersychan and Garndiffaith. At Pontypool and Abersychan there were also women's associations. The Pontypool lodge was an old one, founded as we have seen early in 1838. By 1839 the watchmaker William Lloyd Jones had emerged as its most prominent figure, and much activity focused on his beershop, the Bristol House. The lodge secretary was a certain T.P–. who in August wrote to the General Convention in London expressing the members' determination to 'assume a menacing aspect, such as will strike terror to the heart of the shopocracy and all aristocrats, so as to force them to petition immediately for the Charter'.[107] A little higher in the valley was the Pontnewynydd lodge, founded towards the end of 1838. It met at the beershop kept by its treasurer, the former London journeyman hatter John Lewis Llewellyn.[108] Its principal support came from the workers at the Pentwyn and Golynos forges and collieries in Cwm Du. Still higher in the valley was Abersychan. The lodge met in Britannia House and copies of its resolutions were sent to the *Western Vindicator* by its secretary, William Harris.[109] The members were drawn principally from the British ironworks, the Pentwyn and Golynos furnaces, and the associated mines, collieries and quarries. The fourth association was at Garndiffaith and mainly served the Varteg ironworks.[110] Of the thousand and more workers there it was claimed, not very convincingly, that only 30 had become chartists.[111] No report has been found of any lodge at the head of the valley, where the Blaenavon and Garnddyris works were situated. In June and July 1839 the lodges in the Pontypool district subscribed £15 0s 7½d to the prisoners' fund. Subsequently other small sums came in, including £2 16s raised from a tea-party organised by the Pontypool and Abersychan women.[112] Data on the labour force in the five 'disturbed districts' are summarised in Table 6.6. For 1839 the figures have to be revised upwards somewhat, to allow for the contraction of industry between that year and 1841, and for missing data on those employed at the very small

**Table 6.6: Labour Force at the Ironworks and Collieries**

| Locality | | Labour Force |
|---|---|---|
| *Cardiff hinterland* | | |
| Merthyr district | 15,348 | |
| Pontypridd district | 2,273 | |
| | ———— | |
| | | 17,621 |
| *Newport hinterland* | | |
| Heads of the Valleys district | 14,990 | |
| Blackwood district | 2,909 | |
| Pontypool district | 7,423 | |
| | ———— | |
| | | 25,322 |
| | | ———— |
| | | 42,943 |

works and collieries and on the canals and railways. It may be assumed with some confidence that the industrial labour force in the 'disturbed districts' was in the upper part of the range 40,000 to 45,000. Data on the distribution of the lodges within the five districts are summarised in Table 6.7. The strength of the workers' movement in the hinterland of Newport relative to that of Cardiff was reflected in the progress that chartism made in the two maritime towns.

The Newport WMA was founded in mid-1838 with a cabinetmaker named Hawkins as secretary and a shoemaker named Homer as treasurer.[113] At the beginning of 1839 the former office was taken over by the radical printer, Samuel Etheridge, and the latter by Edward Thomas, grocer, draper and chartist poet.[114] In June Etheridge resigned in protest against the increasing militancy of the lodge, and Thomas relinquished office the following month (though whether or not for the same reason is unclear).[115] Charles Waters, a ship's carpenter, and Edward Frost, a watchmaker and uncle of John Frost, took over the

**Table 6.7**: Working Men's and Women's Associations, 1839, by District

| Cardiff Hinterland | | | Newport Hinterland | |
|---|---|---|---|---|
| *Merthyr* | *Pontypridd* | *Heads of the Valleys* | *Blackwood* | *Pontypool* |
| Merthyr Tydfil | Pontypridd | Rhymney | Blackwood | Pontypool |
| Dowlais | Dinas | Dukestown | Blackwood | Pontypool |
| Aberdare | Nelson | (Star) | (women) | (women) |
| | | Sirhowy | Crumlin | Pontnewynydd |
| | | Tredegar | Fleur-de-lis | Abersychan |
| | | Dukestown (Horse | Argoed | Abersychan |
| | | and Jockey) | Pontllanfraith | (women) |
| | | Ebbw Vale and | Gelligroes | Garndiffaith |
| | | Beaufort | Maes-y-cwmer | |
| | | Rassa | Llanhilleth | |
| | | Victoria | Croespenmaen | |
| | | Blaina | | |
| | | Blaina (women) | | |
| | | Brynmawr | | |
| | | Llanelli | | |

two positions. Etheridge claimed that when he resigned the Newport lodge had 500 or 600 members and was still growing.[116] It is known that William Griffith was enrolled as No. 458 and James Rees as No. 635, both during Etheridge's secretaryship.[117] The headquarters of the lodge was at the Royal Oak in Thomas Street, though it also met at the Old Bush in Commercial Street.[118] A Newport Female Patriotic Association was founded early in 1839 and a sister of William Edwards was among its leading members;[119] in March 300 women turned out to listen to Henry Vincent and to attend a tea-party in his honour.[120] A Democratic Youths' Association was also launched; John Frost's son, Henry, was enrolled as its first member on 14 June.[121] At nearby Caerleon another lodge had been established late in 1838; little is known about it, but it presumably drew some of its members from Fothergill's Caerleon tinworks at which just over 100 people were employed in 1841.[122]

No such progress in the chartist cause was apparent in Cardiff. The first lodge there was opened only in early July 1839. It met at the Red Lion Inn. The tailor, George Williams, was secretary and the committeemen included five other tailors and one shoemaker. John Frost visited the lodge in mid-July. 'He particularly addressed himself to the middle classes', it was reported. He did, however, also visit the docks to hold a meeting with the navvies there. Between 60 and 100 of them heard him out, but only two subsequently appeared at the Red Lion Inn to enrol in the lodge. It was thought that the presence of a Cardiff police officer at the dockland meeting had much dampened the labourers' enthusiasm.[123] All those who joined a lodge were issued with a card or 'ticket'. On it was printed the lodge motto. That for Ebbw Vale and Beaufort, for example, read, 'The man who evades his share of useful labour diminishes the public stock of wealth, and throws his own burthens on his neighbour.' A card also recorded the member's name, lodge number and contributions. The latter were commonly set at fourpence or sixpence a month. There were, as the *Silurian* reported, strong pressures on the workers to enrol:

. . . hints were thrown out to those who had not already joined them, that a dreadful fate awaited them unless they formed part of their body, and great numbers of the workmen were, in consequence, induced to join them. No one was now admitted into the 'lodge' till bound by an oath not to reveal any of their transactions, and considerable alarm was felt by all classes of the community, at the mysterious bearing of those who were initiated.[124]

In many areas something like 'closed shops' were created; that is, men without lodge cards might find it impossible to get, or hold, a job. 'The Men say that it is of no use to seek for work towards Nantyglo unless they are Chartists', one report of October 1839 had it, and according to another the colliers in the neighbourhood of Blackwood 'would not allow any man to be employed there unless he could produce his Chartist Ticket'.[125] Joseph Coles, who worked near Blackwood, described how he came to join a lodge. 'I was going home from my Pay', he said; 'I met some people on the road and they asked me if I was a Chartist, and I said no, — thee hast better join or thee should not work here [they replied].' Coles joined.[126] Stories circulated about the danger in which those without cards might find themselves. 'If', for example,

a poor miner who was not enrolled met with an accident under ground, from the falling of a tram, or other cause, which perhaps broke his leg, men in the same pit, who were chartists, have been known to pass him by, looking him in the face with their candles, and leaving him in his misery unremoved, with the exclamation, 'O let him die; he is not one of us'.[127]

Such stories did not have to be veridical to be effective.

## Notes

1. For the extensive literature on chartism, see J.F.C. Harrison and Dorothy Thompson, *Bibliography of the Chartist Movement, 1837-1976* (Sussex and New Jersey, 1978). A more recent general study of interest is Eva H. Haraszti, *Chartism* (Budapest, 1978).

2. A.R. Schoyen, *The Chartist Challenge. A Portrait of George Julian Harney* (London, 1958), pp. 28-53.

3. For a useful summary of these events, see Schoyen, *Chartist Challenge*, pp. 35-53.

4. David Williams, *John Frost* (Cardiff, 1939), pp. 99-103; *The Rebecca Riots* (Cardiff, 1955), pp. 147-9; and 'Chartism in Wales', in Asa Briggs (ed.), *Chartist Studies* (London, 1959), pp. 220-1.

5. Williams, 'Chartism in Wales', pp. 222-3; *John Frost*, pp. 103-5.

6. *Monmouthshire Merlin*, 4 Nov. 1837 (from *Bristol Mercury*). For a different account see J.T. Ward, *Chartism* (London, 1973), p. 97.

7. Newport Public Library, Chartist Trials 1839-1840, 24 vols. (henceforth Newport Examinations), XIV, doc. 626: evidence of Samuel Shell. Birmingham Central Libraries, Lovett Collection, 2 vols., I, doc. 160.

8. Williams, *John Frost*, p. 106.

9. Ibid., pp. 102-3.

10. British Library, Add. MSS. 37,773, doc. 126, 16 Oct. 1838.

11. Williams, 'Chartism in Wales', pp. 222. For Morgan Williams, Gwyn A. Williams, 'The Making of Radical Merthyr, 1800-1876', in *Welsh History Review*, I, 2 (1961), pp. 184-5.

12. Williams, 'Chartism in Wales', pp. 222-3. R.C. Gammage, *History of the Chartist Movement 1837-1854*, 2nd edn (London, 1894), p. 70.

13. Williams, *John Frost*, pp. 106-8.

14. *Monmouthshire Merlin*, 1 Dec. 1838. *Silurian*, 8 Dec. 1838.

15. Public Record Office, HO.40/40: Disturbances, Glamorganshire, 1838. By this time the People's Charter was available in Welsh translation.

16. Williams, *John Frost*, pp. 119-22; 'Chartism in Wales', p. 227.

17. Newport Public Library, doc. D.4.79, *Address and Rules of the Working Men's Association for benefitting politically, socially and morally the useful classes*, John Partridge (Newport, [1838]), italics original.Compare the *Address and Rules* of the London WMA in the Lovett Collection, Birmingham Central Libraries, reprinted in Dorothy Thompson (ed.), *The Early Chartists* (London, 1971), pp. 50-4.

18. Williams, 'Radical Merthyr', pp. 167, 184-5.

19. For Price see, for example, T. Islwyn Nicholas, *A Welsh Heretic. Dr William Price, Llantrisant* (London, [1940]); John Cule, 'The Eccentric Doctor William Price of Llantrisant (1800-1893)', in *Morgannwg*, VII (1963); Brian Davies, 'Empire and Identity: the "Case" of Dr William Price', in David Smith (ed.), *A People and a Proletariat* (London, 1980), pp. 72-93.

20. Price was, *inter alia*, a leading figure in the Pontypridd Cymreigyddion and donated a substantial prize to its 1837 eisteddfod, see *Merthyr Guardian*, 15 April 1837, 30 June 1838.

21. Evan Powell, *History of Tredegar. Subject of Competition at Tredegar 'Chair Eisteddfod' held February the 25th, 1884* (Newport, 1902), p. 48.

22. Oliver Jones, *The Early History of Sirhowy and Tredegar* (Tredegar

Historical Society, 1969), pp.91-3.
23. [W.N. Johns], *The Chartist Riots at Newport*, 2nd edn (Newport, 1889), pp. 12-13.
24. *Charter*, 10 March 1839. *Western Vindicator*, 20 April 1839. PRO, TS.11/496, Queen vs. Vincent, Edwards, *et al.*, doc. 1621.
25. Newport Examinations, VII, doc. 499: evidence of David Jones. See also *Monmouthshire Merlin*, 23 Nov. 1839.
26. *Merthyr Guardian*, 12 Jan. 1839.
27. *Western Vindicator*, 20 and 27 April 1839, 'The Life and Rambles of W. Edwards, of Newport, Chartist Agitator'.
28. PRO, TS.11/499, doc. 1626, Queen vs. Henry Vincent and William Edwards, Monmouthshire Lent Assizes, 1840. *Monmouthshire Merlin*, 23 Nov. 1839: evidence of David Jones.
29. *Western Vindicator*, 20 April 1839.
30. Idem.
31. *Monmouthshire Merlin*, 23 Nov. 1839: letter of Morgan Williams dd. Merthyr, 25 April 1839. Ibid., 4 May 1839.
32. British Library, Add. MSS. 34,245, vol. I, doc. 20: Hugh Williams to R.K. Douglas, dd. Carmarthen, 4 Feb. 1839.
33. Williams, *John Frost*, pp. 124-7, 131-7.
34. *Western Vindicator*, 6 April 1839. *Monmouthshire Merlin*, 6 April 1839. British Library, Add. MSS. 34,245, vol. I, doc. 195: Frost to Lovett, dd. Newport, 2 April 1839.
35. *Western Vindicator*, 20 April 1839. Williams, *John Frost*, pp. 141-3.
36. See Frost's numerous addresses to his 'constituents of Monmouthshire, Glamorganshire and Stroud', to 'the Chartists of the West of England and South Wales', to 'the Young Men of the West of England and Wales', etc. in *Western Vindicator*, 22 and 29 June, 20 and 27 July, 3 and 10 August 1839.
37. *Western Vindicator*, 6 April and 4 May 1839.
38. *Monmouthshire Merlin*, 23 Nov. 1839: evidence of David Jones. PRO, TS.11/496, doc. 1621: evidence of George Essex.
39. TS.11/496, doc. 1621: evidence of Isiah W. Keys.
40. TS.11/502: letter to the *Merthyr Guardian* (unpublished), dd. Nantyglo, 24 April 1839. Italics original.
41. TS.11/496, docs. 1621, 1622.
42. TS.11/499, doc. 1626.
43. *Silurian*, 11 May 1839. *The Times*, 21 Nov. 1839: evidence of Samuel Etheridge.
44. Gwent County Record Office, Depositions, Quarter Sessions 1840, doc. 32-16: deposition of Samuel Etheridge.
45. No copies of the *Welshman* for 1839 have been located. The article in question was reprinted in *Shrewsbury News and Cambrian Reporter*, 21 Dec. 1839.
46. Cardiff Central Library, Bute MSS, XX/69: Scale to Bute dd. 14 Nov. 1839. Italics original.
47. *Merthyr Guardian*, 19 Jan. 1839, citing the *Sun*.
48. Ibid., 9 Feb. 1839.
49. National Library of Wales, Tredegar Park Muniments, Box 40, No. 2: Williams to A. McKechnie dd. 25 May 1840.
50. *Hereford Journal*, 13 Nov. 1839.
51. *South Wales Argus*, 19 Sept. 1936 and 11 Nov. 1938.
52. See *Merthyr Guardian*, 20 May 1837, for the clash between the Sirhowy Iron Company and the parish authorities of Bedwellty on the occasion of the beating of the bounds in 1837.

53. British Parliamentary Papers, *Children's Employment Commission, Appendix to First Report of Commissioners. Mines*, Part II (1842), pp. 469-580, Report by Robert Hugh Franks (henceforth Franks Report, 1842), and pp. 581-720, Report by Rhys William Jones (henceforth Jones Report, 1842).

54. Harry Scrivenor, *A Comprehensive History of the Iron Trade* (London, 1841), p. 293.

55. *Cambrian*, 29 June 1839.

56. Jones Report (1842), p. 639.

57. Ibid., p. 649.

58. Samuel Lewis, *A Topographical Dictionary of Wales*, 3rd edn (London, 1844), II, p. 217.

59. Charles Wilkins, *The South Wales Coal Trade* (Cardiff, 1888), pp. 74-84. E.D. Lewis, 'Pioneers of the Cardiff Coal Trade', in *Glamorganshire Historian*, vol. 11, n.d.

60. Cardiff Central Library, Bute MSS, XX/75: Scale to Bute dd. 19 Nov. 1839.

61. Charles Wilkins, *The History of Merthyr Tydfil* (Merthyr Tydfil, 1867), pp. 306-8.

62. The first payment on the card was for May, *Morning Chronicle*, 7 Nov. 1839, or for April, Ness Edwards, *John Frost and the Chartist Movement in Monmouthshire* (Abertillery, 1924), p. 34.

63. *Northern Star*, 15 June 1839.

64. *Western Vindicator*, 27 July 1839.

65. CCL, Bute MSS, XX/20: William Thomas to Bute dd. 18 Aug. 1839. *Merthyr Guardian*, 24 Aug. 1839.

66. CCL, Bute MSS, XX/2: Notes as to Chartists delivered by Mr. Hutchins at Swansea Quarter Sessions 1839. The document is undated but the reference to Feargus O'Connor being in Ireland shows that it was written after 4 Oct.

67. Ibid., XX/20: William Thomas to Bute dd. 18 Aug. 1839.

68. Ibid., XX/77: G.R. Morgan to Bute dd. 21 Nov. 1839.

69. Ibid., XX/56: Scale to Bute dd. 8 Nov. 1839. *Western Vindicator*, 27 July 1839.

70. W.H. Smyth, *Nautical Observations on the Port and Maritime Vicinity of Cardiff* (Cardiff, 1840), p 11.

71. E.D. Lewis, 'Cardiff Coal Trade', passim. E.D. Lewis, *The Rhondda Valleys* (London, 1959), pp. 41-3. CCL, Bute MSS, XX/4: Booker to Bute dd. 2 May 1839.

72. CCL, Bute MSS, XX/105: Coffin to Bute dd. 4 Dec. 1839.

73. Morien [Owen Morgan], *History of Pontypridd and Rhondda Valleys* (Pontypridd and London, 1903), pp. 202-5. CCL, Bute MSS, XX/1: examination of Daniel Llewellyn, collier, of Dinas, n.d. but probably Nov. 1839; XX/87: Howells to Bute dd. 25 Nov. 1839; XX/94: Coffin to Bute dd. 28 Nov. 1839.

74. CCL, Bute MSS, XX/21: magistrates for Miskin Hundred to Bute dd. 6 Sept. 1839.

75. *Merthyr Guardian*, 13 July 1839. A church parade held at Llantrisant on 15 Sept. was attended by 300 chartists, but it is unclear where they came from, see CCL, Bute MSS, XX/24: magistrates for Miskin Hundred to Bute dd. 20 Sept. 1839.

76. *Western Vindicator*, 10 Aug. 1839.

77. Ibid., 4 May 1839.

78. CCL, Bute MSS, XX/7: T.W. Booker to Bute dd. 9 May 1839.

79. Ibid., XX/101: J. Bruce Pryce to Bute dd. 3 Dec. 1839. PRO. TS.11/502: evidence of Richard Davies, collier, Llanfabon.

80. *Western Vindicator*, 10 Aug. 1839.

81. Powell, *History of Tredegar*, p. 57.

82. Scrivenor, *Iron Trade* p. 294.

83. *Western Vindicator*, 10 Aug. 1839.

84. Oliver Jones, *Sirhowy and Tredegar*, p. 93. Newport Examinations, XIV, doc. 410: evidence of Esther Evans.

85. Jones, *Sirhowy and Tredegar*, p. 93. Powell, *History of Tredegar*, p. 53.

86. *Hereford Times*, 9 Nov. 1839.

87. Newport Examinations, VI, doc. 475: evidence of John Howells.

88. *Western Vindicator*, 10 Aug. 1839.

89. *Morning Herald*, 14 Nov. 1839: examination of George George.

90. Newport Examinations, XIII, docs. 105, 657. The Beaufort works probably employed about 1,500 persons. This figure is obtained by distributing the Bailey workforce between Nantyglo and Beaufort in proportion to output. *Silurian*, 28 March 1839: evidence of John Powell.

91. *Western Vindicator*, 10 Aug. 1839.

92. Newport Examinations, IV, doc. 384: deposition of William Davies.

93. Ibid., XV, doc, 372: evidence of John Davies.

94. Ibid., XV, doc. 474: evidence of William Howell.

95. Ibid., XV, doc. 620: evidence of Thomas Saunders.

96. *Western Vindicator*, 10 Aug. 1839.

97. Idem.

98. David Mushet, *Papers on Iron and Steel, Practical and Experimental* (London, 1840), p. 820.

99. *Merthyr Guardian*, 4 May 1844.

100. Mushet, *Iron and Steel*, p. 823. Franks Report (1842), pp. 548-9: testimony of Edward Robatham. J.H. Morris and L.J. Williams, *The South Wales Coal Industry, 1841-1875* (Cardiff, 1958), pp. 29, 183. New shafts were sunk at Risca in 1841; the labour force may therefore have been considerably lower in 1839.

101. Scrivenor, *Iron Trade*, p. 294.

102. Newport Examinations, V, doc. 599: evidence of Esther Pugh; doc. 601: evidence of Richard Pugh.

103. *Western Vindicator*, 31 Aug. 1839.

104. Ibid., 27 July 1839.

105. Ibid., 10 Aug. 1839. The sum is probably double entered, and misprinted, under the name of William Barwell, the lodge secretary at the time.

106. *Western Vindicator*, 27 July and 10 Aug. 1839.

107. British Library, Add. MSS. 34,245, vol. II, doc. 91: T.P–. to Convention dd. Pontypool, 2 Aug. 1839. Was T.P–. the 'Mr. P– (a Jew, Socialist and Chartist from Pontypool)' who was active in Bilston, south Staffordshire, in late 1841? See George J. Barnsby, *The Working Class Movement in the Black Country 1750 to 1867* (Wolverhampton, 1977), p. 89.

108. Newport Examinations, VII, doc. 549: evidence of John Maggs.

109. *Western Vindicator*, 27 July 1839.

110. *Western Vindicator*, 29 June 1839 – 'Garn Association'.

111. *Hereford Journal*, 20 Nov. 1839.

112. *Western Vindicator*, 29 June, 27 July and 10 Aug. 1839. It is assumed that the sums listed on 27 July included those previously listed on 29 June.

113. PRO. TS.11/496, doc. 1621: Queen vs. Vincent, Edwards, *et al.*, testimony of Morris Morris.

114. Many examples of Edward Thomas's compositions will be found in the *Western Vindicator*. They range from the lightly introspective ('Born on the mountains/Of Walia was I,/And still her fair fountains/Are my Casteli./Then joy be my partner,/My guerdon be joy,/Thy gloom shall not darken/The Welsh Mountain

boy'), to the ponderously political ('Justice to England, Ireland, Wales,/Justice to Scotia too;/Justice to *all*, o'er hills and dales,/The CHARTISTS seek to do').

115. Joseph and Thomas Gurney, *The Trial of John Frost for High Treason* (London, 1840), p. 518: evidence of Edward Thomas.

116. Gwent Record Office, depositions at Quarter Session, S. 1840, QSD 32-16.

117. Newport Public Library, doc. D.4.79, *Address and Rules*. *The Times*, 12 Nov. 1839.

118. It has been suggested that the Old Bush Inn housed a separate lodge, see [W.N. Johns], *The Chartist Riots at Newport*, 2nd edn (Newport, 1889), p.18.

119. Ibid., p. 16.

120. *Western Vindicator*, 6 April 1839.

121. *Morning Chronicle*, 15 Nov. 1839.

122. Jones Report, 1842, p. 607.

123. CCL, Bute MSS, XX/16: C.C. Williams to Bute dd. 18 July 1839. *Cambrian*, 27 July 1839. *Merthyr Guardian*, 3 Aug. 1839.

124. *Silurian*, 16 Nov. 1839.

125. CCL, Bute MSS, XX/2: Notes as to Chartists delivered by Mr. Hutchins, evidence of Thomas George and A.B. ('a Chartist').

126. Newport Examinations, VII, unnumbered doc: defence of Joseph Coles.

127. *Hereford Journal*, 20 Nov. 1839. Compare *Merthyr Guardian*, 16 Nov. 1839.

# Part III: THE 'DISTURBED DISTRICTS'

Ymunwn Gymry oll,
A'r Saeson yn ddigoll,
  Mewn cyfiawn fael;
I fathru gormes dan
Ein traed, — a Rhyddid lan,
  Fel na bo mwy i'r gwan
  Garcharau gwael.

  (Merthyr handbill, Dec. 1838. PRO, HO.40/40)

But here we come marching
  And ready to dare
The wrath of the gamblers
  Who have dirtied the air,
And here we come singing
  The songs of our ire,
And with torches of beauty
  To set cities on fire.

  (Idris Davies, *The Angry Summer*, Faber and Faber, 1943)

The month it was November and all the storm winds blew,
And as we marched to Newport, full many of us knew
That our comrades would be lying at the rising of the sun
Who'd never feel its warmth again, nor hear our rivers run.

  (Harri Webb, *Rampage and Revel*, Gomer Press, 1977)

# 7 THE ARMING OF THE CLASSES

It was apparent to contemporary observers of the Welsh scene that the November Rising resulted from the deep divisions within society. The editor of the *Silurian* remarked that 'an unnatural and bitter feeling of animosity between the different classes of our people has been sown, and which the late events [of 3-4 November] will in nowise assist to eradicate'.[1] A writer in the *Herald* (who was perhaps an older man, for he still used the language of 'social orders' rather than of 'classes'[2]) made a similar point. It is useless, he urged,

> to disguise the fact, *that, of late years, the distance between the higher and the humbler orders of society has been gradually widening* — or that the interval has been filled up by passions of a most unamiable kind. The result is before the world in this scarcely-extinguished rebellion. Let it not be forgotten, moreover, that the most complete suppression of an attempt at revolution, by no means involves a suppression of those dangerous feelings in which that attempt at revolution took its rise.[3]

It is impossible to know when the idea of the rising first began to take shape. By the early spring of 1839, however, the more militant of the workers' leaders had already taken the position that the class struggle had to be an armed struggle. Weapons were being procured and cached, and information to that effect began to reach the government in London. In the second week of March Mayor Thomas Phillips of Newport notified the Home Office that clubs for the purchase of arms were being formed in south Wales; that two packages of guns and muskets originating from Birmingham had recently been consigned to Pontypool and two to Tredegar; and that the colliers were being incited to violence by agitators who assured them that the soldiers were sympathetic to the workers' cause. 'I am loath to believe that they [the workers] will be hurried into actual insurrection', Phillips wrote,

> but it is certain that sullen discontent marks their appearance [and] that they look with aversion and dislike at their employers . . . The appeal made to the passions of the ignorant and wicked must sooner or later lead to acts of illegality and violence and it seems now

openly avowed that a systematic application of physical force is the means by which the Chartists intend to act on the government and the legislature.[4]

Russell's response was a reasonably prompt though not agitated one. On 23 March he wrote to Capel Hanbury Leigh, Lord Lieutenant of Monmouthshire, calling his attention to the matter and requiring him to alert the magistrates in the county. Russell summarised the legal position, pointing out that 'under the provisions of the Training Act, (60 Geo. 3, c. 1,) . . . all meetings for the purpose of training or drilling to the use of Arms without lawful authority are prohibited; and every person who shall attend any such meeting for the purpose of training or drilling, or of being trained or drilled to the use of Arms, shall be liable to be transported and imprisoned.' The magistrates, he ordered, 'should endeavour to procure depositions with respect to any seditious meetings in their neighbourhood at which any excitements to resist the Laws may be addressed to the people'.[5] Similar letters were sent to six Lord Lieutenants of English counties from which reports of arming had been received. Russell had probably given the report from Phillips less credence than it deserved. The early months of 1839 were those in which William Edwards was vigorously building up the workers' organisations in the Blackwood district, and Phillips, by virtue of his colliery interests there, undoubtedly had a shrewd knowledge of what was taking place. The commander of the troops in northern England, Charles Napier, went to London to meet Russell on 30 March. The current view of affairs at the Home Office, Napier noted, was that the chartists in general lacked both leadership and organisation, and that the arms were being pushed by unscrupulous profiteers. 'If insurrection is going to break out', he commented, 'government is strangely ill informed.'[6] He returned to the north and quietly drew up plans for the deployment of 4,000 men under his command in the event of an uprising. In south Wales, with no such resources at his disposal, Thomas Phillips launched a drive to organise and arm the middle classes in defence of their interests. It was, as it happens, his first step on the path to knighthood.

An anti-chartist meeting was called for 12 April and Christchurch, near Newport, was chosen as its location. Its purpose became apparent when Thomas Phillips moved an address to the Lord Lieutenant of Monmouthshire. He proposed, in effect, the creation of an armed force of volunteers prepared to undertake the maintenance of civil order in the event of a workers' uprising.[7] William Edwards was quick to point out that the middle classes had held 'a physical force meeting'.[8] On 23 April he took Henry Vincent to Blaina where the two addressed a large gathering of chartists. They expounded the principles of republicanism and declaimed against 'the monstrous injustice of Capitalists'. If Vincent was correctly reported, he came remarkably close to calling for an armed insurrection:

when the signal is hoisted on the tops of your beautiful hills, flock in crowds to *our* standard, and *we* will lead you to victory through oceans of fire and water and dust and smoke and blood and thunder . . . We have the *power* so to do, – and the *army* will be on our side . . . therefore we will turn off the Queen, the Parliament, the Law, the Church, – in fact every thing – and every body that dares to oppose us, for we are for *universal liberty*.[9]

On 29 April the ironmasters of Blaina and its neighbourhood held their own anti-chartist meeting at Coalbrookvale. Those present voted an address of loyalty to the queen and heard several impassioned defences of capitalism. A statement, probably drawn up by Crawshay Bailey, was clearly intended as a reply to Edwards and Vincent:

The employment of capital is the barometer of the prosperity of the working classes; but in times of public danger, those who possess this resource are deterred from employing it; and nothing can be more fatal to the happy state of industry in this country than that it should become the scene of disturbance. The violent course proposed by the emissaries of the Charter must lead to bloodshed, the extent of which no man can foresee; the result of which assuredly will be suppression by military force . . . [10]

Edwards and Vincent in the meantime had travelled first to Ponty-pool, on 24 April, and then to Newport the next day. There was much alarm in the Pontypool district. G.S. Kenrick of the Varteg works believed that an uprising was imminent and proposed arming the 'respected householders'. By the second week in May no less than 1,428 special constables had been sworn in at Pontypool and the nearby works.[11] In Newport Mayor Phillips took steps to prevent chartists from speaking there. He declared all meetings banned and swore in the special constables to enforce the ban, thereby earning himself the nickname 'Gag'. Vincent ignored the prohibition and addressed several gatherings before leaving for Bristol.[12] Phillips was not a man to see

authority thus flouted, but more than the personal affront was at issue.
Rumours were already current that the colliers and ironworkers intended an attack on Newport. Indeed, an anonymous writer spelled the
matter out in a letter addressed to Phillips's partner, Thomas Prothero,
at the beginning of May. If 'Gag' interfered with Vincent on his next
visit to Newport, it threatened (rather in the manner of the Scotch
Cattle),

> the Blackwood men will be down the Pontypool men will be down.
> the Myrther men will be down ready for any thing. There are Thirty
> Thousand men there Armed. they could destroy this town in a few
> hours. The feeling of the Blackwood men particularly against gag
> and yourself you have no conception of. if the people shall have
> quiet they wills for quiet, if they are interupted death will follow
> the people are full of revenge they are only watering [i.e. wait-
> ing] for a opportunity your house and gags on their mark [i.e.
> march]. as for gag God help him he is playing a desperate game
> . . .[13]

It was presumably on representations made by Phillips through the
Lord Lieutenant that troops of the 29th Regiment of Foot, 120 strong
in all, arrived in Newport on 2 May.[14]

When Vincent did next appear in Newport it was in circumstances
very different from those envisaged by the anonymous writer. He was
arrested in London on 7 May on the warrant of the Newport magistrates and three days later he, William Edwards, John Dickenson and
William Townsend were brought before the Newport bench and committed for trial. Some 300 colliers from the Blackwood district demonstrated violently in the town, but a like number of specials held them in
check. Lt. Colonel Sir Digby Mackworth, who was present, claimed that
the special constables displayed great gallantry on the occasion.[15]
The anonymous writer saw things differently. This time he addressed
Phillips directly. 'You have gone too far Phillips in taking those persons
by God you have', he claimed;

> you have excited the people far beyond your conception. There are
> spyes from the Hills and all around the country watching your pro-
> ceedings The fellows you are swearing in special constables betray
> you every movement is carried to Frosts there are a great many
> spyes among them they betray you, another thing the Soldiers are
> *not to be trusted* depend upon it you have acted very unwisely . . .[16]

The strength of the middle-class reaction in south Wales undoubtedly took the workers' leaders by surprise. The fact of the matter was that they had no access to information available to the local authorities and could not know that Home Office policy towards the working-class movements was in process of reformulation. The occasion of Lord John Russell's shift in position is readily identifiable. In April the chartist missionary Henry Hetherington made a tour of the flannel towns of mid-Wales. On his return to London he reported to a full session of the General Convention that the towns could turn out 600 armed men and that arming and drilling was being carried on. The Montgomeryshire magistrates, not surprisingly, requested the Home Office for troops. Russell responded by sending three London policemen to Llanidloes. On 30 April rioting occurred in that town and it was taken over by the chartists who held it until troops arrived five days later.[17]

Russell had to move with some dispatch to outflank his critics. On 3 May a royal proclamation against arming was issued. Exhibiting that inverted logic available to officialdom, the proclamation was in fact the authority for the arming of the middle classes. On 7 May Russell wrote to various Lord Lieutenants, mayors and magistrates in south Wales and elsewhere. He approved the formation of associations for the protection of life and property, agreed to arm them at government expense, agreed also to arm the special constables when the local situation warranted it, and authorised the magistrates to search for and seize any arms and other offensive weapons found in the possession of workers believed to be disaffected.[18] In south Wales, certainly, the Home Secretary's instructions only put the stamp of authority on associations that had already been formed on local initiatives. Lord Lieutenant Leigh immediately applied for official recognition of the Pontypool and Monmouth Associations for the Protection of Life and Property. Russell gave his approval to both on 13 May. He issued 50 cutlasses and 50 brace of pistols with ammunition to the Monmouth association, and double those quantities to that of Pontypool.[19] He also sent a further 200 brace of pistols and 200 cutlasses to the Lord Lieutenant of Monmouthshire. They were for the use of the special constables should the situation deteriorate.[20] Six metropolitan policemen were also placed at the disposition of the Lord Lieutenant, to be employed in training the special constables, and a troop of the 12th Lancers was posted to Abergavenny to supplement the troop of the same regiment already stationed in Monmouth.[21]

The volunteers in the Newport area had apparently formed a West

Monmouthshire Association after the Christchurch meeting. They boasted of having helped defend Newport against the colliers on 10 May. On 22 May they mustered at Whitson, a few miles southeast of Newport. William Phillips of Whitson House expressed the political stance of the association. The chartists, he claimed,

> have endeavoured to dissever the union of all classes, and to destroy that reciprocity of kindness and service which has rendered this [Britain] the greatest nation and most prosperous people in the world. Rather let us die in defence of our laws, than witness all that is great and good swamped in a bloody revolution. If these anarchists once succeed, slavery, foreign or domestic, must ensue − either from tyrants, as those democrats who, 47 years since, ruled in France, or from the grasping Russians, or any other power that might choose to trample on our blood-stained and disorganised country. When bad men combine, good men must unite.

Mackworth announced that the association was to be reconstituted as two corps, one of infantry based on Newport and one of cavalry based on the more scattered parishes. Officers were elected to serve under William Phillips, the major commandant. The next muster was set for the following Saturday, and application was immediately made to the Home Office for recognition as a corps of yeomanry.[22] Russell considered the request and turned it down. William Phillips, his pride much injured, left for a spell in Europe.[23] The other Phillips, the Mayor of Newport, played no conspicuous part in these proceedings. Perhaps his political instincts had counselled prudence. He was, however, prosecuting a campaign of his own on the industrial front, and was reported to be encouraging his fellow coalowners to discharge those workers known to be active chartists.[24]

News that the Newport magistrates had issued warrants for the arrest of Henry Vincent, William Edwards and others reached the delegates at the General Convention in London. They responded swiftly. John Frost was ordered home to calm the local leaders. He reached Newport on the evening of 10 May, after the magistrates had completed their committal proceedings. He addressed a crowd that had assembled, urging chartists not to break the law.[25] On 15 May he submitted a report on the situation to the General Convention. The authorities, he wrote,

> declare that they will arm [the special constables] and that they will

put down public meetings by force. One of two things will follow from putting this determination into practice, a complete dispiriting of the people, or an outbreak either of which will be fatal to our cause. I have had the greatest difficulty in keeping the people within bounds, and I am convinced that nothing but my presence could have restrained them.[26]

It is by no means clear that Frost was fully conversant with the situation on the coalfield. He probably depended for his information upon his old friend Samuel Etheridge, who was still secretary of the Newport Working Men's Association. Etheridge, however, was a 'moral force' man who had little contact with the militant leaders in the collieries and ironworks; he denounced violence, argued that chartism offered no threat to property, and refused to believe that workers were arming.[27] In particular, Frost was most probably wrong in thinking that the movement in the valleys was in any danger of collapse or, alternatively, that its leaders might feel pushed into premature revolt.

The Home Secretary's policy of arming the middle classes was found repugnant, expectedly enough, by sections of the aristocratic interest. One of the great landowners in south Wales, the Duke of Beaufort, argued in the House of Lords that only men under 'regular military control' should bear arms.[28] The workers' leaders were hardly likely to see it that way. The *Western Vindicator* carried a different proposal. It purported to have been written by Henry Vincent from Monmouth Gaol.[29] The 'industrious men' of Newport and Monmouthshire were urged to form themselves into 'Legal Armed Societies for the Protection of Life, Labour, and Property', and to ask Lord John Russell for arms. 'I do not know exactly the number you want', the writer remarked,

but I would suggest the following as a commencement:

| | | |
|---|---|---|
| Newport; arms, etc. for | 5,000 | able-bodied men |
| Pontypool and vicinity, arms for | 8,000 | ditto |
| Carleon and vicinity, arms for | 500 | ditto |
| Blackwood, Tredegar, etc. arms for | 10,000 | ditto |
| Nantyglo and its vicinity, arms for | 10,000 | ditto |
| Merthyr Tidvil and neighbourhood, arms for | 20,000 | ditto. |

And so on. These will form a small company of *fifty-four thousand, five hundred men*, ready to turn out in a moment's notice to defend 'life, labour, and property'.[30]

In a less facetious vein the pseudonymous Junius adverted to the matter in an address 'To the Middle Classes of the Iron and Coal Districts of South Wales' —

> The Whig government of England is doing at the present time your unholy work. The crusade which it is now making against the working classes, is the work of the middle classes. It is hurried forward by you. It is backed by you in every possible shape, and you are ever ready with your suggestions and your aid to put down the meetings of the people . . . Do you not enrol yourselves in armed societies? Do you not take to be sworn in as special constables, and wherever and whenever the Government wants you, there you are to be found.[31]

The arming of the middle classes was an overt operation; that of the workers necessarily covert. The information on the latter that became available to the authorities was scant and episodic. In the nature of the case it was in the interests of both buyers and sellers to preserve secrecy. There was apparently a brisk trade in firearms in April. 'Hawkers', it was reported in the *Merlin*, 'find it a good speculation, to bring down weapons of different sorts for sale in this district.'[32] One abortive transaction in Newport revealed something of the demand. On 27 April Joseph Johnson, an ironmerchant from Liverpool,[33] visited the Newport firm of Townsend and Co. He met William Townsend jr. (who was to be arrested soon after). Johnson remarked that his firm could have made much money from the chartists, for it had been dealing in muskets, pistols, cutlasses and matchets in the African and West Indian trades. Townsend said that he was treasurer for the chartists in the district and would pay cash for arms delivered in Newport. Johnson gave a price list and Townsend said that he would take 200 to 300 muskets and 500 to 600 cutlasses. Johnson then refused the order; he was, he claimed, 'disgusted'.[34] Three weeks later another incident attracted attention. Two labourers from the Monmouthshire Iron and Coal Company, Thomas Jones and Henry Fawkner, arrived in Bristol by boat from Newport on 17 May. The next day they made the rounds of the pawnshops in the city. They had bought nine pistols and three powder flasks when they were arrested. On being searched one was found to have between £6 and £7 in his pocket, and the other a copy of the *Western Vindicator*.[35] Among the works owned by the Monmouthshire Iron and Coal Company were those at Victoria. It is therefore all the more interesting to find it reported some weeks later that about 100 of 'the more desperate men' at Victoria had formed a club for purchasing firearms, and had put out tenders.[36]

No estimate of the number of arms obtained by the working-class organisations can be made. It is clear, however, that pikes rather than guns dominated their arsenals. The popularity of the pike resulted largely from the writings of Colonel Francis Macerone, erstwhile aide-de-camp to Joachim Murat, king of Naples. Macerone published his *Defensive Instructions for the People* in London in 1832. A shorter and cheaper edition appeared two years later. He recommended the creation of 'Foot Lancers' armed with specially constructed lances and pikes. A populace thus organised could, he claimed, defeat regular soldiers:

Infantry and artillery must be charged, so as to render their fire comparatively useless, by preventing its being repeated. *Be prompt, and you will destroy them; hesitate and you will be destroyed!* As to cavalry, it will hardly ever be necessary for you to form into squares to resist them; for, armed with my lances or with pikes, you may defy them, and even charge them *in line*, without receiving a scratch.[37]

Henry Vincent had apparently commended Macerone's work to the people of the Blaina district on his visit there in late April.[38] The topic of the foot lancers was, however, a hotly debated one. An articulate opponent of Macerone's views emerged in the person of Alexander Somerville, who had served in the Scots Greys in 1832 and in the 8th Highland Regiment (British Auxiliary Legion) in Spain in 1835-7. He took, so he wrote, 'Colonel Macerone's *Defensive Instructions on Street Warfare*, on which they [insurrectionists] seemed to place all their reliance, and showed them the worthlessness of these, as instructions, against the regular army, and especially against artillery.'[39] His views were published in 1839, in a tract entitled *Dissuasive Warnings to the People on Street Warfare.*[40] Somerville claimed that, as a known radical, he was solicited to join in 'the Welsh insurrection of 1839'; it was, he said, 'to have taken place several times during several months, before it was actually begun . . . '[41] He also claimed that his *Dissuasive Warnings* was translated into Welsh, published at Monmouth, 'sent among the iron and coal workers of South Wales', and that a postponement of the rising was a result.[42] Certainly Somerville's arguments were known in south Wales.[43] Certainly, too, they did not ultimately prevail in the rebel councils. Pikes were extensively manufactured, and were carried by many of those who rose in November.

Useful data on two pike manufactories are available, the one at Pill-gwenlly on the outskirts of Newport and the other at Cwm in Ebbw Vale below Victoria. The Pillgwenlly enterprise was run by John Gibby, a smith at William Evans's foundry, and William Stephens, who worked his own smithy.[44] One witness said that pikes were already being made there 'a good bit after Vincent was taken', a somewhat unhelpful remark.[45] A police search of Gibby's house after the rising turned up his accounts and a set of drawings of pike heads.[46] The accounts appear to cover several months. The basic model of pike cost 1s 6d and this sum was often paid in three instalments of 6d each. Larger payments were also sometimes made by groups, for example, 'William Mogford and men' 3s 0d, 'B. Evans and men' 4s 6d, and 'Ring 8 men' 4s 0d. Gibby was committed for trial on charges of high treason for having made and delivered 50 pikes. Perusal of the accounts suggests that the quantity was about right. Charges against Stephens were dropped for lack of evidence.

The Cwm manufactory operated on a larger scale than that at Pill-gwenlly. It was run by John Owen, who was also to be committed to trial for high treason. His smithy lay near the Ebbw Vale tramroad at Cwm, and he was believed to have appropriated iron from the passing wagons bound for Newport.[47] One of the principal distributors for the Cwm pikes was John Hopkins, a carpenter at the Victoria works.[48] A week before the rising John Owen left his smithy in charge of an assistant. He delivered 53 pikes to the Rassa lodge, near Beaufort, charging 1s 0d each. On the first day of the rising, 3 November, Owen was at Llangynidr in the Usk Valley. He was still on duty, for on a table in the Lion beershop he had drawings of three kinds of pike, and he was evidently anticipating going to Brecon as soon as the rebels occupied it.[49] His movements must surely have had something to do with the 'chartist caves' to which reference is still made in local tradition. In 1884 Evan Powell of Tredegar reported that 'caves in Llangynider mountains were utilised as smitheries for the purpose of forging "pikes" and other weapons'.[50] It has been pointed out that it was neither necessary nor practicable to set up forges in them.[51] It is more likely that the caves were used to store arms, and particularly those intended for the attack on Brecon, which lay only ten miles to the northwest. Certainly it was the practice of the rebels to keep arms cached when not in use; 1,500 pikes and many guns and pistols, for example, were said to be concealed in the cellars of the Royal Oak at Coalbrookvale on the eve of the rising.[52] There were rumours that a few pieces of cannon had been secretly cast at the ironworks. Reports that those who attacked Newport had one or two small pieces seem to be without substance.[53] More convincing were the references to the six or seven pieces believed to be in possession of Dr William Price of Pontypridd; they were said to have been melted down immediately after the rising.[54]

Many of the proceedings of the working men's associations were of a public kind, and informers and even magistrates in person attended and monitored the progress of the workers' movement. The threats of force routinely made by most chartist speakers in south Wales were duly noted in official memoranda and often reported in the local newspapers. If the middle classes were in a state of some consternation in the spring of 1839, by the autumn they had come to view the threats as no more than a particularly ebullient brand of political rhetoric. Indeed, in October it was widely believed that the workers' movement was in decline.[55] When Sir Josiah John Guest visited Cardiff two days before the rising, he felt able to assure the adjutant of the Royal Glamorganshire Militia that chartism was making no progress at Dowlais or in the neighbourhood of Merthyr generally.[56] That a rising did occur shocked the middle classes; that it had been so little anticipated compounded that shock. The correspondent of *The Times* put the matter as well as anyone. This was 'no momentary outbreak', he wrote, 'but a long-planned insurrection, deeply organized, managed with a secrecy truly astonishing . . . If we need proof that the plan has been long matured, the quantity of arms of all description possessed by the deluded men of the hills gives sufficient evidence of the state of preparation.'[57] The correspondent referred to 'the secret Chartist Lodge . . . with its sections, captains, and companies'. It was in fact only at the time of the rising that it was realised that under cover of the working men's associations the militants had built up a different organisation dedicated to armed struggle. Paradoxically, it was the rhetorical threat of force, articulated openly at the lodge level, that provided the screen behind which those committed to the actual use of physical violence could put together the clandestine movement.

William Davies of Blackwood, who for a time after the rising turned Queen's evidence, maintained that the sections had been started to facilitate collection of money for the defence of Vincent, Edwards and the other chartist prisoners.[58] He was probably right that the system was introduced early in the summer of 1839, but he was prevaricating about its original purpose. A copy of a memorandum on sections sent out, so we have assumed, to the lodges, fell into the hands of the magistrates. It was found (together with issues of the *Western Vindicator*, letters from chartist leaders, membership cards for the Newport WMA and other miscellaneous documents) when the house of Samuel Etheridge was searched on 15 November. Since Etheridge resigned his secretaryship of the Newport lodge at the beginning of June, the memorandum had presumably been put out before that date. Perhaps, indeed, it contributed to his decision to resign, for we have seen that he was much alarmed by the growing violence of the working-class movement.

It would have been difficult for the magistrates to have interpreted the memorandum as anything other than a design for insurrection, and the unfortunate Etheridge was committed for trial on charges of high treason and sedition. But Etheridge was able to show that the document was not in his handwriting, and the charge was reduced to one of conspiracy. He was acquitted at the Special Assizes in Monmouth on 16 January 1840, and his papers were returned to him. He showed the memorandum to Feargus O'Connor, who was in Monmouth to follow the trials. O'Connor promptly burned the document.[59] Fortunately for the historian, the Newport magistrates had earlier made copies of it:

Let us form into sections by choosing a good staunch indefatigable brother at the head of each section, that is to say each section to be composed of 10 men who is known to him to be sincere so that the head of each section will know his men the five sections will compose 55 men with *officers* from those 5 officers such as corporals will *chose* a Head so that he may give his 5 officers notice so those 50 men is to be called a bye name then three 50 will compose a company and the three officers will choose a proper person to command the 165 in the Company officers and all such as a Captain then the three companies will compose 495 men and officers which officer will be such as a Brigade General so three Brigades will *chose* a Chief which will be 1485 men and officers which chief officer is to be in the style of a conventional General so by these means the signal W-r can be given in two hours notice within 7 miles by the Head noticing every officer under him till it comes to the Deacon or Corporals to notice his 10 men the officers to have by name and not a miletary [sic] name to prevent the Law.[60]

Clearly the author or authors of the memorandum envisaged a volunteer force emerging from a series of local initiatives, as the more active and committed workers formed sections, chose officers and acquired arms. So critical to the whole operation were the section leaders that they became commonly known, not as corporals, but as captains — 'captains of ten'. It appears to have been usual to provide a new section with an amount of basic documentation, and specifically with what was always known as its 'list'. These were highly incriminating papers, and most were destroyed along with other records in the aftermath of the rising. At least one list, however, did fall into the hands of the magistrates. It was that for Section No. 11 of Blaina, which went into action at Newport where one of its members, Abraham Thomas, was killed:[61]

*No. 11*
|      |                             |
|------|-----------------------------|
|  89  | James James, collier        |
| 161  | Williams James, miner       |
| 177  | Benjamin James, collier     |
| 178  | David Jonathan, ditto       |
| 206  | John Davis Jonathan, ditto  |
| 210  | William Jenkins, haulier    |
| 257  | Abraham Thomas, collier     |
| 312  | Thomas Bowen, ditto         |
| 416  | David Davis, ditto          |
| 482  | John Davis, ditto           |

| | |
|------|-----------------------------|
| 484  | William Davies, collier     |

William Davies, who lived at Nantyglo, headed the section. He was better known as William Yr Hen Waun. He 'assented to become a Captain of 10', it was said, 'by arrangement amongst the others while at work'.[62] This seems to have been in August 1839. The eleven men gave their WMA membership cards to James James, who took them to lodge headquarters at the Royal Oak. Zephaniah Williams asked his son, Llewellyn, to make out the list. James was told that they had been tardy in forming the section, for it was some time since Zephaniah Williams had explained how to have lists made.[63] The implication, perhaps, is that only ten sections had been formed in Blaina in the two or three months since the memorandum had first been circulated.

It will be noted that the members of Blaina Section No. 11 were listed by order of seniority within the local WMA. There is reason to believe that members were assigned a section number on the basis of that seniority, so that James James would have been No. 1 and William Davies, although the captain, No. 11. One Thomas Williams was impressed on 3 November by a Tredegar section operating in Ebbw Vale. He found himself 'walking with a short man No. 6 who had a piece of light coloured ribbon round his arm. The other men called him number 6 . . . ' No. 6 was in fact the captain of the section, and the armband showed that.[64]

All the members of Blaina Section No. 11 were employed at the Brewers' Coalbrookvale works and all but one, John Davis, laboured in the same level. It is apparent from the section list that William Davies had only recently joined the Blaina WMA, and it is unclear why he was chosen to be captain. Certainly he must have been well known to the section, for the dangers of infiltration by informers were understood. Benjamin Green, a native of Colne in Lancashire, testified to the suspicion of strangers. He lodged at the house of section member Abraham Thomas. 'I saw some Bullets at Abraham Thomas a few days before the Sunday [3 November] ', he reported later; 'they appeared fresh casted and he appeared to be very careful of shewing them to us Englishmen because many [of us] do not belong to them.'[65]

The rebel leaders in south Wales were remarkably successful in keeping their activities secret. Much as this furthered their ends, it imposes severe constraints upon the historian concerned to chronicle their struggles. Material on the levels of the military organisation above that of the sections is particularly lacking in both quality and quantity. Only a few weeks before the rising a chartist identified only as 'AB' provided the magistrates with the information that 'all the Chartists in Merthyr and elsewhere (but not yet in Dowlais) are divided into Pickets of Eleven and the Eleventh Man communicates to the other Ten the orders from the Head Committee'.[66] The Head Committee, despite its imposing name, was presumably only the low level of command represented by five section officers and (to use the language of the memorandum) the 'head' who gave them orders. Although the memorandum gave no name to the unit intermediate between the section and the company, for convenience we shall follow various witnesses who described it as the 'troop'.[67] Henry Scale was probably describing the troop officers when he said that they met weekly and sent representatives to still higher 'councils',[68] that is, to the company commands each controlling three troops or fifteen sections in all. One George Thomas (said to 'know the lower classes well') described yet another body to the magistrates. It was 'a Committee which meets at Cyfarthfa who are very particular in excluding common Members from their deliberations'.[69] The Dowlais men were reported to be in communication with it. The Cyfarthfa Committee may have been the highest level of command in the Merthyr district.

A meeting of rebel delegates was held at Dukestown on 28 October 1839. Six attended from Merthyr. They announced that they had 2,000 men armed and ready to move, that is, some four brigades or about 180 sections in all.[70] This figure excluded the men of the Cynon Valley, for the Aberdare delegates refused to commit themselves to a rising on the grounds that they had not recruited sufficient numbers.[71] It may have been the same Dukestown meeting that William Price mentioned in his reminiscences, though the by then aged doctor thought it had been held several weeks before the rising. He recollected that a delegate from Abersychan announced that he could call on 1,600 men. '1,200 of them are old soldiers', the delegate claimed; 'the remaining 400 have never handled arms but we can turn them into fighting men in no time.'[72] The 'old soldiers' cannot all have been veterans of the regular army but had presumably received their training in the rebel ranks. Price's interviewer understood him to say that all the men were from the Abersychan lodge. The command was located there but the sections it controlled must have been those of the entire Pontypool district. The delegate was David Davies, and to judge from the authority with which Price remembered him speaking he was himself the district commander ('conventional general'). One of the brigades within the command was used as a reserve in the attack on Newport on 4 November. Comprising about 500 men, it was at full strength. 'Many of them were armed with guns; about 50', it was said; 'about 200 armed with pikes. Many had short knives, which they carried in their pockets.' It was led by Solomon Britton, a collier from Garndiffaith, near Abersychan.[73]

After the Dukestown meeting, according to the *Silurian*'s reporter, 'it was evident that some plan had been determined upon, as few of the Chartists from that period [onwards] were observed to attend to their work, and reports were rife as to the efforts made by many to procure arms'.[74] In fact another meeting of delegates was held at Blackwood only a few days later, on 1 November, at which it was decided to place the section captains 'under orders to march in military order'. The rising was, in other words, effectively set in motion. The total membership of each lodge was reported, and the numbers announced of those who had guns or pikes and of those who were enrolled in sections and could be considered completely reliable. William Lloyd Jones recorded these numbers and tallied the men ready to fight at 5,000.[75] The figure did not, however, include all the men from the western districts. In particular, with the exception of Dowlais the lodges in the Merthyr district were not represented, their leaders probably being too busy in their own localities to travel far away.

If we accept the full strength of the Pontypool district to have been the 1,600 men claimed by David Davies, then reference to Table 6.6 will show that about one in five of the industrial workers in that locality had enrolled in sections. If, somewhat arbitrarily, we use this ratio as a more general guide, then we may guess that the 5,000 men tallied by William Lloyd Jones comprised the three brigades from the Ponty-pool district, six from the Heads of the Valleys district (perhaps including, for this purpose, Dowlais), and one from the Blackwood district. To these we have to add the four Merthyr brigades announced at the Dukestown meeting, and the sections from Pontypridd district which may have approximated in strength to one further brigade. With all due reservations arising from the inadequacy of the data, then, it is suggested that on the eve of the rising the rebels had some 15 brigades to throw into the struggle.

The meetings at Dukestown on 28 October and at Blackwood on 1 November were apparently ones of the rebel directorate, for no higher level of authority within the insurgent wing of the workers' movement can be identified.[76] Some members of the directorate were already well-known public figures who had espoused the chartist cause and, somewhere along the way, had committed themselves to the armed struggle. Dr William Price of Pontypridd was a prominent local citizen who had hobnobbed in his time with the Crawshays and Guests. It was rumoured in English chartist circles that he had been originally chosen to lead the rising.[77] John Frost was ex-Mayor of Newport and delegate to the chartist General Convention. He was recruited into the directorate only shortly before the rising, and then (we shall see) against his will. This matter, and the hostility which Price evinced for Frost, will be examined further in Chapter 9. Other members of the directorate were men who had made their mark primarily as political organisers. Zephaniah Williams of Sirhowy and Coalbrookvale and William Lloyd Jones of Pontypool had been among the most active in establishing working men's associations in south Wales; only the jailed William Edwards might claim comparable standing in the movement. It will be remembered that Williams was a master collier and mineral agent turned publican, Jones an actor turned watchmaker, and Edwards a preacher turned baker.

David Lewis of Brynmawr, beerhouse keeper, and William Davies of

Blackwood and William David of Dinas, both sons of shopkeepers, were among those members of the directorate who had demonstrated their commitment to the cause at a more exclusively local level, bringing the ironworkers and colliers into the lodges. John Phillips, John Reynolds and Moses Owen are less well-known figures who must have served in much the same capacity. The first was a butcher in Pontypool and the second a Gelligroes haulier turned preacher; of the third nothing is known.[78] These local lodge leaders constituted a particularly important element in the rebel directorate, for they were in constant and direct contact with the mass of the workers whose militancy had been shaped by the shared experiences of strikes and combinations. They had introduced the rhetoric of chartism to the coalfield, but in the lodges a programme of agitation for the reform of Parliament became transformed into one of industrial action in the pursuit of working-class autonomy; as the *Merthyr Guardian* had earlier complained, the men sought 'to take the regulation of wages and hours of labour into their own hands'.[79]

David Davies, John Rees and Richard Rorke constituted a different component of the rebel leadership. Whatever the degree of their participation in the political movement, all had in common a prior involvement in armed struggle of one sort or another. David Davies, collier and presumed commander of the Pontypool district, had served in the British army for 25 years and had fought at Waterloo.[80] His career could doubtless be reconstructed from military records, but this has yet to be attempted. John Rees of Tredegar, mason, better known as Jack the Fifer, led the attack on Newport on 4 November. He seems to have been the John Rees who earlier had emigrated to the United States and, in 1835, left for Mexico to take part in the revolutionary struggle of the Texans against the dictatorship of Santa Anna. He participated in the storming of San Antonio de Bexar when, against all odds, the Texan insurgents wrested the town from its Mexican garrison. Subsequently taken prisoner by the Mexicans, Rees was one of the few to survive the massacre at Goliad.[81] Using bounty money, he recrossed the Atlantic and worked for a time in Manchester and London before returning to Wales.[82] After the November Rising he succeeded in making his way back to Texas where he obtained a commission in the army of the newly independent republic and a grant of land in Indian territory near the Colorado river.

Richard Rorke's story was a different one. A correspondent of *The Times* summed up his career. 'One of the leaders of the [1839] insurrection', he wrote, 'was an Irishman, named Rock (not yet in custody), who is known to have taken part in the Irish rebellion [of 1798], and supposed to have since been mixed up very considerably with Whiteboyism . . . '[83] In the 1830s Rorke was a painter and beer-shop keeper in Newport, and was a founding member of the working men's association there.[84] He and his son Richard, a Blackwood resident, eluded capture until January 1840. They were brought to trial at the following Spring Assizes. Samuel Etheridge was one of those to give evidence. He claimed that the memorandum on sections which had been found in his possession was in the handwriting of Richard Rorke senior, and implied that it related not to the Welsh rising of 1839 but to the Irish one of 1798.[85] Etheridge was presumably trying to clear his own name while not incriminating Rorke. In fact the organisation into sections of ten outlined in the memorandum does not bear any particularly close relationship to that used by the United Irishmen.[86] Nevertheless, the interesting possibility remains, that Rorke was one of those involved in fashioning the military structure of the Welsh workers' movement.

At the Monmouthshire Quarter Sessions in April 1840 the elder Rorke was acquitted largely by reason of his advanced age. 'He had', remarked the chairman of the bench, 'found a very merciful jury.' His son was found guilty of conspiracy and riot and sentenced to six months with hard labour.[87] A few weeks later the old man appeared before the Newport Police Court. This time he was a plaintiff. The *Merlin* somewhat gleefully reported that this 'patriot of the Irish rebellion' had been robbed outside a tavern by a man he had befriended inside; a man to whom he had confided, moreover, 'the sufferings of his dear son Richard in Monmouth Castle, in whose strongholds he is now incarcerated like a felon, because he had been one of the glorious patriots who attacked Newport on the memorable 4th of November'.[88] There, beneath the element of farce, we may perhaps hear an authentic voice of the Welsh rising.

## Notes

1. *Silurian*, 23 Nov. 1839.
2. For the emergence of the 'language' of class under the impact of industrialisation, see Asa Briggs, 'The Language of "Class" in Early Nineteenth Century England', in A. Briggs and J. Saville, *Essays in Labour History* (London, 1960), pp. 43-73.
3. *Hereford Journal*, 20 Nov. 1839 (from the *Morning Herald*). Italics original.
4. PRO, HO.40/45: T. Phillips jr. to Home Sec., dd. 9 and 12 March 1839.
5. British Parliamentary Papers, Accounts and Papers XXXVIII, C.179, 1839:

*Copy of Letter . . . respecting Arms and Training.*
6. W. Napier, *The Life and Opinions of General Sir Charles James Napier,*
*G.C.B.*, 4 vols (London, 1857), II, pp. 5-7.
7. D. Williams, *John Frost. A Study in Chartism* (Cardiff, 1939), pp. 145-6.
8. *Western Vindicator*, 27 April 1839.
9. PRO, TS.11/502: letter to the *Merthyr Guardian*, unpublished, dd.
Nantyglo, 24 April 1839. Italics original.
10. *Report of the Proceedings at the Great Anti-Chartist Meeting, held at*
*Coalbrook Vale, Monmouthshire, on Monday, April 29th, 1839* (Monmouth,
[1839]), title page. *Cambrian*, 4 and 11 May 1839. *Merthyr Guardian*, 4 May
1839.
11. PRO, HO.40/45: British Iron Co. to Home Office, dd. 30 April 1839,
enclosing extracts from William Wood's letter, 27 April 1839. HO.40/45: return
of special constables, dd. 11 May 1839.
12. Williams, *John Frost*, pp. 152-3.
13. PRO, TS.11/502: anon. letter postmarked Newport, 4 May 1839.
14. *Merthyr Guardian*, 11 May 1839.
15. Williams, *John Frost*, pp. 160-1. Among the colliers on this occasion was
Thomas Llewellyn of Fleur-de-lis, who was to be prominent in the November
Rising, see *The Times* and *Morning Chronicle*, 27 Nov. 1839: evidence of
Moses Scard and Isaac Venn. John Lovell of Newport was another to be active in
both demonstration and rising, *The Times*, 11 Nov. 1839. See also *Merthyr*
*Guardian*, 1 June 1839.
16. PRO, TS.11/502: anon. letter postmarked Newport, 18 May 1839.
Emphasis original.
17. D. Williams, 'Chartism in Wales', in Asa Briggs (ed.), *Chartist Studies*
(London, 1959), pp. 229-32.
18. British Parliamentary Papers, Accounts and Papers XXXVIII, C.299,
1839: *Copies of Letters . . . suggesting the formation of Associations for the*
*Protection of Life and Property, etc.*
19. Ibid., C. 559, 1839: *Return of all Associations formed and armed for the*
*Protection of Life and Property* . . . PRO, HO.41/14: Russell to Leigh, two letters
dd. 13 May, and Russell to Leigh, dd. 20 May, 1839. William Needham had taken
the initiative in Pontypool district and by 10 May had 100 stand of arms, PRO,
HO.40/45: Needham to Leigh, dd. 10 May, 1839.
20. PRO, HO.41/13: Home Office to O.C., Militia Staff, Monmouth, dd. 8
May 1839. HO.41/14: S.M. Phillipps to Mayor of Monmouth dd. 12 May 1839.
21. Idem. Also HO.41/14: Russell to Leigh dd. 10 May 1839.
22. *Merthyr Guardian*, 1 June 1839.
23. PRO, HO.41/14: S.M. Phillipps to J.G. Phillipotts dd. 27 May 1839.
HO.40/45:R.J. Blewitt to Home Office dd. 6 Nov. 1839.
24. *Western Vindicator*, 1 June 1839.
25. British Library. Add. MSS, 27,821, doc. 133; Add. MSS, 34,245, I, doc.
430.
26. Add. MSS, 34,245, I, doc. 445.
27. *Silurian*, 11 May 1839. *Western Vindicator*, 8 June 1839.
28. *Hansard's Parliamentary Debates: Third Series*, XLVIII (1839), pp. 134-5.
29. It has been argued that Vincent's gaol letters were in fact written by his
close associate, Francis Hill, see Williams, *John Frost*, p. 183. This was, however,
strongly denied in a letter of 2 Dec. 1839, purporting to be by Vincent, *Western*
*Vindicator*, 7 Dec. 1839. Whatever the truth of the matter, the letters show a
detailed knowledge of rebel affairs in south Wales; whoever wrote them must have
had an informant or informants in the inner councils of the Welsh leadership.
30. *Western Vindicator*, 8 June 1839.
31. Ibid., 24 Aug. 1839.

32. *Monmouthshire Merlin*, 20 April 1839.

33. *Cambrian*, 29 June 1839, carries an article by Johnson.

34. PRO, HO.40/45: deposition of Joseph Johnson, 29 April 1839. PRO, TS.11/496, doc. 1621: deposition of Johnson in the Queen vs. Vincent, Edwards, *et al.* *Merthyr Guardian*, 4 May 1839, reports that Townsend also offered to buy a proportionate number of pistols.

35. *The Times*, 21 May 1839. *Chartist*, 26 May 1839.

36. *Merthyr Guardian*, 24 Aug. 1839.

37. Francis Macerone, *Defensive Instructions for the People: containing the new and improved combination of arms, called Foot Lancers; miscellaneous instructions on the subject of Small Arms and Ammunition, Street and House Fighting, and Field Fortification* (J. Smith, London, 1832), p. 51, emphasis original. 2nd edn with similar title (Richard Carlile jr., London, 1834).

38. *Merthyr Guardian*, 4 May 1839: S.B.R. to ed., dd. Nantyglo, 29 April 1839.

39. [A. Somerville], *The Autobiography of a Working Man* (London, 1848), p. 423.

40. This title is given by Somerville. British Library BM 8831.1.10 is *Warnings to the People on Street Warfare* (London, [1839]).

41. [Somerville], *Autobiography*, p. 422.

42. Alexander Somerville, *Cobdenic Policy. The Internal Enemy of England* (London, 1854), pp. 28-9.

43. Anon. *Riots in South Wales. An Address to the Working Classes of Wales, on the Late Occurrences at Newport, by One of the People* (Swansea, 1840), pp. 5-8.

44. Newport Public Library, Chartist Trials 1839-1840, 24 vols (henceforth Newport Examinations), X, especially doc. 129, indictment; docs. 635 and 636, evidence of William Stephens; docs. 100, 456, 458, evidence of David Herring; doc. 347, evidence of Edward Brickley. *Monmouthshire Merlin*, 14 Dec. 1839. *Morning Chronicle*, 14 Dec. 1839.

45. Newport Examinations, X, doc. 315: testimony of James Cole by letter to W.T.H. Phelps.

46. Ibid., X: papers found by Moses Scard at John Gibby's house.

47. Ibid., XIII, docs. 105, 88, 593: evidence of Llewellyn Powell.

48. Ibid., XIII, docs. 105, 334, 336, 337, 836: evidence of Thomas Arthur. Not surprisingly, John Hopkins himself denied any knowledge of the matter when examined by the magistrates. Compare Earl of Bessborough (ed.), *Lady Charlotte Guest. Extracts from her Journal 1833-1852* (London, 1950), entry for 3 Nov. 1839.

49. Newport Examinations, XIII, docs. 105, 656, 657: evidence of John Thomas and David Jones. *Monmouthshire Merlin*, 7 Dec. 1839.

50. Evan Powell, *History of Tredegar. Subject of Competition at Tredegar 'Chair Eisteddfod' held February the 25th, 1884* (Newport, 1902), p. 57.

51. Oliver Jones, *The Early Days of Sirhowy and Tredegar* (Tredegar Historical Society, 1969), p. 97.

52. Newport Examinations, XI, doc. 401: evidence of James Emery.

53. *Morning Herald*, 5 Nov. 1839, second edition. *Morning Chronicle*, 5 Nov. 1839, second edition.

54. *The Times*, 11 Nov. 1839: evidence of Edward Dory. Newport Examinations, V, doc. 601; XI, docs. 485, 513.

55. Cardiff Central Library, Bute MSS, XX/2: notes as to Chartists delivered by Mr. Hutchins at Swansea Quarter Sessions, 1839.

56. Ibid., XX/34: Capt. Howells to Bute, dd. 2 Nov. 1839.

57. *The Times*, 11 Nov. 1839.

58. Newport Examinations, IV, doc. 384: evidence of William Davies.

59. Gwent Record Office, Depositions at Quarter Sessions, QSD 32-16, deposition of Samuel Etheridge.

60. Newport Examinations, VIII, doc. 830.

61. The list given here synthesises the slightly different versions in *The Times* and *Morning Chronicle*, 28 Nov. 1839, and Newport Examinations, III, unnumbered doc: evidence of James James.

62. Newport Examinations, XV, doc. 481: evidence of James James. Hen Waun was the name of a colliery at Blaina.

63. Ibid., XV, doc. 497: evidence of William Jenkins. *The Times* and *Morning Chronicle*, 28 Nov. 1839.

64. Newport Examinations, XII, docs. 709-10: evidence of Thomas Williams; doc. 522: evidence of Henry Lewis. Other members of the section were Thomas and John Morgan and their brother-in-law William Evans. The captain, No. 6, eluded capture after the rising but Thomas Morgan was apprehended and tried. Compare also PRO, TS.11/500: deposition of Thomas Evans, referring to 'Thomas Jones No. 7 of Pen-y-cae', apparently one of the Ebbw Vale sections.

65. Newport Examinations, XV, doc. 647: evidence of Benjamin Green. Green, significantly, testified only to the activities of a man who was dead.

66. CCL, Bute MSS, XX/2: notes as to Chartists, cited above.

67. See, e.g., *Silurian*, 28 March 1840: Edward Jenkins on the 40 to 50 men under David Howell's command.

68. CCL, Bute MSS, XX/72: Scale to Bute dd. 15 Nov. 1839.

69. Ibid., XX/2: notes as to Chartists, information from Thomas George.

70. Newport Examinations, VII, doc. 399: evidence of James Emery. *The Times*, 20 and 21 Nov. 1839, and *Morning Chronicle*, 21 Nov. 1839: evidence of James Emery.

71. CCL, Bute MSS, XX/72: Scale to Bute, dd. 15 Nov. 1839.

72. Ap Id Anfryn [Gwilym Hughes], *The Late Dr Price (of Llantrisant). The Famous Arch-Druid* (Cardiff, 1896), p. 10, reprinted from *Cardiff Times and South Wales Weekly News*, 26 May 1888.

73. Newport Examinations, VI, doc. 554: evidence of William Watkins. *The Times*, 13 Nov. 1839 and *Morning Chronicle*, 13 Nov. 1839: evidence of William Watkins and Moses Scard.

74. *Silurian*, 16 Nov. 1839.

75. Newport Examinations, IV, doc. 384: evidence of William Davies, and V, doc. 669: evidence of Job Tovey.

76. The most informed sources for those attending the meeting of deputies on 1 Nov. are Newport Examinations, IV, doc. 384, and V, doc. 669. See also CCL, Bute MSS, XX/105: W. Coffin to Bute, dd. 4 Dec. 1839.

77. Birmingham Central Libraries, Lovett Collection, II, doc. 211: enclosure in John Taylor to William Lovett, dd. 10 June 1841. Price took the chair at the important Dukestown meeting of 12 Aug. 1839, at which John Frost, William Lloyd Jones and Zephaniah Williams were among those present, see Newport Examinations, III, unnumbered doc.: evidence of Morgan James, and V, doc. 670: evidence of Job Tovey.

78. Newport Examinations, XIV, doc. 566: evidence of Thomas Morgan.

79. *Merthyr Guardian*, 11 Nov. 1837.

80. Ap Id Anfryn, *The Late Dr Price*, p. 10.

81. I.G.H. Wilks, 'Insurrections in Texas and Wales: the Careers of John Rees', in *The Welsh History Review*, 11, 1 (1982), pp. 67-91.

82. PRO, TS.11/502, doc. 1630: Jas. Brown to Thomas Jones Phillips, dd. Blaina, 7 Nov. 1839.

83. *The Times*, 30 Nov. 1839.

84. *Pigot's Directory* (London and Manchester, 1835), pp. 260, 261. PRO,

TS.11/496, doc. 1621: evidence of Morris Morris.

85. Gwent Record Office, Depositions at Quarter Sessions, QSD 32-16, deposition of Samuel Etheridge. See also Newport Examinations, VIII, doc. 113: evidence of Samuel Etheridge.

86. R.R. Madden, *The United Irishmen, Their Lives and Times*, 2 vols (London, 1842), I, pp. 144-6, 168.

87. *The Times*, 14 April 1840.

88. *Monmouthshire Merlin*, 9 May 1840.

# 8 THE REVOLUTIONARY DESIGN: A WORKERS' REPUBLIC

Late in March 1839 William Edwards — Mad Edwards the Baker as he became known from the violence of his language — took Henry Vincent on a tour of the Blackwood district, stronghold of the most militant of the colliers. A band of about 100 young girls accompanied them into Blackwood itself; 'Here's a health to the Radical boys, May tyranny fail, and freedom prevail', went the refrain of their song. Vincent was mightily impressed by all he saw and heard. 'The scenery is very picturesque', he wrote in his journal;

> Fine fertile hills rising in all directions. I could not help thinking of the defensible nature of the country in the case of *foreign invasion!* A few thousands of armed men on the hills could successfully defend them. Wales would make an excellent Republic.[1]

He could scarcely have foreseen that only seven months later the Welshmen would rise in arms in a bid, as it was reported at the time, 'for seizing the whole of South Wales to erect a Chartist kingdom';[2] to create, as that excellent poet Harri Webb aptly describes it, a Silurian republic.

Numerous commentators on the November Rising referred to the extraordinary secrecy in which it had been planned. The government's own commissioner, Tremenheere, remarked on 'the unusual phenomenon . . . of large masses of the working population capable of contriving and keeping secret from the magistrates and everyone in authority until the moment of execution, a well-organised plan for a combined attack at midnight upon a populous town'.[3] Tremenheere was right; the majority of the populace either actively supported or acquiesced in the rebel cause. Sections were formed, armed and drilled, but the magistrates were quite unable to build up any network of informers within the working-class communities. Much of the difficulty in reconstructing the design of the rebel leaders results from this circumstance. Those who have written on the rising of 1839 have been, for the most part, more concerned to explain it away than to understand it, a matter that will be considered more fully in Chapter 13. Most apparently, few writers have been prepared to allow for the singularity of the early nineteenth-century Welsh experience although this was the subject of vigorous comment in the London *Courier* only two days after the rising. 'We must not omit to take into account the peculiar character and habits of the people at large, in conjunction with the special features of the locality', wrote a columnist. From Newport and Cardiff, he explained,

> are shipped the immense mass of iron and coal produced by the mines, and worked up in the ironworks . . . Large working populations are congregated about the respective seats of these different collieries, but more especially the ironworks, established on a scale so vast, and involving individual properties of amount so enormous, as to be without parallel in the mining industry of the whole world.

The columnist recognised that an insurrection had occurred ('for it cannot be softened down into a mere riot'); that it had mass support ('an almost entire population has been embarked on it'); and that its roots reached deep into the Welsh working-class experience ('a more ignorant, desperate, and, we might almost add, a more disaffected population cannot be found in the empire'). He even had a sharp comment to make on the matter of electoral politics. 'The people were falsely deluded', he remarked,

> into the hope that Parliamentary Reform would produce an amelioration of their social condition; that hope has been disappointed, and will it ever be disappointed so long as the people are led to expect social improvement from the increase of abstract political privileges . . . And however much these scenes of insurrection and blood, which it has been our painful duty to record, may occasion regret and lamentation, do they occasion, we ask, *surprise* . . . ?[4]

It is not necessary to share the columnist's toryism to find his observations salutary. We shall not understand the rising of 1839 if we persist in viewing it, as most historians have, as no more than a violent phase in the chartist agitation for parliamentary reform. It may have been that, but it was much more. It was a fervid expression of the emerging proletarian consciousness in south Wales. There was a sense in which the rising could not fail for, whether in victory or defeat, through their struggle the rebels were to renew history and to make history. 'We must', declared Dr William Price of Pontypridd, strike with all our might and power and strike immediately. The time for hesitating is past and the day of reckoning is at hand . . . Oppression, injustice and the grinding poverty which burdens our lives must be abolished for all time. We must have an understanding of our cause in our minds, the principle of our cause in our hearts, the power of our cause in our conscience, and the strength of our cause in our right arm – strength that will enable us to meet our oppressors boldly, fearlessly, upright on our feet. Remember that freedom is our birthright and for that we are prepared to give our lives. We are the descendants of valiant Welshmen and we must be worthy of the traditions which they have passed on to us.[5]

Where the struggle would lead none of the rebels could have known. The form it took was conditioned as much by the means through which it could be prosecuted as by the ends which it might achieve. 'It is far better', Price urged, 'that we should die fighting for freedom, than live as slaves of greed and opulent wealth.' Some did die. George Shell, 19 years of age, a carpenter, and a member of a Pontypool rebel company chosen for use against Newport, addressed a letter to his parents on the eve of the attack. 'I shall this night be engaged in a struggle for freedom', he wrote, 'and should it please God to spare my life I shall see you soon; but if not grieve not for me, I shall fall in a noble cause.' He was killed in the fighting the following day, a bullet in his chest.[6]

Six months after the rising one of the leaders from the Tredegar district, Zephaniah Williams, produced a short account of it. At the time he was on board a convict ship bound for Australia, and he wrote at the request of its surgeon-commander, A. McKechnie. Williams referred to 'our designed, and proposed plan, to overthrow the present Government of England, and establish a Republican'. Despite the ordeal of his trial, Williams maintained a positive attitude towards the rising. 'Had we been cautious and Judicious in our proceedings', he claimed, 'it would have been a difficult matter to defeat us.' He also remained guarded in his comments. He excused himself from 'giving names of persons concerned in the Affair from reasons which are obvious', and he expressed the hope that the communication 'will not be made use of to my prejudice either to my interest or reputation'. McKechnie must, however, have made the document available to the authorities in south Wales, for it came into the hands of Octavius Morgan, son of Sir Charles Morgan of Tredegar Park and the Newport magistrate most active in the pursuit of wanted rebels throughout 1840. It is difficult to believe that McKechnie was not in violation of the terms on which Williams had agreed to write. However that may be, the document has survived in the Tredegar Park muniments, and any attempt to reconstruct the rebel design must depend heavily though by no means exclusively on it.[7] Three phases or moments in that design are to be distinguished. The first involved destabilisation of the existing bourgeois order in south Wales; the second, seizure of control over the means of production from the ironmasters and coalowners; and the third, defence of the workers' republic against the state. It was only in the third phase that the rebels lost the initiative and south Wales fell under a veritable military occupation.

Bourgeois order in south Wales as elsewhere was sustained by a formidable apparatus of control directed, ultimately, from the Home Office in London: Lord Lieutenants and magistrates, police and special constables, yeomanry, militia and regular soldiers.[8] Through the use of the Stamp Acts and the law of seditious libel, government also exercised a close superintendence of the press, and in 1839 the nearest approach to a Welsh working-class paper was the unstamped weekly *Western Vindicator* published from the west of England.[9] Shortly before the *Vindicator*'s suppression Henry Vincent made use of its columns to decry the situation:

> Oh! the damned press! What an infernal engine it is. That which might be the means of rescuing mankind from bondage and from slavery is used as a formidable means of warping the mind struggling to be free, and of crushing all who endeavour to be honest in their advocacy of the rights of the people.[10]

It was, then, all the more remarkable that by the time of the rising many of the company officials, shopkeepers and other 'respectable individuals from the neighbourhood of the Works' had come to feel their position so precarious that they chose to flee to the relative safety of the countryside rather than stay and face what they believed would be rapine, plunder and devastation.[11] The fact of the matter was that over many months their confidence in public order had been eroded by agitators who threatened 'bloody revolution' (while at the same time concealing the extent of the actual preparations for a rising). The word 'terror' was frequently used at the time. 'Terror?' remarked Vincent; 'an awkward word, but full of meaning. Tyranny that triumphs over every other foe trembles at this!'[12] In a call for strike action in support of the People's Charter, members of the Pontypool Working Men's Association declared, 'There is no arguing with our government nor parliament; we must assume a menacing aspect, such as will strike terror to the hearts of the shopocracy and all aristocrats . . .'[13]

Mad Edwards the Baker became one of the masters of the rhetoric of violence in the early months of 1839. 'I would not give a Tinkers damn for a Chartist who would not stand and have his head cleaved asunder to support the Charter', he told an audience at Pontypool in April.[14] At a meeting at Beaufort later in the same month he denounced the local press; he talked so much of cutting throats that none of the newsmen present dared bring out his pencil.[15] There is an account of the fervour manifest at another meeting in April, at Blaina. The speakers on this occasion ('two vagabondising, levelling, infidel, radical demagogues') were Edwards and Vincent. 'A *spy* a *spy*!' shouted one person when a heckler interrupted the proceedings; 'a *tory* said another; a *whig* cried a third; – down with the *whigs* and the *tories*, – down with little *Jack Russell*; – down with all our tyrants and employers; – down with the Queen, the Lords, the Commons, and every body else who may wish to prevent our being *self-governed* . . .'[16] Years later old Evan Powell of Tredegar was to recollect much the same aspect of the gatherings. 'Meetings were frequently held, in which popular discontent was exhibited to extremes', he wrote;

> speeches were delivered in a most violent and agitated strain. When the wrongs of the working class were pathetically described, the audiences awoke to storms of emotion, and when the leaders described 'the fine old gentlemen of England, with their fine estates, living at a bountiful and luxurious rate, riding to hounds, broaching pipes of malvoisie, issuing pasties of the doe to all and sundry, and leading the ladies forth on hawking excursions,' their indignation knew no bounds.[17]

Serious business was done at the weekly lodge meetings, to which admission was by membership ticket only. Public meetings had a different purpose. They were sometimes poorly attended but they were almost always reported in the local press. They provided, therefore, a channel through which the demagogues could reach out to the middle classes. In the spring of 1839 it was already apparent that the rhetoric of Edwards and others was having its effect. On 22 April Mayor Thomas Phillips of Newport wrote to the Home Secretary to argue that the verbal violence of the agitators might easily lead to undeliberated outbreaks of physical violence. 'In such circumstances', he speculated, 'outrages are committed by a few persons from whom the main body of the disaffected stand aloof whilst the loyal and well disposed are paralyzed by terror.'[18] If the Home Secretary was somewhat alarmed by the report from Newport, those that reached him from the ironworks above Pontypool a few days later would not have been reassuring. The manager of the Varteg works, G.S. Kenrick, was convinced that 'a general rising . . . all the Works stopped, and a great deal of rough work done' was likely early in May, and the manager of the British ironworks at Abersychan was already making preparations to remove his family to safety.[19] It was with some justification that John Frost reported to the chartist Convention in the middle of May that 'the great men . . . are frightened out of the few wits they possess'.[20]

In response to the reports of the disturbed state of affairs in south Wales in April, a detachment of 120 men of the 29th Regiment of Foot was stationed in Newport on 2 May.[21] It remained there until 9 October.[22] In that time no less than 13 soldiers deserted,[23] the cause attributed in some cases to 'tricks of the Chartists'. In fact an organisation seems to have been created to spirit the disaffected soldier away from his regiment. On 27 May, for example, Pte John McDonnald was singled out as a likely defector by William Watkins (who cut pit props for Thomas Powell). McDonnald was taken to a house on Stow Hill, breakfasted, given 6s in cash, and told that civilian clothes would be provided for him to be ready to move under cover of darkness. He was promised a job cutting timber at 15s a week, and was presumably expected to assist in training the rebel sections.[24] McDonald had a last minute change of mind and returned to barracks. Another deserter from the 29th Regiment, however, one Williams, served the rebels as 'drill sergeant and fugleman'. He was among those to lead the assault on the Westgate Hotel on 4 November, and he was among the first to fall.[25] Later rumours that Williams was a government spy, who only claimed to have deserted from the 29th, seem highly unlikely in view of the circumstances of his death.[26] His identity is, however, uncertain. It is possible that he was the John Williams of Merwood in Montgomeryshire who enlisted in the 29th in December 1837, deserted in June 1838, and was arrested at Welshpool the following August, returned to his regiment and branded. He deserted again in February 1839, was arrested in Gloucester in July, and once again returned to his regiment.[27] It is not known whether he was posted to Newport; no report of a third desertion has been found but the record may be imperfect in this respect if indeed he was slain before the hue and cry had been raised.

The men of the 29th Regiment were withdrawn from Newport to

Woolwich because of the extent to which they were becoming disaffected. A company of the 45th Regiment of Foot from Windsor took over immediately. The next day Samuel Victory of Newport treated three privates to rum, interrogated them about their attitudes in the event of an uprising, indicated that they could draw 2s 6d a day if they joined the rebels, and told them how to get in touch with him. A few days later one did, and brought a comrade with him. The two were immediately moved out of Newport to a farm where they were provided with civilian clothes, and the next day they proceeded to Blaenavon. There one fell ill; the other became apprehensive and returned to Newport.[28]

Knowledge that representatives of the workers' movement were attempting to subvert the soldiers was a cause of much disquiet to the middle classes. 'Amongst other dangers which the peaceable inhabitants of this town were exposed to', wrote one Newport correspondent, 'was that of being subject to the chance of desertion by those upon whose fidelity they were entirely dependent.'[29] The magistrates of Crickhowell urged the Home Secretary to increase the number of soldiers in that locality but to build a barracks for them 'in consequence of the constant attempts made by the disaffected to seduce the military from their duty when in billets'.[30]

Certainly the middle classes had cause for alarm. The rebel leaders constantly assured their own men that the soldiers were so sympathetic to the workers' cause that they would either desert or lay down their arms if fighting broke out. 'The soldiers were their friends and brothers', they were told; 'they would not fire upon the people.'[31] In his communication to Dr McKechnie, Zephaniah Williams revealed the rebel plans to deal with the existing military forces in south Wales. The soldiers in Brecon town 'would soon surrender themselves as they were so few not exceeding 30 in number and many of them fresh recruits'; there were 36 soldiers in Abergavenny 'and all with the exception of two was agreeable and anxious to join, provided it was a general outbreak'; and the soldiers in Newport were to be taken on their way back to barracks from the taverns where they tippled away their Sunday evenings.[32] Understandably cautious in the circumstances in which he wrote, Williams made reference only to the rank and file. At a meeting of the rebel leaders shortly before the rising the commander of the Pontypool district, David Davies, had been more explicit. 'I know what the English army is', declared that veteran of Waterloo, 'and I know how to fight them, and the only way to succeed is to attack and remove those who command them — the officers and those who administer the law.'[33] His words were heeded. Instructions were passed down to the lodges that the officers and sergeants should be killed but that the soldiers were not to be harmed.[34]

The events of 4 November in Newport showed that David Davies was in fact correct. However disaffected the soldiers might have been, when stood at arms they unhesitatingly obeyed their officers and directed their fire into the ranks of the workers. Yet the soldiers were undoubtedly disaffected, and that became even more apparent after the rising when the whole of the 45th Regiment was moved into south Wales. In the eight months from late November 1839 to the end of July 1840 over 100 desertions occurred. Not all were politically motivated, but many were.[35] The network for helping deserters appears to have survived the rebel defeat in Newport, for two defectors on 21 November were rapidly supplied with civilian clothes and got out of town.[36] It was in the valley towns, however, where more of the rebel organisation remained intact, that the military authorities faced their worst problems. It was said of the company of the 45th stationed in Dowlais, that 'they have changed clothes with the miners in some instances; many of them have been made drunk by them, and indeed considerable difficulty is felt in keeping up the proper state of military discipline'. It was considered too risky to station troops in Tredegar at all, and armed policemen were put there instead.[37] Clearly the rebel leaders were wrong in believing that the soldiers would be won over; equally clearly, their belief that the soldiers could be won over was not entirely without foundation.

The extent to which the middle classes were alarmed by the susceptibility of the soldiers to the blandishments of the workers was a measure of the extent to which they felt the security of their property and indeed of their persons threatened by a revolutionary upsurge of the people. Thomas Prothero of Malpas Court claimed 'that there was a list of the proscribed gentry and of their houses which were marked for destruction'.[38] This was no mere rumour. Indeed, Zephaniah Williams made no bones about the matter. Some of the rebel forces, he wrote, were to be assigned 'to take and inprison [sic] all the Aristocracy and Magistrates, and if any of them made the least resistance they were to be put to death. There was a certain number which was not to escape death under any consideration whatever likewise all the Police.'[39]

Time and time again the spokesmen for the middle classes voiced the sense of dread and impending doom which they felt. The magistrates of Crickhowell wrote of 'revolutionary violence, and the sword of desolation' in an address to the Home Secretary, and observed,

> These are fearful times, when the hydra head of rebellion stalks forth in military array to subvert our glorious constitution, and to slaughter with the cowardly sword of chartism her Majesty's peaceably disposed subjects . . . In the division and sub-division of property we have clear evidence of the republican principle of equality and fraternity.[40]

But the middle classes failed to appreciate the quite extraordinary degree of revolutionary discipline maintained in the workers' ranks. It was decreed by the rebel directorate that any man taking life or destroying property without authority would be shot or hung.[41] There was, in other words, to be no pillage, and remarkably few instances of random violence in fact occurred when the workers took to arms.

There had been strong pressure within the rebel councils to have a precise list of those to be killed drawn up.[42] This was apparently done, though no copy has survived. It seems that, rather in the manner of the earlier 'scotchings', men were not to be assigned to carry out executions in their own localities. Thus members of the Rassa lodge near Beaufort were amongst those under orders to kill the ironmaster and magistrate Summers Harford of the Sirhowy and Ebbw Vale works, the cashier Prosser at the latter, and the policeman at Nantyglo.[43] The Harfords may have learned of the danger they were in, for as the rising commenced Charles Lloyd Harford and his wife, with their domestic staff, fled to Cheltenham.[44] Certainly one magistrate on the Newport bench was told by a sympathetic rebel that he was marked out for execution, and John Lawrence, a local squire with interests in the ironworks, received an anonymous letter to the same effect.[45]

The list of persons to be killed was probably not a long one if only because those considered enemies of the people were more valuable to the rebels alive than dead. In mid-1839, following the arrests of Edwards, Vincent, Dickenson and Townsend, John Frost had suggested taking hostages and holding them in coalpits as security for the safety of the prisoners.[46] Since Frost advanced the idea quite openly, in speeches and in a broadside, it is unlikely that he intended it to be acted upon. Clearly, however, it found favour with the militant leaders in south Wales. The issue was discussed at the meeting of delegates in Blackwood on 1 November and it was decided that 'they were to secure all the authorities where they met them, to be kept prisoners as hostages'.[47] The decision was rapidly made known in the lodges by the returning delegates.[48] Particularly popular was the suggestion that the hostages should not only be kept in the pits but made to work in them.[49] Not surprisingly, those to be secured included Capel Hanbury Leigh, the Lord Lieutenant of Monmouthshire (who was to have 'one of the direst stalls that could be found for him'),[50] and Mayor Thomas Phillips of Newport.[51] Many of the houses of the 'great men' were to be expropriated. There was talk of making Thomas Prothero's Malpas Court into a poor house,[52] and Tredegar House, seat of Sir Charles Morgan, into a rebel barracks.[53] Other buildings were simply to be destroyed, for example, the Newport town house of the magistrate Lewis Edwards,[54] and Llantarnam Abbey, home of the Deputy Lieutenant and MP for Monmouth Boroughs, Reginald Blewitt. Blewitt is on record as complaining about the lawlessness of the colliers; 'it requires', he wrote, 'some courage to live amongst such a set of savages'.[55] Clearly it was the intention of the 'savages' in question to put that courage to the test.

Had the rising proceeded according to plan, civil authority would rapidly have been set at naught as those who exercised it either fled or were apprehended, and the relatively few regular soldiers in the districts would have laid down their arms after their officers and NCOs had been killed. Neutralisation of the civil and military authorities in south Wales was seen, however, as no more than a first step even though a critical one. The major goals of the rebel leaders were to establish a frontier that could be held against whatever forces of the crown might be despatched against them and, behind that frontier, to achieve a massive mobilisation of the working population in support of the revolutionary regime. The attainment of both goals was dependent upon the speed with which the trained sections could be put under arms and used to 'scour' the valleys.

We have seen that on the eve of the rising the rebels had in all perhaps 15 brigades, or some 7,500 men, committed to armed struggle. Scouring, *ysgwrio*, was a means of winning ironstone and coal by using a rush of water to separate the mine from the rubbish.[56] By analogy, the sections were to 'scour' the working-class communities, pressing all able-bodied men into their ranks. The ironworks and collieries were thus to be brought to a standstill by the all but total withdrawal of labour from them. The first phase of the rising was, in other words, essentially one of industrial rather than military action, and some years later Charles Wilkins of Merthyr could quite correctly look back upon it as one of the earliest general strikes on the south Wales coalfield.[57] The aims of the rebels, however, went far beyond bargaining for better wages or improved working conditions. The matter of the ownership of the very means of production was at issue.

A general concern with the unequal distribution of property was a feature of popular culture that had been raised to the status of a political programme by the levellers of mid-seventeenth-century England. Almost 200 years later the chartists were commonly accused by their opponents of being levellers, and the theme was indeed one frequently pursued by the Welsh radicals in their speeches and writings. At issue, typically, was land. 'How unjust it was', went one complaint, 'that Sir C[harles] M[organ] should have such a large rent-roll, and so many thousands of acres, and others, equally worthy, should not possess an acre!'[58] In the industrial valleys, however, land was less the issue than plant — furnaces, foundries and mineral workings. Among the ironworkers and colliers of the new proletariat, correspondingly new and advanced political ideas were taking shape. It was not only that the concentration of industrial property in the hands of a few was perceived as a *fact*; it was also perceived as a *consequence* and specifically, as a consequence of the exploitation of labour. 'We are the lower orders, and the foundation of society', wrote 'A Blackwood Collier' in June 1839, 'and all the other orders are living upon the labour of the so-called lower orders.'[59] The revolutionary view that the workers should own the value of their labour was one already current in south Wales. In April 1839, for example, the ironworkers and colliers of the Garndiffaith lodge had met to decide that 'the Works do not belong to the present proprietors, but to the Workmen, and that they would very shortly have them'.[60]

It is no longer possible to know how the rebels intended the works should be run under a republican regime. The case of Thomas Powell is, however, instructive. Powell was proprietor of a number of collieries in Glamorgan and Monmouthshire: Gelligaer, Buttery Hatch, Bryn and Gelligroes. He learned that his collieries were to be expropriated, and was much affected by reports that the rebel directorate (the 'council of rapine') had decided that he should work as a coal-cutter at Gelligaer. 'Such', he remarked, 'is the sense of justice of these lawless depredators.'[61] A conversation between the wives of two Gelligaer colliers was widely reported in the local press. The women had gone to pick coal while their husbands were still away with the rebel forces.

'I want some coal, and I don't know what I shall do, now the colliery is stopped', [said the first].
'Oh, do not hesitate to go and take some coal off the trams on the tramroad', [replied the second].

'What will Mr Powell say, if he should hear of it?'

'Oh, never mind him. The Gelligaer Colliery will be my husband's tomorrow, when Newport is taken.'

'Why, then what will then become of our master, Mr Powell?'

'Why, we have worked long enough. Mr Powell may come and cut coal, if he likes it.'[62]

The story of the two women may or may not be veridical, but it probably represents accurately enough the spirit that was in the land in the heady days of the insurrection. Zephaniah Williams himself remarked only that the ironworks were to be 'appropriated' and their production geared to the immediate needs of the rebels.[63] Whether they were to be managed by committees of workers he did not say, nor did he make any reference to the fiscal aspects of the anticipated take-over. Although the evidence is fragmentary, we may be fairly sure that not long before the rising the rebel directorate took steps to maximise the amount of coin in circulation and reduce the number of bank notes, and that instructions on this matter were sent out to the lodges. George Shell of Pontypool was telling people that within two months 'Bank Notes will not be worth a snap of his Finger'.[64] Reports indicate that in many of the ironworks and collieries the men insisted on taking their pay in full, in sovereigns or silver, the week before the rising.[65] On 30 October a message was sent to the president of the Oddfellows in Newport, informing him of the imminence of the rising and advising him to withdraw the society's money (in coin, presumably) from the bank.[66] Whether the rebels intended to close down the banks, or to take them over, we do not know. Thomas Williams, a Newport plasterer and rebel activist, was overheard apparently talking about robbing them.[67] The section captain Jenkin Morgan of Pillgwenlly was ordered to apprehend the Rev. Richard Roberts of Christchurch and hold him and his family prisoners in Newport;[68] we may guess that it was not his pastorate but his position as a manager of the Newport and Caerleon Savings Bank that made his detention important.[69] Certainly the manager of the Tredegar Branch Bank was prepared to take no chances. On the Sunday of the rising he arrived in Abergavenny with all the bank's cash, valuables and securities, having escaped from Tredegar as the rebel sections started mobilising.[70]

If the rising took the form of essentially industrial action in one of its phases, in another it was unambiguously military in character. With their ranks augmented by the impressed (though not necessarily unwilling) men, the rebels planned to launch simultaneous attacks on

Abergavenny, Brecon, Cardiff and Newport. Zephaniah Williams wrote that the first town was to be taken by 5,000 men from Tredegar district ('Rhumny, Tredegar, Sirhowy, Ebbwvale, Beaufort and Nantyglo'); the second by about the same number from Merthyr district; and the third by some 2,000 men from Pontypridd district ('Taff Vale'). The original intention was that Newport should be occupied by the sections already established in and around the town, aided by 'large numbers' of Blackwood men who would join them.[71] For some reason Williams failed to make any mention of the Pontypool forces. It is clear from other sources that these were to secure Pontypool itself and also to move on the town of Usk.[72]

The rebels saw themselves as establishing, *pro tem*, a defensible frontier along the Usk River and the Severn Shore. Newport itself was to be sealed tight. The river, according to Zephaniah Williams, was 'to be blocked up with trading vessels', and plans for the destruction of the Usk bridge were carefully worked out: Jenkin Morgan's section from Pillgwenlly, referred to above, was also detailed to seize Aaron Crossfield's warehouse, the gunpowder from which would be used to blow up the bridge.[73] Unlike Newport, the other towns along the Usk all lay on the left bank, but there is one report which suggests that their bridges were also to be destroyed.[74] Certainly elaborate plans were made for the occupation of Abergavenny and Brecon. Zephaniah Williams provided some detail. Some 100 men with concealed weapons, he wrote, were to enter Abergavenny the day before the rising and obtain lodgings at the public houses where soldiers were billeted. When the main rebel forces entered the town, 'which was intended to be in the Dead of Night, a Signal was to be given to the fresh lodgers who was to open the doors and let them in, and immediately Secure the Soldiers, and arms'. There was, however, rather more to the situation than Williams explained.

No lodges of the working men's association had been opened in those Usk towns which, unlike Newport, were linked with their rural hinterlands rather than with the industrial valleys. Two 'chartists' toured the towns in October, visiting Abergavenny on 19 October and Brecon on 21 and 22 October. One of the two was David Lewis, head of the Brynmawr lodge at Waunhelygen. The other, 'a wild, dottish, hot-headed Irishman', came from Newport; he can have been no other than the senior Richard Rorke. Lewis and Rorke made no effort to conceal their presence in the towns; indeed, they attempted to open lodges in both places.[75] Both men, however, in fact belonged to the rebel directorate, and there can be little doubt that their more serious purpose was to report back to that body on the state of each town. The planning of the attacks presumably proceeded on the basis of these reports.

It was essential to the rebel plans that fresh troops from England should be prevented from entering south Wales, whether by land or sea. The creation of a perimeter along the Usk and the Severn Shore was intended to achieve that purpose. It was, however, an interim measure. In the thinking of the workers' leaders the ultimate guarantee of security was to be found not in the maintenance of territorial frontiers but rather in the creation of an armed populace fully committed to the republican ideal. Much attention was therefore given to the matter of weaponry. In the towns that were to be occupied, Zephaniah Williams pointed out, 'there were a great number of Arms and Warehouses which contained powder likewise on the Hills at the Iron Works, there were many Powder Magazines, which were all to be taken to'. To supplement these sources a raiding party was to cross the Severn by commandeered steamer, seize a powder house on the shore near Bristol, and remove its contents to Newport. Meanwhile the ironworks were to be turned over to the production of cannon and small arms.[76]

Within a week from the start of the rising, so Zephaniah Williams claimed, the rebels should have had 80,000 to 100,000 men at their disposal, well enough armed to resist any body of troops sent against them. Yet even had the rising gone strictly according to plan, scarcely half those numbers of men could have been mobilised from the five rebel districts. Perhaps Williams was indulging in a little hyperbole. Or perhaps it was assumed that the revolutionary upsurge of the people would immediately spread to the disaffected regions of mid-Wales (where the textile workers had risen in arms six months earlier) and west Wales (where the rural guerrilla known as Rebecca had already been born). There was, in any case, another component in the rebel calculations that was of major importance: the English factor. The matter was summed up rather neatly by a contributor to the London *Charter*, shortly after the rising. 'The ultimate design of the leaders does not appear', he wrote,

> but it was probably to rear the standard of rebellion throughout Wales, in hopes of being able to hold the royal forces at bay, in the mountainous district, until the people of England, assured by successes, should rise, *en masse*, for the same objects.[77]

It was John Frost who had assured the rebel directorate that risings in

England and indeed Scotland would be sparked off by the Welsh one. They were not, and the topic is one that must next be considered.

## Notes

1. *Western Vindicator*, 6 April 1839. Italics original.
2. *The Times*, 6 Nov. 1839: communication from Bristol dd. 4 Nov.
3. British Parliamentary Papers, *Minutes of the Committee of Council on Education with Appendices and Plans of School Houses*, Part II (1839-40), p. 208.
4. *Courier*, 6 Nov. 1839. Italics original.
5. Cited in T. Islwyn Nicholas, *A Welsh Heretic. Dr William Price, Llantrisant* (London, 1940), pp. 15-16. I have been unable to locate the source for this speech. In conversation, Islwyn ap Nicholas was unable to recollect it but promised to consult his notes (Aberystwyth, 29 June 1979). His much lamented death occurred before he was able to do so.
6. *Monmouthshire Merlin*, 23 Nov. 1839. *Monmouthshire Beacon*, 7 Dec. 1839. Shell's death inspired a number of writers. 'Vengeance is now our cry. Remember Shell!' urged John Watkins for example; 'We'll live like him – at least we'll die as well.' *John Frost: a Chartist Play in Five Acts* (London, 1841).
7. National Library of Wales, Tredegar Park Muniments, Box 40, doc. 2: Zephaniah Williams to A. McKechnie, dd. 25 May 1840.
8. See David Jones, *Before Rebecca. Popular Protest in Wales 1793-1835* (London, 1973), Ch. 7 and more generally, F.C. Mather, *Public Order in the Age of the Chartists* (Manchester, 1959), *passim*.
9. R.D. Rees, 'South Wales and Monmouthshire Newspapers under the Stamp Acts', in *Welsh History Review*, I, 3 (1962), pp. 301-24.
10. *Western Vindicator*, 7 Dec. 1839. Italics original.
11. For the flight of the middle classes see, for example, the various reports from Abergavenny, Brecon and Newport in *Hereford Times*, 9 Nov. 1839.
12. *Western Vindicator*, 7 Dec. 1839
13. British Library, Add. MSS 34,245, II, doc. 91: WMA, Pontypool, to General Convention, dd. 2 Aug. 1839.
14. Public Record Office, TS.11/499, doc. 1626.
15. *Merthyr Guardian*, 27 April 1839.
16. PRO, TS.11/502: letter to *Merthyr Guardian* (unpublished), dd. Nantyglo, 24 April 1839. Emphasis original.
17. Evan Powell, *History of Tredegar. Subject of Competition at Tredegar 'Chair Eisteddfod' held February the 25th, 1884* (Newport, 1902), p. 57.
18. PRO, HO.40/45: Thomas Phillips to Home Sec., dd. 22 April 1839.
19. PRO, HO.40/45: extracts from Wood's letter, dd. 27 April 1839.
20. British Library, Add. MSS 34,245, I, doc. 445: Frost to Lovett, dd. Newport, 15 May 1839.
21. *Merthyr Guardian*, 11 May 1839.
22. *Cambrian*, 12 Oct. 1839.
23. There were 94 desertions from the whole regiment in 1839, see PRO, WO.25/2917, Record of Desertions, 14 Foot to 43 Foot, 1837 to 1843.
24. *Cambrian*, 8 June 1839.
25. *Bristol Mercury, Monmouthshire, South Wales, and West of England Advertiser*, 9 Nov. 1839. See also *Morning Chronicle*, 7 Nov. 1839. *Merthyr Guardian*, 16 Nov. 1839. Newport Public Library, Chartist Trials 1839-1840,

24 vols (henceforth Newport Examinations), IV, doc. 466: evidence of James Hodge.

26. *Northern Star*, 14 Dec. 1839, reporting W. Cardo.

27. PRO, WO.25/2917. WO.25/2945 and 2946, Register of Commitments. HO.75, Police Gazette and Hue and Cry, 27 Feb. 1839. The only other Williams to have deserted from the regiment was a Thomas, in March 1838; he was apprehended.

28. *Monmouthshire Merlin*, 16 Nov. 1839.

29. *Morning Chronicle*, 15 Nov. 1839.

30. *Monmouthshire Beacon*, 30 Nov. 1839.

31. *Morning Chronicle*, 15 Nov. 1839. Cardiff Central Library, Bute MSS, XX/69: Scale to Bute, dd. 14 Nov. 1839.

32. NLW, Tredegar Park Muniments, 40, 2: Williams to McKechnie, dd. 25 May 1840.

33. Ap Id Anfryn [Gwilym Hughes] , *The Late Dr Price (of Llantrisant). The Famous Arch-Druid* (Cardiff, 1896), p. 10.

34. *Silurian*, 28 March 1840. Brecon Lent Assizes: evidence of Charles Lloyd against Ishmael Evans.

35. PRO, WO.25/2918, Record of Desertions. It was noted of the court-martial of two privates on 2 Dec. 1839, that the evidence failed to connect their desertion with the rebels (as if that was exceptional), see *Cambrian*, 7 Dec. 1839.

36. *Monmouthshire Beacon* and *Merthyr Guardian*, 30 Nov. 1839.

37. *The Times*, 3 Dec.1839. For charges of encouraging soldiers to desert against Daniel Hopkins, miner, of Merthyr, see *Cambrian*, 4 and 11 April 1840.

38. *Morning Chronicle*, 23 Nov. 1839.

39. Williams to McKechnie dd. 25 May 1840, cited above.

40. *Monmouthshire Beacon*, 30 Nov. 1839.

41. Newport Examinations, III, unnumbered doc: evidence of Stephen Fletcher, citing William Shellard. Thomas Ainge Devyr, *The Odd Book of the Nineteenth Century* (Greenpoint, New York, 1882), p. 194.

42. Ap Id Anfryn, *The Late Dr Price*, p. 10.

43. Newport Examinations, XIII, doc. 105: evidence of John Thomas and David Jones.

44. *Monmouthshire Beacon*, 9 Nov. 1839. PRO, TS.11/500: Mayor Dyke to Home Sec. dd. Monmouth, 4 Nov. 1839.

45. *The Times*, 11 Nov. 1839. *Monmouthshire Merlin*, 16 Nov. 1839.

46. David Williams, *John Frost. A Study in Chartism* (Cardiff, 1939), pp. 168-9.

47. Newport Examinations, V, docs. 668-70: evidence of Job Tovey.

48. See for example Newport Examinations, III, unnumbered doc: evidence of Stephen Fletcher against William Shellard of Pontypool. CCL, Bute MSS, XX/1: evidence of Daniel Llewellyn against William David of Dinas.

49. Newport Examinations, XII, doc. 624: evidence of Moses Scard; XV, doc. 348: evidence of Joseph Brown.

50. Ibid., III, unnumbered doc: evidence of Stephen Fletcher. *The Times*, 11 Nov. 1839: evidence of John Prosser. *Monmouthshire Merlin*, 14 Dec. 1839: 'Plans of the Chartists'. E.L. and O.P. Edmonds, *I Was There. The Memoirs of H.S. Tremenheere* (Eton Windsor, 1965), p. 37. W.N. Johns, *The Chartist Riots at Newport*, 2nd edn (Newport, 1889), p. 33.

51. Newport Examinations, VIII, docs. 113, 612-13: evidence of Charles Rogers.

52. Ibid., III, unnumbered doc: evidence of William Phillips.

53. Ibid., V, doc. 670: evidence of Job Tovey.

54. Ibid., VIII, docs. 113, 612-13: evidence of Charles Rogers. *Monmouthshire Merlin*, 23 Nov. 1839. *Salopian Journal and Courier of Wales*, 11 Dec. 1839.

Johns, *Chartist Riots*, p. 34.

55. *Monmouthshire Merlin*, 14 Dec. 1839. Newport Examinations, III, unnumbered doc: evidence of William Phillips. PRO, HO.40/45: Blewitt to Home Sec. dd. 6 Nov. 1839.

56. Powell, *History of Tredegar*, p. 20. John Lloyd, *The Early History of the Old South Wales Iron Works (1760 to 1840)* (London, 1906), p. 46.

57. Charles Wilkins, *The South Wales Coal Trade and its Allied Industries, from the Earliest Days to the Present Time* (Cardiff, 1888), p. 278.

58. Ignotus, *The Last Thirty Years in a Mining District* (London, 1867), pp. 61-2.

59. *Western Vindicator*, 13 June 1839.

60. PRO, HO.40/45: extract from Wood's letter dd. 27 April 1839.

61. *Monmouthshire Merlin*, 30 Nov. 1839. Compare *Merthyr Guardian*, 7 Dec. 1839.

62. *Monmouthshire Merlin*, 30 Nov. 1839. *Hereford Journal*, 4 Dec. 1839. The version of the conversation given here is a composite from the two sources.

63. Williams to McKechnie dd. 25 May 1840, cited above.

64. Newport Examinations, VII, unnumbered doc: Roberts to Phelps dd. 4 Dec. 1839. 839.

65. CCL, Bute MSS, XX/72: Scale to Bute dd. 15 Nov. 1839 (Blackwood); XX/97: Howells to Bute dd. 1 Dec. 1839 (Dinas). *Monmouthshire Beacon*, 9 Nov. 1839: testimony of C.L. Harford (Sirhowy).

66. *Monmouthshire Merlin*, 30 Nov. 1839: evidence of Lewis Lloyd. Newport Examinations, X, doc. 547: evidence of Lewis Lloyd.

67. Newport Examinations, X, doc. 371: James Davies to Mayor Hawkins.

68. Ibid., XII, unnumbered doc: statement by Morgan James.

69. T.M. Hodges, 'The History of the Newport and Caerleon Savings Bank (1830-88)', in W.E. Minchinton (ed.), *Industrial South Wales 1750-1914* (London, 1969), pp. 190-205.

70. *Hereford Times*, 9 Nov. 1839.

71. Williams to McKechnie dd. 25 May 1840, cited above.

72. *Manchester Guardian*, 6 Nov. 1839. Report from Pontypool dd. 4 Nov. to the effect that men had set off in the direction of Monmouth.

73. PRO, TS.11/501, doc. 1629: T.J. Phillips to Maule dd. 22 Nov. 1839. Newport Examinations, XII, unnumbered doc: statement by Morgan James.

74. Lady Charlotte Guest, it seems, heard a rumour that the Abergavenny bridge was to be destroyed, see Earl of Bessborough (ed.), *Lady Charlotte Guest. Extracts from her Journal 1833-1852* (London, 1950), entry for 4 Nov. 1839. There were eight bridges on the stretch of river between Newport and Abergavenny alone, though most were very modest constructions, see PRO, TS.11/497, doc. 1623: Plan of the Canals and Railroads communicating wih the Town of Newport, Monmouthshire, 1839, G.E. Madeley, London.

75. *Hereford County Press and Shropshire Mail*, 26 Oct. 1839. *Hereford Journal*, 30 Oct. 1839. *Hereford Times and General Advertiser*, 2 Nov. 1839. *Cambrian*, 2 Nov. 1839.

76. Williams to McKechnie dd. 25 May 1840, cited above.

77. *Charter*, 17 Nov. 1839.

# 9 THE ENGLISH CONNECTION AND THE AGONY OF FROST

On 14 September 1839 John Frost, ex-magistrate and ex-Mayor of Newport, used his casting vote to ensure the dissolution of the General Convention of the Industrious Classes. The Convention had been meeting intermittently in London and Birmingham since 4 February and over that period Frost had become more and more closely associated with its militant wing. In a number of public pronouncements he had adopted positions as extreme as those held by any delegate. Early in May, for example, he had dwelled on the possibility of mutiny in the army and a month later had both written and spoken of taking as hostages those who oppressed the people.[1] The dissolution of the Convention has been well described as the result of a coalition of those who contemplated a direct resort to force and those who were simply disillusioned with the struggle.[2] Frost most surely belonged to the first category. The evidence, however, is of a particularly refractory kind. Much of it is hearsay, and much of it is partisan and recriminatory; some is pure fabrication. It is possible, nevertheless, to reconstruct, albeit tentatively, something of that network of intrigue and conspiracy of which Frost found himself a part.

Alexander Somerville, who had seen active service with the British Auxiliary Legion in Spain from 1835 to 1837, was thought to be sympathetic to the chartist cause. He claimed that he was asked to join the Welsh rebels. He refused, and in an attempt to avert a rising wrote his *Warnings to the People on Street Warfare*. It was, he said, translated into Welsh and widely circulated in the disturbed districts. The implication of his evidence is that the approach was made to him in the spring of 1839, for he reported that shortly before the rising Frost had told Henry Hetherington that but for the effect of the *Warnings* a recourse to arms would have been made six months earlier. Somerville admitted, however, that he learned nothing of the detailed plans of the rebels, and he casts no further light upon the events of early November in Wales.[3] Little more revealing, though certainly more curious, was the testimony of the shoemaker William Cardo, delegate for Marylebone in the General Convention. Late in the summer of 1839 Cardo came under the spell — the word is quite apposite — of the radical tory and obsessive Russophobe David Urquhart. In a series of conversations Urquhart

162

convinced Cardo that the current unrest in the British Isles was being fermented by Russian agents. Cardo thereupon confessed to the existence of 'a plan for simultaneous outbreaks in the long nights before Christmas'. A Polish emigrant, he said, was responsible for the military side of the movement and would himself 'have the command in the mountains of Wales'. The conversations were memorialised by Urquhart's associate, the barrister George Fyler, who was present throughout. His memorandum bears the same date, 22 September 1839, as a letter on the matter which he routed through Lord Anglesey for the attention of the Prime Minister or Home Secretary (but which no one took seriously until the rising had occurred).[4]

The Polish emigrant was Major Bartlomiej Beniowski, who had deserted the Russian army for the Polish resistance in 1830 and who subsequently went into exile in France and Egypt before settling in England in or about 1836.[5] Beniowski was a leading member of the London Democratic Association and a most unlikely candidate for the role of Russian agent in which Urquhart and the Urquhartites had eagerly cast him.[6] The rising in south Wales, however, only confirmed them in their view. It must have been at Urquhart's instigation that Cardo arrived in Newport ten days after the attack on that town, having announced his intention of finding out what had really happened.[7] Cardo was apprehended on 15 November and brought before the Newport magistrates. They were clearly puzzled when Cardo informed them that the Welsh rising was the result of 'Russian agency' and subsequently identified Beniowski — who they had not heard of until then — as the agent in question.[8] It is quite possible that there had been talk in London of sending the Pole to Wales, for he was a man of much military experience and had contributed articles on urban warfare to the London *Democrat* in the spring of 1839. There is, however, no evidence whatsoever that Beniowski was actually involved in the rising in November.[9]

The fact of the matter was that in the late summer of 1839, as the General Convention lurched towards dissolution, a number of coteries were formed in London. Some remained committed to reform through a reformed Parliament and others contemplated a revolutionary refashioning of society. On all sides, however, the talk was of armed struggle in the pursuit of whatever goals. One such coterie included P.M. McDouall (delegate for Ashton-under-Lyne), R.J. Richardson (for Manchester) and John Taylor (for Newcastle, Carlisle and elsewhere). If Somerville is to be believed, the three boldly surveyed Woolwich arsenal with a view to seeing how it could best be seized.[10] Frost's position in all of this was a rather special one, for it was generally recognised that his 'constituents' were already far advanced in their preparations for a rising. Wales was seen, in W.E. Adams's memorable phrase, as 'the cockpit of the kingdom',[11] and from this circumstance Frost undoubtedly gained a certain amount of kudos.

On his release from gaol in mid-1840 William Lovett, former secretary of the General Convention, carried out his own investigation of Frost's stance in 1839. During the final session of the Convention, Lovett learned, Frost made it known to a number of his fellow delegates that it was very difficult to restrain the Welshmen from rising immediately and marching upon Monmouth to release the chartist prisoners held there. Peter Bussey of Bradford pledged his support to Frost in the event of the Welshmen taking to arms, and agreed to bring the local organisations in Yorkshire and Lancashire to a state of readiness.[12] William Ashton, a Barnsley weaver who was in London at the time of the dissolution, gave a somewhat different but essentially compatible account of affairs. Frost, he claimed, was a member of a group that met to commit itself to 'a rising in arms of the people'. His associates included Peter Bussey (delegate for the West Riding of Yorkshire), William Burns (for Dundee) and, once again, John Taylor.[13] Ashton thought that 3 November was mooted as the date of the risings; either he added this detail from hindsight or it was by sheer coincidence that it was the day that the march on Newport was in fact commenced.[14] Both Lovett and Ashton wrote long after the time in question. We shall see, however, that their accounts accord well with the subsequent sequence of events.

The date of John Frost's return from London to Newport is uncertain, but he had arrived there before the end of September. He involved himself in a flurry of writing. On 28 September he addressed letters to the Lord Lieutenant of Monmouthshire and to at least one of the local magistrates. In them he urged an improvement in the treatment of the prisoners in Monmouth — Vincent, Edwards, Dickenson and Townsend — and gave as his reason, that 'the agitation has now subsided'.[15] It may be that Frost was dissimulating, but it seems more likely that, after the heady days in London, Frost needed to convince himself that the situation in south Wales was not beyond his control. A Newport draper, petty bourgeois by background and lower middle class by achievement, Frost had been no more than an occasional intruder into the ironworking and mining districts. Nothing in his numerous letters to the *Western Vindicator* throughout 1839 suggested that he was particularly sensitive to the proprieties and aspirations of the new proletariat. His appeals were always for reason, and he directed them to the good tradesmen and farmers and artisans of Monmouthshire for the most part. The world of the Scotch Cattle with their disguises and bellowings and trashings and beatings was one that he never would and never could enter. The attitude of the rebel leaders in the valleys towards him was incalculable until put to the test. And so Frost set down his ideas on the prosecution of the struggle ahead for publication in the *Western Vindicator*[16] and, apparently in fine fettle, left Newport for the valleys to convince the ironworkers and colliers to accept his leadership.

In the first week of October he addressed meetings in the Blackwood and Tredegar districts. He had heard, he told his audiences, that the rising had virtually started and that men were already under arms. He was glad to find that this was not so. The time was not ripe, for the men of Scotland, Lancashire and the west of England were not yet ready to move. 'They were not all to expect to be generals', he told them; they should accept him as their commander and await his orders. He, Frost, would offer himself as candidate for Monmouthshire at the next parliamentary elections, and he wanted 30,000 men in sections of ten to be ready to support him at the hustings.[17]

The ironworkers and colliers were somewhat less than enthusiastic about Frost's programme. His reception at Blaina on 3 October was a mixed one. When he told them to await his orders they shouted, 'now! tonight! tonight!' When he argued that the time was not yet ripe for a rising they replied, 'today! today!' And when he promised that as their member of Parliament he would no longer argue for restraint if universal suffrage had not been won within a month, they yelled, 'Well done, – now, now is the time.'[18] Clearly Frost was not attuned to the mood of the men. They, in turn, were no doubt much perplexed by Frost's posture. It was not only that he seemed to be trying to deflect the movement from its insurrectionary course but that he was doing so in public, even to the extent of speaking openly of the organisation into sections. It became imperative to subject Frost to the revolutionary discipline. Immediately after the Blaina meeting the rebel leaders assembled privately at the King Crispin beershop near Brynmawr. Their deliberations lasted into the early hours of the morning of 4 October.[19] We may be reasonably sure that Frost was there, and that it was the episode he referred to when he was interviewed in Monmouth Gaol on 1 December. 'What was I to do?' he asked. 'I went up the mountains a few months ago; on that occasion the men surrounded me and said, "Mr. Frost, if you will not lead us, neither you nor your family shall live in Newport; we are beginning to suspect you".'[20]

The workers' leaders were unlikely to have been interested in Frost's ambition to represent them in a Parliament whose authority they were seeking to reject. Nevertheless, they needed to have Frost with them for he and he alone was in contact with revolutionary groups in England. Frost, moreover, possessed a kind of experience otherwise lacking in the rebel leadership. He had served in local government as town councillor, magistrate, Poor Law guardian and Mayor, and he had not only been the one active Welsh delegate in the General Convention of the Industrious Classes but had been elected president of that body's final session. He was, in other words, seen as having the qualities that would make him a very acceptable president of the workers' commonwealth, and subsequently he was indeed cast in just that role.[21]

We may be reasonably sure that Frost, whether persuaded by the blandishments or the threats of the rebel leaders, committed himself to their cause at the Brynmawr meeting of 3-4 October. At that time he had already accepted an engagement to attend a dinner at Bury in Lancashire on 14 October. It was to honour the Bury delegate to the Convention, Dr Matthew Fletcher.[22] We may also be reasonably sure that Frost was encouraged to fulfil the engagement, and to use the occasion to ensure that his associates in the north of England and Scotland were making preparations to rise whenever the Welshmen did. On 8 October Frost penned a letter to the *Western Vindicator* in which, perhaps to confuse the authorities, he announced that he would visit Merthyr and Pontypool.[23] In fact he must have left south Wales for Manchester a day or so later.

In the weeks after the dissolution of the Convention the closest associates of Frost — Bussey, Burns and Taylor, if we accept Ashton's testimony — had taken their commitment to an armed uprising with varying degrees of seriousness. Burns had returned to Dundee, where moderation prevailed among the chartists; there he adopted the rather ambiguous stance that the people should never threaten violence unless they were prepared to use it.[24] Taylor had remained in hiding in London, for a warrant for his arrest had been issued, and he claimed to have been virtually incommunicado in the period.[25] Only Bussey appears to have appreciated the gravity of the situation. He attended a meeting of delegates from the West Riding of Yorkshire at Heckmondwick on 30 September. According to Lovett, Bussey informed the assembly that the Welshmen were preparing to rise. Several present thought it premature, but the majority expressed a determination to come out in support.[26] Bussey himself, however, seems already to have had grave reservations about the enterprise. William Ashton had travelled north with him from London earlier in September and from their conversation had become convinced that, when it came to the point, Bussey would renege on his agreement with Frost. Ashton's forebodings were so strong that he decided to sit out the events in France. Before taking a steamer from Hull, however, he informed William Hill of his fears: 'that Frost was, to his certain knowledge, engaged upon a dangerous enterprise, and that he had good means of knowing that he was in danger of being sold by some of those with whom he was associated'.[27] Ashton charged Hill, who was editor of the *Northern Star*, with getting a warning to Frost through Feargus O'Connor. Hill failed to do so; he said that O'Connor was in Ireland, that he did not know Frost's address, and that in any case he would not entrust so dangerous a communication to the mails.[28]

Of these matters Frost knew nothing when he arrived in Manchester in the second week of October. He anticipated meeting John Taylor there but the doctor, although scheduled to attend the Bury dinner, did not turn up.[29] William Burns of Dundee did. Bussey was apparently not expected in Manchester, but Frost had arranged to visit Yorkshire the next week. Indeed, he and Bussey were billed to appear in Halifax on 21 October.[30] In fact Frost fulfilled his engagements at neither Bury nor Halifax. A courier from Wales caught up with him in Manchester.[31] The information he brought was that the Welsh directorate had taken a firm decision to call their men out at the beginning of November, and that Frost should return to south Wales immediately.

We do not know when the directorate met to make final the date of the rising, through it must have been within a day or two either side of 10 October. Zephaniah Williams referred to the occasion but gave no date. 'As soon as the day was agreed, and fixed upon for the attack', he wrote, 'Messages were despatched to the North of Wales with the information, also the North of England, from thence Despatches were to be sent to Scotland.'[32] Feargus O'Connor, who was in Ireland at the time, subsequently obtained an account of Frost's hasty departure home. 'A pack of the most reckless, cowardly, and blood-thirsty scoundrels that ever lived', he wrote, referring to what can only have been the directorate in south Wales,

constituted the 'Central Board', who had so far assumed to themselves all power and control over Frost's person as to send a delegate post-haste from London to Bury, where he [Frost] was to have attended a public dinner, to order him to proceed forthwith to Wales.[33]

Frost did indeed leave Lancashire with little delay. Burns must already have been in Manchester, for Frost was able to give him the news. On his way back to Dundee Burns called on Robert Lowery in Newcastle, and told him of the imminence of a rising. He betrayed none of the details of the plan, however, but he did assure Lowery that O'Connor was not involved ('for they did not think he was to be trusted').[34] Frost had not seen Bussey, but it seems clear that he sent the Welsh courier on to Bradford to put the Yorkshireman in the picture. For reasons which will become apparent below, an informed guess may be made that the courier was Charles Jones of Welshpool. A warrant for his arrest had been issued early in May 1839, after the uprising in the mid-Wales town of Llanidloes, but he had evaded capture. Like many others of those involved, he probably went into hiding in south Wales. If O'Connor was right that he travelled to Lancashire via London, it must have been because the alternative route through Birmingham was considered unsafe; certainly a hue and cry for him had earlier been raised in that town.[35]

Frost also passed through London on his return from Manchester to Newport. He probably hoped to contact Taylor there. Apparently he failed to do so. He did see his close friend, Henry Hetherington, and a remark he made passed into the lore of the chartists. 'I am', Frost said, 'a doomed man.'[36] Frost must indeed have felt the gravest presentiments of disaster. He had assured the Welshmen that there were English and Scots leaders committed to the armed struggle and, even if against his better judgement, had agreed to act as a go-between. By mid-October Frost must have known that there was little chance that any of the English or Scots leaders could bring out significant numbers of men by 3 November. He cannot have relished taking the one course of action that seemed open to him: that of making a break with the directorate whose members he had encouraged in their resolve to take to arms.

Frost was back in Newport by 19 October, for on that day he wrote to one of the town's magistrates, probably the Rev. James Coles. It was as if Frost felt a need to establish the continuity of his current position with the one he had held prior to the Brynmawr meeting, for in the letter he stressed how he had been trying to calm the ironworkers and colliers when he addressed them in Blaina and Blackwood in the first week of October.[37] Three days later he penned a communication to the *Western Vindicator*. It was an address to 'The Farmers and Tradesmen of Monmouthshire', and clearly Frost was attempting to restate the tenets of the political struggle. 'What', he asked, 'is it which has rendered the labouring classes of this country so discontented? What has produced that deep and powerful feeling which a spark would now ignite from one end of the country to the other?' His answer was a ringing indictment of bourgeois society:

> Their labour is taken from them by means of the law; it is given to a set of idle and dissolute men and women; those who produce not, are clothed in purple and fine linen, and fare sumptuously every day, while the labourer is fed with the crumbs which fall from the table of the rich.

Frost went on to make an indirect plea for the release of the political prisoners in Monmouth, for he continued to believe that their incarceration was one of the principal causes of unrest in south Wales:

> The French people, previously to the revolution, were led by some of the most benevolent men in the world; they sought for a change in the most oppressive laws that ever existed. The government fancied that if it could destroy the leaders, that all would be well. In many instances it succeeded; and what was the consequence? Leaders ten times more violent.[38]

This was all very stirring: an honest and indeed bold statement of a radical position. Frost had, however, to convince not the farmers and tradesmen but the ironworkers and colliers that their cause should, after all, be prosecuted through political and not armed struggle. Frost needed an ally within the directorate, and he looked to Dr William Price of Pontypridd. He calculated that Price might take a rather more detached view of the situation than most of the rebel leaders, for the doctor was himself of middle-class background, had been a student in London, and on one of his subsequent visits to that city was introduced by Frost to the delegates at the General Convention.[39] Yet Frost was taking a gamble, for in joining the directorate at the beginning of October he had effectively displaced Price from the titular leadership of the movement. On 26 October Frost sent a messenger, Isaac Morgan, to Price to suggest a meeting in Newport the following morning.

Price turned up. Frost asked him if he intended bringing his men out. Price asked to see the full plans for the rising. Frost said that he did not have them; they were in Etheridge's printing office. Price stated that he would not move until he knew exactly what was intended, and who was to be killed. 'What', said Frost, 'do you want us to kill the soldiers – kill a thousand of them in one night?' Yes, Price answered, 'a hundred thousand, if it is necessary'. Clearly, if Price's recollections are to be trusted, the meeting was not going the way Frost had hoped. 'Dear me', said Frost, 'I cannot do it, I cannot do it', and he cried like a child, so Price reported, and spoke of heaven and hell. Price cursed him, and put his own position very clearly: 'You shall not put a sword in my hand and a rope round my neck at the same time. If I take a sword in my hand I will use it, and no one shall take it from me but at the cost of my life.'[40] Price probably represented Frost's anguish accurately enough for a little over a month later, from a cell in Monmouth Gaol, Frost was to confess, 'I was not the man for such an undertaking.'[41] But Price seems scarcely to have given Frost the chance to explain the dilemma he was in. The doctor was extremely suspicious of Frost and believed that he had someone concealed in the room listening to the whole conversation. The gist of what was said, Price claimed, was subsequently relayed to one of the Newport magistrates, the Rev. James Coles.

There was a meeting of the rebel directorate at Dukestown the next day, the 28th. Frost, apparently, did not attend.[42] Perhaps Price communicated his suspicions of Frost to the members, but the proceedings were not made public and we cannot be sure. Certainly, however, the delegates felt some action was called for. A deputation of workers from the hills visited Frost in Newport. They told him, so report had it, 'that they began to doubt his sincerity or courage, and as they were determined to put it to the test, they would insist on his joining them at once and making preparations for an immediate attack'. One can only guess at Frost's agony, but it was perhaps as much out of fear as conviction that he agreed to accompany the men back to the hills. Their invitation was obviously a pressing one. Frost's family was apparently not at home, but such was the urgency of the moment that he 'left a message at his house that if he did not return by a certain day, they might know what would happen'.[43] The confrontation must have occurred on 31 October, for Frost did indeed take up his residence in Blackwood on that day and attended a meeting of the directorate held there on the next.[44] Once again proletarian discipline had prevailed.

More light is shed on the episode by a somewhat curious report that appeared in the *Western Vindicator*. It was written on 12 November, putatively by Henry Vincent from Monmouth Gaol, though the real identity of the author became a matter of concern even in the Home Office.[45] Since it was impermissible for the *Vindicator* to carry news, the report was cast in the form of a dream-narrative. Its ultimate source must have been someone who was present at the meeting of the delegation of workers with Frost on 31 October. 'Moral means', said a tall man (of most commanding aspect),

> have failed to produce any effect on our hard and callous-hearted rulers — by physical means are our friends [that is, the Monmouth political prisoners] withheld from us — by physical means they shall be restored to us again. Your fears of the utility of this step will avail nothing. We are determined. Our desire for liberty shall not now be quenched. You have your option, to go with us or desert us. That you will not do the latter we are confident, for you are our best friend. Look at our numbers, and no longer tell us we are premature and ill-prepared . . .

The others present signalled their support of the speaker. Frost's resolve crumbled. Whatever thoughts he had of Bussey and Burns and Taylor, and their lack of preparation, must have been put aside. 'Men of Wales', Frost replied,

> the same spirit which in former times animated your forefathers, I find exists among you. That the government would drive you to this I have long feared; but I have ever advised you to be peaceable, hoping, vainly hoping, that your rulers would be induced to listen to your prayers. They have not done so. I cannot dispute that you have tried every means possible. Let the dread sequel then take its course. If you are determined, 'twould be vain of me to advise. I am content.[46]

Frost was to remain at Blackwood until he entered Newport with the rebel columns on the morning of 4 November. To the bitter end William Price maintained that Frost was trying to abort the attack, delaying the advance on the town in order to give the authorities there time to put it in a state of defence.[47] But this seems hardly borne out by the facts. Once securely in the embrace of the insurgents, Frost appears to have been swept along by the revolutionary impulse. He addressed the Blackwood colliers on 2 November, and urged that 'the Gentlemen they were under should be brought there and put in the dungeon to work where they were — and be made to work for the same wages and pay the same taxes as they did and see how they liked it'.[48] It was scarcely the speech of a man shrinking back from a position he had adopted however reluctantly. Indeed, it is somewhat ironical to find that Frost's detractors were later to accuse him of falsely raising the morale of the rebels by referring to imaginary letters from the soldiers in Newport stating that they would not open fire on the workers; from leaders in England asserting that they were ready to rise; and (quite unbelievably) from Lord Anglesey, agreeing to support the movement![49]

While these changes had been taking place in south Wales, events in the north of England had followed a logic of their own. The Welsh courier who Frost had sent from Manchester to Bradford must have made contact with Peter Bussey on or about 15 October. The York-shireman took immediate steps to summon John Taylor from London. The courier he sent was unquestionably Charles Jones of Welshpool, and it is difficult to believe that he was not the very person who Frost had despatched to Bussey from Lancashire. Again probably to lessen the risk of detection, Jones opted to travel to London by steamer from, it must be assumed, Hull. Unfortunately the steamer was wrecked, and it took Jones well over a week to reach the capital. Through the good offices of Henry Hetherington he made contact with Taylor on 29 October, informed him of the date of the Welsh rising, and asked him to go to Bradford immediately. Taylor left London in great haste, but not before he had written a letter to Frost to say that he would be at his post but that he was astonished not to have been given earlier warning of the plan to rise.[50]

In the meantime Bussey had realised that he could not bring out his men by early November. He despatched a messenger of his own to south Wales to ask that the rising be postponed for ten days.[51] The messenger reached Newport on 2 November, and was taken to see Frost in Blackwood. He was, according to William Davies who escorted him there from Newport, a tall, young working man.[52] Lovett confused him with the courier to London, Charles Jones, but otherwise probably reported his reception in Blackwood quite accurately. Frost said that the directorate had set the rising in motion the previous day and that he, Frost, 'might as well blow his own brains out as to try to oppose them or shrink back'.[53] The messenger returned to Newport the same day, and on 3 November started his journey back to Bradford via Monmouth, Worcester and Birmingham.[54] The episode, however, had another and rather curious aspect to it. Whoever his contacts in Birmingham were, Bussey's messenger entrusted them with information about his mission. Presumably unknown to him, they were converted Urquhartites, and they passed the information on to George Fyler in London. He, in turn, with David Urquhart's approval, communicated it to Lord Melbourne, the Prime Minister. The messenger, Fyler wrote, had passed south through Birmingham on 31 October, and north on 3 November. With the request for the postponement of the rising he also carried the cryptic statement,

> I hunt in the mountains of Scotland, on Sunday or Monday, but if the hounds wont hunt there, I shall hunt on Monday or Tuesday in Yorkshire; and if the hounds shall fail me there, I shall proceed immediately to join your pack.[55]

Clearly the allusion was to projected attempts to mobilise the men of Scotland and the north of England in the week of the Welsh rising, though whether the message emanated from Bussey or from another of the northern leaders can no longer be determined.

John Taylor arrived in Bradford from London perhaps late on 30 October or early the next day. Bussey confirmed the date of the Welsh rising, said that he had sent a messenger to Frost to request more time, asked Taylor to proceed to Newcastle or Carlisle to organise the men there, and said that he would inform Taylor about the date as soon as the messenger arrived back from south Wales. Taylor then proceeded to Newcastle, put the local leaders into the picture, and busied himself, as he wrote, 'preparing my men for some move without telling them what'. News of the failure of the attack on Newport reached him before any message had arrived from Bussey.[56]

Taylor's account of the situation in Newcastle is compatible with that given by Thomas Devyr, sub-editor of the *Northern Liberator*. Devyr said that the Newcastle men were expecting news to reach them through Birmingham, but that it was only with the arrival of *The Times* for 5 November that they knew that the Welshmen had taken to arms. On the strength of the earliest reports in *The Times*, placards were put up in Newcastle: 'The hour of British Freedom has struck! John Frost is in possession of South Wales at the head of 30,000 men!' Delegates from 65 districts around Newcastle rapidly assembled to await further news from Wales, but dispersed just as rapidly when it became known that the attack on Newport had failed.[57]

In Dundee William Burns was, if that was possible, even more out of touch. Taylor had written to him from Newcastle to say, cryptically, that he had arrived there from London 'to give lectures on Chemistry, explaining the nature of explosive forces', and that he wanted Burns to go to Newcastle to assist him. Burns once again consulted Robert Lowery, who happened to be in Dundee. He told Lowery that he knew 'something was to take place soon in Wales', and asked his advice on what to do. The next day news of the events in Newport reached Dundee and Burns went into hiding.[58]

Taylor and Burns had both been awaiting word from Bussey, though it is unlikely that they could have organised more than token outbreaks even had the date of the Welsh rising been put back by ten days. Bussey, in turn, awaited the return of his messenger from south Wales. There was considerable activity in the Bradford district, however. A full study of the topic is needed, for it has been shown that a certain urgency was felt; there was talk of attacking barracks on 3 November, and many were busily engaged in casting bullets.[59] But large numbers of regular soldiers were deployed in the north of England and their commander, Major General Charles Napier, boasted that they constituted the 'largest force in England'. On 1 September he had referred to the 'Chartist steam' and predicted that 'it will be up again in two months or more, when dark nights begin and work slacks', and presumably he held his troops in readiness as those dark nights set in.[60] Be that as it may, Bussey decided that, whatever the news from Wales, it was impossible to have the Yorkshiremen under arms by early November. On 1 November, claiming to be ill, he sent George White of Leeds around the West Riding towns to say that the rising had been put off.[61] His messenger probably arrived back from south Wales on 4 or 5 November, to report that the Welshmen would by then have risen. Some steps were taken to revive the Yorkshire movement and bring the men out the following weekend, but then news of the disaster in Newport arrived. All plans were cancelled and Bussey himself went into hiding.[62] There were to be no risings in Scotland or the north of England, or for that matter anywhere else, to synchronise with the Welsh one.

Zephaniah Williams claimed that all he knew of the preparations being made in England, or of the English leaders, came either from Frost or from one of the Welsh messengers 'after he had returned from there giving them the intelligence of our preparations and the fixed time'. From their reports Williams understood that 'there was every preparation possible making — particularly London, Bath, Yorkshire and Lancashire where they were strong and courageous'.[63] The messenger in question may have been Charles Jones for, if he returned to south Wales after seeing Taylor in London on 29 October, the information he carried was indeed that Taylor and Bussey both were 'strong and courageous'. The fast coaches from London took only 26 hours to reach London, so Jones may have reported to Frost before the meeting of delegates held at Blackwood on 1 November. If so, Jones was sent back to London almost immediately, for he was there on 6 November when he made known his belief that the Yorkshire men had either risen or were about to rise.[64]

It is necessary at this point to recapitulate briefly, and attend more closely to the unfolding plans for the rising. We have argued that Frost committed himself to the armed struggle at the Brynmawr meeting of 3-4 October, but that the firm decision to rise at the beginning of November was taken when he was away in the north of England. Returning to south Wales, he tried to distance himself from the rebel leadership and did not attend the meeting of the council at Dukestown on 28 October. It was, however, at this meeting that delegates from all over the coalfield agreed upon the final (or so they assumed) plan of campaign. Abergavenny, Brecon, Cardiff, Newport and Usk were to be occupied simultaneously. The men were to be mobilised on the Sunday and Monday, and to go into action on Tuesday, 5 November.[65] Undoubtedly the fact that 5 November was Guy Fawkes' day dictated its choice. The ancient festival of Hallow-e'en had merged into the commemoration of the Gunpowder Plot to produce a veritable saturnalia. 'It was always a scene of much riot and confusion', it was remarked specifically of Newport, where a winter fair also added its quota to the excitement. The streets were taken over by bands of persons who might violently assault the policemen during the brief regime of licence.[66]

The rebel leaders responsible for operations in the eastern sector of the coalfield set up their headquarters at Blackwood on 30 October. Among others, Zephaniah Williams and William Lloyd Jones arrived there that day and Frost the next, after the deputation of workers had confronted him in Newport.[67] Frost, then, was present at the rebel council held in Blackwood on 1 November. It was attended by delegates from most if not all the lodges in the Heads of the Valleys, Blackwood and Pontypool districts, but the Merthyr district was represented only by Dowlais, and Dr William Price apparently did not attend.[68] Frost addressed the members on the state of affairs in England and spoke optimistically of Trowbridge and other places in the west country being ready to rise. He also put forward, perhaps for the first time, his plan to stop all the coaches leaving south Wales. The failure of the Irish and Welsh mails to reach their various destinations in England, he suggested, would be a signal for the risings there.[69] Most remarkably, the delegates were persuaded to abandon the plan of attacking the Usk towns and Cardiff simultaneously.

Frost said, according to Zephaniah Williams, 'let me have two thousand armed men and Z[ephaniah] W[illiams] with them, and we will accomplish Our object with little trouble and as for Brecon and Abergavenny we will afterwards soon secure them'.[70] Frost's intention was not to cancel other operations but rather to bring the occupation of Newport forward by a day. Mayor Thomas Phillips had learned of the rebels' change of plan by the 3rd. 'It has come to my knowledge', he wrote to his opposite number in Monmouth, 'that they have planned a general rising which is immediately to take place tonight, tomorrow night, and Tuesday night having been respectively named as the periods of attack.'[71] Tuesday, a reporter in Newport learned, 'was the original day, but it was afterwards altered to Monday'.[72]

That Frost was able to persuade the delegates at Blackwood to accept the revised plan suggests that at least some of his reasons were cogent ones. We can be reasonably sure what they were. First, Frost doubted whether the rebel sections in and around Newport, though supported by the colliers from Blackwood, were sufficient to take and hold Newport. He wanted to throw into the attack the men from the Heads of the Valleys and the Pontypool districts even if they had to be almost immediately redeployed in other sectors. Second, Frost was apprehensive — and rightly so, as it turned out — that Newport would be put into a state of defence before the attack was launched, for his connections there were so extensive that he must have known that leaks had occurred. (It will be recollected that on 30 October the president of the Newport Oddfellows had been informed of the imminence of the rising.) And third, Frost may also have had it in mind that the soldiers tended to drink heavily on Sunday nights at taverns throughout the town,[73] and that the large winter fair that was to open there on Monday might make the authorities less sensitive than usual to the rising excitement of the citizenry.[74]

Some 25 lodges were represented at the Blackwood meeting and estimates of the number of delegates present vary from 30 to 50. John Reynolds, the preacher-haulier, presided. If there was opposition to Frost's revised plan we know nothing of it. 'At that meeting', wrote Devyr (who wrongly thought that it had been held in Merthyr), 'the delegates of three sections of country arranged to advance on Newport, the nearest military station, on the night of the 3d.'[75] We have seen that the number of pikemen and gunmen were tallied and those ready to fight reckoned at about 5,000 (Chapter 7). All those impressed, it was agreed, should be required to find arms; if they could not procure pikes or guns then they should turn out with mandrils, bludgeons or whatever. The men should proceed to the rendezvous in their sections and then accept the orders of those appointed to lead the attack. A rendezvous at Abercarn in the Ebbw Valley was suggested, but rejected as too inconvenient for the Pontypool men. Risca was chosen instead. The men from the Heads of the Valleys were to operate as an integrated division, and link up with the men from the Blackwood district at Risca around midnight. A junction with the Pontypool men would then be effected at the Cefn, near Newport.[76] The delegates were empowered to start mobilising their lodge members immediately, but not to make known until Sunday the fact that Newport was to be the first target.

The meeting of the directorate ended at about 5 p.m. and the delegates dispersed. Lewis Rowland, secretary at Maes-y-cwmer and Gellideg, had convened a meeting of his lodge by 8 p.m. the same evening. Some 40 attended. 'I have news today – we must all provide arms', he announced, and asked all those who were prepared to move to raise their hands. Lists were compiled. The soldiers will all lay down weapons, he assured the men. Jacob Thomas, a shopkeeper, was present. He was a sympathiser but not a member. Why, he had the temerity to ask Rowland, were arms needed? 'Such things are wanted to meet such like you', he was told; 'if a poor man was to get £5 of goods of you, you would arrest him immediately unless he paid you.'[77]

Lewis Rowland was unusually zealous. Most of the delegates set to work the next day, the 2nd. The Argoed lodge, for example, was assembled at William Williams's beerhouse on Saturday night. Names were called out by sections and the captains were required to stay at the lodge overnight. One, George Beach, urged everyone to procure arms by the next day. William Edmunds, blacksmith and preacher, paid the large sum of 10s to the lodge to buy himself out; he was, he said, a man of peace, but he had been told he might be killed if he did not show support. The men met by sections on Sunday morning, and reassembled at the lodge, about 100 strong, in the afternoon. George Reed, a shoemaker, had been sent by Frost to address them. He explained the plan of action in detail. They were going to march on Newport that night, stop the mail and other coaches, and seize all the arms there. They would then remain in Newport to help guard the town.[78] At Croespenmaen lodge things did not proceed quite so smoothly. The lodge was convened on Saturday evening and the septuagenarian David Stephens took the chair. He said that the men should choose captains over each ten of them; that they should all procure arms; and that they would soon be called upon. He was, he added, under oath not to reveal further details at that time. Many of the men refused to commit themselves in such

circumstances, however, and the meeting broke up in some disarray.[79]
The *Silurian* reported the rush to join the movement on the eve of the
rising:

> On Saturday, great numbers were induced, through fear, to attend at
> the different lodges, when the price of the Chartist cards was
> enhanced to half-a-crown [2s 6d], and to such an extent were the
> fears of the workmen wrought upon, that it is said upwards of three
> hundred from one Iron Work, paid their half-crowns on that night,
> and were informed of the intended operations of the party.[80]

A rush there certainly was, but the new recruits were not as unwilling
to join as the report implies. In Blaina, for example, Zephaniah Williams
and his son Llewellyn were busy throughout Saturday enrolling late-
comers and assigning them to sections. Zephaniah Williams spoke of the
parties of soldiers in Wales and said that they were insufficient in
numbers to stand up to the workers. Section captains like Isaac Tippins
took the men into the lodge room to pay 1s for a pike; others like
Thomas Farraday (whose brother William was to die in the fighting)
helped arrange loans for those who wished to purchase guns. Williams
said that he would announce the plans the next day and refused to issue
the weapons until then lest the men should get drunk and behave fool-
ishly.[81]

At the Brynmawr lodge Ishmael Evans, a patchman, and David Lewis
('King Crispin'), also swore in many new members on Saturday. There
would be a 'rise' the next day, Evans told the members, but the destin-
ation could not be revealed until then. There would also be risings in
other parts of Wales and in England. Everyone should procure arms.
The soldiers would be no problem; no harm should be done to any but
the officers and sergeants, who must be killed. Lewis reiterated the
points. 'All must go, rich and poor . . . Nothing but the sea could stop
them . . . If we win, we win, if not we shall be slaves and transports for
life.' A number of guns were distributed. We have good marksmen,
Lewis added, who will pick off the officers, soldiers and 'rulers' (presumably the magistrates); then the rest of the soldiers will change
sides.[82] When Peter Bussey's messenger arrived in Blackwood from
Bradford late on Saturday to ask that the rising be postponed for ten
days, it is quite apparent why Frost could only reply that he might as
well shoot himself as try to hold back his men.

## Notes

1. For Frost's role in the Convention, see David Williams, *John Frost. A Study in Chartism* (Cardiff, 1939), Chs. 5 and 6.
2. A.R. Schoyen, *The Chartist Challenge. A Portrait of George Julian Harney* (London, 1958), p. 87.
3. [A. Somerville], *The Autobiography of a Working Man* (London, 1848), pp. 422-3. A Somerville, *Cobdenic Policy. The Internal Enemy of England* (London, 1854), pp. 28-30.
4. George Crawshay, 'The Chartist Correspondence', *Free Press Serials*, Sheffield, XIII [1856], pp. 1-2, letter dd. London, 22 Sept. 1839, and pp. 11-12, Narrative by Mr. Fyler, of the same date. For the fate of the letter, see pp. 2-6, various communications. George Crawshay of Gateshead was the youngest son of William Crawshay (died 1834) of Cyfarthfa. It is unclear how the documents came into Crawshay's hands.
5. Peter Brock, 'Polish Democrats and English Radicals 1832-1862', in *The Journal of Modern History*, XXV, 2 (June 1953), pp. 146-7. Schoyen, *Chartist Challenge*, p. 62.
6. Crawshay, 'Chartist Correspondence', p. 3, Mr Ross, of Bladensburg, on the chartist organisation. [D. Urquhart], 'Chartism; a Historical Retrospect', in *The Diplomatic Review*, XXI, 3 (July 1873), pp. 222-4. Urquhart made his view widely known. Beniowski was treated very roughly by his fellow exiles at a meeting of the Friends of Poland in London on 29 Nov. 1839, but the chartists present supported him, see *Morning Chronicle*, 30 Nov. 1839.
7. *The Times*, 18 Nov. 1839, reporting Commissioner of Police, Birmingham, to Mayor Hawkins of Newport, 13 Nov.
8. *Monmouthshire Merlin* (henceforth *Merlin*), 16 Nov. 1839. PRO, HO.40/45: Mayor Hawkins to Home Office dd. 16 Nov. 1839.
9. For a fuller discussion of this matter, see Williams, *John Frost*, pp. 246-50.
10. Somerville, *Autobiography*, p. 423. Somerville, *Cobdenic Policy*, pp. 29-30.
11. W.E. Adams, *Memoirs of a Social Atom* (London, 1903), p. 196.
12. William Lovett, *The Life and Struggles of William Lovett in his Pursuit of Bread, Knowledge and Freedom* (London, 1876), pp. 238-41.
13. *National Reformer*, 19 April 1845. Ashton referred only to F–, B–, T– and B–. The identifications are those made by Feargus O'Connor, *Northern Star*, 3 May 1845.
14. We shall argue that the date of the Welsh rising was originally set for 5 November, and that the decision to muster on the 3rd and attack Newport the next morning was not taken until 1 November.
15. Joseph and Thomas Gurney, *The Trial of John Frost, for High Treason* (London, 1840), pp. 515-16.
16. *Western Vindicator*, 5 Oct. 1839.
17. *Merthyr Guardian*, 19 Oct. 1839. Newport Public Library, Chartist Trials 1838-1840, 24 vols (henceforth Newport Examinations), V, doc. 670: evidence of Job Tovey.
18. *Merthyr Guardian*, 19 Oct. 1839.
19. Idem.
20. *Shrewsbury News and Cambrian Reporter*, 7 Dec. 1839.
21. A proclamation was said to exist naming Frost President of, oddly enough, 'the Executive Government of England', Newport Examinations, XI, doc. 401: evidence of James Emery. Just after the rising a letter arrived in Monmouth addressed to 'His Mightiness John Frost, Lord Protector of South Wales', *Merlin*, 16 Nov. 1839. Clearly some clarification in the matter of title would have become

necessary!

22. *Northern Star*, 28 Sept. 1839.

23. Williams, *John Frost*, p. 198.

24. Alexander Wilson, *The Chartist Movement in Scotland* (Manchester, 1970), pp. 103-4.

25. Birmingham Central Libraries, Lovett Collection, II, doc. 211: enclosure in Taylor to Lovett, dd. 10 June 1841. *Northern Star*, 19 Oct. 1839.

26. Lovett, *Life and Struggles*, pp. 238-9.

27. *National Reformer*, 19 and 26 April 1845. *Northern Star*, 3 May 1845.

28. *National Reformer*, 10 May 1845. *Northern Star*, 17 May 1845. For a useful discussion of Bussey's activities, see A.J. Peacock, *Bradford Chartism 1838-1840* (York, 1969), pp. 28-34.

29. *Northern Star*, 28 Sept. 1839.

30. Ibid., 19 Oct. 1839.

31. Frost explained his failure to appear at the Bury dinner on the grounds that he was detained in Manchester, idem.

32. National Library of Wales, Tredegar Park Muniments, Box 40, doc. 2: Zephaniah Williams to A. McKechnie, dd. 25 May 1840.

33. *Northern Star*, 3 May 1845.

34. [Robert Lowery], 'Passages in the Life of a Temperance Lecturer', see B. Harrison and P. Hollis (eds.), *Robert Lowery. Radical and Chartist* (London, 1979), p. 155.

35. Williams, *John Frost*, pp. 156-8.

36. Repeated by Feargus O'Connor, *Northern Star*, 3 May 1845.

37. *Charter*, 8 Dec. 1839.

38. *Western Vindicator*, 26 Oct. 1839.

39. Lovett Collection, cited above, II, doc. 211: enclosure in Taylor to Lovett, dd. 10 June 1841.

40. Ap Id Anfryn [Gwilym Hughes], *The Late Dr Price (of Llantrisant). The Famous Arch-Druid* (Cardiff, 1896), pp. 10-12.

41. *Shrewsbury News and Cambrian Reporter*, 7 Dec. 1839.

42. *Silurian*, 16 Nov. 1839.

43. *Morning Chronicle*, 19 Nov. 1839: report from Newport dd. 16 Nov.

44. Newport Examinations, V, doc. 599: evidence of Richard Pugh; V, doc. 670: evidence of Job Tovey; IV, docs. 383-5: evidence of William Davies.

45. PRO, HO.41/15: S. M. Phillipps to Visiting Justices, Monmouth Gaol dd. 23 Nov. 1839.

46. *Western Vindicator*, 16 Nov. 1839.

47. Ap Id Anfryn, *The Late Dr Price*, p. 11.

48. Newport Examinations, XII, doc. 624, and PRO, TS.11/496: evidence of Moses Scard, citing Thomas Llewellyn, miner, Fleur-de-lis.

49. *Silurian*, 16 Nov. 1839. *Morning Chronicle*, 19 Nov. 1839.

50. Lovett Collection, cited above, II, doc. 211. PRO, HO.40/44: Robert J. Edwards to Normanby, dd. 6 Nov. 1839. Edwards was in service in Hetherington's house and sent information directly to the Home Office.

51. Idem.

52. Newport Examinations, IV, docs. 383-5: evidence of William Davies; V, doc. 670 evidence of Richard Pugh.

53. Lovett, *Life and Struggles*, pp. 238-41.

54. W.N. Johns, *The Chartist Riots at Newport*, 2nd edn (Newport, 1889), p. 34. A direct coach from Newport to Birmingham, put into service soon after the rising, was able to complete the journey in eleven hours, see *Merlin*, 14 Dec. 1839.

55. Crawshay, *Chartist Correspondence*, p. 2: letters to Melbourne and Normanby dd. 10 and 11 Nov. 1839.

56. Lovett Collection, cited above, II, doc. 211.
57. Thomas Ainge Devyr, *The Odd Book of the Nineteenth Century* (Greenpoint, New York, 1882), pp. 194-6.
58. Lowery, *Passages*, pp. 155-6.
59. Peacock, *Bradford Chartism*, p. 33.
60. W. Napier, *The Life and Opinions of General Sir Charles Napier, G.C.B.*, 2nd edn (London, 1857), II, pp. 82, 88.
61. Lovett Collection, cited above, II, doc. 211. Taylor, Lovett and others believed that White had been sent round Yorkshire by Feargus O'Connor. This cannot have been so, see Peacock, *Bradford Chartism*, pp. 32-3.
62. Peacock, *Bradford Chartism*, pp. 34, 48-9. Peacock probably misreads Taylor's evidence on this matter.
63. Williams to McKechnie, dd. 25 May 1840, cited above.
64. PRO, HO.40/44: R.J. Edwards to Normanby, dd. 6 November 1839.
65. *Cambrian*, 9 Nov. 1839, from a correspondent in Cardiff, 6 Nov. *Hereford Times*, 9 Nov. 1839. *The Times*, 26 Dec. 1839.
66. *Merlin*, 11 Nov. 1837. W.N. Johns, *The Chartist Riots at Newport*, 2nd edn (Newport, 1889), p. 34.
67. Newport Examinations, IV, docs. 383-5: evidence of William Davies; V, docs. 599, 670: evidence of Richard Pugh and Job Tovey.
68. Dr.William Price was apparently in Blackwood earlier in the day but did not attend the meeting. Newport Examinations, V, doc. 601: evidence of Richard Pugh.
69. Newport Examinations, IV, docs. 383-5: evidence of William Davies; IV, doc. 436: evidence of James Harford; IV, doc. 466: evidence of James Hodge. At Frost's trial defence counsel tried to demonstrate the infeasibility of the plan, see Williams, *John Frost*, pp. 278-9. Williams tended to accept counsel's arguments. Chief Justice Tindal, however, summed up the matter very astutely, see Gurney and Gurney, *Trial of John Frost*, pp. 755-7. The Milford Haven-London Royal Mail coaches passed through Newport daily, but mail coaches also plied other routes, for example, from Merthyr to Abergavenny.
70. Williams to McKechnie, dd. 25 May 1840, cited above.
71. PRO, TS.11/500: Phillips to Dyke, dd. Newport, 3 Nov. 1839.
72. *Hereford Times*, 9 Nov. 1839: report from Newport dd. 5 Nov. [E. Dowling], *The Rise and Fall of Chartism in Monmouthshire* (London, 1840), p. 39, put it just the wrong way round; 'the "rise" ', he wrote, 'was to have taken place on the preceding [i.e. succeeding] Tuesday, but was deferred [i.e. brought forward] till Sunday night, or early on Monday morning.'
73. Williams to McKechnie, dd. 25 May 1840, cited above. Williams offers this to explain the choice of Sunday night. His remarks are, however, inconsequential and we have to assume that he referred to the revised and not the original plan.
74. 'Lord' George Sanger, *Seventy Years a Showman* (London, edn of 1938), pp. 32-7. Sanger's memory played him tricks; he thought that the rising had occurred at Whitsuntide.
75. Devyr, *Odd Book*, p. 194. An Irishman living in Newcastle-on-Tyne might not seem a good witness, but in America Devyr had become acquainted with John Rees (Jack the Fifer).
76. Newport Examinations, IV, docs. 383-4: evidence of William Davies; V. docs. 668-70: evidence of Job Tovey; V, doc. 672: evidence of Susanna Tovey.
77. Ibid., XIV, docs. 526, 651: evidence of Lewis Lewis and Jacob Thomas.
78. *The Times*, 7 Nov. 1839. Gurney and Gurney, *Trial*, pp. 265-92: evidence of Matthew Williams. *Morning Chronicle*, 30 Nov. 1839: evidence of Joseph Coles. Newport Examinations, VII, unnumbered doc: defence of Joseph Coles; XIV,

doc. 394: evidence of William Edmunds.
  79. Ibid., XV, doc. 569: evidence of Thomas Morgan and Herbert Davies. See also *Merlin*, 28 March and 4 April 1840.
  80. *Silurian*, 16 Nov. 1839.
  81. Newport Examinations, XV, docs. 342-3: evidence of Thomas Bowen; doc. 479: evidence of Benjamin Davies.
  82. *Silurian*, 28 March 1840. *Cambrian*, 4 April 1840.

# 10 THE 'RISE': THE MARCH ON NEWPORT

*Y cyfodiad*, the 'rise' as it was known in the English of south Wales, began on 3 November 1839. The word *cyfodiad* differs significantly in meaning from *gwrthryfel*, 'rebellion', or *terfysg*, 'insurrection, riot'; it carries more the sense of 'a beginning, a start' (and *atgyfodiad* means 'resurrection'). The 'rise' was not a preliminary to the creation of the workers' commonwealth, it was its creation. We have already remarked on the urgency with which the lodge officials registered people in the days before the rising, issuing them with cards or 'tickets' as if to confer virtually a new citizenship on them. At the Blaina lodge, for example, John Davis (himself No. 451) testified to having seen 'the people all signing – hundreds of them'. Rachell Howell was one who went there to obtain a card (No. 753) for her husband from Zephaniah Williams. 'When I gave my husband's name', she reported,

> he asked me if I would have a card. I said, 'Yes, if you please, Sir.' He gave me a card. I asked him what it was for. He told me that it would be better for him [her husband] to have one than to be without it, because it would keep us without danger.[1]

Subtle and not so subtle pressure was brought to bear on recalcitrant workers. Elizabeth Jones of the Blaina women's lodge was advised 'not to sleep with her husband till she had made him a Chartist'.[2] Most of those who failed to enrol in a lodge and thereby to place themselves in rebel jurisdiction felt, however, that it was their lives that were in danger and not just their conjugal rights. 'The consequence for those that stayed behind', Zephaniah Williams warned them, 'would be, that they might live for a little time, but that their lives would be miserable, because they might die like dogs', and it was reported that none who stayed 'escaped insult except a favoured few, who were supposed to have had offices assigned them at home during the absence of the *army*'.[3] In such large centres as Beaufort, Blaina, Brynmawr, Dukestown and Nantyglo captains were appointed to remain behind and watch carefully those who had failed to respond to the muster. The 'spy' at Nantyglo, for example, was Edward Tippins whose brother Isaac was a captain at Blaina.[4] In the smaller collier communities it seems that the women watched out for the recalcitrants. William

183

Davies, who had been very active in the Blackwood lodge, was seen there early in the afternoon of 4 November. 'Ah turn coat', a group of women shouted; 'you do stop at home and send people to Newport to the slaughter.'[5]

An armed citizenry was central to the concept of the workers' commonwealth, of the 'Silurian' republic. Only a populace totally mobilised for the defence of its autonomy might hope to withstand the forces that would be unleashed against it. The commonwealth was conceived in arms and born in arms. On 3 November there were good pikemen and gunmen in numbers fully sufficient to attain the immediate military objectives of the rebels, that is, to establish a frontier along the Usk and the Severn Shore. The thousands of men who mustered, as towns and villages all over the coalfield were scoured, and who joined the columns often armed with no more than a stick, were not needed to do battle immediately. They were, however, required visibly to affirm their adherence to the cause. Those who would not do so voluntarily were impressed wherever they could be found. The *modus operandi* of the press gangs, not surprisingly, was similar to that of the herds of Scotch Cattle. It was vividly described by one contemporary writer:

A band of 40 or 50 Chartists, armed with pikes, guns and other mortal weapons, march to a house, and if the door is not instantly opened to them they at once attack and demolish it. They then enter the house in a body, and demand that the master and every other man on the premises join their ranks, stating that no harm shall come to the women or children, as they are sworn not to injure them. If the master refuse he is then seized and dragged forth, placed in the centre of the band, and a file of men behind him with presented pikes, and thus marched off.[6]

Not all the men who turned out were heroes, but some were. None desired martyrdom even in the cause of freedom, but there were those among them who were to find it.

It was an army of irregulars that marched on Newport (see Map 10.1). Men carried a little bread and cheese in their pockets. By the time that was eaten it was assumed that they would be in possession of the town where, as Frost said, there were plenty of flour warehouses and deer in Sir Charles Morgan's park that the butchers in their ranks could deal with.[7] No one could have anticipated that the weather on the night of 3-4 November was to be some of the worst that people remembered. Torrential rain drenched the men to the skin and made it impossible to

**Map 10.1: The South Wales Rising of 1839, Showing the Main Lines of March**

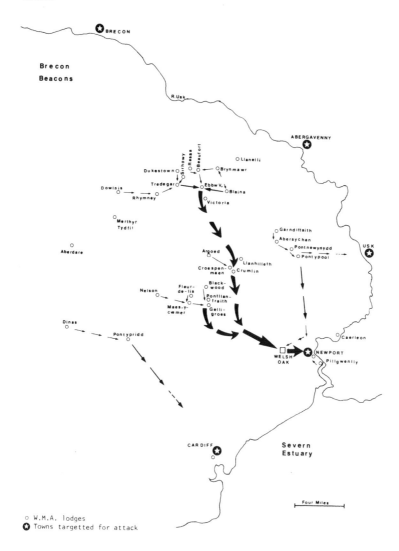

O W.M.A. lodges
O Towns targetted for attack

keep the powder dry. If any excuse was needed for forcing the publicans along the routes of march to open their establishments, the
weather provided it. But as the men attempted to dry off a little, time
was being lost. In the circumstances it is remarkable that so many wet,

tired though seemingly not too dispirited men were converging on Newport not indeed in the small hours of Monday morning, but as dawn broke. How many there were we cannot really say. Townspeople who gave evidence before the magistrates seemed to be in a measure of agreement that 5,000 men, give or take 1,000, had actually entered Newport, but no one was in a position even to guess the numbers that were still on the march.[8] It was an impressive piece of organisation, and no small part of the credit must go to William Lloyd Jones of Pontypool, 'a thorough, good fellow', so Dr William Price believed.[9]

It was presumably as a result of Frost's change of plan that William Lloyd Jones was assigned a special responsibility for overseeing the muster in the three eastern districts of the coalfield. His task was to ensure that the lodges were bringing out their men on time and that it was everywhere clearly understood that Newport was to be the first target and was to be occupied in the early hours of Monday morning. On Sunday Jones made a long tour of the valleys on horseback. He left Pontypool at dawn, was in Abersychan at 7 a.m., Blaina at 10, Tredegar at 3 p.m., Blackwood at 6, Crumlin at 7.30, and back in Pontypool by about 10.[10] The report he gave Frost when he passed through Black-wood must have been an encouraging one, for almost everywhere the local leaders had matters well in hand. But, perhaps most reassuring of all, he was able to tell Frost that a column from Tredegar was already approaching Blackwood. It was commanded by John Rees, better known as Jack the Fifer.

Whether the council of 1 November decided the matter, or whether it was decreed by a caucus of the more senior leaders, John Rees of Tredegar had been chosen to direct the attack on Newport. We have seen that he was, apparently, a veteran of the Texan war of independence who had taken part in the storming of San Antonio in 1835, when ill-equipped irregulars wrested control of the town from its garrison of regular Mexican soldiers.[11] It was, then, essential that nothing happened to delay Rees's arrival at the forward position to be set up in preparation for the entry into Newport. Rees entrusted his close friend, the collier David Jones (Dai the Tinker), with the task of completing the muster in Tredegar and its neighbourhood and, with a party of his own well-trained pikemen and gunmen, moved off in the mid-afternoon of Sunday.[12] They travelled by tram. Elizabeth Walters of Argoed testified that trams full of armed men approached there not long after 6 p.m., and within the hour they had arrived in Blackwood.[13] Among those who travelled down with John Rees was, it seems, the deserter from the 29th Regiment, Williams. He took an active part in setting up the forward position and a few hours later was to die in the fighting. In Blackwood and district the muster was everywhere well advanced by the time of Rees's arrival. The colliers' lodges were scattered along the valleys of Rhymney, Sirhowy and Ebbw, and across the hills that separated them. No plan had therefore been made to assemble the men of the district at any one central point. Each lodge was to move in sections to the forward position by whatever route its captains thought best. In the early part of Sunday evening that position was generally assumed to be the Cefn, only some two miles outside Newport, where the Pontypool men were to join the other columns. It was probably as a result of a reappraisal of the situation by Rees and Frost that the Cefn was realised to be so near Newport that scouts from the town would be able to keep the rebel movements under constant surveillance. The Welsh Oak at Ty'n-y-coed |was chosen instead. It was a mile or so below Risca, where the columns from the Heads of the Valleys would arrive, but still some five miles from Newport. An advance party was despatched from Blackwood to carry out a number of preliminary tasks. Some of its members took up stations at the Welsh Oak at about 10 p.m., to ensure that all columns halted there.[14] The remainder, a section or two in strength, proceeded to Rigby's midway between the Welsh Oak and the Cefn. There they were to close the road to prevent scouting parties from Newport approaching the forward position. They were in fact scarcely in position before two men sent out by Mayor Thomas Phillips rode straight through their ranks, at about 10.30 p.m.[15]

The colliers of the Blackwood district were mustering on a schedule that, in accordance with plan, would bring them to Risca, or the near-by Welsh Oak, at about midnight. In Argoed, to the north of Blackwood, there were perhaps about ten sections in all. The quarryman Matthew Williams, who was to be badly wounded in the fighting, belonged to one captained by a collier he knew only as Harry.[16] Another collier, George Beach, seems to have commanded several sections.[17] The muster commenced early Sunday evening and the women took to the streets in a ritual wailing for the departing men. That not everyone displayed a proper enthusiasm for the cause is illustrated by the case of the coal-cutter, John Walters. A party of men under George Beach, many of them colliers from the Hafod-yr-isclawdd Levels above Argoed, assembled outside his house. 'There is a man here', one of them said, 'and we shall have him out; he shall not stop here to make fun of us . . . he shall not make fun of our wives, that we are all gone and he left here.' Beach broke open the door and his men threatened Walters with guns and pikes. 'Move from here', they ordered. 'I will not go',

Walters replied; 'besides I have no money, and it is no good to travel about the country without money.' Beach gave him a shilling, but Walters was adamant. 'Go I will not, and if you intend to kill me, kill me here, for I am sure if I go along with you I shall be killed, and it will be less trouble for my friends to take me from here to be buried than from anywhere else.'[18] Walters was unceremoniously bundled out of the house.

Walters appears to have been no more than a recalcitrant individual who preferred the comforts of his home to a night on the roads. In the nearby Croespenmaen lodge we have seen that a more serious situation had developed, a faction there having refused to accept the authority of the captains. A group of those committed to the rising mustered at the Navigation Inn, Crumlin, at about 7 p.m. on Sunday. Shortly after William Lloyd Jones arrived there on horseback. He asked who they were. Old David Stephens was their leader, they replied, but the lodge members were not agreed among themselves. It may be that Jones instructed the Argoed men to intervene, for certainly some of Beach's colliers scoured Croespenmaen and as late as 10 p.m. one Argoed section apparently led by David Lloyd was still active there.[19] By that late hour, however, most of the Argoed and Croespenmaen men were well on their way to the Welsh Oak. It was probably the most advanced of their sections that arrived at Newbridge at about 8.30 p.m., proceeded to scour it for both men and weapons,[20] and then, their numbers increased by others who had drawn up to them, scoured Abercarn at about 10 p.m.[21]

In Blackwood itself men had been arriving from outlying areas throughout the afternoon of Sunday and by 3 or 4 p.m. 200 to 300 were already assembled at the Coach and Horses.[22] Soon the lodge women, pledged to 'fight with our husbands for the Chartists unto death', began their wailing.[23] By early evening there were enough men in the town, as William Davies remarked, 'to eat Newport'. Wearing his red cravat, the preacher-haulier John Reynolds announced that he had been in Newport and that the soldiers there were ready to join them. John Frost said that the men should follow him down to the Cefn where Zephaniah Williams would join them with 5,000 workers from the Heads of the Valleys and William Lloyd Jones with 2,000 from around Pontypool.[24] Much activity followed the arrival of John Rees with the Tredegar pikes and guns. Frost announced that it was time to scour Blackwood but there was some resistance to the suggestion presumably from those who feared to see the Tredegar men used for that purpose. The problem was resolved when George Turner of Blackwood volunteered to carry out the task with local sections; he was later to take the men he pressed by way of Pentwyn Mawr and Newbridge to the Welsh Oak.[25]

Frost left John Reynolds in command of the Blackwood column. He and John Rees almost certainly travelled together to the forward position, for none of the Blackwood men subsequently examined by the magistrates could testify to seeing Frost between that place and the Welsh Oak. Presumably the two chiefs followed the Sirhowy tramroad through the little populated lower reaches of the valley, their progress virtually unnoticed. They seem to have reached Risca Bridge at about 11 p.m. and to have met the column from Argoed and Croespenmaen there. Guns were fired off and there was much cheering. The commotion was heard by the two scouts from Newport who had passed through the rebel patrol at Rigby's. They turned back to take the information to the mayor, and one of them was severely wounded as they ran the gauntlet of the patrol a second time.[26] Frost and Rees, with the Tredegar, Argoed and Croespenmaen men, reached the Welsh Oak just after midnight.[27]

Meanwhile Reynolds conducted the Blackwood column through Pontllanfraith, where another 200 men had been mustered, to Gelligroes to effect a junction with the sections there. The preacher was clearly a formidable man who brooked no failure. He spotted Thomas Morgan in Gelligroes, without a weapon. 'You have nothing in your hand, you ought to be hanged', he said, and slapped Morgan across the face.[28] From Gelligroes the column followed the Rock tramroad which ran on the side of the river opposite the Sirhowy line. At Nine Miles Point, where the two tramroads joined, they met another column. Again guns were fired and there was cheering. The time was about 10 p.m.[29] The second column could only have been that from Pontaberpengam, Fleur-de-lis and Maes-y-cwmer in the Rhymney valley. The men of Fleur-de-lis and Aberpengam had been efficiently mustered by Thomas Llewellyn in the early part of Sunday evening. He was a man of considerable standing among the rebels, for he was one of those who had led the tumultuous protest in Newport when William Edwards, Henry Vincent and the other chartist prisoners had been brought before the magistrates there just six months earlier.[30] Effecting a junction with the Maes-y-cwmer men, Llewellyn had brought the column through Bryn to Gelligroes and thence along the Sirhowy tramroad to Nine Miles Point.[31]

The combined columns led by John Reynolds and Thomas Llewellyn must have entered Risca hard on the heels of Frost and Rees.

They spent some time there, however, scouring the neighbourhood, different parties following the line of the turnpike road, the tramroad and the canal.[32] In this action they were assisted by local sections based on the nearby Pontymister works and led by Isaac Phillips (alias Williams).[33] Meanwhile the Tredegar, Argoed and Croespenmaen men established themselves at the Welsh Oak. By this time Frost was physically exhausted. In his mid-fifties and unaccustomed to physical exertion, he had found the march from Blackwood a strenuous one. He was probably becoming concerned, moreover, about the general progress of the muster, for he had no news of the columns from the Heads of the Valleys. Williams, the deserter from the 29th, rode back to Risca. He met the forward sections of Blackwood district men even before he reached there. He told them that Frost was awaiting them, that arms and ammunition would be available in plenty when they reached Newport, and that some of the soldiers had left that town for Pontypool (or, by another report, Abergavenny).[34] 'How the devil do you keep hanging back there', he said; 'why don't you come on faster . . . you are eno' to eat Newport.' He found Reynolds in Risca, still searching for arms and men. Frost, he told him, was ailing. He, Williams, had a horse for him, but he needed to find a saddle in Risca. 'Come my lads', he exhorted the men, 'hurrah my lads, you ought to have down at Newport at 12 o'clock, Mr. Frost is waiting for you.'[35] A certain urgency communicated itself to the captains. One of them, George Tillett, formed up his guns to push the men forward. 'Don't keep behind', he told them; 'every man that deserts will be shot. Recollect, that all you that is not with us when the morning comes there will be a bright eye kept, and everyone that is missing will be shot.'[36]

Williams the Deserter returned to the Welsh Oak. He was able to bring Frost the good news that the Blackwood columns were approaching. They marched into Tŷ'n-y-cwm between midnight and 1 a.m., more or less on schedule. The nonagenarian Israel Firman, the Philadelphian who had become a traditional *consuriwr* (more a shaman than a conjurer), later turned queen's evidence. He provided the magistrates with a veritable roll of honour of the local captains who so successfully carried out the muster. It included, among others, Edmund Edmunds (mine agent), Henry Harris (beerhouse keeper) and John Barrill (collier, who blew the bugle during the march), all of Pontllanfraith; William Williams (collier) of Pentwyn; George Beach (collier) of Argoed; Thomas Nailer (collier) of the Bryn; Griffith Evans (blacksmith) of Gelligroes; and George Tillett (collier).[37] Frost might well have felt encouraged, but Williams the Deserter also brought back bad news, that there was no sign of the arrival at Risca of the columns from the Heads of the Valleys.

Frost was in a quandary. Clearly he felt reluctant to continue the advance on Newport until other columns had arrived; indeed, to have done so would have been quite contrary to the spirit of the revised plan. Yet with every hour that passed the element of surprise was being lost. Tactically, Frost undoubtedly took the wrong decision, for the men he had at the Welsh Oak were already sufficient to overwhelm Newport. Instead Frost chose to immobilise them there — for four or five hours as it turned out — while he went ahead to try to establish contact with the Pontypool columns. According to one witness, a very reliable one, Frost left the Welsh Oak before 1 a.m. With a small party of only about five men he proceeded to High Cross, just beyond the Cefn, where the Pontypool columns were expected to appear.[38] We shall see that Frost did finally make contact with them, but it was not until about 6 a.m. that he returned to the Welsh Oak.[39] The men from the Heads of the Valleys had been arriving there two and three hours earlier, and joining the Blackwood contingents in their long wait. Clearly Frost had made a series of decisions that spelled disaster. Dr William Price recognised this, and was led to claim 'that Frost wanted to destroy the Chartist movement, and that he kept his men for hours in the rain in order to give the soldiers time to fill the Westgate'.[40] The accusation was preposterous, but so too was Frost's conduct of the operation. All that can be said in his defence is that the columns from the Heads of the Valleys did indeed fail to maintain schedule, and the reasons for this should now be considered.

According to the original plan of campaign, the men from the Heads of the Valleys were to carry out the occupation of Abergavenny on 5 November. Under the revised plan they were assigned to the attack on Newport, a day earlier. On the original plan they were to assemble at Brynmawr, on the revised plan at Ebbw Vale.[41] It is presumed that John Rees was originally to take part in the attack on Abergavenny; on the revised plan we have seen that he was to lead that on Newport. Clearly there was a risk in the situation, for it was by no means sure that such radical changes in plan could successfully be made at such short notice. Initially, in fact, the muster across the Heads of the Valleys did proceed on schedule. That schedule, however, was not maintained for long.

Early on Sunday Zephaniah Williams sent a messenger to John Frost in Blackwood, to say that the Blaina men would muster at 6 p.m.[42]

They began to assemble at the Royal Oak in Coalbrookvale between 5 and 6 p.m. They were addressed by a tall, thin man who spoke no Welsh. He had been sent there by Frost. 'Every one who intended to be a turncoat march out', he said. No one did. They were to muster on the mountain between Blaina and Ebbw Vale immediately, he told them. Everyone must carry arms and should take some bread and cheese, for 'he didn't think they would be back for a few days'. They should not tell their wives too much for fear of making them uneasy, but they were going to release the political prisoners from Monmouth and incarcerate instead those who had put them there. Zephaniah Williams then addressed the men in Welsh. There would be thousands of men on the mountain, he said. Everyone should be sure to take weapons; 'he did not think they would be wanted as their numbers would frighten the people and the soldiers but that if the soldiers fired upon them then they were to use their weapons and kill them'. They should not worry about their wives and children, Williams told them; 'we have provided for them as well or better than usual'. It was only those who refused to join the rebels who had real cause for alarm, for 'spies' would be watching them. The briefing over, pikes which had been stored in a cellar were distributed to those who had paid for them. By 7 p.m. the men of Blaina and Coalbrookvale, Zephaniah Williams with them, were assembled on the slopes of Mynydd Carn-y-cefn. There, in the heavy rain, they waited for the columns from the western works to arrive in Ebbw Vale below.[43]

No men had further to travel than those from Dowlais. The intention, we may suppose, was that they should scour the upper reaches of the Rhymney Valley to prevent those trying to evade the muster from finding refuge in the borderlands between the Merthyr and Heads of the Valleys commands. Dowlais sections were moving across the hills by late afternoon on Sunday.[44] By one report they were about a brigade strong, but only 100 or so of them armed.[45] At the Rhymney Upper Furnaces it is possible that a party turned south to scour the Lower Furnaces and Bute works, and then proceeded to the Welsh Oak by way of the Rhymney Valley.[46] The remainder descended into the upper Sirhowy Valley and joined the muster there. Tredegar, Sirhowy and Dukestown were the scenes of great activity. Throughout Sunday the men had been meeting by sections in the beershops, and John Rees (the Fifer) and David Jones (the Tinker) held long conversations at the Globe Inn.[47] When Rees left by the Sirhowy tramroad to join Frost in Blackwood, Jones took charge. Many middle-class residents fled the neighbourhood, among them the ironmaster Charles Lloyd

Harford, his wife and their domestic staff. They left Sirhowy early on Sunday evening, for they were in Monmouth by 11 p.m. When they had departed, Harford said, the furnaces had all been blown out and 'there were already assembled large masses of miners etc. (and of his own men some thousands) armed, ammunitioned, and ready for action'.[48] We have seen that the manager of the Tredegar Branch Bank also succeeded in escaping, removing all the cash and other valuables to Abergavenny; it seems unlikely that the rebels intended this to happen.

Twyn-y-Star was designated the muster ground and one observer estimated that 5,000 or 6,000 people had assembled there by 7 p.m.[49] Reece Meredith, who was to be killed in Newport, called over the names of the captains.[50] Among them was Benjamin Richards, a Tredegar shoemaker, who had travelled backwards and forwards over several nights to maintain contact with Frost in Blackwood. He was a man dedicated to revolutionary violence. 'He would sacrifice his Body to the ruin of the place', he told people. If they won the day he would take the lives of William Homan, superintendent of police at Tredegar, and his family; of his assistant William Davies; and, for good measure, of 'all the Tories'.[51] As for the soldiers, he 'should like to see them', Richards said; 'we would soldier them'. At 6.30 p.m. he was busily fixing pike heads to their shafts, assisted by several members of his section: colliers, miners and other shoemakers. They proceeded to the muster at about 7 p.m.[52]

Soon after 7 p.m. the magistrates, policemen and special constables who had been sworn in were obliged to watch helplessly as the rebels paraded through the neighbourhoods in columns. 'The inhabitants', remarked one middle-class writer, referring to the middle-class inhabitants, 'were completely at their mercy.'[53] But there was no rioting and no looting. In the very fact of their discipline it became apparent that rebel rule was something other than mob rule. While Zephaniah Williams was anxiously awaiting their arrival in Ebbw Vale, the men of Tredegar and its neighbourhood celebrated their strength. There was time even for debate. Some advanced the view that the columns should proceed to Newport by way of the Sirhowy Valley, leaving Zephaniah Williams to move his men down the Ebbw Fawr independently. Perhaps it was a manifestation of local patriotism, perhaps a recognition that more time would be lost in making a junction with the Blaina men. In the event it was decided to keep to plan. At or a little before 10 p.m. the columns, in files of six, crossed the hill and descended on Ebbw Vale.[54] By the time they arrived Zephaniah Williams had been awaiting them for some three hours, and John Frost and John Rees were already approaching Risca.

In the upper reaches of Ebbw Fawr there were two lodges, the Rassa, and the Ebbw Vale and Beaufort. At the former the muster was already in progress by about 6 p.m., when sections scoured the houses along the Rassa railroad. 'It was all the same in every corner of the world', one of those who tried to run away was told. At about 8 p.m. a party entered Rhyd Chapel to muster the men at prayer. 'Myn Diawl', exclaimed a pikeman; they should all get out 'or they should have it'. Cheers were given as the column crossed the bridge into Beaufort at about 8.30 p.m.[55] By then Beaufort had already been scoured. Two men who refused the muster were said to have been shot.[56] A section led by a collier, George George, had impressed the men from Carmel Chapel, near the ironworks, at about 8 p.m.[57] The musters in both Rassa and Beaufort were clearly behind schedule, for it had been intended that they should join the Ebbw Vale sections at 7 p.m., in a field near the ironworks.[58]

We have seen that the columns from the head of the Sirhowy did not arrive in Ebbw Vale until about 10 p.m., and it seems that Zephaniah Williams waited until then to move the Blaina men off Mynydd Carn-y-Cefn.[59] The situation in Ebbw Vale, however, was still not regarded as satisfactory and both divisions joined in scouting it. The furnaces were put out. 'Let them be stopped to the devil', Zephaniah Williams was heard to remark, 'that is the fittest for them.' But then he must have been acutely aware of the passage of time. He talked of trying to find steam engines to take the men down the Beaufort tramroad.[60] The scheme did not materialise and a correspondent of the *Merlin* watched the columns move off; they marched, he reported, in discrete parties, not *en masse*.[61] At the Victoria works, only two miles below Ebbw Vale, the pikemakers had laboured all through the previous night.[62] Williams halted there briefly, perhaps while the local men turned out. 'I hope there is no danger that we do go down to be killed', he was heard to remark.[63]

The first party of men from the Heads of the Valleys, over 100 strong, arrived at Pontaberbeeg between 11 p.m. and midnight, and forced the proprietor of the Hanbury Arms to open his house. Captains tried to urge the men on; we must be at Newport by 2 a.m., Thomas Davies, an Ebbw Vale collier, told them. Zephaniah Williams looked around for a horse, without success, and it was already 1 a.m. when he finally left.[64] Meanwhile the forward sections had reached Llanhilleth at about 11.30 p.m. and Newbridge at about 1 a.m. They forced the landlord of the Newbridge Inn to open. Some of them were from

Dowlais. A Tredegar man declared that they had begun the wrong way. The landlord's wife readily agreed; it was, she said, wrong to rise on a Sunday. 'Oh! not for that', the man replied; 'we ought to have brought Floman's and Will the captain's heads down on the spears.' We may perhaps recognise in the speaker none other than Benjamin Richards, whose feral concern with the policemen William Homan and William Davies has already been noted.[65]

By this time Zephaniah Williams was far behind. He did not arrive at Llanhilleth until between 1.30 and 2 a.m. He went to the Coach and Horses and the landlord thought that he was decidedly low in spirits. 'They were very late', Williams remarked, 'and they ought to be at Newport sooner than they would be.' Fortunately he was able to procure a horse and two trams there, and in that manner he proceeded to the Welsh Oak with as many of his companions as could scramble aboard.[66] There was, however, at least one other party that was moving down behind Williams. David Jones (the Tinker) was with it. He arrived at the Newbridge Inn at about 3 p.m. and took a hurried meal there: 'the last bread and cheese', he said, 'he might ever want'.[67] There is no evidence to show why Jones was so delayed. An informed guess is that he had led a detachment from Pontaberbeeg some miles north into the Ebbw Fach, to scour the neighbourhood of Abertillery.[68]

Zephaniah Williams arrived by tram at the Welsh Oak between 3 and 4 a.m. on Monday.[69] Some of the companies from the Heads of the Valleys had probably preceded him there, others had yet to come in. Several parties stopped briefly at John Jones's house in Risca in the early hours of the morning, to dry off.[70] All were halted at the Welsh Oak to await Frost's return there. Although the projected time schedule for the attack on Newport was no longer feasible, the rebel forces from the Blackwood district and the Heads of the Valleys had at least effected a juncture. It remained only for the Pontypool companies to come in.

Frost had said that he expected 2,000 men from the Pontypool district to participate in the occupation of Newport. The figure was a notional one. Many of the rebel units in the district were to be used to garrison Pontypool itself, to seize the town of Usk and, should the situation be auspicious, to spearhead a march on Monmouth. It seems likely that only two companies (each of 165 men at full strength) were to be put into the attack on Newport, and that a brigade (of some 500 men, commanded by Solomon Britton) was to be held in reserve near the town. In the event only one company, its men drawn from the Pontnewynydd and Pontypool lodges, actually went into action at Newport.

Men of the Pontnewynydd lodge were assembling at John Lewis Llewellyn's beerhouse between 8 and 9 p.m. on Sunday night. By about 9 there were some 50 present, a troop of five sections under the command of John Thomas (Jack the Sailor). They moved off to join the muster at the Pontypool race-course.[71] In Pontypool itself William Shellard, a master shoemaker, was in charge of affairs pending the return of William Lloyd Jones from his day-long tour of other rebel centres. The men reported to Jones's house, the Bristol, whence Shellard directed them to the race-course. They should be assembled there by 10 p.m., he told them.[72] By that time Jones had arrived there. He took over command, leaving Shellard in charge in Pontypool. Jones's men, about 150 strong by then, moved to the New Inn on the Newport turnpike road, where Jones formed them up in files of five, pikes first, guns second and others behind.[73] Near Croesyceiliog, the Pontypool brewer, Barnabas Brough, and currier, Thomas Watkins, were taken prisoner. They were put in the custody of a troop commanded by George Shell.[74] The column passed through Croesyceiliog at about 11.30 p.m. and reached the Marshes turnpike gate, on the very outskirts of Newport, at about 1 a.m. on Monday morning.[75] There they were met by a troop from Pillgwenlly, south of Newport.

The Pillgwenlly men were dockworkers for the most part, stone-cutters, masons, blocklayers and labourers. Patrick Hickey mustered a section of Irishmen there at about 10 p.m. on Sunday night. It went to John Lewis's house at the Pottery, where several other sections were assembling at the direction of Jonathan Palmer and William Jewel, both stone masons. They divided into two parties. One followed the canal along the Newport wharfs and the other skirted the town to the west. They were reunited at the Marshes Gate where they awaited the arrival of the Pontypool men.[76] It may be assumed that the men from Pillgwenlly, with their better knowledge of the town, were to act as guides to the Pontypool columns. Clearly, however, no move was to be made in the direction of Newport until word had been received from Frost.

John Frost, we have seen, had in fact left the Welsh Oak at about 1 a.m. to establish contact with the Pontypool forces, and expected to find them near the Cefn. There was some confusion in the planning, for the Marshes Gate was almost three miles distant from the Cefn. At 3.30 a.m. the Pontypool and Pillgwenlly men were still waiting to hear from Frost. Finally William Lloyd Jones decided to retrace his steps towards Pontypool to meet the next company which by then should have been drawing up.[77] Before leaving he instructed his captains to move their men along the lane that led from the Marshes Gate through Pen-y-lan to the Risca and Newport road near the Cefn. They did so, but with much hesitation, and halted several times and talked about turning back. They had, understandably, a sense that all was not well. They reached the Cefn between 5 and 5.30 a.m. and finally made contact with Frost.[78] They followed him into the Welsh Oak at about 6 a.m.[79] With Frost's return to the Welsh Oak preparations were made immediately to resume the march on Newport. Pikemen rounded up the irregulars from barns, cowsheds, farmhouses and wherever else they had sought shelter. 'Come be off', said one, 'it's time to go.' The men complained that they would catch their death of cold. 'If you don't come', he replied, 'I'll send in half a dozen guns and make you go.'[80] On the road guns were tested and Frost brought the Tredegar pikemen and the gunmen to the head of the column.[81] It was scarcely daylight when a patrol of special constables from Newport saw the vanguard of the rebels, a troop of about 50 pikemen, approaching Pye Corner. The patrol was able to seize two stragglers. One, Lewis Thomas, was helping along his companion, the 71-year-old Thomas Bowen; both were from Dowlais and by then they had been on the march for over 13 hours.[82] Two or three sections of men from the Blackwood district slipped into the Three Horseshoes at Pye Corner to refresh themselves. The Pontllanfraith captain, Edmund Edmunds, followed them in. 'March on', he said; 'what the Devil do you want to drink beer and spirits. Do you want to get drunk? You do know that this is our day, go on — that is Frost's orders.'[83]

The columns followed the tramroad through Tredegar Park. One of the gatekeepers watched them pass. The pikes were in front, the guns next. 'They were very tidy together', he remarked. He put their number at no less than 3,000, no more than 5,000, and thought that there were about 300 guns.[84] A halt was called at Cwrt-y-bella weighing machine, no more than a mile from the centre of Newport. The columns extended back almost a mile along the track, to the Waterloo turnpike gate and beyond. At Cwrt-y-bella John Rees (the Fifer), David Jones (the Tinker) and a third man who was almost certainly Williams (the Deserter) took command and marshalled the assault group. Witnesses differed as to the precise formation used. One reported that pikemen were drawn up six abreast with a gunman on each flank, so making files of eight. Another thought that the pikes were drawn up five abreast, with a gun on the right of every other file.[85] Three youths who arrived on the scene from Newport were questioned about the soldiers. It was learned from them that a detachment had been sent from the barracks at the Union Poor House to the Westgate Hotel in the centre of the town, from which Mayor Thomas Phillips had decided to direct the defence of the town. 'Yes, for to go on and say they meant to have the Westgate by and by for themselves', John Rees told one of the youths. 'We want the Westgate', a man shouted, to which a wit replied, 'I want a waistcoat, for mine is damned wet.'[86]

From Cwrt-y-bella the columns proceeded past the Fairs to the turnpike gate on Stow Hill, immediately above the town centre. A short distance to the left lay the Union Poor House, where some 200 stand of arms were kept.[87] Captain Richard Stack, with magistrate Lewis Edwards in attendance, had 30 or so men of the 45th Regiment drawn up. The remainder of his company, another 30 under Lieutenant Basil Gray, had joined the mayor and the special constables in the Westgate at about 8.15 a.m.[88] The rebels ignored Stack's party. 'Let us go towards the town, and show ourselves to the town', Frost was heard to say, and the assault group started down Stow Hill towards the Westgate.[89]

It was said that on their arrival at Stow Hill the columns from the hills were to use rockets as a signal for the sections in Newport itself to go into action.[90] One witness some miles away claimed to have seen several fired off, but that was earlier in the morning.[91] By the time the columns had reached Stow Hill rockets would have been of little use, for it was broad daylight. Again, the failure to maintain schedule had jeopardised other operations. We know most about the local section led by Jenkin Morgan, a Pillgwenlly milkman. He was a man dedicated to the cause who had been heard to say that 'he would like to see every one that would not join the Chartists, mown down like grass'.[92] Attached to his section were the rebel pikemakers of Pillgwenlly, John Gibby and his Irish assistants, Edward Brickley and David Herring.[93] Morgan's orders had been transmitted to him by Charles Waters, ship's carpenter at the dry dock and sometime secretary of the Newport Working Men's Association. Morgan was to take prisoner the Rev. Richard Roberts of Christchurch, and his family, and then to seize and hold (pending further orders) Aaron Crossfield's gunpowder warehouse at Cinder Hill wharf. It was Morgan's understanding that the rebel columns from the hills would arrive outside Newport by 1 or 2 a.m., that they would take the Union Poor House where the soldiers were stationed, and that he was to be ready to move into action when the rockets were fired. His section took up a position east of the Usk, not far from Christchurch, soon after midnight. At 3 a.m. the men went home, convinced that nothing would occur that night. At 6 a.m. Morgan was making his milk round as usual and some of his men were pulled out of their beds at

8 a.m. with the news of 'thousands and thousands of colliers coming down'.[94]

The attack on the Westgate Hotel was begun at about 9.10 on Monday morning by 200 or 300 men of the assault group. They had been drawn up in front of the building by John Rees while most of their comrades were still moving down Stow Hill. From within the hotel Lt. Gray observed the assailants form from column into line 'very steadily'.[95] Assisted by 'powder monkeys' who carried charges and ammunition in bags,[96] the guns directed their fire on the windows, and under its cover pikemen forced a way into the building through the main door. Another party passed through the Catholic chapel and reached the hotel's yard by a rear entrance.[97] For a time the assailants had the initiative, but the soldiers enfiladed the street with their fire and commanded that of the rebels. The men in front of the Westgate were forced to fall back. Fierce fighting, however, continued within the building. The pikemen attempted to force the soldiers' positions whenever the smoke cleared but, as Lt. Gray testified, 'they always faltered when they encountered their own dead, and then received our fire'.[98] The attack lasted for about 15 minutes, and had to be abandoned.

On 2 January 1840 Gray, newly promoted captain, gave evidence before the Special Commission in Monmouth. He testified that the soldiers in the Westgate had each been issued with 22 rounds of ammunition but that they fired on an average only three. Her Majesty's officers were not necessarily honourable men and there is reason to think that Gray was prevaricating, fearing the charge that he had used unnecessary force. He admitted that his soldiers had stripped the rebel dead of their ammunition, but denied that any of it was used at the Westgate.[99] He failed to mention that, in the course of the attack, a small boy slipped out of the hotel and returned from the Union Poor House with his pockets full of cartridges.[100] Nor did Gray mention that, while surgeons treated the wounded defenders of the Westgate, the rebels were left unattended. Even that scourge of the chartists, Edward Dowling, was affected by the scene. 'Many who suffered in the fight', he wrote, 'crawled away; some exhibiting frightful wounds, and glaring eyes, wildly crying for mercy, and seeking a shelter from the charitable; others, desperately maimed, were carried in the arms of the humane for medical aid; and a few of the miserable objects that were helplessly and mortally wounded, continued to writhe in tortures, crying for water . . .'[101] But the soldiers tried to drive away those who came to succour the rebel wounded, and throughout Monday threatened to shoot those attempting to carry away the rebel dead.[102]

Casualties among the defenders had in fact been comparatively light; only Mayor Thomas Phillips, two special constables and Sgt Daily of the 45th were officially acknowledged to have been seriously injured in the assault. But the military never revealed the full extent of its wounded. Rumours circulated that at least nine soldiers had been slain and were buried with full military honours.[103] There was no truth in them. Certainly, however, two weeks after the engagement a number of soldiers were still recuperating in the Union Poor House.[104] Rebel casualties were much higher. No complete roll call of the dead can be made, for badly wounded men managed to travel considerable distances. William Jones, a Sirhowy miner shot in the side, was assisted to Blackwood, took a tram to Tredegar, another to Talybont on the Usk, a canal boat to Brecon, and was arrested as he neared Trallong where his bride-to-be lived.[105] He was, as it happened, to recover from his wounds, but there were reports that six men, miners or colliers, had died in Caerleon, another four in Tredegar, and so forth.[106] No one really knew where and when men drew their last breaths. But nine rebels lay dead in and around the Westgate and twice that number and more succumbed in other parts of Newport. They included Williams the Deserter, shot by Gray and said to have been the first to fall (see Appendix I).[107]

When the fighting had started Zephaniah Williams was still at the top of Stow Hill. John Frost was with the assault group, but reports had it that he disappeared as soon as the firing began.[108] He himself later admitted to their truth. 'The moment I saw blood flow', he said, 'I became terrified and fled.'[109] Frost was not, nor ever had been, a man of the sword. The attack was directed by John Rees from the front of the hotel. Forced back by the soldiers' fire, and himself wounded in the hand, Rees made some attempt to rally his men.[110] 'Thank God we have cut at them and knocked down 3 or 4 and they have not lost one of us', he said, apparently unaware of the extent of the carnage.[111] By then, however, the retreat had begun. It was subsequently represented by anti-rebel writers as a rout. It is by no means clear that it was. At 11 a.m. a correspondent of *The Times* wrote that the rebels had 'almost entire possession of the town' and that firing was still going on; 'what the end of it will be', he added, 'God only knows'.[112] At 2 p.m. a correspondent of the *Morning Herald* penned an account of the 'most ferocious and bloody' fighting at the Westgate, but referred to the town as still in rebel possession. In another despatch an hour later, however, he implied that the rebels had finally evacuated the town but only, he thought, to return to the attack after nightfall. They did not, and the next day the same correspondent gave a summary of the situation. 'Finding themselves worsted', he reported, 'and that, from the position occupied by the military, the consequences were almost certain death, the chartists retreated to the fields, where they divided themselves into regularly-organized parties.'[113] The truth of the matter is that some of the rebels were seized with panic and did indeed flee back to the hills in total disorder, but others regrouped on the outskirts of Newport and were prepared, if so directed, to return to the attack. We know that there were columns still moving towards Newport. When the fighting started in Newport a second company from the Pontypool district was at Malpas Court, a mile and a half north of the town. Some of its sections had mustered in Abersychan only some five hours earlier.[114] Impressing men as it advanced, the company passed through Pontypool at about 5 a.m. and reached Croesyceiliog at 8. There William Lloyd Jones had been awaiting its arrival. At 9 a.m. Jones halted the company at Malpas Court, where he was joined by James Aust and a section or two mustered from between there and Caerleon.[115] The column proceeded to the Marshes Gate, where Jones directed it through Pen-y-lan towards the Cefn and High Cross.[116] It is difficult to understand why he did so. Perhaps it was intended that the company should be held in reserve. However that may be, Jones was still in the neighbourhood of Pen-y-lan when a collier gave him news of the disaster at the Westgate. It was not long after 10 a.m.[117] The men should stand firm and Dr William Price would arrive with his cannons, Jones said; if they fled the soldiers would follow them into the hills, and he and others would be hung.[118]

Behind Jones's company a still larger force was moving from Pontypool towards Newport. It was a brigade drawn from the ironworks and collieries around Abersychan. It numbered about 500 men, 200 of them pikes and 50 guns, and it was led by Solomon Britton of Garndiffaith. The brigade had passed through Pontypool at about 6 a.m. and was at Croesyceiliog when the fighting started in Newport.[119] Britton himself went into Newport to see what had happened, but it is unclear whether his men took up positions outside the town or returned to Pontypool.[120] On Sunday evening large bodies of rebels were still congregated along the Risca road. They were not, apparently, in retreat, but it is no longer possible at this remove of time to say who they were and what their intention was.[121]

Edward Dowling, nephew of Deputy Lieutenant Reginald Blewitt and proprietor of the *Monmouthshire Merlin*, was one of the first to write about the attack on Newport. It was his opinion that 'if the [rebel] chiefs had been firm, and the town assaulted in various parts, the few brave men in the Westgate and at the barracks would have come forth for its protection'. But, he admitted, the odds were against the soldiers 'when in conflict with thousands of infuriated men'. The failure of the rebels to take Newport was in part a result of the severity of the weather, for if the assault had been made in the night 'it must have been successful, and flaming houses would have proclaimed the town's doom, and the insurgent's [sic] triumph'. But Dowling did not exonerate the rebel commanders from responsibility for the failure. 'Even when the attack had been made', he argued, 'if the leaders were not the veriest dolts that ever attempted to guide the councils and direct the movements of men, temporary success, at least, might have crowned it.'[122]

Dowling's judgements were harsh ones, but they were not without substance. A number of disastrous decisions were indeed taken by the rebel chiefs. The plan agreed upon at the Dukestown council of 28 October should not have been so radically revised, on Frost's prompting, only four days later at a meeting of delegates which did not even represent the whole coalfield. Political and military objectives, moreover, were insufficiently distinguished. Well-trained and well-armed men were used to scour the valleys and bring about a massive demonstration of workers' power when they should have been swiftly deployed to secure the bridges and other strategic points, to neutralise the soldiers and to seize stores of arms and powder. The severe weather conditions were no excuse for the men of the Sirhowy Valley, under David Jones, moving into Ebbw Vale several hours behind schedule. Zephaniah Williams could have led the Blaina men down to Risca notwithstanding the failure of the Sirhowy forces to appear on time. Frost lost all the advantages of a night attack upon Newport when he chose to halt the rebel companies from the hills at the Welsh Oak until he had made contact with the Pontypool men. John Rees, in choosing to lead a frontal, daylight assault on the strongly defended Westgate Hotel, rejected the tactically more appropriate option of taking over the town and containing the soldiers within the Westgate Hotel and the Union Poor House under siege conditions. And finally, in predicating all other operations upon the success of the attack on Newport, local initiatives were discounted. However impotent the civil authorities in towns like Tredegar and Pontypool might have seemed, it was a tactical blunder to leave their elimination until the local companies returned (victorious, it was presumed) from Newport; the 'rise' had indeed begun the wrong way, as we have seen one rebel captain to have remarked. The events of the morning of 4 November in Newport were not necessarily the end of the 'rise' but they were a singularly inauspicious start to it.

## Notes

1. *Monmouthshire Merlin* (henceforth *Merlin*), 30 Nov. 1839: evidence of John Davies and Rachel Howell. Newport Public Library, Chartist Trials 1839-1840, 24 vols, henceforth N[ewport] E[xaminations]. NE, XV, doc. 372: evidence of John Davies; doc. 474: evidence of William Howell.
2. *Monmouthshire Beacon* (henceforth *Beacon*), 11 Jan. 1840: evidence of Thomas Sanders.
3. Idem: evidence of Thomas Bowen. *Silurian*, 16 Nov. 1839 (italics original).
4. Idem. NE, XV, docs. 342-3: evidence of Thomas Bowen.
5. NE, VI, doc. 423: evidence of Mary George.
6. *Merthyr Guardian*, 23 Nov. 1839.
7. NE, V, docs. 46a, 672: evidence of Susanna Tovey.
8. For example, NE, III, notes on evidence, Thomas Dyer and Moses Scard; IX, doc. 411: evidence of Thomas Evans. Joseph and Thomas Gurney, *The Trial of John Frost, for High Treason* (London, 1840), p. 344: evidence of John Parsons.
9. Ap Id Anfryn [Gwilym Hughes], *The Late Dr Price (of Llantrisant). The Famous Arch-Druid* (Cardiff, 1896), p. 10. The aged Price remembered the Pontypool man, however, as John Jones.
10. See David Williams, *John Frost. A Study in Chartism* (Cardiff, 1939) pp. 212, 218-19. To the sources cited by Williams should be added, NE, XV, doc. 647: note on cover re. Ann Thomas; XI, doc. 393: evidence of Sarah Edmunds; VIII, doc. 562: evidence of Herbert Davies. The times given by witnesses are usually approximations. Many people had clocks in their houses, which they set by the works, but few carried watches on their persons.
11. I.G.H. Wilks, 'Insurrections in Texas and Wales: the Careers of John Rees', in *Welsh History Review*, 11, 1 (1982), pp. 67-71.
12. A useful account of the muster in and around Tredegar is to be found in Oliver Jones, *The Early Days of Sirhowy and Tredegar* (Tredegar Historical Society,1969), pp. 101-2. Jones had the advantage of having talked with a survivor of the rising, David Jones (Dai Golchi), who still lived in Tredegar in the early 1900s, ibid., pp. 108-9, and see also Hywel Francis and David Smith, *The Fed. A History of the South Wales Miners in the Twentieth Century* (London, 1980), p. 194.
13. *Merlin*, 30 Nov. 1839; NE, VII, doc. 677: evidence of Elizabeth Walters. NE, IX, doc. 414: evidence of Mary Farraday.
14. *Merlin*, 7 Dec. 1839: evidence of Ann Thomas. Ibid., 23 Nov. 1839: evidence of Catherine and Mary Charles.
15. Gurney and Gurney, *Trial*, pp. 257-64: evidence of Thomas Walker.
16. Ibid., pp. 265-92; *The Times*, 7 Nov. 1839: evidence of Matthew Williams.
17. NE, VI, doc. 450: evidence of Job Harris; VII, unnumbered docs: statements by William John Llewellyn and Joseph Coles.
18. *The Times*, 30 Nov. 1839, NE' VII, docs. 677-80: evidence of John and Elizabeth Walters. NE, VII, docs. 693, 802: evidence of Thomas Watts.
19. NE, VIII, doc. 562, XI, doc. 369, XV, doc. 569: evidence of Herbert Davies; XV, doc. 443: evidence of Daniel Thomas; XV, doc. 569: evidence of Thomas Morgan; XII, docs. 448-9: evidence of Evan and Hannah Harris. *Merlin*,

28 March and 4 April 1840: examination and trial of David Stephens.
　20. *The Times*, 9 Dec. 1839; *Beacon*, 14 Dec. 1839, NE, XI, doc. 663: evidence of Mary Thomas.
　21. *Courier*, 9 Nov. 1839, from an Abercarn correspondent, 7 Nov.
　22. NE, V, doc. 669: evidence of Job Tovey.
　23. NE, IX, doc. 414: evidence of Mary Farraday; V, doc. 670: evidence of Job Tovey.
　24. Gurney and Gurney, *Trial*, pp. 361-72; NE, XV, doc. 444: evidence of William Harris. Gurney and Gurney, *Trial*, pp. 297-311: evidence of James Hodge.
　25. Idem. NE, XIV, doc. 581: evidence of Amy Phillips; XIV, unnumbered doc: evidence of George Ashman.
　26. Gurney and Gurney, *Trial*, pp. 257-64: evidence of Thomas Walker.
　27. *Beacon*, 23 Nov. 1839: evidence of Catherine Charles. *The Times*, 9 Dec. 1839; *Beacon*, 14 Dec. 1839; NE, XI, doc. 508: evidence of John Jones. *The Times*, 7 Nov. 1839; Gurney and Gurney, *Trial*, pp. 265-92: evidence of Matthew Williams. NE, XV, doc. 619: evidence of Thomas Saunders.
　28. NE, XIV, doc. 566: evidence of Thomas Morgan.
　29. NE, IX, doc. 5: evidence of Israel Firman (in *Reg.* v. *Fisher et al.*); *Merlin*, 7 Dec. 1839: evidence of Firman (in *Reg.* v. *Harris*). *Beacon*, 28 Dec. 1839: evidence of Benjamin Strickland.
　30. *The Times* and *Morning Chronicle*, 27 Nov. 1839: evidence of Moses Scard.
　31. *The Times*, 16 Nov. 1839; NE, XII, doc. 616: evidence of George Evans. NE, XII, doc. 616: evidence of John Rapps. *The Times*, 25 Nov. 1839; NE, XII, docs. 476, 525: evidence of John Hughes and Lewis Lewis. See also PRO, TS.11/496.
　32. NE, V, doc. 553: evidence of Charles Maisley.
　33. NE, XIII, docs. 108, 333, 381, 389, 445, 446, 511, 652, 666, in the examination of Isaac Phillips.
　34. A detachment of a corporal and four men had indeed been sent from Newport to Pontypool on Sunday, see Williams, *John Frost*, p. 225 and Frost must have received intelligence of this after his arrival at the Welsh Oak.
　35. Gurney and Gurney, *Trial*, pp. 309, 369: evidence of James Hodge and William Harris. NE, IV, doc. 466: evidence of James Hodge; XIV, doc. 566: evidence of Thomas Morgan; IX, doc. 5: evidence of Israel Firman. Firman mistakenly thought that Williams the Deserter was William Davies of Blackwood.
　36. *Merlin*, 7 Dec. 1839: evidence of Israel Firman.
　37. NE, IX, doc. 417: evidence of Israel Firman.
　38. NE, XV, doc. 619: evidence of Thomas Saunders.
　39. Gurney and Gurney, *Trial*, pp. 265-92: evidence of Matthew Williams; pp. 347-51: evidence of Barnabas Brough; pp. 369-70: evidence of William Harris.
　40. Ap Id Anfryn, *The Late Dr Price*, p. 11.
　41. Geographical considerations dictate the assumption that Brynmawr was the base for the attack on Abergavenny, but see the account of the rebel plans in *Silurian*, 9 Nov. 1839, in which Brynmawr is named as a major assembly point (which it was not, under the revised plan).
　42. NE, V, doc. 670: evidence of Job Tovey.
　43. NE, XV, docs. 342-3, 372, 474, 479, 481, 584, 607: evidence of Thomas Bowen, John Davies, William Howell, Benjamin James, James James, John Phillips and Edward Richards.
　44. Cardiff Central Library, Bute MSS, XX/35: J.J. Guest to Bute, dd. Dowlais, Sunday eve., 3 Nov. 1839. Earl of Bessborough (ed.), *Lady Charlotte Guest. Extracts from her Journal 1833-1852* (London, 1950), entry for 3 Nov.

1839.
45. *Courier*, 18 Nov. 1839, 'from accounts which have reached us'.
46. E.E. Edwards, *Echoes of Rhymney* (Risca, 1974), p. 23. James Davies, *The Chartist Movement in Monmouthshire* (Newport, 1939), p. 25.
47. *Beacon*, 16 Nov. 1839, from a Tredegar correspondent. O. Jones, *Early Days*, p. 101.
48. PRO, TS.11/500: Mayor Dyke to Home Sec., dd. Monmouth, 4 Nov. 1839. *Beacon*, 9 Nov. 1839.
49. *Beacon*, 16 Nov. 1839.
50. NE, V, docs. 564-5: evidence of John Morgan.
51. The Tredegar ironworks paid its own police and Samuel Homfray appointed them, see PRO, HO.40/57: Bute to Home Sec. dd. 10 Oct. 1839.
52. NE, XIV, docs. 110, 410: evidence of Esther Evans. HE, XIV, doc. 476a and *Morning Chronicle*, 23 Nov. 1839: evidence of John Cullimore and W. Homan.
53. *Beacon*, 16 Nov. 1839.
54. Idem. CCL, Bute MSS, XX/57: Howells to Bute, dd. 8 Nov. 1839, reporting W. Homan.
55. *Silurian*, 28 March 1840; *Cambrian*, 4 April 1840: trials of John Jones, labourer, David Howell, miner, Walter Meredith, collier, William Price, collier, William Williams, miner and John Thomas, tailor.
56. *Beacon*, 9 Nov. 1839, from Abergavenny, 6 Nov.
57. NE, X, docs. 682-3: evidence of Thomas Waters.
58. *Merlin*, 16 Nov. 1839, from an eye-witness.
59. Gurney and Gurney, *Trials*, pp. 311-16: evidence of George Lloyd. *Merlin*, 30 Nov. 1839: evidence and re-examination of Thomas Sanders.
60. *Merlin*, 16 Nov. 1839. NE, XV, docs. 342, 607: evidence of Edward Richards; XV, doc. 546: evidence of George Lloyd.
61. *Merlin*, 16 Nov. 1839.
62. CCL, Bute MSS, XX/35: Guest to Bute, dd. 3 Nov. 1839. Bessborough (ed.), *Lady Charlotte Guest*, entry for 3 Nov. 1839.
63. *Merlin*, 30 Nov. 1839: evidence of James James.
64. Ibid., 30 Nov. 1839, NE, XV, docs. 374, 520: evidence of Simon Leonard; VI, docs. 461-3: evidence of George Hitchins.
65. *The Times*, 9 Dec.; *Beacon*, 14 Dec. 1839; NE, XI, doc. 663: evidence of Mary Thomas
66. NE, XV, doc. 617; Gurney and Gurney, *Trial*, pp. 323-6; *Merlin*, 30 Nov. 1839: evidence of James Samuels. NE, XV, doc. 629: evidence of Henry Smith.
67. *The Times*, 9 Dec.; *Beacon*, 14 Dec. 1839; NE, XI, doc. 663: evidence of Mary Thomas.
68. NE, misc. loose papers, has a note that a small rebel group was in Abertillery.
69. *Merlin*, 30 Nov. 1839: evidence of Thomas Sanders.
70. *Beacon*, 28 Dec. 1839: evidence of John Jones.
71. NE, VII, doc. 452: evidence of Keziah Harris; XIV, doc. 575: evidence of John Parry.
72. *Merlin*, 23 Nov. 1839: evidence of R.T. Johnson and James Emery.
73. NE, XI, doc. 401: evidence of James Emery. Gurney and Gurney, *Trial*, pp. 378-81: evidence of John Parry.
74. Ibid., pp. 347-51: evidence of Barnabas Brough. See also [B. Brough], *A Night with the Chartists, Frost, Williams and Jones. A Narrative of Adventures in Monmouthshire* (London, [1847]), reprinted in Dorothy Thompson (ed.), *The Early Chartists* (London, 1971), pp. 228-40.
75. *Merlin*, 23 Nov. 1839; evidence of William Rousell. Gurney and Gurney,

*Trial*, p. 380: evidence of John Parry.
76. NE, XII, unnumbered doc: evidence of David Evans; doc. 447: evidence of Edward Harris; XIII, docs. 354, 523, 590: evidence of William Chambers, John Lewis and John Pollock. Clearly the belief that the Irish remained aloof from the rising cannot be sustained, for which see *Merlin*, 23 Nov. 1839: 'The Irish in Monmouthshire'.
77. NE, XI, doc. 500: evidence of David Jones.
78. *The Times*, 11 Nov. 1839: evidence of Brough.
79. Gurney and Gurney, *Trial*, pp. 283-4: evidence of Matthew Williams.
80. NE, XV, doc. 619: evidence of Thomas Saunders.
81. Gurney and Gurney, *Trial*, pp. 310, 361-72: evidence of James Hodge and William Harris. NE, V, unnumbered doc., signature illegible.
82. *Morning Chronicle* and *The Times*, 14 Nov.; *Merlin*, 16 Nov. 1839: evidence of Isaac Venn and Thomas Beckingham. NE, loose papers, notes on Thomas Edwards, Job Harris, *et al*.
83. NE, VII, doc. 649: evidence of Edmund Thomas.
84. NE, IX, doc. 411; *Morning Chronicle*, 24 Dec. 1839: evidence of Thomas Evans.
85. NE, XIV, docs. 596, 598, 632, 643a: evidence of Thomas Pritchard and Samuel Smith. Gurney and Gurney, *Trial*, pp. 214-15: evidence of T.B. Oliver.
86. Gurney and Gurney, *Trial*, pp. 204-12: evidence of John Rees and James Coles.
87. [E. Dowling], *The Rise and Fall of Chartism in Monmouthshire* (London, 1840), p. 39.
88. Ibid., p. 40. Gurney and Gurney, *Trial*, p. 247: evidence of Basil Gray.
89. Ibid., pp. 169, 177: evidence of Samuel Simmons.
90. PRO, TS.11/501, doc. 1629: T.J. Phillips to Maule dd. 22 Nov. 1839.
91. Gurney and Gurney, *Trial*, pp. 352-4: evidence of Thomas Watkins.
92. NE, XII, doc. 437: evidence of Maria Harper.
93. NE, X, docs. 347, 455-8: evidence of Edward Brickley and David Herring.
94. NE, XII, docs. 488, 840: evidence and signed statement of Morgan James; doc. 344: evidence of Jane Branson.
95. Gurney and Gurney, *Trial*, p. 248: evidence of Basil Gray.
96. [Dowling], *Rise and Fall*, p. 41.
97. 'Ground Plan of the Westgate Hotel', lithograph, Quarter Master General's Office, Horse Guards, 1839.
98. Gurney and Gurney, *Trial*, pp. 170-254, 528-32: especially evidence of Samuel Simmons, Richard Waters, T.B. Oliver, Henry Evans, Daniel Evans, Thomas Phillips, Basil Gray and Henry Williams. [Dowling], *Rise and Fall*, pp. 40-3.
99. Gurney and Gurney, *Trials*, p. 250.
100. W.N. Johns, *The Chartist Riots at Newport*, 2nd edn (Newport, 1889), p. 42.
101. [Dowling], *Rise and Fall*, p. 43. *Merlin*, 9 Nov. 1839, and compare CCL, Bute MSS, XX/37: Watkins to Bute, dd. 7 Nov. 1839, p. 4.
102. Johns, *Chartist Riots*, p. 44.
103. *Northern Star*, 7 Dec. 1839.
104. Gurney and Gurney, *Trials*, p. 359: evidence of John Harford.
105. NE, IX, docs. 702, 703: evidence of Jonas Williams and William Voss.
106. *Bristol Mercury*, 9 Nov. 1839. *Merlin*, 9 Nov. 1839.
107. CCL, Bute MSS, XX/37: Watkins to Bute, dd. 7 Nov. 1839; XX/57: Howells to Bute, dd. 8 Nov. 1839. *Hereford Times*, 9 Nov. 1839.
108. *Hereford Journal*, 13 Nov. 1839. *Merthyr Guardian*, 7 Dec. 1839.

109. *Shrewsbury News and Cambrian Reporter*, 7 Dec. 1839.
110. NE, VI, doc. 728: evidence of J.W. Wright. Thomas A. Devyr, *The Odd Book of the Nineteenth Century* (Greenpoint, New York, 1882), p. 194.
111. NE, XIV, docs. 598, 632: evidence of Samuel Smith.
112. *The Times*, 2nd edn, 6 Nov. 1839.
113. *Morning Herald*, 6 Nov. 1839.
114. NE, XI, doc. 719: evidence of William Williams.
115. NE, XI, docs. 500, 516, 608: evidence of David Jones, Christopher Kidner and John Richards. *The Times*, 11 Nov. 1839: evidence of John Phillips. *Merlin*, 9 Nov. 1839: evidence of John Richards, John Dallimore, Christopher Kidner and John Matthews; 16 Nov. 1839: evidence of David Jones. Gurney and Gurney, *Trial*, pp. 391-4: evidence of John Matthews. James Aust had apparently been influenced by the Urquhartites, and believed that when the revolution came The Russians would move in. But, he said, 'he would rather be under a Russian government, than under the present Government'.
116. NE, XI, doc. 719: evidence of William Williams.
117. NE, XI, doc. 516: evidence of Christopher Kidner.
118. NE, XI, doc. 513: anon. statement; doc. 388: evidence of Edward Dorey.
119. *Merlin*, 16 Nov. 1839: evidence of David Jones and William Watkins.
120. Ibid., evidence of Moses Scard.
121. *Morning Herald, Morning Chronicle, The Times*, 6 Nov. 1839, variously presenting information from a mail coach guard.
122. [Dowling], *Rise and Fall*, pp. 46-7.

# 11 ALL THE QUEEN'S MEN: SOLDIERS, MAGISTRATES AND POLITICIANS

When news of the events of 4 November reached the more militant of the chartists in Scotland and the north of England, it seemed that the Welshmen had made 'a miserably poor job of it'. Why, it was asked, 'did they no tak t' th' hills and stand it out like men?'[1] In London a special meeting of chartists was held on 16 November to consider the situation. One man recently returned from south Wales hesitated to address the gathering lest he should put the rebel leaders into jeopardy. 'He would only tell them', he said,

> that the Welsh had not been beaten [cheers]. He was a Welshman himself, and he knew that his countrymen were not cowards. The fact was that the men who entered Newport were fitter at the time for an hospital than for a battle, after the fatigue and hunger which they had endured. They were not beaten yet.[2]

The truth of the matter is that the events of 4 November created such a pitch of excitement among the populace that, at this remove, it is extremely difficult to distinguish what was unfounded rumour from what was factual report. The situation in each of the five 'disturbed districts' requires review.

It was, on the face of it, unlikely that the rebels would renew the attack on Newport at least until they had regrouped in the hills. Within 24 hours, however, the situation had already changed to their disadvantage, for on Tuesday morning a troop of the 10th Hussars, issued with 1,500 rounds of ball cartridge, reached Newport by packet boat from Bristol.[3] Nevertheless a large rebel force was assembled at Pontaberbeeg in the Ebbw Valley on Tuesday afternoon and by the evening it had apparently moved down to Abercarn. In the Blackwood district, too, attempts were being made to muster the men again. Panic swept Newport and many of its citizens prepared to flee. The soldiers were stood at arms and plans made to establish positions at Risca Bridge and Marshes Gate, commanding the two northern approaches to the town.[4] No attack materialised.

The situation in the Pontypool district was a confused one, for its three brigades were dispersed and their commanders — William Lloyd

Jones, Solomon Britton and, it is presumed, David Davies — were out of touch with each other. We have seen that one of Jones's companies, from Pontypool and Pontnewynydd, took part in the fighting in Newport, and that a second was on the outskirts of the town at the time. The third, under William Shellard, appears to have remained in Pontypool to watch the situation there. We have also seen that Britton's brigade, from Abersychan and its neighbourhood, was moved up to Newport in its entirety, as a reserve. The third brigade, also recruited in and around Abersychan, was most probably commanded by the veteran of Waterloo, David Davies. It was mustered on Sunday evening and went into action a little before midnight, stopping the blasts at the British, Pentwyn and Golynos, and Varteg works and impressing the men there into its ranks.[5] The brigade moved through Pontypool at about 3 a.m. on Monday morning and apparently took the road leading to Usk.[6] It was assumed by those on the spot that it was destined for Monmouth, but we may be sure that it was to take up a position somewhere near Usk pending the arrival of instructions from the rebel commanders in Newport. News of its advance reached Usk. Some 180 special constables were sworn in and ordered to defend the bridge there until troops could be obtained.[7]

It was the intention that, as soon as Newport was secured, Britton's brigade and Jones's two companies were to return to Pontypool and carry out a phased series of operations there, first, to seize the police station; second, to appropriate all the arms and ammunition that could be found in the town; and third, to occupy the mansions of Lord Lieutenant Leigh and Deputy Lieutenant Blewitt, taking both men prisoner if they could be found. The two brigades were then to be held ready to join the third outside Usk and proceed towards Monmouth if the plan to attack that town was activated.[8] By 9 a.m. on Monday Shellard was convinced that Newport had been taken. 'The soldiers are all disarmed this hour ago, and Newport is in possession of the Chartists', he told people; 'I suppose we are determined to have it now; we have tried long enough by peaceable means.'[9] The lodge women began their own muster. They were, it was thought, ready to go to Newport for plunder and 'in many cases they appeared more eager than the men'.[10] But the authorities in Pontypool had not been inactive. John Roberts, the police superintendent, had ridden to Abergavenny to alert the Lancers stationed there; the pensioners had been called out and issued with guns and bayonets; and the special constables had been sworn in. Leigh succeeded in obtaining a corporal's party from the company of the 45th in Newport and a permanent guard of 80 men was established at his house and another of 50 men at the police station.[11] When news of the defeat in Newport reached Pontypool all rebel operations were suspended, but the pensioners and special constables could not be stood down until a company of the 45th Regiment arrived in the town on 12 November.[12]

On 4 November the Merthyr magistrates sent scouts out to report on the situation along the heads of the valleys. They brought back information that men had marched both to Newport and Abergavenny.[13] The latter item misrepresented the facts but was not entirely without substance. We have noted that under the original rebel plan the attack on Abergavenny was to be launched from Brynmawr, only nine miles away. Under the revised plan some of the Brynmawr sections, whether a majority or not is unknown, were switched to the attack on Newport. They mustered in Brynmawr and Nantyglo early on Sunday evening, assembled at Twyn-y-cynnordy at about 6 p.m., and moved through Beaufort to join the other columns from the heads of the valleys at Ebbw Vale.[14] But the two local leaders, David Lewis and Ishmael Evans, remained behind. Their assignment was almost certainly to infilter other of their men into Abergavenny in preparation for the attack on that town to be launched on 5 November, by companies returning from Newport. The hundreds of refugees (works officials, shopkeepers and others) who were pouring into Abergavenny provided excellent cover for the operation. Amongst them, one correspondent reported, were 'many Chartists'.[15] Three of them can still be identified. Charles Lloyd, Thomas Hopkins and Owen Williams, all members of Brynmawr lodge, entered the town in the early hours of Sunday.[16] They may have been the strangers who were reported to be treating soldiers to drink, to the alarm of the magistrates.[17]

The attack on Abergavenny was never launched, the tactical errors in Frost's revised plan being again demonstrated. On Sunday evening the Crickhowell magistrates, learning of the muster of the men in the hills, requisitioned soldiers from the barracks at Brecon. A detachment of the 12th Regiment of Foot entered Crickhowell late that night, and on Monday marched into Brynmawr and Nantyglo, where they established camp. Three magistrates travelled with the soldiers, John Gwynne, Joseph Bailey and William Stretton. Suspected rebels were rounded up thoughout Monday night and the magistrates examined them. Warrants were issued for the arrest of Zephaniah Williams, David Lewis and Ishmael Evans. Williams had, of course, gone to Newport, but Lewis and Evans were picked up on Tuesday morning.[18] With the assistance of the military, civil authority had re-established itself in the neighbourhood of Brynmawr with remarkable alacrity. Abergavenny, moreover, had been swiftly put into a state of defence: 500 special constables were sworn in, and a magistrate there boldly countermanded War Office instructions that the troop of the 12th Lancers quartered in the town should proceed to the aid of Usk.[19] Everywhere the rebels had lost the advantage of surprise.

The progress of the 'rise' in the Pontypridd district was much affected by the differences of opinion between Dr William Price and John Frost. The three lodge heads, Price of Pontypridd, William David of Dinas and Thomas Giles of Nelson were all present in Blackwood on 1 November for the meeting of delegates, but it seems that Price spoke with Frost just before it began and as a result decided not to attend.[20] We can only guess that Price learned that Frost intended to make changes in the plan agreed upon at the previous Dukestown meeting, and refused to have anything to do with them. It is certain that none of the Dinas and Pontypridd men took part in the march on Newport, but those of Nelson did.

Thomas Giles and his deputy William Owen, both colliers and the latter an ex-soldier, mustered about 300 men from the collieries around Nelson. 'You must attend to what I tell you seriously', Giles informed them on Sunday evening;

> every man that is now here is bound to be at Newport and go down with me tonight — every man that will turn back on his journey will be a dead man before 12 o'clock tomorrow and any man that stops in his house tonight will be one and all dead men before 12 to-morrow — all the pits shall be broken to pieces and closed on the people in the levels — and every man must plunder every house as we go along and search for guns.

The Nelson men arrived at the Welsh Oak soon after midnight, well on schedule, and were among those who entered Newport.[21]

On the night of the march on Newport and throughout Monday, 4 November, William Price and William David had their men scouring the lower Rhondda and the neighbourhood of Pontypridd, and stopping all the works.[22] The Dinas coalowner Walter Coffin subsequently made extensive inquiries into the proceedings, but was unable to penetrate the conspiracy of silence. Many years later Owen Morgan, who was able to talk with survivors of the period, gave some account of the matter. It was his understanding that the Rhondda phalanx (as he called it) was to assemble around midnight and then 'dash lupon

Cardiff' in the early hours of the morning.[23] Several contemporary reports may, then, be veridical. They indicate that on the night of 4-5 November the Rhondda and Pontypridd men were to proceed first to to Caerffili, where they were to be reinforced by companies from Blackwood district freed (by the anticipated victory in Newport) to participate in an attack on Cardiff.[24] It was believed, with what truth we cannot say, that Price had had a number of cannons cast for the assault.[25] In the event no men from Blackwood arrived in Caerffili, for obvious reasons, but news of the disaster in Newport did. Although Price and David made some attempt to continue the muster, the enthusiasm of the Taff Valley populace rapidly waned and many took to the hills and woods to escape impressment. Their predicament was satirised by a contemporary balladist:

Mae son yn Nantgarw fod y Chartist yn d'od,
A phob un a'i elfen am gilo ta'r co'd;
Mae Harriet o'r felin, Shon Tomos y Crydd,
Ac hen Ddic o'r Turnpike am ffoi t'a Chaerdydd.
Dafydd Shon Isaac a chydaid o fwyd,
A lefodd dair noswaith yn Nghraig y Berthlwyd.[26]

The march on Cardiff had to be abandoned. The town would, in fact, have proved difficult to take. When reports of the muster in the Taff Valley reached its mayor, C.C. Williams, he drew upon every available resource for its defence. The pensioners, special constables, staff of the Carmarthenshire Militia and a recruiting party of the 41st Regiment were all stood at arms. Field pieces were positioned to command all entrances to the town and Captain Foulger of the United States ship *Warsaw* landed twelve of his gunners to help man them. Scouting parties were sent out to report on the progress of the rebels, and bell-ringers and buglers were ready to alert the citizens should an attack be imminent.[27]

By 5 November only the Merthyr men – *gwyr Merthyr* – might still have saved the 'rise'. Of the four brigades there only one, from Dowlais, had been put into the attack on Newport. This was in accordance with plan, or so an investigative reporter who visited Merthyr in December found. 'Their apparent failure in joining the main body in their attack upon Newport', he wrote of the other brigades, 'was not through any apathetic feeling, or want of unison in action, but from design, it being believed by the leaders that those who marched were fully sufficient to capture Newport.'[28] Once the 'rise' was in progress it had in fact become very widely known that the Merthyr men were intended to attack not Newport but Brecon. There were even reports that the march on Brecon had commenced.[29] It had not, but there is reason to believe that (as in the case of Abergavenny) a number of men did secretly enter the town, to await the arrival of the columns from Merthyr. If so, they were sent there not from Merthyr but from the Rassa and Beaufort lodges. The evidence is tenuous. On 3 November a group of men from Beaufort were assembled at Llangynidr, on the way to Brecon. Among them was the Cwm pikemaker, John Owen, who certainly anticipated going on to Brecon. 'If the Chartists would gain the victory at Brecon and the next places Abergavenny and Newport', he told the group, 'he would put his spike into a sheep or some fowl and when he did follow the Chartists that they might know that he did kill a man put it into somebody.'[30] Another group of Rassa and Beaufort men did enter Brecon on Tuesday morning. At the trials their defence was that they were rebel deserters, which may or may not have been the case.[31]

A seemingly reliable report has it that the Merthyr men were not to move until they received information, by mounted messenger, of the success of the attack on Newport, and that it was anticipated that this would arrive in time for them to take over the town of Merthyr itself in the small hours of Tuesday morning. *Y ni gwmpwm ar y Dre* was said to be their password, 'we will fall on the Town'.[32] In fact they received news not of the success but of the failure of the assault on Newport. Nevertheless a muster was called for around daybreak on Tuesday. By 7 a.m. 500 or 600 men were assembled on Twyn-y-Waun above Dowlais. The ironmaster Guest showed considerable courage in going to address them and thought he had dissuaded them from proceeding with whatever was their plan. One group did, however, cross the hill to Rhymney where they stopped the blasts at the Bute works and mustered the ironworkers.[33] News of their action reached the magistrates in Nantyglo, and the detachment of the 12th Regiment took up positions above the turnpike road to oppose any move of the Merthyr men into that neighbourhood.[34]

It was, it seems, only the most committed of the Merthyr men who were mustering. Knowledge of the events in Newport had created widespread demoralisation, and under cover of darkness on Monday night and Tuesday morning many workers had taken to the hills and woods to avoid being drafted.[35] The rebel committee in Merthyr took steps to bring some order into the situation by calling a meeting for 6 p.m. on Tuesday, at Pen-yr-heolgerrig. The leader writer for the *Merthyr*

*Guardian* thought that it needed 'only one word' to persuade the men to rise and the magistrates were ready to requisition a company of the 12th Regiment from Brecon.[36] The militants opened the meeting with the proposal that they should 'strike while the iron is hot'. But the 'moral force' men were there, presumably including Morgan Williams who had been away from Merthyr over the weekend making arrangements to purchase the press on which the *Udgorn Cymru* was soon to be printed. The majority of the men were persuaded to disband and to return to work the next day.[37] 'Go home and be quiet', they were told; 'our friends at Newport have jumped over the hedge too soon.'[38]

By the end of the first week in November it was obvious that the 'rise' had stalled. The very conception of Frost's revised plan was such that the one reverse in Newport inevitably jeopardised every subsequent phase. At the time of the 'rise' the depot companies of the 12th Regiment in Brecon were about 400 strong,[39] the company of the 45th in Newport about 70,[40] and the troops of the 12th Lancers in Monmouth and Abergavenny each consisted of 36 men.[41] The rebels succeeded neither in neutralising these forces nor in preventing the arrival of reinforcements. We have seen that a troop of the 10th Hussars landed in Newport the day after the attack. On 6 November the Newport magistrates learned from the Home Office that eight more companies of the 45th were on their way to south Wales by forced marches from Winchester, and that a brigade of the Royal Horse Artillery, with field pieces and ammunition wagons, was being moved in by Great Western Railway.[42] Within a few days it could be reported that Newport 'now presents completely the appearance of a military station'.[43]

Colonel James Considine, a very distinguished soldier, was appointed 'Officer in Command of the Troops in the Disturbed Districts of Wales'. Once a junior officer in the Monmouthshire Infantry, he had recently returned from a mission in Tunis where he had held the local rank of Major General.[44] He systematically deployed his troops across the coalfield, sending one company of the 45th to relieve Pontypool on 12 November and drafting two others to control the Taff Valley from Cardiff to Merthyr.[45] By the middle of November south Wales was under a *de facto* military occupation, but to the civil and military authorities it was still by no means clear that the rebels had abandoned all hope of recovering the initiative they had so briefly held. Report after report of continuing activity in the hills appeared in the press. There was fresh alarm in Merthyr on 9 November and 'many persons expected a rising'.[46] Four days later the district still remained in a state of turmoil and the men were said to be meeting 'in very large numbers in their secret lodges'.[47] On 15 November report had it that 'manifestations of further attempts at rebellion have been apparent'; that 'in several works the men have not returned to their usual occupations'; that 'the mountainous districts are still in a most feverish state'; and that 'secret lodges are held almost nightly'.[48] Rumours came in that the Hirwaun men were in arms, had stopped work and had put out the blasts,[49] and that the Blackwood men were meeting in the levels to plot another rising.[50] The Varteg workers were reported to be meeting in their thousands, and Pontypool braced itself for another attack.[51] Colonel Considine was said to have remarked that 'he came to Newport with contempt for the Chartists, but he now thinks, if they attack they will be too much for the troops there, numerous as they are'.[52] At the end of November he ordered combined exercises to be carried out around Newport in the expectation that news of them would have a salutary effect on the workers in the hills. So realistic was the simulated attack of infantry, cavalry and artillery upon Newport that many of its citizens closed their shops and prepared to flee.[53]

It is clear, then, that the 'disturbed districts' remained highly disturbed despite the presence in them of a formidable military force. But the fact of the matter was that the rebel command was rapidly destroyed and the conditions were not such as to permit a new leadership easily to emerge. One correspondent remarked that the civil authorities in south Wales were 'afraid to apprehend the rioters without the presence of the military',[54] but that entailed no long delays over much of the coalfield. With an infantry company and cavalry troop in the town, the Newport magistrates began their examinations on 5 November.[55] We have seen that the three magistrates who accompanied the detachment of the 12th Regiment to Brynmawr and Nantyglo were able to start work on the same day. The magistrates in Brecon, depot of the 12th, were examining prisoners by 7 November and those in Pontypool began four days later, assured of the imminent arrival of a company of the 45th.[56]

Rewards of £100 were offered for the apprehension of the rebel chiefs. John Frost was arrested in Newport on the evening of 4 November.[57] Three days later William Lloyd Jones was taken in Crumlin.[58] John Lewis Llewellyn was caught near Swansea on 13 November, as he was boarding a coach for Carmarthen,[59] and on 21 November Zephaniah Williams was found in Cardiff, already embarked on a ship bound for Portugal.[60] In female attire, Dr William Price escaped via Cardiff, Liverpool and London to Paris,[61] and John Rees (the Fifer) and William David both reached the USA.[62] So, too, did a Llanhilleth rebel. He lived underground for three months, fed by his butties who smuggled him out in a tram when the police finally arrived.[63] David Jones (the Tinker) vanished to no one knows where, to reappear in Tredegar in the mid-1850s.[64] The destruction of the rebel command was thus both swift and total, and the *Merthyr Guardian* accurately represented the policy of the magistrates:

> . . . our chief desire at present is that *every leader* be brought to the bar of justice, and that the eyes of every operative may soon be opened, that they may see they have been nothing more than the *dupes* of bad and designing men. We confidently look for the speedy return of right feeling, and the spread of sound principles amongst our labouring population; but we cannot shut our eyes from the fact that, to this end, it is absolutely necessary that traitorous proceedings of the leaders of rebellion be effectually stopped by the strong arm of the law. *They*, – the leaders, – and not any real or substantial political or social grievances, are the chief evil against which the operatives have to contend. We trust that evil will speedily *be removed*.[65]

The magistrates were both eager and anxious to see eradicated the threat to bourgeois life and property which the rebels had presented; they were, quite understandably, acting in their class interest. The whig politicians in London viewed the matter rather differently. While hastening to despatch troops to south Wales, the Home Secretary was not oblivious to the fact that the rising could be seen as a serious failing in his office's responsibility for the maintenance of law and order. He took the decision to safeguard the image of the whig administration by attempting to minimise the gravity of the situation in south Wales. On 7 November he wrote to the mayor of Newport accordingly, suggesting that

> it would be advisable to make a *selection* of the prisoners to be committed for trial: That the worst offenders, (that is, those who took the most active and leading part in the late Outrage) should be committed, and the rest discharged on their recognizances, to appear and answer any charge which may be brought against them.

Normanby was quite specific; the number to be committed, he felt, should not exceed 20.[66]

The tory press was quick to scent a cover-up, and rumour soon had it that the government was involved in a conspiracy to pervert the course of justice. The whig ministers, one leader writer argued,

> intend to compromise the matter, by letting their co-labourer in the field of reform, Mr. Frost, escape, on condition of him taking himself off from the shores of England. There cannot be a doubt that such a course would be vastly agreeable to the court fribbles who are lounging away our liberties: for, mixed up as they are with this Chartist rebellion, things in no way conducive to their case would to a certainty come out should the prisoners be fairly brought before the honest and independent judges of the land.[67]

Be that as it may, the magistrates in south Wales were in no mood to accommodate the wishes of the Home Secretary by exercising restraint in the prosecution of the rebels. Already by the end of November 23 rebels had been committed for high treason by the magistrates sitting in Newport, and one by those in Pontypool. Six others were posted as wanted on the same charge. On a variety of lesser but still serious charges — sedition, riot, conspiracy, burglary, illegal arming, administering illegal oaths, inducing soldiers to desert and the like — the Newport bench had committed a further 12 persons for trial, the Brecon bench 13 and the Pontypool bench 19. Other prisoners had been summarily convicted on charges of vagrancy, and others bound over (see Appendix II). In the early weeks of December there was no sign that the zeal of the magistrates was abating; indeed, those in the Glamorgan valleys were only then commencing their formal examinations.[68]

Although engaged in judicial proceedings the magistrates did not hesitate publicly to express their indignation at what they saw as a totally unwarranted challenge not only to middle-class hegemony but to the Crown itself. No one was more shrill than Octavius Morgan, son of Sir Charles Morgan of Tredegar Park, who had returned in haste from the Netherlands to assume his civic duties in the crisis. 'In all my reading', he announced,

> I have not met an analogous case — a case in which a ruthless mob, not urged by distress, not impelled by want, not irritated by oppression, had emerged from their fastnesses to plunder and destroy an unoffending town; a band, too, led by men who were traitors, not only to their Sovereign, but to their homes and their fellow-townsmen. Had it not been for the special interposition of a merciful

Providence, this town would now be in ruins, its inhabitants butchered in cold blood, and the whole nation in a state of open rebellion.[69]

Only two days after the attack on Newport Reginald Blewitt wrote to the Home Secretary urging him to appoint a Special Commission to try the rebels, and at the head of a deputation he proceeded to London to argue the case in person.[70] In this course of action Blewitt had the support of most of the south Wales magistrates, who felt that the more immediate the trials the more rapidly would the turmoil in the hills subside. Normanby proved receptive to the idea, probably because his influence over special commissioners would be greater than that over regular Assize judges. On 19 November a Special Commission of Oyer and Terminer and of Gaol Delivery was issued under the Great Seal.[71] Lord Chief Justice Sir Nicholas Tindal, Sir James Parke and Sir John Williams were appointed the commissioners, and the proceedings opened in Monmouth on 10 December when the grand jury was sworn in. Two companies of the Rifle Brigade and several of the 19th Regiment of Foot were drafted into south Wales to strengthen Considine's command at this critical time.[72]

The jurisdiction of the Special Commission extended to Monmouthshire and Glamorganshire but not to Breconshire, where no prisoners had been committed for high treason.[73] The Attorney-General, Sir John Campbell, decided to bring only 19 treason cases to the grand jury, reducing the charges against others of the prisoners to ones of riot and conspiracy. On 11 December the grand jury found true bills of treason against 14 of the 19, namely, John Frost, Charles Waters, John Lovell, Richard Benfield, John Rees, George Turner, Zephaniah Williams, Edmund Edmunds, Jenkin Morgan, Solomon Britton, William Lloyd Jones, James Aust, John Rees (the Fifer) and David Jones (the Tinker), the last two not yet in custody. It found true bills of burglary against four of the others and no bill in one case.[74]

The trials began on the last day of 1839. The 14, together with 'a great multitude of false Traitors whose names are to the said Jurors unknown to the number of two thousand and more', were charged with 'levying war against the Queen in her realm'. Tindal carefully defined the concept of treason. The crime, he observed,

in its own direct consequence, is calculated to produce the most malignant effects upon the community at large; its direct and immediate tendency is the putting down the authority of the law, the shaking and subverting the foundation of all government, the loosening and dissolving the bonds and cement by which society is held together, the general confusion of property, the involving of a whole people in bloodshed and mutual destruction . . . Gentlemen, an assembly of men, armed and arrayed in a warlike manner with any treasonable purpose, is a levying of war, although no blow be struck; and the enlisting and drilling and marching bodies of men are sufficient overt acts of Treason, without coming to a battle or action. And, if this be the case, the actual conflict between such a body and the Queen's forces must, beyond all doubt, amount to a levying of war against the Queen . . . [75]

Frost was accorded the honour of the first trial, appropriately enough since he had been president-designate of the workers' republic. Zephaniah Williams was taken next, and then William Lloyd Jones, again appropriately enough in the absence of John Rees (the Fifer). The prosecution concerned itself almost exclusively with the attack on Newport and no attempt was made to lay bare the full extent of the rising; indeed, it is difficult to read the proceedings without concluding that they were carefully conducted to avoid doing just that.

On 8 January 1840 there was general astonishment when Chief Justice Tindal summed up for an acquittal of Frost. 'What he meant', the Attorney-General wrote in his diary that day, 'the Lord only knows . . . Chief Justice Tindal is a very honourable man, and had no assignable reason for deviating from the right course. Yet from the beginning to the end of his charge he laboured for an acquittal.'[76] But Campbell need not have worried. The jury consisted not of colliers or ironworkers but of twelve good and true men of some property — haberdashers, butchers, ironmongers, farmers and the like — and it was not unduly swayed by the summing up. On 8 January it gave a verdict of guilty against Frost. Judge Parke then took the trial of Zephaniah Williams and a guilty verdict was returned on 13 January, and Judge Williams took that of William Lloyd Jones and the same verdict was returned on 15 January.[77]

If the Attorney-General had suspected Tindal of bowing to political pressures from London, his suspicions were soon to be strengthened. He was instructed that the trials must not be allowed to drag on. On 15 January he plea-bargained with the nine remaining persons in custody on charges of treason. 'The Attorney-General of this great country', wrote one observer of the process, 'making himself cheap with solicitors' clerks, was condescending to enter into a compromise with persons charged, and eventually by their own confession convicted of the highest crime against the state.'[78] Waters, Morgan, Rees (not the Fifer), Benfield and Lovell all changed their pleas to guilty on the understanding, it seems, that they would receive sentences of at most three years' imprisonment.[79] In a move that took everyone by surprise the Attorney-General then asked for a jury to try Edmunds, Aust, Turner and Britton, but declined to call any evidence; there was, he said, doubt about whether Edmunds and Aust had joined the rebel ranks voluntarily and doubt about the identity of both Turner and Britton. The four men were immediately released without, it was noted, 'a word of admonition even from the bench'.[80]

On 16 January sentences of death were passed on the eight found or pleading guilty of high treason, but Waters, Morgan, Rees, Benfield and Lovell were told that mitigation would be recommended in their cases.[81] Tindal left for London immediately. Again to everyone's surprise the other two judges dealt with the 30 or so cases of conspiracy and riot with extraordinary despatch, completing all business within the space of several hours. A few cases had to be traversed to the next Assizes but almost all the prisoners had been induced to plead guilty and no evidence had to be taken. The heaviest punishments handed out were ones of a year's imprisonment with hard labour.[82] Before the Special Commission was closed Parke chose to address them. 'You, prisoners at the bar', he said,

> have all either confessed your crimes or have been found guilty. Your crimes carry with them the character of misdemeanors. But for the merciful interference of the Crown, you would have been responsible for great offences. The clemency of the Crown, and the merciful proceedings on the part of its law officers, have prevented the outrages committed by you on the 4th of November from being punished as they would otherwise deserve. I hope sincerely that the clemency of the government and the leniency of the court will not be lost, but that the country will experience the most beneficial results from them.[83]

The political undertones in the address were unmistakable. 'The almost indecent haste of the Crown lawyers to shuffle off the indictments one after another', wrote an observer, 'suggested that a Normanby jail delivery was being enacted at Monmouth, and that magistrates are scarcely to be protected after the discharge of an onerous and dangerous duty.' It would, he added, 'be impossible to describe the indignation of the country magistrates at this abandonment of duty upon the part of the Crown'.[84]

It is unlikely that the magistrates felt physically menaced by the rebels who had been freed, though there had been threats ('Ye serpents, ye generation of vipers . . . there are Samsons in Cambria . . . Remember Emmet he was hung, so was Norbury shot . . . ').[85] It was partly that their professional pride was injured. Normanby sensed this, and on 21 January wrote to express his appreciation of their valuable services.[86] Whatever his letter did to assuage their feelings was probably undone when, on 1 February, the death sentences on John Frost, Zephaniah Williams and William Lloyd Jones were commuted, on a technicality, to transportation for life.[87] But there were still rebel leaders at large, and it was no longer clear to the magistrates whether there was any point in continuing the pursuit. At the beginning of February, for example, the whereabouts of John Rees (the Fifer), David Jones (the Tinker) and seven or eight other wanted men became known. Octavius Morgan felt that the efforts of the magistrates were paralysed by the results of the Special Commission. 'We hold it', he informed the Home Secretary,

to be worse than useless, and indeed consider ourselves hardly authorised to apprehend and commit even on such strong evidence as we have heretofore done, and as we can now do, those parties on so serious a charge as that of High Treason and Rebellion, if although a true bill may have been found by the Grand Jury, they are afterwards to be discharged without any evidence being adduced against them, or if after having undergone some trifling punishment for so serious an offence, they are shortly again to be set at large, and turned loose upon society to scoff at the Law.[88]

Octavius Morgan went so far as to claim that a change was discernible in the mood of the colliers, for 'the prevailing impression among them now is that the Chartists are stronger than the Government, since the Government did not dare to carry the sentence of the Law into execution . . . ' It is difficult to resist the conclusion that it was a similar perception that led Justice Maule to pass savage sentences against the rebel prisoners appearing before the Brecon Lent Assizes. In particular, David Lewis and Ishmael Evans of the Brynmawr lodge, who were charged with the administration of unlawful oaths and with incitement to violence, were sentenced to seven years' transportation. It was the maximum penalty allowed, and the good judge made it clear that the prisoners were fortunate; in his opinion they were guilty of high treason and might well have faced the death penalty.[89]

At the end of 1839 and beginning of 1840 Considine's army remained almost 2,000 strong.[90] The Guests of Dowlais, who had taken refuge in London in mid-November, returned in December to take comfort from the company of the 45th billetted in their stables. Seymour Tremenheere arrived in Pontypool on Christmas Eve to find barricades at each approach to the town manned by soldiers who checked all traffic, and Capel Hanbury Leigh's house protected by a sergeant's guard with sentinels posted around it.[91] Yet Considine was not without his problems. Fraternisation between soldiers and workers continued to the prejudice of military discipline and it was obvious that the military occupation had done nothing to reconcile the populace to the established order.[92] The rebel chiefs had been arrested or had fled, but resistance was emerging once more at the local level, as in the days of the Scotch Cattle. Indeed, not only were the terroristic methods of the Cattle being revived, but so was the name. Those who had readily testified against their leaders received death threats, in some cases signed by the 'Scotch Bull'. In the collieries the men struck work whenever the outcasts appeared and the coalowners were obliged to isolate them in their own levels.[93] William Harris was beaten almost to death near Blackwood.[94] James Hodge and others went to Newport and threw themselves on the mercy of the magistrates; Israel Firman was provided with a passage to London for himself, his wife and family.[95] Barnabas Brough, the Pontypool brewer, went out of business when the workers boycotted all beershops and inns supplied by him.[96] Thomas Prothero distrained a hay rick belonging to the wife of the Pillgwenlly captain, Jenkin Morgan, for rent owing. It was set on fire the next day.[97] A week or so later several ricks belonging to the Newport manufacturer J.J. Cordes were burned; the immediate occasion is not known but he was notorious for having made all his workmen sign a disclaimer of their support for chartism.[98]

Although in armed struggle the workers of the coalfield had acquired a new sense of their strength, they had signally failed to topple the regime of the ironmasters and coalowners. As the economy took a sharp turn downwards in the early months of 1840, so the class struggle once again manifested itself in industrial action. Between January and May the price of south Wales bar iron on the London market fell by almost 13 per cent, and the ironworkers accepted a 15 per cent cut in wages.[99] The proprietors of the sale-coal collieries attempted to lower the price paid for a ton of coal cut by 2d. The colliers did not accept the reduction. At the beginning of June they struck work in Monmouthshire and eastern Glamorganshire, and in some places held out for as long as 14 weeks. The company shops refused credit and families were brought to starvation level. Colliers were obliged to beg the ironworkers for food. 'The labouring classes depend on and help one another in these extreme cases', commented the agent at Argoed.[100] At almost every colliery the owners were finally forced to give way, agreeing to introduce a sliding scale based on the selling price of coal at Cardiff. 'The Masters have been completely beaten by their men', conceded the Marquess of Bute, 'in a way that never happened to them before.'[101] The success which the workers enjoyed was unusual, but otherwise the situation on the coalfield might be said to have returned to normal.

## Notes

1. [Robert Lowery] , *Passages in the Life of a Temperance Lecturer*, see B. Harrison and P. Hollis (eds.), *Robert Lowery, Radical and Chartist* (London, 1979), p. 156.
2. *Monmouthshire Merlin* (henceforth *Merlin*), 23 Nov. 1839.
3. *Bristol Mercury*, 9 Nov. 1839.
4. [Edward Dowling] , *The Rise and Fall of Chartism in Monmouthshire* (London, 1840), pp. 45-6. Newport Public Library, Chartist Trials 1839-1840, 24 vols, henceforth N[ewport] E[xaminations] , NE, V, doc. 669: evidence of Job Tovey.
5. *Manchester Guardian*, 6 Nov. 1839, from a Pontypool correspondent. *Monmouthshire Beacon* (henceforth *Beacon*), 23 Nov. 1839: evidence of Lewis Morris, Henry Smith, Edward Carroll and Thomas Lewis. *The Times*, charges against Thomas Lewis and Edmond Richards. *Morning Chronicle*, 13 Nov. 1839: evidence of James Price. NE, XI, doc. 719: evidence of William Willams.
6. *Manchester Guardian*, 6 Nov. 1839. *Merlin*, 16 Nov. 1839: evidence of David Jones.
7. J.H. Salter, 'James Henry Clark of Usk, and His Times', in *Monmouthshire Medley*, II (1977), p. 36.
8. NE, XI, doc. 405: evidence of James Emery. *Merlin*, 16 Nov. 1839: evidence of William Watkins.
9. *Beacon*, 23 Nov. 1839: evidence of C.J. Phillips and S. Fletcher.
10. *Merlin*, 16 Nov. 1839.
11. Idem. NE, VII, doc. 610: evidence of John Roberts.
12. *Merlin*, 16 Nov. 1839.
13. Earl of Bessborough (ed.), *Lady Charlotte Guest. Extracts from her Journal 1833-1852* (London, 1950), entry for 4 Nov. 1839.
14. *Silurian*, 28 March 1840: evidence of David Griffiths, John Phillips, Rosser Thomas and William Williams.
15. *Hereford Times, Merthyr Guardian, Silurian*, 9 Nov. 1839.
16. *Silurian*, 28 March 1840: evidence of Charles Lloyd.
17. PRO, HO.40/45: Rev. William Powell to Home Sec. dd. 6 Nov. 1839.
18. *Beacon*, 9 Nov. 1839. *Silurian*, 9, 16 and 23 Nov. 1839.

19. *Merthyr Guardian, Beacon, Silurian*, 9 Nov. 1839. *Hereford Journal*, 13 Nov. 1839.

20. NE, V, doc. 601: evidence of Richard Pugh. CCL, Bute MSS, XX/105: Coffin to Bute, dd. 4 Dec. 1839.

21. PRO, TS.11/502: evidence of Richard Davies. Bute MSS, XX/133: Williams to Bute, dd. 17 Dec. 1839.

22. Bute MSS, XX/94: Coffin to Bute, dd. 28 Nov. 1839; XX/103: Coffin to Bute, dd. 3 Dec. 1839. There was a report that Caerffily was scoured, and the works stopped, late on Sunday night, see *The Times*, 6 Nov. 1839. It is probable that there was a confusion in the source between Caerffili and Pontypridd.

23. Morien [Owen Morgan], *History of Pontypridd and Rhondda Valleys* (Pontypridd and London, 1903), pp. 202-5.

24. Bute MSS, XX/56: Scale to Bute, dd. 8 Nov. 1839; XX/50: C.C. Williams to Bute, dd. 7 Nov. 1839; XX/137: C.C. Williams to Bute, dd. 18 Dec. 1839.

25. NE. V, doc. 601: note on Price's cannons; XI, doc. 388: evidence of Edward Dorey; XI, doc. 513: anon. memorandum.

26. Morien, *History of Pontypridd*, pp. 204-5. Harri Webb has kindly supplied an English version: There's talk in Nantgarw that the Chartists are on the way/ And each with his gear in the woods has hidden away;/Harriet the Mill, John Thomas the Snob alike/With Old Dick the Gateman to Cardiff will hike./Dafydd Siôn Isaac with a sackful of food/Wept three full nights at Craig y Berthlwyd.

27. Bute MSS, XX/38, 50, 137: C.C. Williams to Bute, dd. 4 and 7 Nov. and 18 Dec. 1839. *Morning Herald*, 6 Nov., *Cambrian*, 9 Nov. and *Courier*, 18 Nov. 1839. The *Warsaw* of New York was the first foreign ship to put into the Bute Docks, see *Cambrian*, 2 Nov. 1839.

28. *The Times*, 26 Dec. 1839.

29. Bessborough, *Lady Charlotte Guest*, entry for 5 Nov. 1839. *Morning Chronicle* and *Morning Herald*, 6 Nov. 1839. *Hereford Times* and *Western Vindicator*, 9 Nov. 1839.

30. NE, XIII, docs. 105, 656-7: evidence of David Jones and John Thomas.

31. *Silurian*, 28 March 1840 and *Cambrian*, 4 April 1840: evidence of Edward Jenkins, etc.

32. *The Times*, 26 Dec. 1839.

33. Bute MSS, XX/42: Guest to Bute, dd. 5 Nov. 1839; XX/43: Thompson to Bute, dd. 5 Nov. 1839. Bessborough, *Lady Charlotte Guest*, entries for 4 and 5 Nov. 1839.

34. *Beacon*, 9 Nov. 1839.

35. *The Times*, 26 Dec. 1839. Evan Powell, *History of Tredegar. Subject of Competition at Tredegar 'Chair Eisteddfod' held February the 25th, 1884* (Newport, 1902), p. 59.

36. *Merthyr Guardian*, 9 Nov. 1839. Bute MSS, XX/42: Guest to Bute, dd. 5 Nov. 1839.

37. Bessborough, *Lady Charlotte Guest*, entry for 5 Nov. 1839. Bute MSS, XX/42: Guest to Bute, dd. 5 Nov. 1839; XX/43: Thompson to Bute, dd. 5 Nov. 1839; XX/56: Scale to Bute, dd. 8 Nov. 1839.

38. *Courier*, 18 Nov. 1839.

39. *The Times*, 6 Nov. 1839. The companies of the 12th Regiment were landed by steamer at Aberystwyth in mid-1839. Crowds assembled to witness the rare event. The troops, it was reported 'were well aware of the cause of being so hastily embarked for Wales, and at once supposed that the countless numbers they observed were "Welsh Chartists", prepared to oppose their landing'. The *Cambrian*, 24 Aug. 1839, enjoyed a little fun at the expense of the nervous soldiers.

40. *Merlin*, 9 Nov. 1839.

41. *Beacon*, 9 Nov., *The Times*, 11 Nov., and *Hereford Journal*, 13 Nov. 1839.

42. PRO, HO.41/15: Home Sec. to Mayors of Bristol and Newport, and Lord Lieutenant of Monmouthshire, dd. 5 Nov. 1839. *The Times*, 8 and 9 Nov. 1839. *Morning Chronicle*, 8 Nov. 1839. *Merthyr Guardian*, 9 Nov. 1839. *Merlin*, 16 Nov. 1839.

43. *The Times*, 13 Nov. 1839.

44. PRO, Army List, 1839, p. 60. HO.40/15: Home Office to Merthyr magistrates, dd. 13 Nov. 1839. *The Times*, 8 Nov. 1839. *Merthyr Guardian*, 16 Nov. 1839. *Merlin*, 15 Feb. 1840.

45. *The Times* and *Morning Chronicle*, 14 Nov. 1839. *Merlin* and *Beacon*, 16 Nov. 1839.

46. Bessborough, *Lady Charlotte Guest*, entry for 9 Nov. 1839.

47. *The Times*, 15 Nov. 1839, from Newport, 13 Nov.

48. *Hereford Journal*, 20 Nov. 1839, from Newport, 15 Nov.

49. *The Times*, 21 Nov. 1839, from Newport, 20 Nov. *Morning Chronicle*, 21 Nov. 1839, from Newport, 19 Nov.

50. NE, VI, doc. 757: T.M. Llewellin to W.T.H. Phelps, dd. 3 Dec. 1839.

51. *The Times*, 18 and 20 Nov. 1839. *Merthyr Guardian* and *Beacon*, 23 Nov. 1839.

52. W.Napier, *The Life and Opinions of General Sir Charles James Napier, G.C.B.*, 4 vols, 2nd edn (London, 1857), II, p. 96. Napier thought Considine too good a soldier to have made such a remark, but he would not have been the first indiscreet general.

53. *The Times*, 29 Nov. 1839. *Merthyr Guardian*, 7 Dec. 1839.

54. *Morning Chronicle*, 14 Nov. 1839.

55. *Merlin*, 9 Nov. 1839.

56. *Beacon*, 9 Nov., *The Times*, 13 Nov., *Merlin*, 16 Nov. 1839.

57. Gurney and Gurney, *Trial*, pp. 417-23: evidence of Thomas Jones Phillips.

58. *Merlin*, 9 Nov. 1839.

59. *The Times*, 15 and 21 Nov. 1839.

60. *Merlin*, 23 Nov. 1839.

61. Ap Id Anfryn [Gwilym Hughes], *The Late Dr Price (of Llantrisant). The Famous Arch-Druid* (Cardiff, 1896), pp. 12-13.

62. I.G.H. Wilks, 'Insurrections in Texas and Wales: the Careers of John Rees', in *Welsh History Review*, 11, 1 (1982), pp. 85-6. Morien, *History of Pontypridd*, p. 205. Rees took a commission in the army of Texas and appears never to have returned to Wales. David is said to have returned in 1845, an American citizen.

63. *South Wales Argus*, 24 May 1933. *Weekly Argus*, 19 Sept. 1936.

64. Oliver Jones, *The Early Days of Sirhowy and Tredegar* (Tredegar Historical Society, 1969), pp. 108-9.

65. *Merthyr Guardian*, 23 May 1839 (italics original).

66. PRO, HO. 41/15: Home Office to Mayor of Newport, dd. 7 Nov. 1839 (italics original).

67. *Blackburn Standard*, 20 Nov. 1839.

68. Bute MSS, XX/93, 101: J. Bruce Pryce to Bute, dd. 28 Nov. and 3 Dec. 1839.

69. *Merlin*, 23 Nov. 1839.

70. *The Times*, 7 Nov., *Morning Chronicle*, 12 Nov. 1839.

71. Gurney and Gurney, *Trial*, p. 3.

72. *Salopian Journal*, 18 Dec., *Merlin*, 28 Dec., *The Times*, 31 Dec. 1839.

73. *The Times*, 26 Nov. 1839.

74. Gurney and Gurney, *Trial*, p. 12. A plan was believed to exist to kidnap witnesses at Usk, on their way to Monmouth. The authorities foiled any such attempt by assembling many of them at Newport and sending them to Monmouth

under armed escort, NE, XXIV, docs. 773-4: Phelps to Maule, dd. 23 and 24
Dec. 1839.
  75. Gurney and Gurney, *Trial*, pp. 5, 9.
  76. Mrs Hardcastle (ed.), *Autobiography of John, Lord Campbell*, 2 vols
(London, 1881), II, p. 127.
  77. Gurney and Gurney, *Trial*, p. 767.
  78. *Beacon*, 25 Jan. 1840 (from *Gloucester Chronicle*).
  79. *Morning Chronicle*, 16 Jan. 1840.
  80. *Beacon*, 25 Jan. 1840.
  81. Gurney and Gurney, *Trial*, pp. 772-3.
  82. *Morning Chronicle*, 18 Jan., *The Times*, 20 Jan., 1840.
  83. *Morning Chronicle*, 18 Jan. 1840.
  84. *Beacon*, 25 Jan. 1840.
  85. *The Times*, 5 Dec. 1839: letter dd. Welshpool, 1 Dec.
  86. *The Times*, 30 Jan. 1840, from Newport, 27 Jan.
  87. Gurney and Gurney, *Trial*, p. 778.
  88. National Library of Wales, Tredegar Park Muniments, Box 40, doc. 31:
O. Morgan to Normanby dd. 9 Feb. 1840.
  89. *Silurian*, 28 March 1840.
  90. PRO, HO.50/16: Distribution of the Army, January 1840.
  91. Bessborough (ed.), *Lady Charlotte Guest. The Times*, 27 Nov. 1839. E.L.
and O.P. Edmonds, *I Was There. The Memoirs of H.S. Tremenheere* (Eton,
Windsor, 1965), pp. 37, 39.
  92. *The Times*, 26 and 30 Dec. 1839. The companies of the 45th Regiment
in south Wales had three desertions in Jan. 1840 (when soldiers were often
confined to camp during the trials), nine in February, twelve in March and
twelve in April, see PRO, WO.25/2918, Record of Desertions.
  93. NLW, Tredegar Park Muniments, Box 40, doc. 31: O. Morgan to Normanby
dd. 9 Feb. 1840. *Beacon*, 15 Feb., *Cambrian*, 22 Feb. 1840.
  94. *Merlin*, 29 Feb.1840.
  95. *The Times*, 30 Jan., *Merlin*, 1 Feb. 1840.
  96. R. Nichols, 'Some Rare Books with Pontypool Associations', in
*Monmouthshire Medley*, II (1977), pp. 107-8.
  97. *Silurian*, 25 Jan., *Merthyr Guardian*, 1 Feb. 1840.
  98. *Beacon*, 8 Feb. 1840. Newport Museum and Art Gallery, doc. dd. 2 May
1839.
  99. Harry Scrivenor, *A Comprehensive History of the Iron Trade* (London,
1841), p. 409. J.H. Morris and L.J. Williams, *The South Wales Coal Industry
1841-1875* (Cardiff, 1958), pp. 248-9.
  100. British Parliamentary Papers, *Children's Employment Commission.
Appendix to First Report of Commissioners. Mines*, II, pp. 526, 536, 545, 546:
testimony of William Jenkins, Samuel Jones, William Evans and John Price.
  101. Morris and Williams, *South Wales Coal Industry*, p. 249.

# Part IV: CONSIDERATIONS

They walked this road in seasons past
When all the skies were overcast,
They breathed defiance as they went
Along these troubled hills of Gwent.

They talked of justice as they strode
Along this crooked mountain road,
And dared the little lords of Hell
So that their future should be well.

Because they did not count the cost
But battled on when all seemed lost,
This empty ragged road shall be
Always a sacred road to me.

(Idris Davies, *Tonypandy and Other Poems*, Faber and Faber, 1945)

There are many more names to remember
And some that will never be known
Who were loyal to Wales and the gwerin
And defied all the might of the throne.

(Harri Webb, *Rampage and Revel*, Gomer Press, 1977)

# 12 THE PECULIARITIES OF WALES

The level of contemporary chartist comment on the events of 1839 in Wales was regrettably low, seldom moving beyond a search for scapegoats. Bussey betrayed Frost, O'Connor betrayed Frost, Ashton betrayed Frost, Frost betrayed the workers – the permutations were seemingly inexhaustible. Few attempted any real analysis of the situation. All honour must go, then, to 'One of the People', the pseudonymous author of *An Address to the Working Classes of Wales on the Late Occurrences at Newport*. The text was originally written in Welsh and much of it probably before the rising, for the author intended to publicise the view of Alexander Somerville that an armed citizenry could not combat regular soldiers. Suppose, the writer speculated, the workers seized Newport and the country about it, how could they hope to hold out against the forces of the crown, 'men whose very trade is war', and defend the town against artillery that would rapidly have reduced it 'to a mass of smoking ruins tumbling about the heads of its unfortunate inhabitants'.[1] The confidence of the rebel leaders, he argued, can only be understood with reference to the peculiar circumstances of the ironworkers and colliers, that is, to their solidarity ('amity of sentiment and thought') and to their organisation ('facility of forming . . . extensive combinations').

The confidence of the rebel leaders was misplaced, the author of the *Address* argued, because it rested upon the assumption that the workers of England and Scotland were similarly united and similarly well organised. But, he admonished his countrymen,

this estimate of your capacity of general combination throughout the country is wrong, and you might, and indeed ought already to have learned from experience, that, though it may hold good in the mining and manufacturing districts, the rule does not apply to the kingdom at large'.[2]

Specifically, the writer argued, the Welsh leaders had over-rated the 'power of general combination of *different trades*'. Mark this distinction, he said. At best the Welshmen might have expected the operatives of Birmingham, Manchester, Sheffield and a few other 'populous places' to join them, but on these localities 'would be brought to bear all the military force in England'. You might be told, he cautioned his countrymen,

> that the working classes of England are intelligent — that they are enlightened, and know their rights. I wish it were so . . . Go beyond these districts, and you will find that the mass of the population neither know, nor care for political rights . . . Do not, then, be led away by exaggerated and confident assertions, that the people of this or that district are ready to join your cause.[3]

The author of the *Address* was linking the fact of the Welsh rising with the peculiarities of the Welsh industrial experience. Attention has been drawn to these peculiarities in earlier chapters. The natural resources of south Wales — coal, iron ore, limestone, water power — specified the relative narrowness of the range of productive activities. Ironworking and mining dominated the economy. The circumstances of Welsh history, of the *longue durée*, were such that, while it was largely the Welsh peasantry that supplied industry with its labour, it was English entrepreneurs who provided the capital. In the shorter term rapidly expanding markets for iron, both insular and overseas, dictated the rapidity with which industrialisation proceeded in south Wales, and it will be recollected that between the late 1780s and the early 1820s the proportion of pig iron produced there rose from 18 to 40 per cent of the British total. Industrial capitalism did not develop uniformly within the British Isles. In a sense there was no British Industrial Revolution, but a number of industrial transformations that occurred at different paces and on different (sometimes convergent, sometimes divergent) trajectories in different regions. Nowhere was the impact of industrialisation so revolutionary as in south Wales and nothing signalled this more plainly than the general uprising which took place there in the autumn of 1839. Not even a local outbreak occurred in the industrial regions of England and Scotland to divert the attention of government from its Welsh problem.

We have seen that, on the assurances of John Frost, the rebel leaders in south Wales did indeed come to believe that simultaneous risings would occur in England and Scotland. They did not and could not, for at the time nowhere else in the British Isles did that peculiar conjuncture of circumstances exist that not only enabled the Welshmen to rise but made their rising if not inevitable, at least highly likely. It is not much to be wondered at, wrote one hostile commentator, that the untaught Welshmen of the Iron Works should have taken up arms. Ignorant themselves of the real strength of the country, and flattered by their wicked deceivers into a high opinion of their own importance, they began to think that they alone constituted the 'Nation,' and as such conceived their recourse to arms as fully justified.[4]

The wife of the Dowlais ironmaster, Lady Charlotte Guest, already immersed in her translations of medieval Welsh romances, put the matter a little differently. 'I do not believe', she wrote, 'that any but Welshmen could be brought up to such a pitch of enthusiasm.'[5]

In the late eighteenth and early nineteenth centuries the great ironworks had sprung up where previously there had been no more than the occasional farm. Only in the few small towns fringing the coalfield had communities of artisans existed before the advent of industry, and it was not out of them that the new working class was made. Unlike the artisans, the ironworkers and colliers of south Wales were not victims but products of the capitalist system.[6] They were as much part of that system as were the ironmasters and coalowners. But ironworkers and colliers on the one hand, and ironmasters and coalowners on the other, were linked together within the system in a relationship that was inherently conflictive. In the class struggle the interests of labour were inevitably pitted against those of capital. The forms which the class struggle took were specific in time. In the period of early industrialisation in south Wales a generation of workers rioted sporadically against the price of food.[7] Three decades later the next generation used the weapon of the strike to seek redress of grievances whilst the herds of Scotch Cattle terrorised those who collaborated with the class enemy. Over those three decades the class struggle had quite apparently intensified. The workers acquired a deepening sense of solidarity and a growing capability of collective action; they were becoming increasingly conscious, in other words, of their identity as a class. In 1839 the class struggle finally assumed the form of armed struggle.

The extent of the development of the productive forces, the intensity of the class struggle, and the level of class consciousness are linked phenomena. The last two, however, are not simple functions of the first, for both may be moderated by the hegemonic impulses of the bourgeois state. Through such institutions as schools, churches and press the worker might be inducted into the values of bourgeois society and thereby led to acquiesce in the *status quo*. We shall argue that in the south Wales of the early nineteenth century the high degree of linguistic and cultural exclusivity – of distinct nationality – effectively shielded the workers from such influences, with the result that it was precisely there that the class struggle did finally take the advanced form of armed struggle. Late in 1839 a writer in the *Morning Chronicle* saw the point. The rising in Wales, he remarked, 'took place under circumstances more favourable for the Chartists than can be expected elsewhere', for it resulted not only from 'the nature of the occupations', that is, of ironworking and mining, but also from 'the distinction of language between the high and lower classes', that is, from the conjuncture of national and economic factors in the development of class.[8]

By hegemonisation we mean the extension of the values of the (English) bourgeoisie to all classes of society in order to establish a consensual basis for state power.[9] The obstacles to the dissemination of such values in south Wales in the early nineteenth century were formidable ones. In the remembrance of the Welsh people England remained the historic enemy even if, as one ironmaster claimed of the Pontypool district, 'the old traditions about Glyndwr and Prince Llewellyn and other ancient heroes, are becoming fainter and fainter'.[10] The Welsh peasant's 'hereditary resentment against every one who speaks the English language' was noted and dutifully deplored in 1830.[11] It was a trait that the peasants carried with them to the coalfield. 'The working people over the hills in this parish', claimed Elizabeth Todd of Merthyr, 'are strongly against, not only the English language being taught, but against the English also.'[12] Friendly societies attached to the Order of True Ivorites forbade the use of English at their meetings.[13]

A writer in the unionist tradition deplored 'the feeling which makes, of an imaginary line dividing a Welsh county from an English one, a real barrier between persons equally British, living under the same laws, affected by the same interests'. He observed that 'the lower classes of Wales avow such feelings, by designating English persons coming among them *"foreigners"* . . . '[14] In the Newport of the mid-1840s the time was remembered when there was 'a strong prejudice entertained by the primitive inhabitants against the "foreigners" who came to settle in the town . . . Exclamations were common enough, shocking to ears polite, such as "ein Sais Jaul", which meant, literally translated, "Old English Devils".'[15] Evan Powell wrote of the objections of leaseholders in Tredegar who were dispossessed by the ironmasters. 'Prejudice stimulated by national prejudice also strengthened these objections', he remarked. 'Who are these foreigners, children of Hengist and Horsa, that lay claim to our possessions?' the victims asked; 'we, who are the natives and real owners, cannot stretch out a foot, without being trod upon.'[16] G.S. Kenrick told of the Staffordshire workers who had been brought to the neighbourhood of Pontypool at the time of the strike of 1822. 'The Aborigines', he reminisced, 'considered it to be such a wanton unjustifiable invasion of their territory that many severe battles were the consequence; and at the pays the Staffordshire men frequently went to bed with the fear that they should be murdered before morning.'[17] In 1829 the Bute ironworkers attempted to expel all the Englishmen from the district.[18] But issues of nationality were, as always, inextricably linked with the conditions of labour. Many of the English and indeed other immigrants were rapidly assimilated into Welsh proletarian culture even to the extent of adopting the older language, and many of them took their place in the rebel ranks in 1839.

The major conduits for the transmission of the English language and of bourgeois values were the schools, and these were remarkably few in south Wales. In 1839 there were 47 elementary schools ('Common Day Schools') and 33 kindergartens ('Dame Schools', which were essentially day-care centres) in the five central parishes of the coalfield. Tremenheere estimated that over 70 per cent of working-class children received no schooling whatsoever. Many of those who did, moreover, attended irregularly and intermittently, that is, for only two or three years and then only for some months in the year. The quality of the instruction was for the most part very poor indeed. 'It is manifest', commented Tremenheere (who knew nothing of hegemonisation but made the point none the less), 'that, under the most favourable circumstances, the instruction offered to the children of the labouring classes in the day-schools of this district could not be expected to have much permanent effect in disciplining the mind, raising the taste and habits, and correcting the disposition.'[19]

Among the workers of the coalfield receptivity to the written word was clearly low. 'Of the few who have learned to read at all', Tremenheere reported, 'a large proportion confine themselves to the restricted literature of their own language.'[20] Statistical data are lacking and literacy is notoriously difficult to define, but in 1841 the Children's Employment Commissioners interviewed a number of well-informed witnesses. The overseer of Llancaiach colliery maintained that nearly half the men could read Welsh but very few English ('which keeps them all in the dark'). Their wives and daughters he thought 'excessively ignorant'.[21] Of the 70 men at Top Hill colliery it was said that not one in ten could read at all, and then seldom in English, and at

Penllwyn and Gellideg the proportion was reckoned at less than a third.[22] Of the 400 workers aged 18 or under at the Cyfarthfa collieries and mines, the overman estimated that a quarter at most could read even to the extent of knowing the alphabet.[23] The schoolmaster at Hirwaun praised the Sunday schools but noted that, since Welsh was the preferred language, English was even declining.[24] Much to the point, Tremenheere observed that English newspapers had virtually no circulation in the working-class communities.[25]

Hugh Seymour Tremenheere was a London civil servant, newly appointed Inspector of Schools. On 18 December 1839 he was instructed by the Council on Education to proceed to Herefordshire and Monmouthshire, there to consider applications for the erection of school houses at Ross, Archenfield and Monmouth with regard to the general state of education in those districts.[26] This in fact was a cover; his secret instruction was to inquire into the causes of the rising.[27] In south Wales he used 'strict caution' in contacting magistrates, iron-masters and coalowners, enjoining them to run no risk of his inquiries 'getting before the public in any manner'.[28] His activities nevertheless roused the suspicion of the workers and it was rumoured that he had come to south Wales to count their children because the government intended to have one in ten 'put out of the way'.[29] The gist of Tremenheere's subsequent report to the government was that the rising should be seen as the result of ignorance, and that the more complete pacification of Wales would be achieved through the schoolroom rather than the barracks; through hegemonisation, that is, rather than coercion.[30]

Others looked to pursuing the same goal through the churches rather than the schools. The author of a report on 'The Spiritual State of the Disturbed Districts in Monmouthshire' argued the case. 'If the wealthy capitalists who have heaped up their tens and hundreds of thousands', he wrote,

> can spare little or nothing to promote the best and highest interests of the masses they have congregated, the question still remains, whether our legislators will look on with equal indifference? Will they trust to coercion? — and, if so, are they prepared to meet and provide for that expenditure, which coercive measures, carried out upon such a scale that will give a prospect of efficiency, must inevitably occasion? Hitherto, the country has found such remedies, if remedies they can be called, very costly ones. As a mere matter of state economy — all higher considerations overlooked — can there be a reasonable doubt that the wisest course would be to provide the

Church with the means of sending her ministers as messengers of peace, and ambassadors of Christ among them.[31]

Schools or churches or whatever, the issue was summed up by a writer in the *Morning Herald* only a few days after the rising. 'Other correctives than the bayonet and the gallows', he urged, 'must be administered, before the danger to the institutions of society can be pronounced to have passed away.'[32] In the 1840s a series of parliamentary commissions were to establish the basis for the massive expansion of education in Wales, and thereby for the spread of the English language throughout its populace. But that lay in the future. In 1839 it is clear that the language of the mass of the workers in south Wales was Welsh and that their culture was predominantly an oral one. The rising was a manifestation of the new proletarian class consciousness, but within that consciousness was subsumed an historic sense of nationality. Proletarianisation was a product of the shared experience of the workplace with its attendant dangers and physical traumas. It was a product of the marginality of the conditions under which the working-class family reproduced itself: of wages, prices, housing, truck and the rest. And it was a product of the workers' perception of the discrepancy between the total value of their labour on the one hand and the value of that part returned to them in wages and benefits on the other. What was peculiar to Wales, however, was the intensity of the class struggle, and that resulted from the fact that the centuries old pattern of the Welsh experience had asserted itself once again in the new industrial context. The oppressed came for the most part from Wales and the oppressors for the most part from England.

After the annexation of Wales to England by the acts of 1536 and 1542 only three institutions of state remained that were in any sense peculiarly Welsh. One of these, the Council of Wales and the Marches, fell victim to the English revolution of 1688. The second, the Courts of Great Sessions, survived Edmund Burke's projected Oeconomy Bill of 1780 intended to achieve 'more perfect' union of Wales with England, to be finally abolished in 1830. Only the Principality survived, though after George Augustus Frederick became king in 1820 no Prince of Wales was created until 1841. The Principality remained of some legal significance in the nineteenth century, for example, to those Welsh landowners resisting the Crown's claims to unenclosed wastes and commons,[33] but to the affairs of industrial Wales it had singularly little relevance. There were those who argued that the causes of the rising of 1839 were to be found, if not in the disappearance of the old Welsh institutions, at least in the decline of the traditional leadership that those institutions had underpinned. 'For more than thirty years', one writer urged, only a few days after the attack on Newport,

> the great iron masters, desirous to supplant the political influence of the ancient families, have striven to alienate the people from their hereditary chiefs . . . Their devices now recoil on their own heads. The miners can discover no reason why they should render that reverence to strangers like Guest and Crawshay and Blewitt, which they have been taught to deny to Mackworth, to Meyrick, and to Morgan, names which have so often marshalled their fathers to victory.[34]

The 'alienation' of the ironworkers and colliers, however, resulted more from their perception that landowners and capitalists alike saw any threat to their regimen as a threat to civil government as such. The working-class struggle was, in other words, equated with treason. In April 1839 Crawshay Bailey had presided over a meeting in Coalbrook-vale at which the matter was spelled out. The assembled ironmasters, tradesmen and artisans presented an address to the queen, 'observing with regret the efforts now making to create insubordination among the working classes of society, and discontent with their condition, thereby setting at defiance all established authority, and by means of violence and terror to alter the laws and disturb the settlement of property'. Those who subscribed to the address begged 'humbly to lay at the foot of the throne an assurance of our firm and unalterable determination to support the just prerogatives of the Crown, and the constitutional privileges of Parliament'. One speaker at the meeting referred his audience to 'the turbulent spirit of discontent that at the present time prevails throughout Europe, nay, throughout the civilised world'. Why, he asked them, 'need I direct your attention to the state of feeling of other nations, when if we look at home, we shall find our own domains are infested with the same disease?'[35]

The fact of the matter was, that the Welsh working-class experience was not a replica of the English one. The level of alienation from English institutions (of Crown, Parliament and Law) was higher and conversely, the level of hegemonisation into English bourgeois values (of property, trade and empire) was lower. Mayor Thomas Phillips of Newport had seen the problem clearly, a full eight months before the rising. In south Wales, he informed the Home Secretary, 'the moral influence which ought to belong to the government and without which the government itself cannot exist is altogether at an end amongst a very numerous class of the community'.[36] The rising proved him right, for it demonstrated that in at least one part of Wales government no longer rested on the consent of the governed but on access to superior resources of coercion.

The peculiarities of the industrial transformation in Wales were such as to produce the conditions for armed struggle. In their bid for autonomy the workers challenged not only the regimen of landowners and capitalists but the very apparatus of the centralist state, the very concept of the 'united kingdom'. The peculiarities of the industrial transformation, however, were also such as to produce the conditions for an upsurge of cultural particularism among the new bourgeoisie. Weakly articulated and riven with ambiguities and contradictions, this particularism was to be one of the sources of modern Welsh nationalism. Its development was a signal that a Welsh national bourgeoisie was struggling to be born. We shall refer to the phenomenon as 'cambrianism'. Its proximate sources are to be found in the patriotic societies of the later eighteenth century, Cymmrodorion, Gwyneddigion, Cymreigyddion and Caradogion, but the cambrianists rejected the radicalism and republicanism of their predecessors while retaining their cultural goals. It was not, however, that cambrianism was totally apolitical; indeed, it was on the highly political but scarcely radical issue of the Courts of Great Sessions that the cambrianists cut their teeth. At issue was whether a 'more perfect' union of Wales with England would entail the total assimilation of the Welsh to the English identity.

Burke had abandoned his Oeconomy Bill in 1782 in the face of unexpectedly fierce Welsh opposition; 'care had been taken to poison the minds of the Welch', he claimed rather mysteriously.[37] Ultra-unionist ideologies did not, however, die with it. In the early nineteenth century John Frederick Campbell, second Baron and first Earl Cawdor, largest of the landowners in west Wales, revived Burke's campaign to abolish the Courts of Great Sessions. His hope, he had written in 1828, 'is in a stricter union with England, and in the incorporation of Wales with other English counties . . . into English circuits'.[38] The *Cambrian Quarterly Magazine and Celtic Repertory* was launched at the beginning of 1829 to debate such issues. Significantly, Sir Charles and Lady Morgan of Tredegar Park were among its sponsors. The editor contemplated the time when 'the memorials of the intellect that *had been active* in Wales will be annihilated . . . and in the stead will be left a waste, a desert, without culture, and without fruit'.[39]

The debate on the Welsh courts was opened immediately. A barrister on the Welsh circuit referred to 'Lord Cawdor's vituperations, passing

sentence on our privileges', and argued that justice could not be satis-
factorily administered if the courts were abolished.[40] The president of
the London Cymreigyddion went further, arguing that even with the
courts Welshmen (and no doubt Welshwomen) were effectively denied
the right of trial by jury, for few jurymen knew English and court
interpreters seldom conveyed the subtleties of the proceedings in their
translations. 'In Hindoostan', he observed,

> where the inhabitants generally understand no other language than
> their own, it was essentially necessary that persons intended for the
> administration of judicial affairs there, should previously qualify
> themselves by acquiring a proficiency in the Hindoostanee, and why
> should the ancient Britons . . . be refused a right which is even
> granted by the government to the black Asiatic?[41]

The matter of the courts thus led inevitably into that of language.
The issue was a highly divisive one. There were those like the Plymouth
ironmaster at Merthyr, Anthony Hill, and the Cyfarthfa manager, P.
Kirkhouse, who argued that the Welsh language stultified intellectual
development as well as being the medium for the transmission of 'prej-
udices and bad customs'.[42] The author of the leading article in the
*Cambrian Quarterly Magazine* for July 1830 took up the topic. 'It
has been somewhat fashionable of late', he claimed,

> amongst a certain class of persons who choose to arrogate to them-
> selves all the light that ever dawned on the Principality, to talk per-
> petually about the necessity of enlightening the Welsh by abolishing
> the Welsh language, and of assimilating Wales in every respect with
> England.[43]

There were, however, few cambrianists who cared even to speculate
that the process of political union might be reversed. The pseudonymous 'Senwod' deplored what he saw as a sort of false consciousness
('mistaken nationality') and argued that complete union was still compatible with cultural diversity:

> When a nation is merged in another larger, or more powerful; when it
> has no longer a distinct government, court, or senate, it may still
> claim a distinctive existence through a national literature . . . It is
> time that England and Wales should amalgamate completely, which
> by no means infers an extinction of the latter's noble tongue, or

striking features, or manners of any kind worthy of preservation.[44]

In a prize winning essay submitted to the London Cymreigyddion from a haven in St John's College, Cambridge, J. Bray berated the Welsh gentry. 'Are they, because Wales is merged in the British empire', he asked,

unable to feel, and think, and act as Welshmen — as ancient Britons, expelled from their fair patrimony by the arm of the more powerful and successful Saxon, and doomed to inhabit the less hospitable and fruitful region of Cambria?[45]

Such were the contradictions in cambrianism, however, that Bray could proceed to argue that Welsh be allowed and even encouraged to die in order that Wales might be reborn, resplendent with its own university, while a reviewer of Bray's essay saw in the programme 'only a mean and cowardly imitation of the autocrat of Russia's attempt to denationalise Poland by the abolition of its language'.[46]

The cambrianists were sensitive to racist attitudes then current in England. One writer regretted the antipathy towards the English language that was widespread among the Welsh populace, but asked where the fault lay. 'Where should we point out to them', he remarked, 'an English work that ever deigns to speak of them without adopting the full contumelious tone of the conquest, ridiculing their poverty, and denying them all intellect and virtue.'[47] Not all, however, were quite so defensive. A circular issued by the London Cymreigyddion in 1839 assured the public that the causes of both nationality and language in Wales were flourishing ones. 'There is not', it proclaimed,

a descendant of the Ancient Britons who would hesitate for a moment in making a patriotic effort to preserve their distinctive identity as a people inviolate, *and to perpetuate their language*, by making it the means of communicating useful and scientific knowledge.[48]

The real strength of cambrianism is not, perhaps, witnessed in such debates but rather in the proceedings of the numerous local societies — the *cymdeithasau taleithiol* — that sprang up in Wales in the early nineteenth century. The aging Iolo Morganwg was active in some of the earliest to be founded on the coalfield: the Pontypridd Cymreigyddion in 1814 and the Merthyr Cymreigyddion in 1821. It was, however, the Abergavenny Cymreigyddion that emerged in time as the most prestigious of them all. It is the subject of an excellent recent study.[49] It was founded in 1833 by Thomas Price, Carnhuanawc, pioneer of pan-Celticism and precursor of modern Welsh historiography. The list of the society's early presidents sounds like a roll call of south Wales indus-trialists and landowners: Sir Josiah John Guest in 1835, Benjamin Hall in 1837, Sir Charles Morgan in 1838. The wives of both Guest and Hall were much influenced by Thomas Price. Lady Charlotte Guest is best known for her splendid translations of medieval Welsh tales, *The Mabin-ogion* (London, 1838-49). Augusta Hall adopted the pseudonym Gwen-ynen Gwent and among other good works saved the manuscripts of Iolo Morganwg for posterity. She came to practise, it was said, 'a species of mild Welsh Sinn Feinism', and ran Llanover Park as a traditional Welsh household.[50] The ball given there to celebrate the fourth anniversary of the Abergavenny Cymreigyddion was a veritable orgy of Welshness. Welsh dress was worn, banners bearing strange Welsh devices adorned the walls, and a bevy of harpists provided an appropriate background of sound.[51] Benjamin Hall himself (grandson, it will be recollected, of the Richard Crawshay who founded Cyfarthfa), gave his name to Big Ben but should also be remembered for his advocacy of Welsh interests in the forum beneath it.[52] As for Sir Charles Morgan, he was accorded the honorific of 'Most Honourable Ivor of the Ivors', commemorating at one and the same time his maternal descent from Ifor Hael, 'Ivor the Generous', and his constant patronage of Welsh cultural causes.[53]

The favoured toasts of the Cymreigyddion societies were *oes y byd i'r iaith Cymraeg* and *Cymru fu, sydd, ac a fydd*, in effect, both the lan-guage and the nation shall endure. Ultra-unionists might deplore such sentiments but they were unlikely to see in those who raised their glasses any threat to the British state. At the Abergavenny eisteddfod of 1838 a prize of 60 guineas was offered for the best essay on the influ-ence of Welsh tradition on the literature of Europe. Among the seven who subscribed the money were Capel Hanbury Leigh, Lord Lieutenant of Monmouthshire, and three members of Parliament from south Wales, R. J. Blewitt, the newly knighted Sir Benjamin Hall and W.A. Williams.[54] Indeed, the activities of the cambrianists became so clothed in respectability that in 1848 Queen Victoria was to donate a prize of £25 to the Abergavenny eisteddfod in the name of Albert Edward, the six-year-old Prince of Wales. It was for an essay on the history of the language and literature of Wales.[55] On this hangs a story.

Dr William Price was a good cambrianist who had himself given a prize of no less than £10 to the Cymreigyddion eisteddfod at Pontypridd in 1837.[56] In 1841 Victoria created her month-old child Prince of Wales. The bards celebrated his titular succession from Llywelyn ap Gruffydd, slain by the English in 1282 and generally accounted the last Welsh prince. In that same year, 1841, William Price (back in Wales from exile in Paris) named his first-born child Gwenhiolen Hiarhles Morganwg, 'Gwenllian Countess of Glamorgan'. She was such, Price claimed, by descent from Rhys ap Gruffydd, lord of south Wales until his death in 1197, and the doctor later sponsored an eisteddfod in Pontypridd for Gwenllian's investiture. We regard Price's elevation of his daughter to a fictitious nobility as a highly idiosyncratic form of protest against English domination. In this we follow Brian Davies rather than John Cule, who diagnosed from the gesture the onset of schizophrenia.[57]

William Price was one of those rare creatures, a cambrianist who readily embraced the working-class struggle. Through the societies and the eisteddfodau they sponsored, something of the cultural ferment did communicate itself to the petty bourgeoisie and even, in towns like Merthyr, to the fringes of the working class.[58] There were those who had a vision of the Welsh worker steeped in the values of cambrianism. One writer in 1838 depicted a Wales 'whose *colliers, labourers*, and mechanics are often devoting those hours to the harp, and the extempore verse, which the English of the same grade give to drinking, blasphemy, and Radicalism'. Perhaps, however, the writer was indulging in a little sarcasm, for he signed himself 'An Old Cambrian with Two Eyes'.[59] In general the cambrianists were locked into a completely bourgeois view of society. In 1829, for example, the editor of the *Cambrian Quarterly Magazine* had briefly noticed the recession in the iron industry. 'In common with every friend of humanity', he wrote, 'we deeply deplore the distress under which the *middling classes* of tradespeople are suffering in Wales: in the iron district, we grieve to say, the distress is unparalleled.' But what of the ironworkers and colliers? The writer had not entirely lost sight of them. He felt assured, he said, that 'the morality of the Principality is strong enough to prevent those senseless and degrading scenes of brutalized anarchy, which have lately disgraced some parts of the empire'.[60]

The magnitude of the upheaval that came ten years later left the cambrianists dismayed and confused. The reaction of some was to affirm the loyalty of the Welsh workers to the English government and attribute the rising to agitators from England.[61] One writer who was penning a vigorous defence of Welsh culture at the time of the outbreak added a hasty footnote: he threw John Frost in with Henry Vincent as Englishmen whose 'poisonous artifices and misrepresentation' had led the 'refuse' of Wales into insurrection.[62] The editor of the *Merthyr Guardian* felt obliged to addess himself to this travesty. He expressed his respect for the motives of those 'jealous for the honour and loyalty' of their countrymen, but thought their apologetics to be nonsense. 'If', he wrote, 'the English traitors have been active in their mischief, the Welsh Insurrectionists have equalled them in their lawless | zeal.'[63]

There were others who showed an ambivalent attitude towards the rebels. 'Ap Llewellyn' wrote in the *Carmarthen Journal*. He dutifully deplored the rising as a 'blot on the escutchion of the Principality', but his reasoning was somewhat unexpected. The 'bold men of the mountains', he wrote, 'marched down the hills and then marched up again.' They were scared by the presence of a handful of soldiers. 'Is it that the descendants of those who triumphantly bore the Tudor from Milford Haven to Bosworth Field are shrunk in heart, in nerve, or in limb?' he asked. With a mixture of horror and fascination he explored an alternative scenario. 'What might have been the result', he suggested, 'of determined conduct amongst even a small part of the insurgents (and about "the hills" is assembled the *elite*, as to physical force, of the youths of South Wales) it is terrible to think. What might have been the issue of one desperate rush . . . ?'[64]

Ap Llewellyn's speculations reveal one of the fundamental contradictions of early nineteenth-century Welsh cultural nationalism. The cambrianists revelled in the historic struggles of the Welsh against Saxon domination, and saw Llywelyn ap Gruffydd and Owain Glyn Dŵr and even Henry Tudor as heroic figures of the past. Nor was resistance to the Romans too remote for celebration. 'Our ancestors the Silurians − the inhabitants of Gwent and Morganwg', Morgan Evans reminded the Cardiff Cymreigyddion, 'fought until the soil was drenched with their blood before they yielded up their country to the invader.'[65] But even the contemporary struggle of the Circassians against the Russian advance into Western Caucasus could win the enthusiastic support of cambrianists. 'What Welshman', wrote one,

> can read of their desperate triumphs without being carried back in imagination to the days of the Owens, Gryffydds, and Llewellyns who so long defended their native hills from the overwhelming force of Foreign invaders? The Circassians are sure of the sympathy of every generous mind; but to the breast of a Welshman their spirit-stirring exploits, from the power of patriotic association, come home with irresistible force.[66]

When it was the Welsh workers who took up arms against their oppressors, however, the mood changed. The attack upon Newport, said the coalowner Thomas Prothero, was like 'the irruption of a horde of American Savages upon some hostile village'.[67]

## Notes

1. 'One of the People', *Riots in South Wales. An Address to the Working Classes of Wales on the Late Occurrences at Newport* (Swansea, n.d.), p. 4.

2. Ibid., pp. 3-4.

3. Ibid., pp. 16-17.

4. *Silurian*, 16 Nov. 1839.

5. Earl of Bessborough (ed.), *Lady Charlotte Guest. Extracts from her Journal 1833-1852* (London, 1950), entry for 9 Nov. 1839.

6. The distinction is one made and subtly explored by Craig Calhoun, *The Question of Class Struggle* (Chicago, 1982), Ch. 1.

7. D.J.V. Jones, *Before Rebecca. Popular Protests in Wales 1793-1835,* Ch. 1 and especially p. 32.

8. *Morning Chronicle*, 15 Nov. 1839.

9. See, of course, the various writings of Antonio Gramsci, and particularly Q. Hoare and G.N. Smith (eds.), *Selections from the Prison Notebooks of Antonio Gramsci* (New York, 1971).

10. G.S. Kenrick, *The Population of Pontypool and the Parish of Trevethin; situated in the so-called 'Disturbed Districts'* (London, 1840), p. 12.

11. *Cambrian Quarterly Magazine*, II, 5 (Jan. 1830), p. 51.

12. British Parliamentary Papers, *Children's Employment Commission. Appendix to First Report of Commissioners. Mines*, Part II (1842), pp. 469-580, Report by Robert Hugh Franks (henceforth referred to as Franks Report, 1842) and pp. 581-720, Report by Rhys William Jones (henceforth Jones Report, 1842). Franks Report (1842), p. 507.

13. Franks Report (1842), p. 509: testimony of J.C. Wolrige.

14. *Cambrian Quarterly Magazine*, V, 18 (April 1833), p. 172.

15. [J. Scott], *The Ancient and Modern History of Newport, Monmouthshire* (Newport, 1847), p. 61.

16. Evan Powell, *History of Tredegar. Subject of Competition at Tredegar 'Chair Eisteddfod' held February the 25th, 1884* (Newport, 1902), p. 24.

17. Kenrick, *Population of Pontypool*, pp. 12-13.

18. E.W. Evans, *The Miners of South Wales* (Cardiff, 1961), p. 31.

19. British Parliamentary Papers, *Minutes of the Committee of Council on Education with Appendices and Plans of School Houses*, Part II (1839-40), pp. 207-18, Report by Seymour Tremenheere (henceforth Tremenheere Report, 1840), pp. 209-11.

20. Ibid., p. 212.

21. Franks Report (1842), pp. 528-9: testimony of Richard Andrews.

22. Ibid., pp. 527-8, 543: testimony of Jonathan Isaacs and Morgan Thomas.

23. Ibid., p. 503: testimony of P. Kirkhouse.

24. Jones Report (1842), p. 635: testimony of John Dixon.

25. Tremenheere Report (1840), p. 212.

26. Ibid., p. 207: instructions dd. Whitehall, 18 Dec. 1839.

27. E.L. and O.P. Edmonds, *I Was There. The Memoirs of H.S. Tremenheere* (Eton Windsor, 1965), p. 37.

28. Glamorgan County Record Office, Cardiff, Dowlais Iron Company, Letter Books 1782-1860, '1839, R-Y, ff. 695-6: Tremenheere to J.C. Wolrige dd. 31 Dec. 1839.

29. Edmonds, *I Was There*, pp. 37-8.

30. Tremenheere Report (1840), is the only part made public. The secret material has not been located. Kenrick, *Population of Pontypool*, is based on the material he supplied to Tremenheere.

31. *Salopian Journal and Courier of Wales*, 11 Dec. 1839.

32. *Morning Herald*, in *Hereford Journal*, 20 Nov. 1839.

33. See, e.g., the meeting of Welsh landowners in London on 28 March 1838, at which much emphasis was placed on the significance of the Principality, *Merthyr Guardian*, 7 April 1838. For the background, see Francis Jones, *The Princes and Principality of Wales* (Cardiff, 1969), especially Ch. 4.

34. *Courier*, 9 Nov. 1839: Julius to Editor.

35. *Report of the Proceedings at the Great Anti-Chartist Meeting, held at Coalbrook Vale, Monmouthshire, on Monday, April 29th, 1839* (Monmouth, [1839]), p. 11.

36. PRO, HO.40/45: T. Phillips jr. to Home Sec. dd. 12 March 1839.

37. *The Speeches of the Right Honourable Edmund Burke, in the House of Commons, and in Westminster Hall*, 4 vols (London, 1816), II, p. 357.

38. 'Letter of Earl Cawdor to Lord Lyndhurst, Lord Chancellor of England, on the Administration of Justice in Wales', in *Cambrian Quarterly Magazine*, I, 1 (Jan. 1829), pp. 23-4.

39. Ibid., I, 1 (Jan. 1829), p. 2. Italics original.

40. [R.G. Temple], 'Welsh Judicature', ibid., I, 3 (July 1829), pp. 249-59.

41. Ibid., II, 6 (April 1830), p. 252.

42. Franks Report (1842), pp. 503, 508: testimony of P. Kirkhouse and Anthony Hill.

43. 'The Peasantry of Wales', in *Cambrian Quarterly Magazine*, II, 7 (July 1830), p. 273.

44. 'The Antique, the Picturesque and the Literary Spirit in Wales', ibid., V, 18 (April 1833), pp. 172-3.

45. J. Bray, *Essay on the Means of Promoting the Literature of Wales* (London, 1840). One of the adjudicators of the essay was Sir Benjamin Hall.

46. *Cambrian*, 30 Nov. 1839.

47. 'Vindication of the Welsh Character', in *Cambrian Quarterly Magazine*, II, 5 (Jan. 1830), p. 51.

48. *Cambrian*, 30 Nov. 1839. Italics original.

49. Mair Elvet Thomas, *Afiaith yng Ngwent* (Caerdydd, 1978).

50. Herbert M. Vaughan, *The South Wales Squires* (London, 1926), p. 130.

51. *Monmouthshire Merlin*, 28 Oct. 1837.

52. *Dictionary of Welsh Biography down to 1940* (London, 1959), p. 334.

53. *Merthyr Guardian*, 13 and 20 Oct. 1838. See also Francis Jones, 'An Approach to Welsh Genealogy', in *Transactions of the Honourable Society of Cymmrodorion* (1948), p. 441.

54. Thomas, *Afiaith yng Ngwent*, pp. 15-23.

55. Ibid., pp. 95-6.

56. *Merthyr Guardian*, 15 April 1837.

57. Brian Davies, 'Empire and Identity: the "Case" of Dr William Price', in David Smith (ed.), *A People and a Proletariat* (London, 1980), pp. 72-93. John Cule, 'The Eccentric Doctor William Price of Llantrisant (1800-1893)', in *Morgannwg*, VII (1967), pp. 98-119.

58. Gwyn A. Williams, *The Merthyr Rising* (London, 1978), pp. 81-7.

59. *Merthyr Guardian*, 20 Oct. 1838. Italics original.

60. *Cambrian Quarterly Magazine*, I, 4 (Oct. 1829), p. 504. Italics original.
61. See, e.g., *Carmarthen Journal*, 6 Dec. 1839: letter from 'Fair Play'.
62. *Cambrian*, 30 Nov. 1839.
63. *Merthyr Guardian*, 23 Nov. 1839.
64. *Carmarthen Journal*, 6 Dec. 1839.
65. *Merthyr Guardian*, 6 April 1839.
66. *Silurian*, 30 May 1840.
67. *Monmouthshire Merlin*, 23 Nov. 1839.

# 13 THE RISING REVIEWED

To those of whiggish disposition the south Wales rising of 1839 naturally appeared an aberration, a manifestation of violent passions and lawlessness quite alien to the English – or 'Anglo-Saxon' – temperament. It had no place in that vision of progress, under the constitution, towards a condition of individual liberty and social harmony. Instinctively, then, the inclination of the whig Ministers of the Crown in London was to discount the magnitude of the upheaval. The attack on Newport had to be the subject of judicial proceedings, but no end would be served by exposing to public view the full ramifications of the Welsh workers' movement. The government prosecutors decided that it was enough to show that there had been an attack on Newport, that it was premeditated, and that John Frost led it with the assistance of Zephaniah Williams and William Lloyd Jones. The proceedings of the Special Commission will be searched in vain for any investigation of the origins of unrest; the transcripts contain no references to scotchings and strikes, or wages and truck. The rising was seen as antithetical to the spirit of English history, and of Welsh too, for the destiny of Wales was believed to be in union with England.[1] In the whiggish tradition the rising thus became, first, 'Frost's rebellion', and then simply the 'Newport Riots'.[2] As such it virtually disappeared from the mainstream of British historiography. By 1938, when E.L. Woodward contributed *The Age of Reform 1815-1870* to the Oxford History of England, the rising earned itself one brief paragraph in a book of some 650 pages.

It might be thought that the story of the rising would fare rather better at the hands of those writing, in some sense or other, within the tradition of chartism or, later, socialism. R.G. Gammage's *The History of the Chartist Movement* was a pioneering work first published in 1855.[3] The author devoted half a chapter to 'The Welsh Insurrection'. It was sympathetic in approach but not particularly enlightening, for the author relied almost entirely upon the transcripts of the trials and therefore reproduced the biases of the carefully staged proceedings. There was something of a swell of interest in chartism in the 1910s.[4] Two books by young scholars who knew each other, both published posthumously, presented a sharp contrast in treatment of the Welsh rising. Mark Hovell gave four pages to it, characterising the attack on Newport as 'the most formidable manifestation of physical force that

Chartism ever set on foot'.[5] Julius West wrote with equal brevity. He saw, rightly, that the rising resulted from the peculiarities of the situation in south Wales, but convinced himself 'that 200 would be a generous estimate of the number of rioters' and that accounts of bodies of armed men in the hills 'may well have originated by some citizen of Newport losing his way and coming upon a strange man or two in the darkness'.[6]

In 1924 a serious attempt to establish a context for the rising was made by Ness Edwards, then a militant socialist and activist in the South Wales Miners' Federation. He saw in 1839 'the first independent political working-class movement in South Wales', a result of the 'insurrectionary fervour . . . being generated in the hearts and minds of the working-class'. But Edwards remained locked into the view of the actual rising that had been evolved in the course of the trials, and continued to assign far too much importance to the part played in it by John Frost.[7] Regrettably, he made no use of the transcripts of the examinations conducted by the Newport magistrates, although these had been found in the office of a colliery proprietor in 1915 and deposited in the Newport Museum and Art Gallery.

In the event it was the centenary of the rising that stimulated a new wave of interest in it. The borough librarian and the museum curator in Newport jointly produced an excellent catalogue of the sources available for a study of the Welsh movement, including the transcripts of the magistrates' examinations.[8] James Davies was commissioned to produce a general history of chartism in south Wales, and David Williams a biography of John Frost. Davies succeeded in depicting, for the first time, something of the extent to which the mass of ironworkers and colliers were mobilised in the working-class cause, but nevertheless persisted in writing of the 'Newport Riots' and assuming an apologetic stance. 'We may not approve of the methods adopted by the Newport rioters of a century ago', he wrote; 'neither did a large number of their comrades in the Moral Force Party.'[9] It is, however, David Williams's study of Frost that has largely pre-empted the field over the last four decades.[10]

It was almost inevitable that a biographer of Frost would perpetuate the view that the Newport draper was the central figure in the rising. David Williams did just that. His basic approach to the rising is best summed up in his own words, penned some years later: 'on Friday, November 1, a meeting of delegates at Blackwood determined upon a great demonstration at Newport to take place the following Sunday night . . . There was a scuffle in front of the Westgate Hotel, where, unknown to the Chartists, troops had been stationed.'[11] In Williams's writings the ironworkers and colliers are shadowy figures, lacking unity, completely undisciplined and fatally deluded by a sense of their own power.[12] As Gwyn A. Williams has recently remarked, 'on industrial militants, David Williams's sympathy faltered; his favourite adjective for them was "unsavoury" '.[13] It is all the more strange, then, that it was while he was working on the biography of Frost that David Williams discovered, in the Tredegar Park Muniments, the letter from Zephaniah Williams to A. McKechnie in which the rebel design was out-lined. David Williams rightly regarded it as something of a 'scoop' and was dismayed when Ness Edwards proceeded to publish it in a south Wales newspaper to show that 'the march on Newport . . . was the first stage in an effort to establish a republic in this country'.[14] But in truth Williams was somewhat embarrassed by the document, for it accorded ill with his thesis that the march on Newport was intended only as a monster demonstration. In consequence, he made little use of it, suggesting that it was written 'probably to curry favour with the auth-orities, by supplying them with a reasonable version of the purpose which the Chartists had in mind'.[15] Just how Zephaniah Williams, con-demned to transportation for life and already on board convict ship, might have thus endeared himself to the authorities defies imagination.

In the event it was an English socialist, G.D.H. Cole, who first grappled with the conceptual difficulties in David Williams's study. In 1941 Cole published an essay on John Frost in which he argued that the rising was planned while Frost was in London and that upon his return to south Wales he was confronted 'with a revolutionary movement which it was beyond his power to control'.[16] Cole saw quite clearly the implications of this view. The rising, he wrote, 'was local in its inspira-tion . . . the outcome of the same inhumane conditions in the South Wales collieries and ironworks as had produced the Merthyr Rising of 1831 and the violence of the secret "Scotch Cattle" during the succeed-ing years'. It was not Frost who organised the rising but, Cole specu-lated, 'some successor of Dick Penderyn whose name history does not record, or some group of leaders who were themselves the victims of the desperate oppression of the Guests and Crawshays . . . '[17] In this study we have argued the essential correctness of Cole's approach.

The Welsh workers, we have said, were products rather than victims of the capitalist system. Whatever changes they sought were changes within the framework of the new world of industry. There is no indica-tion in the evidence that the ironworkers and colliers were in any way influenced by luddite ideas. But the workers were certainly concerned with more than collective bargaining for higher wages. Their purpose was to take control over the determination of the conditions of labour generally. In pursuit of this goal their struggle with those who owned the means of production brought them into an inescapable conflict with the state, which existed to maintain the *status quo*. In the event the government in London approved the arming of the middle classes while the workers looked to the creation of an autonomous republic, a commonwealth − or commune − of armed citizens. To the revolutionary design of the workers the English connections were of critical importance. Had risings comparable in extent and organisation to the Welsh one occurred simultaneously in other parts of the realm, then the bourgeois state might well have disintegrated under strains it could not withstand. Any such expectations were, however, chimeric: the trajectory of English working-class history, we have argued, was not that of Welsh.

Set against the peculiarly Welsh past (and most proximately the great strikes of 1816, 1822 and 1830, the clandestine activities of the Scotch Cattle, and the Merthyr Rising of 1831), the insurrection of 1839 ceases to look like the aberration that whig historiography required it to be. In south Wales the class struggle quite apparently did, in 1839, take the advanced form of armed struggle. The workers did, quite deliberately, pit themselves against the forces of the Crown. The whig government at the time knew it, the tory opposition knew it, the local authorities in south Wales knew it, the editors knew it, and only a tendentious reading of the evidence could suggest otherwise.

The rising of November 1839 was one of industrial workers. It occurred, however, in a country that was still predominantly a peasant one. That the peasantry did not engage in the struggle was, we argue, fortuitous: an accident of history rather than a determinate condition. At the core of the Welsh peasant experience was the unremitting effort of small farmers to subsist on marginally productive lands while at the same time supporting, through the various forms in which their incomes were appropriated, a gentry. As land came into ever shorter supply and farms became too small to be economic, so the numbers of landless labourers grew. It is clear that, had it not been for the growth of industry in Wales, mass emigration must have occurred. In 1870 Charles Wilkins of Merthyr argued a further percipient thesis, that if industrialisation averted emigration, it also enfeebled the revolutionary impulse of the peasantry. The 'necessities of the coal and iron works' created jobs. Had this not been so, he argued, 'the results of the want of employment' could have been momentous in impact:

Thousands of men now loyal might be tempted to emulate the unemployed Welshmen of the days of Prince Llewelyn and Owen Glyndwr. The patriotism that is content with the exhibition of the leek on St. David's Day, with the mental joust and tourney of eisteddfodau, and the laudations of their beloved country in patriotic verse, might by similar influence be stimulated to try once more to wrest Wales from English rule.[18]

Be that as it may, Welsh peasant unrest did break into open revolt with the emergence of the rural guerrilla bands known as Rebecca. Their earliest known operations against tollgates and tollgate collectors took place in west Wales in 1839. It was not, however, until late 1842 that the movement achieved vigorous growth.[19] Many workers made their way to the countryside as the iron industry contracted in the early 1840s, and perhaps they were the catalyst. By 1843 Rebecca existed in most of the rural Welsh counties. Thomas Campbell Foster, special correspondent of *The Times*, virtually attached himself to the rebeccaites. Convinced of the racial inferiority of the Welsh, Foster was nevertheless sensitive to their grievances and paid tribute to 'the boldness of enterprise, rapidity of movement, unity of purpose, dexterity of execution, and celerity of retreat, by which the manoeuvres of these Cambrian Cossacks have been distinguished'.[20]

Foster envisaged the rebeccaites setting up a Welsh 'imitation-parliament', appointing Welsh-speaking magistrates, denouncing the oppression of the 'Saxons', declaring that 'Wales shall be a nation' – and then being transported for life to Australia![21] He was not, of course, wholly serious, but local peasant councils did spring into existence. Foster was permitted to attend a session of one, at Cwm Ifor near Llandeilo Fawr on 21 July 1843 (or what it proclaimed 'the first year of Rebecca's exploits, A.D. 1843'). The assembly dealt with matters of tollgates, tithes, rents and poor law, and among its resolutions was one not to allow Englishmen to be employed as land agents in south Wales.[22] Anti-English feeling was clearly running high. A letter of warning was addressed to the toll-farmer Thomas Bullin in December 1842. It was signed 'Becca and children' and included the general observation that, 'it is a shamefull thing for us Welchman to have the sons of Henegust, have a Dominion over us, Do you not remember the long knives which, Henegust hath invented to kill our own fore fathers . . .'[23]

Once again the government had to despatch its infantry, cavalry and artillery to Wales.[24] Colonel James Love, appointed to command the force, made it his key aim to prevent the rural guerrillas from making common cause with the industrial workers of Glamorgan and Monmouthshire. He had reason to be alarmed, for by mid-1843 Rebecca bands were already active on the fringes of the coalfield, led by such men as John Jones (Shôni Sgubor Fawr) of Merthyr and David Davies (Dai'r Cantwr) who had worked in Tredegar.[25] The forthcoming study of the period by Brian Davies will reveal the extent to which a conjunction of workers and peasants was a possibility. There is, however, no gainsaying the fact that four years separated the peak of Welsh industrial unrest in 1839 from that of peasant unrest in 1843. Those so inclined may wish to contemplate the consequences, had the workers and peasants of Wales marched to precisely the same revolutionary beat in those critical years.

The struggle of 1839 was a class struggle. For all its flirtation with cultural nationalism, the south Wales bourgeoisie remained firmly attached to the trinity of Crown, Parliament and Law which manifestly existed to protect the interests of property. Concerns with the preservation of the Welsh language and the promotion of Welsh literature had no functionality in the revolutionary politics of the period (since the language was a living one for the working class, and 'literature' was largely oral). Yet such were the peculiarities of Wales that the class struggle there did take on many of the specific features of a revolutionary national movement. Perceiving their oppressors as alien oppressors, the workers aspired to a condition of self-determination that entailed separation from the bourgeois state. Industrialisation produced the first serious challenge to the English dominion in Wales since, perhaps, the fifteenth century. Contemporary observers, we have seen, remarked on that fact. Precisely because their view was a contemporary one, however, they were yet unable to discern the way in which an age-old encounter was resurgent in a new and revolutionary form of struggle; they had no historical precedents to consult. For our part we shall leave the last word to the excellent Dr William Price of Pontypridd, for he knew that 1839 was a beginning, not an end; that the 'Silurian' republic was a once and future republic. 'Today', he proclaimed in 1839, 'we are fighting for something more than our own freedom — for that of our children and the children of our children.'[26]

## Notes

1. For some of these themes see, most recently, J.W. Burrow, *A Liberal*

*Descent: Victorian Historians and the English Past* (Cambridge, 1981).

2. E.L. and O.P. Edmonds, *I Was There. The Memoirs of H.S. Tremenheere* (Eton Windsor, 1965), p. 37. [W.N. Johns], *The Chartist Riots at Newport*, 1st edn (Newport, 1884).

3. R.G. Gammage, *The History of the Chartist Movement, from its Commencement Down to the Present Time*, 1st edn (London, 1855; and previously issued in seven parts, London, 1854-5).

4. See e.g. E. Dolléans, *Le Chartisme, 1830-1848*, 2 vols (Paris, 1912-13). H. Schlüter, *Die Chartisten-Bewegung* (New York, 1916). F.F. Rosenblatt, *The Chartist Movement in its Social and Economic Aspects* (New York, 1916).

5. M. Hovell, *The Chartist Movement* (Manchester, 1918), pp. 177-80.

6. J. West, *A History of the Chartist Movement* (London, 1920), pp. 141-6. West's figure of 200 'rioters' must have come from the *Northern Star*, 7 Dec. 1839, which reported that the actual assault on the Westgate Hotel was carried out by about that number of men.

7. Ness Edwards, *John Frost and the Chartist Movement in Wales* (Western Valleys Labour Classes, Abertillery, 1924).

8. John Warner and W.A. Gunn, *John Frost and the Chartist Movement in Monmouthshire* (Newport: Chartist Centenary Committee, 1939).

9. James Davies, *The Chartist Movement in Monmouthshire* (Newport: Chartist Centenary Committee, 1939).

10. David Williams, *John Frost. A Study in Chartism* (Cardiff, 1939). See also the adaptation into Welsh, V. Eirwen Davies, *John Frost a Therfysg Casnewydd* (Caerdydd, 1969).

11. David Williams, *A History of Modern Wales* (London, 1950), p. 237. Compare David Williams, 'Chartism in Wales', in Asa Briggs (ed.), *Chartist Studies* (London, 1959), p. 241.

12. Williams, *John Frost*, p. 289.

13. Gwyn A. Williams, 'Locating a Welsh Working Class: the Frontier Years', in David Smith (ed.), *A People and a Proletariat* (London, 1980), p. 45.

14. Personal communication, David Williams to Wilks dd. 26 Sept. 1955. *Daily Argus*, 18 April 1939; *Weekly Argus*, 22 April 1939.

15. Williams, *John Frost*, p. 288, and compare Williams, 'Chartism in Wales', pp. 240-1.

16. G.D.H. Cole, *Chartist Portraits* (London, 1941), p. 146.

17. Ibid., p. 161.

18. Charles Wilkins, *Wales, Past and Present* (Merthyr, 1870), pp. 334-5.

19. David Williams was far happier investigating rural rather than industrial unrest. *The Rebecca Riots* (Cardiff, 1955), remains pre-eminent in the field. His account, nevertheless, reflects many of the presuppositions of bourgeois historiography, and there is need for a re-examination of Rebecca in the light of more recent analyses of peasant uprisings.

20. *The Times*, 22 Aug. 1843.

21. Idem.

22. Ibid., 24 July 1843, and for another council at Pontyberem, between Carmarthen and Pontarddulais, ibid., 27 July 1843.

23. For a facsimile of the letter see Williams, *Rebecca Riots*, facing p. 212.

24. *The Times*, 22 July 1843. Williams, *Rebecca Riots*, pp. 212-14.

25. Williams, *Rebecca Riots*, pp. 247-9, 254-8.

26. T. Islwyn Nicholas, *A Welsh Heretic. Dr William Price, Llantrisant* (London, 1940), p. 16.

## APPENDIX I: THE REBEL DEAD

No complete list of the rebels slain can be compiled, since only those who died in and around the Westgate Hotel, in the immediate aftermath of the fighting, were identified. The following have been noted.

CODD, John. Codd's wife wrote from Pembrokeshire to say that she had learned of her husband's death in the fighting and needed proof in order to claim benefits.

DAVIES, David. Of Waunhelygen, Brynmawr.

DAVIES, —. Son of David Davies of Waunhelygen.

DAVIES, Evan. Collier, residence unknown.

DAVIS, John. Carpenter, of Pontnewynydd.

EVANS, William. Miner, of Tredegar.

FARRADAY, William. Collier, of Blackwood.

JONATHAN, John. Probably of Blaina.

GRIFFITHS, William. His lodge number was 657, and he belonged to section 5 of No. II division. Several sources state that he was from Merthyr.

LANSDOWN, Robert. No further information available.

MEREDITH, Reece. Of Tredegar.

MORGAN, David. Tinker, of Tredegar.

MORRIS, John. Miner, residence unknown.

SHELL, George. Carpenter, of Pontypool.

THOMAS, Abraham. Collier, of Blaina.

THOMAS, Isaac. Of Nantyglo, but may be in error for Abraham Thomas.

WILLIAMS, —. Deserter from the 29th Regiment of Foot.

WILLIAMS, William. Of Cwmtillery.

'WILLIAM ABERDARE'. No further information available.

'JOHN THE ROLLER'. Of Nantyglo.

[Sources: *Bristol Mercury*, 9 Nov. 1839. *Cambrian*, 16 Nov. 1839. *Merthyr Guardian*, 9 Nov. 1839. *Monmouthshire Merlin*, 9 and 16 Nov. and 28 Dec. 1839. *Morning Chronicle*, 8 Nov. 1839. *Silurian*, 9 Nov. 1839. *The Times*, 11 Nov. 1839. Newport Examinations, V (Reece Meredith); XI (John Davis). W.N. Johns, *The Chartist Riots at Newport*, 2nd edn (Newport, 1889), p. 44.]

# APPENDIX II: COMMITTALS AND TRIALS

The magistrates in south Wales were not far into their examinations before it was noticed that they were drawing no clear line between chartists and rebel chartists (*Charter*, 17 Nov. 1839). Men like Samuel Etheridge and Ebenezer Williams of Newport were arrested because they were known to have been active in the working men's associations. A few rebels from the hills were arrested before they had left Newport and, in the absence of witnesses against them, were summarily convicted under the vagrancy laws. Most of their comrades in arms, however, had rapidly distanced themselves from the town and sooner or later returned to their homes. They were effectively beyond the reach of the law. A few it is true, were apprehended, but it was seldom that satisfactory witnesses could be found to testify against them. In places like Tredegar and Ebbw Vale magistrates — ironmasters for the most part — found it virtually useless to conduct examinations. They preferred to join the Newport bench, on the theory that witnesses would be the more co-operative the further they were from their homes, cowed by the unfamiliar surroundings. A few of the rebel leaders could be identified, warrants issued for their arrest, and rewards offered, as in the cases of John Frost, David Jones the Tinker, William Lloyd Jones, John Rees the Fifer and Zephaniah Williams. Others, such as William Jones of Sirhowy and John Lovell of Newport, were prosecuted with confidence since their wounds were considered proof of their involvement in the fighting. The treason trials, however, depended heavily upon a few witnesses who, by intimidation and offers of immunity, turned queen's evidence.

The following lists compile the available data on prisoners dealt with by the various benches of magistrates, the Special Commission and the Assizes. To the best of my knowledge extensive transcripts of the magistrates' examinations exist only for Newport, though the activities of other benches were sometimes mentioned in the press. I believe the lists to be reasonably complete for Monmouthshire and Breconshire, but I have been unable to construct comparable lists for Glamorganshire (where, in any case, only the rebel sections from the Nelson area actually went into action). It should be borne in mind that the jurisdiction of the Special Commission did not extend to Breconshire. I estimate that between 60 and 70 per cent of the prisoners examined were discharged, often for lack of evidence. In this way some of the important rebel captains, like Edward Tippins of Nantyglo, slipped through the hands of the magistrates. I have not attempted to list those discharged, for the information on them is usually minimal.

### Monmouthshire

*Abbreviations.* MEN: magistrates' examinations, Newport. MEP: magistrates' examinations, Pontypool. MEV: magistrates' examinations, various centres in the valleys. SC: Special Commission.

AUST, James. 25, master gardener, Caerleon. MEN 6 Nov: high treason. SC: true bill for high treason; prosecution withdrawn.

BALL, Thomas. –, collier, Abersychan. MEP 18 Nov: riot. Usk Quarter Sessions: acquitted.

BARRETT, John. –, –, –. MEN 8 Nov: vagrancy; 1 month.

BARRILL, John. –, collier, Pontllanfraith. 18 Nov: reward of £25, for high treason. Eluded capture.

BATTEN, John jr. 18, collier, Gelligroes. MEN 30 Nov: illegal arming. SC: acquitted.

BEACH, George. –, collier, Argoed. MEN 28 Nov: treason, *in absentia*. Eluded capture.

BEATTY, Wright. –, –, –. MEN 8 Sept. 1840: riot and conspiracy. Disposition of case not found.

BENFIELD, Richard. 20, miner, Sirhowy. MEN 7 Nov: high treason. SC: true bill for high treason; pleaded guilty; sentenced to death 16 Jan; commuted to life; reduced to 3 years.

BOLTON, Thomas. –, collier, –. MEP 11 Nov: riot and conspiracy. Usk Quarter Sessions: acquitted.

BRITTON, John. –, collier, Garndiffaith, MEP 11 Nov: riot and conspiracy. Usk Quarter Sessions: acquitted.

BRITTON, Solomon. 23, collier, Garndiffaith. MEN 11 Nov: high treason. SC: true bill for high treason; prosecution withdrawn. Re-arrested for intimidating witnesses; sent to Pontypool for examination for riot and conspiracy. Disposition of case not found.

BUCKNELL, Charles. –, collier, –. MEP 11 Nov: riot and conspiracy. Usk Quarter Sessions: acquitted.

CHARLES, John. –, sawyer, –. MEP 11 Nov: riot and conspiracy. SC: pleaded guilty; 3 months with hard labour.

COLES, Joseph. 24, collier, Argoed. MEN 28 Nov: burglary and riot.

SC: pleaded guilty to riot and conspiracy; 6 months with hard labour.

COLLINS, Morgan. −, −, Ebbw Vale. MEV 23 Nov: unlawful combination and conspiracy. Disposition of case not found.

DAVIES, Thomas. 25, collier, Pontllanfraith. MEN 26 Nov: theft. SC: remanded to Monmouthshire Lent Assizes; acquitted 27 March.

DAVIES, Thomas. 28, collier, Ebbw Vale. MEV 13 Nov: riot and conspiracy. SC: acquitted.

DAVIES, Thomas. 33, sawyer, Newport. MEN 7 Nov: high treason. SC: pleaded guilty to riot and conspiracy; 4 months with hard labour.

DAVIES, Thomas. −, −, −. MEP 11 Nov: riot and conspiracy. SC: pleaded guilty to riot; bound over for five years, £50.

DAVIES, William. −, son of Roger Davies, shopkeeper, Blackwood. Reward of £25, for high treason. MEN 5 Dec: conspiracy and riot. Turned queen's evidence, discharged.

DAVIS, Isaac. −, −, −. MEP 11 Nov: riot and conspiracy. Usk Quarter Sessions: bound over for five years, £50.

EDMUNDS, Edmund. 34, mine-agent, Pontllanfraith. MEN 18 Nov: high treason. SC: true bill for high treason; prosecution withdrawn.

EDWARDS, Evan. 24, watchmaker, Tredegar. MEN 21 Nov: high treason. SC: found guilty of making bullets; 1 month.

EDWARDS, Thomas. 28, collier, Argoed. MEN 28 Nov: burglary and riot. SC: pleaded guilty to riot and conspiracy; 4 months with hard labour.

ETHERIDGE, Samuel. 61, beerhouse keeper, Newport. MEN 19 Nov: high treason, reduced to conspiracy. SC: not guilty by direction.

EVANS, Griffith. −, blacksmith, Gelligroes. MEN 5 Dec: riot; bound over, £50.

FISHER, John. −, −, Gelligroes. MEN 30 Nov: conspiracy; bound over, £50.

FROST, Edward. −, watchmaker, Newport. MEN 9 Nov: examined; bound over to the Assizes if charged, £200 and two sureties of £100 each.

FROST, John. 54, linen draper, Newport. 4 Nov: reward of £100, for high treason. MEN 5 Nov: high treason. SC: true bill for high treason; found guilty 8 Jan; sentenced to death 16 Jan; commuted to transportation for life 1 Feb. Conditional pardon 1854, went to USA. Full pardon 1856. Died near Bristol 1877.

GEORGE, George. 37, collier, Ebbw Vale. MEN 12 Nov: high treason. SC: true bill of burglary; pleaded guilty to riot and conspiracy; 6

months with hard labour.

GIBBY, John. 30, blacksmith, Pillgwenlly. MEN 12 Dec: high treason.
SC: pleaded guilty to riot and conspiracy; one year.

GROVES, Charles. 17, apprentice painter, Newport. MEN 11 Nov:
bound over to the Assizes if charged, £50. Turned queen's evidence,
discharged.

HARRIS, Henry. –, –, –. MEP 11 Nov: riot and conspiracy. SC:
bound over for five years, £50.

HARRIS, Job. 28, collier, Argoed. MEN 28 Nov: burglary and riot.
SC: pleaded guilty to riot and conspiracy; 3 months with hard labour.

HAVARD, William. –, labourer, –. MEP 11 Nov: riot and conspiracy.
SC: pleaded guilty to riot and conspiracy; 2 months with hard labour.

HORNER, Moses. 21, collier, Pontllanfraith. MEN 26 Nov: theft. SC:
remanded to Monmouthshire Lent Assizes; discharged 27 March.

HORNER, William. 18, collier, Pontllanfraith. MEN 26 Nov: theft.
SC: remanded to Monmouthshire Lent Assizes; discharged 27 March.

KEYS, John. –, –, –. MEP 13 Nov: bound over to appear if charged,
£100.

KEYS, Thomas. 29, collier, –. MEP 11 Nov: burglary and riot. SC: true
bill for burglary; bound over to keep the peace, £50.

JAMES, John. –, –, –. MEN 8 Nov: vagrancy; 2 weeks with hard
labour.

JEWEL, William. 25-30, stone mason, Pillgwenlly. 29 Nov: reward of
£10, for high treason. Eluded capture.

JONES, David. –, collier, Tredegar. 7 Nov: reward of £100, for high
treason. MEN 7 Dec: examined *in absentia*, high treason. SC: true
bill for high treason, *in absentia*. Eluded capture.

JONES, William. –, quarryman, Pontnewynydd. MEN 8 Nov: vagrancy,
14 days with hard labour.

JONES, William. 25, collier, Sirhowy. Examined Brecon, 3 Nov. Removed to Newport. MEN 11 Dec: riot and conspiracy. SC: guilty of
misdemeanor; bound over to keep the peace.

JONES, William Lloyd. 30, watchmaker and beerhouse keeper, Pontypool. 7 Nov: reward of £100, for high treason. MEN 8 Nov: high
treason. SC: true bill for high treason; found guilty 15 Jan; sentenced
to death 16 Jan; commuted to transportation for life 1 Feb. Conditional pardon 1854. Died Launceston, Tasmania, 1873.

LEWIS, Thomas. 33, collier, Abersychan. MEP 18 Nov: riot. SC:
pleaded guilty to riot and conspiracy; 3 months with hard labour.

LLEWELLYN, John Lewis. 49, beerhouse keeper, Pontnewynydd. 7 Nov: £100 reward, for high treason. MEN 19 Nov: sedition. SC: pleaded guilty; traversed to Monmouthshire Lent Assizes. Pleaded guilty to misdemeanor; bound over, £500 and two sureties of £100 each.

LLEWELLYN, Thomas. 44, collier, Fleur-de-lis. MEN 25 Nov: treason and sedition. SC: guilty of riot and conspiracy; 3 months.

LLEWELLYN, William John. 29, collier, Argoed. MEN 28 Nov: burglary and assault. SC: pleaded guilty to riot and conspiracy; 9 months with hard labour.

LOVELL, John. 41, gardener, Newport. MEN 9 Nov: high treason. SC: true bill for high treason; pleaded guilty; sentenced to death 16 Jan; commuted to life; reduced to 3 years.

MEREDITH, Amy. 45, collier's wife. –. MEP 11 Nov: burglary and riot. SC: true bill for burglary, bound over to keep the peace for 5 years.

MEREDITH, James. 11, collier, –. MEP 11 Nov: burglary and riot. SC: true bill for burglary; bound over to keep the peace for 5 years.

MOORE, James. 20, labourer, –. MEP 18 Nov: riot and conspiracy. SC: pleaded guilty; one year with hard labour.

MORGAN, Jenkin. 40, milkman, Pillgwenlly. MEN 20 Nov: high treason. SC: true bill for high treason; pleaded guilty; sentenced to death 16 Jan; commuted to life; reduced to 3 years.

MORGAN, Thomas. 26 .collier, Tredegar. MEV 23 Nov: unlawful combination and conspiracy. SC: found guilty; 3 months with hard labour.

MORRIS, John. –, –, –. MEN 8 Nov: vagrancy, one month.

OWEN, John. 28, blacksmith, Cwm. MEN 28 Nov: high treason. SC: found guilty of making weapons; 6 months with hard labour.

PALMER, Jonathan. 30-40, stone mason, Pillgwenlly. 29 Nov: reward of £10, for high treason. Eluded capture.

PARTRIDGE, John. 44, printer, Newport. MEN 7 Nov: treason. SC: pleaded guilty to riot and conspiracy; 6 months with hard labour.

PHILLIPS, Isaac. 18, collier, Pontymister. MEN 7 Dec: riot and theft. SC: acquitted.

PILLINGER, Edward. 28, collier, –. MEN 21 Dec: riot and conspiracy. SC: found guilty of misdemeanor; bound over to keep the peace for 5 years, £50.

REES, John. 40, miner, Tredegar. MEN 7 Nov: high treason. SC: true bill for high treason; pleaded guilty; sentenced to death 16 Jan; commuted to life; reduced to 3 years.

REES, John. –, mason, Tredegar. 7 Nov: reward of £100, for high treason. MEN 7 Dec: examined *in absentia*, high treason. SC: true bill for high treason, *in absentia*. Eluded capture.

RICHARDS, Benjamin. 41, shoemaker, Tredegar. MEN 21 Nov: high treason. SC: pleaded guilty to riot and conspiracy; 6 months.

RICHARDS, Edmund. 39, labourer, –. MEP 18 Nov: riot and conspiracy. SC: pleaded guilty to riot and conspiracy; 3 months with hard labour.

RORKE, Richard sr. 82, painter, Newport. MEN 27 Jan: riot and conspiracy. Usk Quarter Sessions: acquitted, 7 April.

RORKE, Richard jr. 24, –, Blackwood. MEN 27 Jan: riot and conspiracy. Usk Quarter Sessions: found guilty, 6 months with hard labour, 7 April.

ROWLAND, Lewis. 37, collier, Maes-y-cwmer. MEN 28 Nov: sedition. SC: pleaded guilty to riot and conspiracy; 1 year with hard labour.

SHELLARD, William. 36, master shoemaker, Pontypool. MEP 18 Nov: high treason. SC: traversed to Monmouthshire Lent Assizes, found guilty on two counts of conspiracy; 18 months with hard labour, and then to be bound over to keep the peace, £500 and two sureties of £100 each.

STEPHENS, David. 78, –, Croespenmaen. MEN 21 March: riot and conspiracy. Monmouthshire Lent Assizes: pleaded guilty; bound over to keep the peace, £500 and two sureties of £100 each.

TOMLINS, George. –, –, –. MEP 11 Nov: riot and conspiracy. SC: bound over to keep the peace for 5 years, £50.

TURNER, Frederick. –, –, –. MEP 11 Nov: riot and conspiracy. SC: bound over to keep the peace for 5 years, £50.

TURNER, George. 37, collier, Blackwood. MEN 15 Nov: high treason. SC: true bill for high treason; prosecution withdrawn.

VICTORY, Samuel. –, –, Newport. MEN 14 Nov: assisting soldiers to desert. Monmouthshire Lent Assizes: no true bill found.

WATERS, Charles. 26, ship's carpenter, Newport. MEN 5 Nov: high treason. SC: true bill for high treason; pleaded guilty; sentenced to death 16 Jan; commuted to life; reduced to 3 years.

WILLIAMS, David. –, –, –. MEP 11 Nov: riot and conspiracy. Disposition of case not found.

WILLIAMS, Ebenezer. –, tiler and beerhouse keeper, Newport. MEN 13 Nov: bound over, £50.

WILLIAMS, William. 29, collier, Ebbw Vale. MEV 11 Nov: conspiracy and burglary. SC: no true bill found.

WILLIAMS, Zephaniah. 44, innkeeper, Coalbrookvale. 6 Nov: reward of £100, for high treason. MEN 26 Nov: high treason. SC: true bill for high treason; found guilty 13 Jan; sentenced to death 16 Jan; commuted to transportation for life 1 Feb. Conditional pardon 1854. Died Launceston, Tasmania, 1874.

## Breconshire

*Abbreviations*. MEB: magistrates' examinations, Brecon. BLA: Brecon Lent Assizes.

EVANS, David. 31, roller, Brynmawr. MEB: unlawful combination and sedition. BLA: 2 years with hard labour and then bound over for 2 years, £50.

EVANS, Ishmael. 51, labourer, Brynmawr. MEB 7 Nov: unlawful oaths and incitement to violence. BLA: 7 years transportation.

GODWIN, James. 41, mason, Brynmawr. MEB 24 Dec: unlawful combination. BLA: 2 years with hard labour and then bound over for 2 years, £50.

HABBAKUCK, Henry. –, –, Rassa. MEB: riot. BLA: prosecution withdrawn.

HOWELL, David. –, miner, Rassa. MEB 11 Nov: unlawful assembly and sedition. BLA: acquitted.

JONES, John. 49, labourer, Rassa. MEB 9 Nov: unlawful assembly and sedition. BLA: 10 years imprisonment.

KIDLEY, Thomas. 24, labourer, Brynmawr. MEB 27 Nov: unlawful combination. BLA: 2 years with hard labour and then bound over for 2 years, £50.

LEWIS, David. 37, shoemaker and beerhouse keeper, Brynmawr. MEB: unlawful oaths and incitement to violence. BLA: 7 years transportation; freed from Millbank Penitentiary mid-1841 because of extreme ill health.

MEREDITH, Walter. 41, collier, Rassa. MEB 9 Nov: unlawful combination and sedition. BLA: 2 years with hard labour and then bound over for 2 years, £50.

POWELL, Thomas. 28, miner, Dukestown. MEB 16 Nov: illegal arming and assembly. BLA: prosecution withdrawn through non-appearance of witnesses.

PRICE, William. 27, collier, Rassa. MEB 9 Nov: unlawful combination and sedition. BLA: 2 years with hard labour and then bound over for 2 years, £50.

THOMAS, John. 48, tailor, Rassa. MEB 9 Nov: unlawful combination and sedition. BLA: not guilty by direction.

WILLIAMS, William. 34, miner, Rassa. MEB 9 Nov: unlawful combination and sedition. BLA: 2 years with hard labour and then bound over for 2 years, £50.

# INDEX

*Conventions.* Throughout this book anglicised forms of Welsh place-names have been used. The Welsh equivalents are, however, given in the index immediately after the form used, e.g. Cardiff/Caerdydd.
  Persons known to have been active in the rising of 1839 are indicated by an asterisk, e.g. Meredith, James*. In view of the frequency with which many names occur, such persons are further identified by their lodge affiliation when this is known, e.g. Davies, David* (Abersychan).